THE

PUBLICATIONS

OF THE

SURTEES SOCIETY

VOL. 225

THE

PUBLICATIONS

OF THE

SURTEES SOCIETY

ESTABLISHED IN THE YEAR

M.DCCC.XXXIV

VOL. CCXXV

THE KEELMEN OF
NEWCASTLE UPON TYNE
1638–1852

EDITED

BY

JOSEPH M. FEWSTER

THE SURTEES SOCIETY

THE BOYDELL PRESS

First published 2021

A Surtees Society Publication
published by The Boydell Press
an imprint of Boydell & Brewer Ltd
PO Box 9, Woodbridge, Suffolk IP12 3DF, UK
and of Boydell & Brewer Inc.
668 Mt Hope Avenue, Rochester, NY 14620–2731, USA
website: www.boydellandbrewer.com

ISBN 978-0-85444-081-8

ISSN 0307-5362

A catalogue record for this book is available
from the British Library

Details of other Surtees Society volumes are available
from Boydell & Brewer Ltd

The publisher has no responsibility for the continued existence or
accuracy of URLs for external or third-party internet websites referred
to in this book, and does not guarantee that any content on such
websites is, or will remain, accurate or appropriate

This publication is printed on acid-free paper

Printed and bound in Great Britain by
TJ Books Limited, Padstow, Cornwall

Dr Joseph Fewster sadly died a few days after submitting his manuscript to the society. The society's editors are grateful to his widow, Elizabeth Fewster, and daughter, Helen Fewster, for their assistance in seeing this volume through the press. They would also like to thank Dr M.M.N. Stansfield of the University of Durham's Archives and Special Collections for his assistance.

CONTENTS

PREFACE

The principal source of material concerning the keelmen is a large body of manuscripts held in Tyne and Wear Archives under the accession number 394 and roughly sorted into 40 files consisting of petitions to the magistrates, minutes of the magistrates' and employers' discussions, letters, wages settlements, legal documents and other material. Everything of significance in these files (apart from material relating to the prosecution of individual offenders) together with items from the Cotesworth and Ellison papers, also preserved in these archives, has been included in the documents printed below, together with items held in the North of England Institute of Mining and Mechanical Engineers, the Newcastle City Library, the Northumberland County Archives, Durham County Record Office, Durham University, and the British Library. The State Papers and Home Office papers in the National Archives include reports from the magistrates on strikes and other disturbances involving the keelmen and appeals for military assistance. The author wishes to thank the staff of all these repositories for making their records available to him.

The Surtees Society volume CV (1901), *Extracts from the Records of the Hostmen's Company of Newcastle upon Tyne*, edited by F.W. Dendy, contains many references to the keelmen, but the Hostmen seldom entered the text of petitions or other documents concerning these men into their books. An exception is the keelmen's petition of *c*.1699 concerning their proposed charity, but here a gloss attributing the keelmen's poverty to their improvidence is added to the text (Dendy, pp. 154–5, *cf.* **Document 8**, below). Disputes over the Keelmen's Charity figure largely in this valuable volume, but Dendy evidently did not know of the part that Daniel Defoe played in them. Thus Dendy placed the *Case* and *Further Case* relating to the keelmen between 1707 and 1709 (pp. 172–77), but both these items (not in the Hostmen's books), which can be attributed to Defoe, were published either at the end of 1711 or beginning of 1712 (**Document 27**, note 1). In the Introduction below, reference has been made to a few items in the Hostmen's records (now preserved in the Tyne and Wear Archives) which Dendy did not include in his publication. After the Hostmen withdrew from the Charity, there is little in their records about the keelmen, but, as will be seen from the documents, there is considerably more to be found in other sources, leaving plenty of scope for the fuller picture that this volume seeks to offer. With records stretching over a long period, the keelmen must be one of the best documented workforces in the country. More information about them can be found in the present writer's *The Keelmen of Tyneside: Labour Organisation and Conflict in the North-East Coal Industry, 1600–1830* (Boydell Press, Woodbridge, 2011).

ABBREVIATIONS

DCRO	Durham County Record Office
HO	Home Office Papers
NA	Northumberland Archives
NCL	Newcastle City Library
NEIMME	North of England Institute of Mining and Mechanical Engineers
SP	State Papers
TNA	The National Archives
TWA	Tyne and Wear Archives

INTRODUCTION

The keelmen, a colourful, cohesive and often turbulent workforce, were once a distinctive feature of Tyneside. Their task was to convey the coal produced in the collieries adjacent to the River Tyne downriver in small barge-like craft known as keels and to cast it aboard ships in the lower reaches, whence it was exported mainly to London and other east-coast ports, or to markets overseas. Keels had evidently carried coal on the Tyne long before they were the subject of royal decrees in 1384 and 1389,[1] but it was in the latter part of the sixteenth century, when diminishing supplies of wood increased demand for coal as an alternative fuel, that the trade rapidly expanded and brought about an influx of labour into Tyneside. The keelmen's work was essential to the coal trade, on which the prosperity of the region largely depended, until they were increasingly superseded by mechanical inventions in the course of the nineteenth century.

The Tyne keel, 'caulker-built', *i.e.* constructed with flush-fitting planks, was oval in shape, 42 feet long and 19 feet wide with a draught of four and a half feet. It was propelled by means of a huge oar worked by two men and a boy, while the skipper in unison with them steered with a shorter oar at the stern. The keel was equipped with a large square sail and eventually with a more sophisticated fore and aft rig to be used according to the weather, and the crew would also take advantage of ebb and flood tides to assist their passage. In shallow water, a man on each side of the keel drove it forward with long poles, a procedure which, like rowing the craft, demanded much exertion and great strength.[2] To cast the coal into the ship's hold was equally laborious, even more so when the ship had high port holes, or when both keel and ship were being tossed and

---

1   *Calendar of Patent Rolls, Richard II, 1381-85* (London, 1897), p. 449; *1388-92*, p. 30, whereby keels of greater capacity than 'of old' were to be destroyed and their measure was to be 'according to ancient custom'.

2   This procedure was known as 'setting'; see **Document 322**, keelmen's petition, 23 October 1819, footnote.

pitched in strong winds and great swell. The work involved danger. Numerous hazards such as shoals, submerged wrecks, the mooring gear of ships, and projections from the banks into the river had to be negotiated or avoided, often in darkness or dense fogs, and if, as frequently, the keels were over-loaded, 'the danger in storms and strong tides was very great'.[3] In the lower reaches of the river, where the keels were even more exposed to vagaries of tide and violence of gales, they were liable to be 'spoyled, sunk, driven into the sea and lost'.[4] Widows of keelmen were always numerous, and many of their husbands undoubtedly perished in the course of their work.

Most of the keelmen and their families lived in Sandgate, just outside the city walls of Newcastle, where they formed a closely-knit community with their own customs, dialect and dress. John Wesley, who visited Newcastle in 1742, described Sandgate as 'the poorest and most contemptible part of the town', and there are various other descriptions of the squalor and disorder prevalent there.[5] Many keelmen were natives of Scotland and could be identified by their blue bonnet, once a common Scottish head-dress. A report from Newcastle in or about 1638[6] states that most keelmen and watermen were at that time Scotsmen or from parts of Northumberland that were notorious for lawlessness. In the early eighteenth century, the Mayor of Newcastle mentioned 'the many Scotch young fellows who come hither to work att the keels for

---

3   **Document 293**, Petition, 28 September 1819. Accounts of storms often mention the sinking of keels, *e.g.* the following extract of a letter from George Liddell to William Cotesworth, 23 March 1717/18 (Cotesworth Papers, CP 1/26): 'We have had a new winter begun of late. You know well enough what great winds we have had of late and yet on Wednesday night our keels went down in order to cast on Thursday morning, but finding the wind likely to rise, such as could did cast and severall that could not were sunk, and none got up till Friday morning. On Friday night it rained till ten violently and betwixt that and 5 in the morning it snowed furiously so that it laid a foot thick on the ground and a storm of wind at North East by which many keeles were sunk.' Nothing is said of the fate of the crews of these craft, but their chance of survival under these conditions could not have been great.

4   F.W. Dendy, *Extracts from the Records of the Hostmen's Company of Newcastle upon Tyne,* Publications of the Surtees Society, CV (1901), pp. 110–11, petition to the Lord Protector, 1656.

5   Nehemiah Curnock, *Journal of the Reverend John Wesley* (8 vols, London, 1909–16), iii, pp. 13–14; J. Fewster, *The Keelmen of Tyneside: Labour Organisation and Conflict in the North-East Coal Industry, 1600-1830* (Woodbridge, 2011), pp. 4–5.

6   **Document 1**.

the sumer only', and the keelmen themselves stated that in winter (when the export of coal stopped), 400 of their total number of 1600 were then in Scotland 'wither they go always to their families'.[7] Although a seasonal migration evidently continued,[8] a census of keelmen made in 1740 shows that many Scotsmen had by that date settled in and around Newcastle.[9]

The keelmen were employed by fitters, members of the Hostmen's Company of Newcastle, incorporated by royal charter in 1600 with an exclusive right to vend coal on Tyneside. The fitters were themselves contracted to the coal owners to provide keels and men to transport the coal to the ships. Each keelman was bound to his fitter for a year. The bond was enforceable at law: bound keelmen were liable to prosecution and imprisonment if they deserted their work, and anyone who then employed them risked prosecution. During a prolonged strike in 1750, the fitters published the names of 829 keelmen bound to them, together with a threat to potential employers.[10] Although to some extent the bond gave the keelmen security of employment for a year, it did not bind the fitter in any way, and as it was not a mutual contract the question of its legality could be raised.[11]

The keelmen were paid by the tide and according to the distance travelled. A keelman reckoned a tide by the time taken from leaving the staith (the loading point) to his return. A long or 'ship tide' might take fifteen to seventeen hours.[12] The several wage settlements set out below show the dues payable to the keelmen from each stage or 'ratch' of the river together with owners' wages, an allowance from the coal owners mainly for beer, regarded as essential to the

7 Jonathan Roddam to Sir John Delaval, 6 July 1710, TNA, SP 34/12/92; *A farther case relating to the poor Keelmen, c.*1712, Dendy, *Records of the Hostmen's Company*, p. 176.

8 Edward Hughes, *North Country Life in the Eighteenth Century, the North East, 1700-1750* (Oxford, 1952), p. 252.

9 TWA 394/10, see **Documents 100–23**.

10 NCL, J. Bell, *Collections relative to the River Tyne: its Trade and the Conservancy thereof*, vol. I, *f.* 12, 28 April 1750, **Document 123**.

11 **Document 394**, Keelmen's Third Address, 14 November 1822. A correspondent in the *Tyne Mercury*, 10 December 1822, described this contention as 'the hackned cry that we have heard from the beginning of these dissensions', and argued that the bond imposed obligations on the employer to provide work and pay to those bound to him, but no clauses to this effect were included in the bond.

12 R. Oliver Heslop, 'Keels and Keelmen', manuscript article, NEIMME, NRO 3410/ZD/71.

keelmen's toil. They frequently complained about the quality of the beer supplied, generally in can houses owned by the fitters' servants, and also about the beer that the shipmasters gave when their ships were being loaded. Any work that the keelmen did at the staithes was also paid in liquor. An attempt to commute these payments into cash was made in the settlement of 1792, but it seems with little enduring success.[13] The sums stated in these settlements were per keel, not to each man. For a long tide, the crew (a skipper, two men and a boy) would receive 13s 4d., and for a shorter distance or bye-tide the lesser sums set out in these settlements, which also included payments for various contingencies that might arise. The boy would get a pittance contributed by the other members of the crew.

Poverty was an ever-present condition among the keelmen, and many stricken by sickness, accident or old age, as well as numerous widows and orphans, faced destitution. In 1699, 'sensible of the pincheing wante and extremities which they and their familyes often groane under', the keelmen authorised their employers to retain a small sum from their wages each tide to provide a fund for the relief of those in need.[14] The scheme at first worked well, and by 1701 a hospital containing 60 dwelling rooms, a club room and an office had been erected at a cost in excess of £2000. Soon, however, disputes broke out over the Hostmen's management of the fund, the keelmen alleging that there was a difference of £955 between the Hostmen's calculation of expenditure and their own.[15] The Hostmen responded that the keelmen were 'mightily mistaken', but the men continued to distrust them and resisted their attempts to tighten their control over the Charity which, however, under their own management, eventually fell into chaos. Large sums were spent in public houses at the behest of some of the skippers, and the keelmen began to suspect their manager of false accounting. They demanded that the workmen on the hospital should not be paid unless they verified their bills on oath, and were particularly incensed when the Hostmen

---

13   DCRO, D/CG6/1247, A.H. Matthewson, staithman at Dunston 1819–33, stated that for loading at the staith the keelmen 'got nothing for it but drink'. According to a correspondent in the *Gateshead Observer*, 24 April 1849, this was the practice at most of the staithes. Andrew Mitchell had feared that this would happen, **Document 200**, *Address to the Keelmen* (1792).

14   **Document 8**, Petition, *c.*1699.

15   TWA, GU/HO/1/2, Hostmen's Minute Book, 1654–1742, fol. 504; Dendy, *Records of the Hostmen's Company*, pp. 166–7.

discharged some of these accounts without that security.[16] Outbreaks of industrial trouble, especially the strike of 1710, worsened relations between the keelmen and the Hostmen, who alleged that part of the charitable fund had been diverted to support those imprisoned for riot during that disturbance.[17] Daniel Defoe, who visited Newcastle about this time, encouraged the majority of the keelmen to seek a charter of incorporation to govern the Charity themselves and bring to justice those who had misapplied the funds. Defoe's vehement denunciations of the Hostmen and magistrates in his *Review* and other publications are printed below.[18] The keelmen accordingly petitioned the Queen for incorporation. Their petition was referred to the Attorney General for consideration, but the magistrates and Hostmen entered a caveat against it and promoted a bill in parliament whereby the mayor, five senior aldermen, the governor of the Hostmen's Company and the two MPs for Newcastle, William Wrightson and Sir William Blackett, were to be incorporated as governors of the Charity with power to examine on oath any who had retained money from the men's wages, and in case of deficiency, to levy double the amount by distress.[19] As will be seen from their correspondence printed below, William Carr and Nevile Ridley, who were involved in preparing the measure, were genuinely anxious that the keelmen should receive justice. The bill addressed many of the keelmen's concerns, indeed to such an extent that the fitters petitioned against it,[20] but the keelmen, now determined to cast off all dependence on Hostmen and magistrates, also petitioned against the bill. Despite all opposition against it, the bill passed the Commons.[21] Both keelmen and fitters addressed further petitions opposing it to the House of Lords, but although it was pronounced fit to pass, the motion for a third reading was defeated.[22] Since both

---

16 TWA, Cotesworth Papers, CJ/3/6; TWA, 394/5, Affidavit of Timothy Tully, 10 November 1710; British Library 8223E9(32), *Case of the Poor Skippers and Keelmen*; Dendy, pp. 178–9.

17 **Document 29**, 'Reasons to be offered against the keelmen's having any grant for Incorporacon unless under the government of the Mayor and Aldermen of Newcastle only'.

18 **Documents 23–6**.

19 House of Lords Record Office, manuscript copy of the bill.

20 See **Document 53**.

21 *Journals of the House of Commons*, 17, p. 160. For the correspondence concerning the passage of the bill through the Commons and petitions against it, see **Documents 29–55**.

22 *Manuscripts of the House of Lords*, n.s. IX, pp. 230–1; *Journals of the House of Lords*, XIX, p. 426.

keelmen and fitters were opposed to the measure it would have proved unworkable had it passed into law. Meanwhile, the keelmen's petition for incorporation had proved fruitless, and the fitters, not surprisingly after the abuse they had suffered from Defoe, determined to cease collecting the contributions for the Charity.[23] When the stock was divided amongst those who had contributed to the last there was insufficient to give each man a shilling.[24]

Various attempts to revive the Charity proved abortive. Both Hostmen and magistrates constantly feared that the keelmen would gain independent control of the fund, which might then be diverted to promote 'mutinies'. When it was rumoured in 1719 that the keelmen might make another attempt to gain incorporation, the Hostmen predicted 'entire ruin not only to this Company but the Corporation and trade in generall'.[25] The keelmen for their part feared that if the Hostmen gained control of the Charity they would, as Defoe had argued, thereby be able to tighten their power over them in their employment. In 1722, the Hostmen and magistrates drew up elaborate rules to govern the Charity, but when the Hostmen sought exclusive control the scheme was wrecked.[26] A further attempt to revive it in 1728 was short-lived,[27] and initiatives in 1759 and 1765 came to naught.[28]

In 1768, during a strike on account of the overloading of the keels, the keelmen obtained the services of Thomas Harvey, an attorney, who undertook to organise them into a society which, besides serving the purposes of a charity, would regulate their conditions of work, particularly regarding the keel-load. Harvey drew up a deed of settlement to found the society, and a levy was imposed on the crew of each keel to raise funds to obtain an Act of Parliament to establish it. The magistrates and fitters, alarmed at Harvey's influence over the keelmen, especially as these proceedings were carried on under a cloak of secrecy, resolved to forestall them by preparing the outline of a bill to regulate the Charity, and refused to handle the keelmen's money until authority from parliament was

---

23 TWA, GU/HO/1/2, Hostmen's Minute Book, 1654–1742, fols 604, 606, 22 January 1712/13, and 5 May 1713.

24 *Account of the Keelmen's Hospital* (Newcastle, 1829).

25 TWA, GU/HO/1/2, Hostmen's Minute Book, 1654–1742, fol. 664; Dendy, p. 186.

26 TWA, GU/HO/1/2, fols 695–6; Cotesworth Papers, CP/1/56, 57, 88, 90: George Liddell to Cotesworth, 9 September 1722, 17 March 1722/3.

27 TWA, GU/HO/1/2, fol. 724; Dendy, p. 205.

28 Dendy, pp. 206, 209.

obtained. The keelmen unanimously rejected their masters' proposal, which would commit 'the absolute superintendancy, conduct and management' of their contributions to the Hostmen, and petitioned the House of Commons in favour of Harvey's plan.[29] Edward Mosley, a magistrate and fitter, and Thomas Waters, also a fitter, attended the Commons committee appointed to consider the keelmen's petition. Much attention was given to their complaint about the overloading of the keels, but Harvey stated that the Charity was necessary because 'great numbers of the keelmen employed at Newcastle are natives of Scotland, and from the mode of binding, hiring and service are not…allowed to gain settlements in the Parish of All Saints where most of them reside'. Mosley confirmed that it was 'the custom to pass Scotch keelmen and their families to their own country on their becoming indigent', but he believed that they were given parochial relief until their settlements were discovered. The committee resolved that the existing Act regulating measurement of the keels ought to be amended, and that it was expedient that a bill should be introduced for the relief of the keelmen and their families residing in and about Newcastle.[30] Harvey drafted a bill to deal with both matters, but altered his original plan for the Charity by making void the deed of settlement and establishing a new fund. The fitters would still deduct money from the men's wages but would be liable to examination on oath before the mayor and two aldermen, and any sums embezzled or misapplied would be recovered by distress. The keelmen governors would be empowered to sue and might them-selves be sued.[31] The fitters resolved that the bill, which put power in the hands of 'a sett of people who ought not by any means to be trusted', should be resisted in every particular. Harvey, realising that his bill had no chance of success, abandoned it in favour of a measure proposed by Rose Fuller, MP for Rye, to regulate the keel-load.[32] The Hostmen thereupon offered to promote a bill which would place the Charity under gentlemen who would see it properly administered, but the keelmen declined. The Hostmen concluded that no bill was better than one disagreeable to the keelmen,[33] and thus, once again,

---

29 See **Document 130 ff.**, 1768–70, below.

30 *Journals of the House of Commons*, 32, pp. 777–9.

31 TWA, 394/29.

32 For the fitters' comments on Fuller and his bill, see **Documents 164–8**, March–April 1770.

33 TWA 394/29, J. Airey to Mosley, 24 March 1770.

the attempt to establish the Charity on a firm foundation ended in failure.

Meanwhile, in 1730 about 200 keelmen had formed a Benefit Society, but through lack of support were obliged to admit non-keelmen. This body kept control of the hospital building, but by 1770 it had fallen into disrepair, while membership of the Society had shrunk to scarcely 100, mostly old men 'fitter to be supplied themselves than to support others'. During the next decade under better management membership increased, benefits to the distressed were doubled, funeral costs and legacies were advanced, and the building was repaired.[34] In an *Address to Young Keelmen* (1781), the secretary of the Society warned them of a 'cruel kind of oeconomy' whereby keelmen could not obtain a parochial settlement in Newcastle, even if they had laboured as 'indented servants from year to year for forty or fifty years'. To avoid 'the deplorable situation of the aged and starving keelmen', he urged them to join the Society in their health and strength, otherwise, overtaken by infirmity, sickness or old age, they would have no alternative but to beg or starve.[35]

A few years later, an 'Acting Committee' of keelmen, assisted by a schoolmaster, recently appointed secretary of the Hospital Society, drew up plans to deal with these ever-present circumstances, and to ensure that an aged or infirm keelman, instead of being 'forsaken by his former friends and left destitute', could look forward to 'a comfortable maintenance for life' in a new hospital which it was proposed to build. It was clearly intended that this new association would seek to regulate the terms of the keelmen's employment, and various suggestions were made to prevent the overloading of the keels. A somewhat naive optimism marked some of these proposals

---

34 Alexander Murray, *Account of the Keelmen's Hospital and Society* (1781), see **Document 184**. That the membership included non-keelmen was a potential source of conflict. In January 1773, William Smith was presented for attempting to create discord in the Company by asserting that the tradesmen kept up the box and the keelmen 'lay upon it and consumed the money gathered by the tradesmen'; that the keelmen drank their money in summer and lay on the box in winter. Smith was expelled by a large majority, but in February 1792, at a general meeting of the keelmen, it was agreed by 30 votes to 21 that in future only keelmen should enter the Society and that landsmen who had entered since the last meeting should have their money returned (TWA, CH.KH/1, Minute Book of the Hospital Society, 1740–1842, pp. 113, 166). The local historian Richard Welford wrote in the front of this book 'a record of squabbling and disorder'.

35 See **Document 184**.

which had wrecked previous schemes, and it was well that the committee accepted a suggestion from Nathaniel Clayton, the town clerk, that the mayor should be governor of the proposed society and that four gentlemen of Newcastle should be among the trustees. As the scheme progressed, Clayton's input became dominant, and eventually the plan to be submitted to parliament placed the Charity under the mayor, certain aldermen, the MPs for Newcastle, and the governor, stewards and other members of the Hostmen's Company – very similar to what had been proposed in the bill of 1712. The keelmen's role was much reduced from what they had originally intended and, instead of a specific remedy against the overloading of the keels, was the bland formula 'that some mode which shall be deemed most effectual shall be adopted by the Bill to prevent all overmeasure and any grievance or oppression arising therefrom'.[36]

The keelmen proceeded to petition the House of Commons for a bill to establish a permanent fund for their support, and after Clayton had confirmed statements in the petition as to the inadequacy of parochial relief, leave was granted, and a bill prepared by Sir Matthew White Ridley and Charles Brandling, MPs for Newcastle, and Charles Grey, MP for Northumberland, was introduced. After some amendments, it passed the Commons and, without further amendment, the Lords. It received the royal assent on 11 June 1788.[37]

'The Society of Keelmen on the River Tyne' thus constituted was governed by 21 Guardians. The two MPs for Newcastle, the mayor, recorder, sheriff, four senior aldermen and the governor and stewards of the Hostmen's Company were always to be included in that number. The remaining nine Guardians were to be fitters, chosen annually by the keelmen's stewards, elected by their fellows. The Guardians were incorporated and empowered to make byelaws, provide a hospital for the destitute, grant pensions to widows and allowances for funeral expenses. Contributions were to be deducted from the wages of each keel-crew, and both fitters and collectors were to be liable to examination upon oath. In case of embezzlement or misapplication of the funds, the deficit was to be levied by distress. The off-putters at each staith were to swear that to the best of their skill and judgement they would cause the keels to be 'fairly and justly loaded after the due and accustomed rate of

---

36 See **Document 184 ff.**, 1786–8.
37 *Journals of the House of Commons*, 43 (1788), pp. 201, 440, 444, 498, 545.

eight chaldrons to each keel'.[38] A copy of the oath was to be filed in the town clerk's office and made available for inspection by the keelmen, but the vague formula left plenty of room for dispute, and was hardly 'the most effectual mode' of preventing this persistent grievance. Although any off-putter who deliberately caused the keels to be overloaded could be prosecuted for perjury, the keelmen could not sue, and most of the Guardians, directly or indirectly involved in the coal trade themselves, were unlikely to be willing to do so. However, arrangements were made to put the Act immediately into effect. The oath was administered to the off-putters, the keelmen's stewards were elected, and a collector was appointed to gather the contributions, which were fixed at a halfpenny for every chaldron transported. The cost of obtaining the Act, in excess of £200, was the first charge on the fund, and to allow it to accumulate no charitable disbursements were made until July 1791. The Guardians then decreed a weekly allowance of five shillings to the temporarily sick or disabled, three shillings to the superannuated, one shilling and sixpence to widows without children, two shillings to widows with two children, and two shillings and sixpence to those with a greater number of children. Funeral allowances were fixed at £2 in respect of a keelman, his wife or widow, and ten shillings for a child under fourteen years of age, if the father was dead.[39]

The newly elected keelmen's stewards proceeded to consult the men in their respective works on several articles. The substance of the replies were incorporated into a petition to inform the Guardians of the 'real state of the people'.[40] This petition, signed by 229 keelmen, called for payment in cash for any work the keelmen did at the staithes, and, instead of the beer provided by the shipmasters, payment of 1s. 4d. per keel. As some keels were still being overloaded, the petitioners asked that an inspector be appointed 'to bring any offputter who does not fulfil his duty to justice to be punished for perjury'.

The same expectation that the Guardians would act in the industrial as well as in the charitable sphere is evident in another representation addressed to them, 'in the name of the people at large', by the Committee of the Keelmen. They begged that the stewards be ordered

38 For the text of the Act see TWA 394/54, and J. Brand, *History and Antiquities of… Newcastle upon Tyne*, 2 volumes (London, 1789), I, p. 655.
39 TWA 394/54, Guardians' Minute Book, 1788–95.
40 For the articles and petition, see **Documents 190** and **192**.

to inspect the off-putters at the several staithes to see justice done to all parties, and that the Guardians would 'empower the off-putter not to load a keel unless she swims fair'. They also called on the Guardians to petition parliament to have the keels fairly weighed and measured, and suggested that the off-putters at Sunderland should be required to take the same oath as those at Newcastle, a measure which they declared would remove 'a great oppression'. They requested that a clerk should be appointed to oversee all receipts and disbursements for the Charity. They hoped that a new hospital, which the Guardians had discretion to build, would have more attention paid to utility and less to ornament, as in the existing one.[41]

These hopes were soon disappointed. The Guardians took no action regarding overmeasure or payments in liquor, and they neither commissioned a new hospital nor improved the old one, which remained, without assistance from the recently established charitable fund, in the care of the Society founded in 1730. Heavy demands were being made on the fund which, in July 1795, besides assisting those suffering from temporary illness, was supporting 102 superannuated keelmen, 53 widows and seven orphans.[42] Its revenues were at the same time being reduced, as the colliers were increasingly being loaded directly from spouts constructed at staithes in the lower reaches of the river, thus dispensing with the services of keelmen. The Guardians recommended that for the benefit of the fund a charge of three farthings per chaldron should be imposed on coal so loaded, but the coal owners refused.[43] Pressure on the fund continued to increase. In 1815, payments to claimants amounted to £2,235, and remained at that level during the next three years, while the deficit between income and expenditure grew so great that it seemed the Charity could not survive without extra help.[44] As part of the terms agreed to end a strike by the keelmen in 1819, the coal owners agreed to donate £300 immediately to the fund (which was struggling to support 138 superannuated members, 182 widows, six orphans and 22 sick), and to grant a farthing on every chaldron of coal exported from the Tyne. The grant was confirmed by an Act of Parliament which received the royal assent on 8 July 1820.[45]

---

41 See **Document 193**.
42 TWA 394/54, Guardians' Minute Book, 1788–95, enclosure, 2 September 1795.
43 TWA 394/54, Guardians' Minute Book, 1788–95, 22 November 1794.
44 See **Document 293**; Keelmen's petition, 28 September 1819.
45 **Document 317**; *Journals of the House of Commons*, 75 (1819–20), pp. 44, 145–6, 354, 423.

Those receiving grants from the Charity could not gain any additional assistance they might need from the parish. In 1803, three stewards of the Charity were impressed into the navy and were therefore unable to grant certificates to keelmen in their respective works who had become infirm. These men had to wait, without help from their parish, until new stewards had been elected. 'Parochial relief as to keelmen is done away', the Mayor of Newcastle declared.[46] Even if some keelmen could claim parochial relief, the amount they received from the Charity was deducted from what they would otherwise have had from the parish, which left them no better off than the other poor. According to a letter of 23 May 1815 to the *Newcastle Courant,* the keelmen regarded this as a great hardship, and on that account other bodies of workers did not form societies similar to the keelmen's.[47] When the Charity's revenue was cut off by the keelmen's strike of 1822, the superannuated keelmen, widows and orphans of keelmen in the Township of Swalwell were refused relief from their parish of Whickham, but the magistrates at Gateshead ruled that until the claimants' allowance from the fund was restored, each parish or township in which the keelmen were 'legally settled' must provide for them.[48]

As the use of keels diminished and the export of coal increased, the coal owners' grant became the Charity's chief source of revenue. In 1829, for example, the keelmen's contribution amounted to £1,037 and the coal owners' to £798, but in 1866 the keelmen's had fallen to £232 against the coal owners' £1,856, while the total fund, which in 1829 stood at £2,953, had increased to £11,505 in 1866. The number of superannuated keelmen receiving support steadily declined from 154 in 1829 to 83 in 1866, and the number of widows, 190 in 1829 (and a maximum of 206 in 1832), progressively decreased thereafter to 100 in 1866. Allowances of £2,295 in 1829 fell to £1,416 in 1836, but then rose to £2,014 in 1866.[49] In January 1872, the Act 24 & 25 Victoria (1861), which abolished dues levied by charities on goods transported by ships, came into effect and deprived the fund of its main revenue. Gross income which in 1871 had totalled £2,732 fell immediately, and by 1874 was reduced to £790, while expenditure on 44

46 TNA, ADM 1/2141, Thomas Clennell to Adam Mackenzie, 23 May 1803.
47 NEIMME, ZD/70, pp. 25–9, press cutting. Keelmen who had been born in the parish would have a legal settlement there and could therefore claim parochial relief, but his would not apply to those born elsewhere.
48 Petition, 21 December 1822; N. Clayton to R. Nicholson and J. Potts, 28 December 1822, **Documents 416** and **417**.
49 NEIMME, ZD/70; TWA 394/57.

superannuated keelmen, 87 widows and two orphans amounted to £874, plus £111 for management.[50] In 1876, only 63 keelmen were still contributing by the tide and the continuance of their occupation was being increasingly threatened. The Society still had capital of £11,254, accumulated mainly from the coal owners' grant and investments, and it was suggested that it should be reconstituted as a friendly society 'more in consonance with the requirements of the present day'.[51] During the next decade keelmen and their old-style keels virtually disappeared from the river, but the Charity had served its purpose in assisting the many members of their community in need.

The Hospital Society, meanwhile, had continued its independent existence. A hundred years after its inauguration it had 300 members and £600 invested,[52] but in 1852 its stewards announced that, on account of 'the decay of the keelmen's trade', the Society was in 'extreme poverty'. Allowances to the sick had been discontinued and the meagre resources applied to funeral expenses. There was no money to repair the clock tower, badly damaged when struck by lightning, and the stewards were forced to petition the town council and appeal to the public for assistance.[53] In 1898, the lease of the ground on which the hospital stood expired, and the Corporation took over the building, which in 1890 had needed at least £163 for repairs. Those who had occupied rooms for at least 20 years were allowed to stay at a weekly rent of sixpence, but by that time no keelmen remained among the tenants.[54] The building still stands, a memorial to a remarkable attempt at self-help by a community well acquainted with poverty.

The keelmen's employers and the magistrates had to deal with a workforce which they regarded as 'too ready to rise and become tumultuous upon the least pretence',[55] but masters, magistrates

---

50 NCL, press cutting with information on the Charity 1864–74 supplied by the Secretary to the Treasury in response to a request by Joseph Cowen MP, attached to booklet by William Brockie, *The Keelmen of the Tyne*, n.d.

51 Press cutting, *c*.1876, *ibid*.

52 *Account of the Keelmen's Hospital* (Newcastle, 1829). There are a number of items relating to the hospital in TWA, including minute book 1740–1842, cash book 1771–97, and register of members 1769–1888 (CH.KH/1; CH.KH/2/4; CH.KH/5).

53 Petition, 1 September 1852, **Document 421**.

54 TWA, MD/NC/77/1, Newcastle Corporation Estate and Property sub-committee Minute Book, no. 1, p. 1, 5 December 1890; 18 November and 8 December 1898, pp. 123–4; Dendy, introduction, lii.

55 TNA, SP 36/83/2/9, 21 April 1746, a commonly expressed sentiment.

and men were united in opposition to the impressment of keelmen into the navy. As a body of physically robust men, skilled in navigating craft on a difficult and dangerous waterway, the keelmen were a desirable target for the press gangs which from time to time visited the region. The keelmen readily claimed that keel-work was a nursery for seamen, and that some of the finest men in the navy came from their midst, but they were particularly belligerent in resisting enforced recruitment into that service.[56] Normally, on account of the importance of the coal trade, they were protected against impressment, and without such a safeguard issued by the Admiralty they refused to work, but when shortage of men for the navy grew acute, the Admiralty ordered protections to be ignored. Thus, in May 1803, the press gang made a sudden swoop and seized more than 50 unsuspecting keelmen, whereupon the rest stopped work. The material printed below concerns the difficult negotiations by members of the coal trade and local MPs with the Admiralty, the agreement to procure substitutes, and how this arrangement was interpreted on Tyne and Wear between 1803 and 1811.[57]

Many documents in this volume concern strikes by the keelmen. The grievances which provoked these stoppages are set forth in the keelmen's petitions, but it is worth considering some of the issues, and conduct of the parties concerned, in more detail. Several of the strikes featured demands for an increase of wages, and restoration of allowances that had been withdrawn. In 1719, the magistrates declared that the keelmen's call for an additional four shillings per tide would amount to six or seven thousand pounds annually, 'a burthen too great for the coal trade to bear', and when strikers sought a wage increase in 1750, the magistrates rejected 'very extravagant demands that could not be complied with'.[58] In 1791, the keelmen struck because their wages were proving inadequate 'on account of the high advance of the necessaries of life'. A general meeting of the coal owners and fitters, 'after much deliberation', granted a small increase to the above-bridge men, and resolved that

---

56   'It is well known that during the last war, besides furnishing our quota as required for the service of the state, the navy was supplied with a number of its best seamen from our body' (Second Address of the Keelmen, 15 October 1822); Nicholas Rogers, *The Press Gang: Naval Impressment and its Opponents in Georgian Britain* (London, 2007), p. 40.

57   See **Documents 252 ff.**, concerning the impressment of keelmen, 1803–11.

58   TNA, SP43/57, Magistrates to the Secretary of State, 30 May 1719; TNA, SP36/112/141–2, Robert Sorsbie to Duke of Bedford, 30 April 1750.

payments in drink for certain tasks should be commuted into cash.[59] The high cost of provisions triggered another strike in February 1800, but the magistrates brokered a settlement whereby each crew would receive an allowance of 2s. 6d. per tide while the average price of wheat and rye remained above a certain level. This 'bread money', intended to be a temporary arrangement, became a permanent part of the keelmen's wages.[60] By 1809 the keelmen were complaining that even if they were to have as much work as they could do, 'the very high price of every article connected with housekeeping' would render their existing wages barely sufficient.[61] The coal owners and fitters were prepared to make an addition to the wages of the keelmen stationed above bridge, but not to those below. This resulted in a prolonged strike accompanied by 'great disorder and some acts of violence',[62] but although deployments of troops on land, and measures to protect keels manned by substitute workers on the river, kept the keelmen in check, they did not bring them back to work. The employers, evidently anxious to avoid further disruption to trade, suddenly announced that they were prepared to reconsider the keelmen's demands, provided they returned to work. The settlement that followed gave all the keelmen an immediate increase in their wages and a further deferred addition to the wages of the above-bridge men – a considerable victory for the keelmen.[63]

The keelmen suffered from various proceedings, which, as some of them remarked, were 'probably unknown to the Gentlemen who are our supreme masters by the subtlety of their under agents'.[64] The fitters' servants, the keelmen alleged, abused them 'beyond all reason' at the staithes, made use of their employers' keels, and engaged men, 'not capable of their labour', to navigate them, thereby endangering lives.[65] One of the fitters explained

59 Andrew Mitchell, *Address to the Society of Keelmen* (1792), see **Document 200**; Resolutions of the Coal Owners and Fitters, 26 September 1791; Further Regulation. See **Documents 195** and **199**.

60 *Newcastle Courant*, 15 February 1800; NEIMME, Easton Papers, East/4, p. 31, Minutes of meeting of Fitters and Coal Owners, 30 September 1809.

61 TWA 394/37, Petition, 29 August 1809.

62 Isaac Cookson to William Charleton, 3 November 1809 (NCL, J. Bell, *Collections relative to the River Tyne: its Trade and the Conservancy thereof*, II, fols 96–7).

63 For details of the strike, the tactics employed and settlement agreed, see **Document 208 ff.**

64 Representation of 30 Skippers and Keelmen, 1788, **Document 192**.

65 Second Remonstrance of the Keelmen, 1719, **Documents 69**.

that servants were employed to see that the keelmen took in the proper amount of coal at the staithes and delivered it to the ships, for 'without being well looked after, [they would] frequently imbezel and dispose of coals in their way down to Shields'.[66] In 1750, the keelmen complained that staithmen deliberately delayed them in order to gain the sixpence, which was intended to provide drink for those who loaded the keels manually, for use of the spout instead. This delay could result in the keelmen having to 'go down to Shields in dark and stormy nights to the danger of our lives', besides the loss of a tide, which cost them 13s. 4d.[67]

The keelmen complained that they were obliged to spend more than they could afford in waiting for orders at 'can-houses' where their beer was supplied and part of their wages paid. To enhance their profits, the can-house keepers, who were all the fitters' servants and one of the keelmen's 'many degrees of masters', would supply them with a brew called 'savage beer or beer for savages' (for which they were charged 'the gentleman's price'), and if they were 'slow in drinking', would abuse and threaten them that they would be turned out of their keels.[68] In the wages settlement of 1791–2, it was agreed that every keelman was to be free to purchase liquor wherever he pleased and 'not at any particular can or public house', but, according to a staithman who was employed at Dunston between 1819 and 1833, most of the collieries both on the Tyne and Wear still allowed their agents to keep public houses where the workmen were paid part of their wages in money and part in drink.[69] This gave the staithman opportunity of 'setting his own interest at variance with that of his employers' by engaging an excessive number of men who would be supplied with liquor at his public house.[70] In 1849, despite what had been agreed in 1792, keelmen at many staithes were being paid for some tasks in liquor or tobacco.[71]

---

66 Edward Mosley's notes of evidence to be given to the Commons' committee, 1770, see **Document 158**.

67 Explanation of the keelmen's grievances, 1750, **Document 118**.

68 *Ibid.* In 1710, the keelmen complained that they were 'obliged by several fitters' servants to spend in drink, or they will stop some of their money for it, and sometime for trash liquor for which they must leave as well as the money for it' (Cotesworth Papers, CJ 3/6, Minutes of the Keelmen's grievances), **Document 12**.

69 For the 1791–2 settlement, see **Document 195 ff.**; DCRO, D/CG6/1247, A.H. Matthewson, Memorial of Services, 1819–33, reproduced by permission of Durham County Record Office.

70 Matthewson's Memorial.

71 *Gateshead Observer*, 24 April 1849.

The overloading of the keels, a flexible means of lowering the price to the shipmaster instead of a direct reduction that would be difficult to reverse, involved frequent hardship for the keelmen. The customary keel-load of eight Newcastle chaldrons, each weighing 53 hundredweights, on which the keelmen's pay was based and custom duties assessed, was indicated by a nail or plate fixed by customs officers on the side of the keel. An overloaded keel would sink, partially or totally submerging these indicators, but there was room for error in this somewhat rough and ready system. An old wet keel when loaded would naturally sink lower than one that was new and dry, and the keelmen themselves stated that long experience had shown that 'on account of the strength or weakness of the water' it would take 'three parts of a chalder more to put a keel to her marks' at one part of the river than at another.[72] Even so, if the keels were grossly overloaded there could be no mistake. Overmeasure involved additional labour for the keelmen without extra pay, danger in navigating overloaded craft, and, as the ships were filled in fewer keel-loads, reduction of their potential earnings. The coal owners and magistrates generally promised redress when the keelmen complained about this practice, but the redress was invariably short-lived. Although the Articles of 1744, signed by magistrates and fitters, decreed that no keel should be obliged to take in more than the King's measure (eight Newcastle chaldrons), one of the keelmen's chief complaints in their strike of 1750 concerned overmeasure which, according to an observer, was so great that they 'could scarce keep the keel above water'.[73] After another strike for the same reason in 1768, the lawyer Thomas Harvey, as mentioned above, tried to obtain an Act of Parliament to regulate the keel-load as well as to establish the keelmen's Charity. When he found that his proposed bill would not succeed, he joined Rose Fuller, MP for Rye, who proposed to bring in a bill to deal solely with over-measure. The coal owners and fitters petitioned against Fuller's bill, but it proceeded no further than the second reading, and was not renewed in the next session.[74] The Act which established the keelmen's Charity included a provision to oblige the off-putters to

---

72 Petition of the Committee of Keelmen to the Guardians of the Charity, **Document 192**.

73 For Articles of 1744, see **Document 114**, footnote; Keelmen's explanation of their grievances, 1750, **Document 118**; William Brown to C. Spedding, 30 April 1750, **Document 115**.

74 See **Document 184 ff.**, 1786–8; *Journals of the House of Commons*, 32, pp. 904, 908.

swear that they would cause the keels to be fairly and justly loaded, but, soon after they had taken the oath, some keels were still being overloaded.[75] Likewise, in April 1820, 'notwithstanding the oath administered to the offputters', the keelmen were said to be carrying overmeasure as great as had been a cause of a strike a few months previously, and in 1822 they declared that they were generally being obliged to transport an extra chaldron which reduced their wages by 2s. 6d. per tide.[76]

The coal owners manipulated the measure according to the exigencies of trade, which also determined another part of their policy that impacted on the keelmen – regulation of the vend.[77] Although combinations of coal owners, fitters and shipmasters to raise the price by restricting output, or retarding the loading or dispatch of the colliers, were illegal and often unstable – they seldom, if ever, included all concerned in the trade – they continued, albeit intermittently, in one form or another. In 1710, the keelmen estimated that such a contract between coal owners and fitters was costing each keel-crew more than £10 or £12, and the Common Council attacked the combination, which, besides reducing the Corporation of Newcastle's revenues and curtailing trade in general, was occasioning great hardships to many keelmen and their families for want of employment.[78] In 1718, the keelmen complained of a contract 'by which our keeles are not onely consined to lye by for one halfe the year idle, but also when shipps doe come must not be loaden out of their turnes', and a year later they repeated that the long contract rendered them unable to maintain themselves and their families, 'our wages being so low, and the measure so great'.[79] In 1738, the fitters, with the connivance of the coal owners and shipowners, proportioned their vends every month so that those who exceeded their quota were to stop loading ships until those who had fallen short had vended their share. Some fitters had to turn over ships they were about to load to others, and

---

75 Petitions to the Guardians of the Charity, 1788, see **Document 192**.
76 Archibald Reed to John Buddle, 5 April 1820, **Document 333a**; Keelmen to Adam Askew, 18 October 1822, **Document 363**.
77 The 'vend' was the gross sale from collieries in the Northumberland and Durham coalfield.
78 Petitions to the Magistrates, **Document 13**; Common Council Book, 1699–1718, **Document 15**.
79 Petition, April 1718, TWA 394/7; Second Remonstrance of the Keelmen, **Document 69**.

restrictions were imposed on the loading of 'irregular ships'.[80] These arrangements resulted in some keelmen getting too much work while others were deprived of employment. A number of 'indigent, suffering skippers' declared that 'by reason of the want of busyness' they and their families were on the point of starving for lack of the necessities of life, and others complained that the combination prevented them working 'at all times that ships required coales'.[81] Thus, while the fitters were doing 'everything in their power to contribute to the good of the trade', the keelmen enforced a strike.[82] There was an incompatibility of interest, at least in the short term, between the keelmen, who would welcome an abundant supply of coal giving them plenty of work, and their employers, who sought to prevent a glutted market with falling prices and the risk that some collieries would go out of business.

The loading of the colliers by means of spouts constituted the most serious threat to the keelmen. These devices, down which the colliery waggons emptied their coal, had long been used to load keels, but in the later eighteenth century staithes were erected with spouts designed to load ships, thus dispensing with keelmen. At first, only small ships that could venture up the undredged river to staithes at various points below Newcastle could be loaded in this manner, but in the first quarter of the nineteenth century larger ships were increasingly being loaded by spout and by a new device, 'the drop', whereby the colliery waggon was lowered over the ship and emptied into her hold. Since no ship could pass through the low arches of the bridge at Newcastle, it was the keelmen employed in the lower reaches of the river who were menaced by these developments. The keelmen complained of spout-loadings in their strike of 1771, after which the matter lay dormant until 1794, by which time the method was making 'amazing progress', with nine staithes, nearly all with two spouts, already in action, while more staithes were being erected for that purpose.[83] The keelmen's employment was being so much reduced that they could not earn sufficient to support themselves and their families. They enforced a strike and demanded that loading by spout should cease, but the coal owners and fitters unanimously

---

80   Dendy, pp. 194–9; TWA, GU/HO/2, Hostmen's Minute Book (in which there is additional material).

81   Petitions, 4 and 9 May 1738, **Documents 87** and **92**.

82   Dendy, pp. 198–9.

83   Matthew Ridley to George Ward, 14 June 1771, **Document 170**; Keelmen's Address to the Public, 9 August 1794, **Document 207**.

rejected this demand as 'a direct infringement of property' and of their legal right to ship their coals in the most eligible manner.[84] Faced with this intransigence, a party of keelmen demolished the spouts serving four collieries, an action that the majority, who only wanted employment, repudiated. Having failed to obtain the least concession, they eventually returned to work.

The issue rose again in 1819 when the keelmen enforced another strike mainly because of 'very great privations from want of employment' on account of 'the vend by spout having increased so much of late'. They therefore begged that no ship be allowed to load more than six keel-loads (48 Newcastle chaldrons) at any spout, and that a penny for every chaldron so loaded should be donated to their Charity. The coal owners and fitters totally rejected this request as 'a violation of private property and of the principles on which all trade is carried on'. Although, as part of the settlement to end the strike, the employers agreed that a farthing on every chaldron of coal shipped whether by keel or by spout should be donated to the Charity, they adamantly adhered to the principle of unfettered use of the spouts.[85] This resulted in the 'long stop' of 1822, when the keelmen held out for almost ten weeks but failed to achieve restriction of spout-loadings or to gain any other concession, a stance which, to the keelmen's wrath, the local newspapers enthusiastically endorsed.[86] The importance of the spouts was clearly demonstrated, as coal exports in ships so loaded actually increased during the strike, which proved that the keelmen's long exercised power to bring the coal trade to a complete standstill had disappeared.[87] The strike was remarkable not only for its unprecedented length, and the collateral damage done to other local industries, but because only those keelmen employed below Newcastle bridge were directly affected by the spouts. Although the keelmen's customary solidarity

---

84 *Newcastle Courant*, 2 August 1794; Address to the Public setting out the Coal Owners' case, 30 July 1794, **Documents 205-6**.

85 Petition of the Keelmen, 28 September 1819, **Document 293**; Resolutions of the Coalowners, 2 October 1819, **Document 299**; Terms offered to the Keelmen, 20 October 1819, **Document 317**.

86 The keelmen accused the coal owners of bribing 'the mercenary editors of the public papers' which were united in denouncing the strike and advocating coercive measures against the keelmen, see Third Address of the Keelmen, 14 November 1822, **Document 394**. See also Maurice Milne, 'Strikes and Strike-Breaking in North East England, 1815–44: the Attitude of the Local Press', *International Review of Social History*, 22 (1977), pp. 226–40.

87 *Tyne Mercury*, 19 November 1822, **Document 396**.

was on the whole maintained, intimidation certainly prevented many of the above-bridge men returning to work. Intimidation was a feature of most keelmen's strikes, and a keelman who broke ranks was liable to be brutally beaten, as were any substitute workers who fell into the keelmen's hands.

The worst outbreak of violence in which the keelmen played a major part occurred in the Newcastle food riot of 1740. This began as a protest led by the pitmen against the high price of corn and the merchants who were perceived to be profiting thereby. Eventually the keelmen, made idle by the stoppage of the collieries, joined the pitmen 'in terrible numbers, armed with all sorts of weapons'. The climax came when the local militia in a panic opened fire, killing one man and wounding others, whereupon the mob launched a violent assault on the Guildhall where the magistrates were assembled. The building, 'a large and beautiful fabric', was sacked and left a 'perfect ruin', the municipal records were thrown to the winds and the treasury robbed of more than £1200. The magistrates, though terrified, were not harmed. The arrival of three companies of soldiers by a forced march from Alnwick, where they had received the magistrates' urgent plea for help, scattered the rioters before they could carry out their threats of further destruction.[88]

Such an outburst of violence by the keelmen was unprecedented, but at other times the magistrates of Newcastle, often with those of Northumberland and Durham, had the difficult task of dealing with these hundreds of robust men during the many strikes they enforced. The local militia was no match for them and sooner or later in the course of a strike the magistrates appealed to the government for military assistance. The coal trade was so important to the nation as a whole that the request was usually granted, though the central authorities and the local commander occasionally made it clear that the military were not at the magistrates' beck and call.[89] The strategy employed is fully described in the documents printed below, but, although it generally prevented major disorder, it seldom brought strikes immediately to an end. In 1770, the keelmen claimed that when they had protested against oppressions imposed upon them, especially with respect to overmeasure, several keelmen had been killed or wounded by soldiers drawn up against them 'under the

---

88 Cuthbert Fenwick to the Duke of Newcastle, 27 June 1740, **Document 96**; Brief for the Crown against the rioters, **Document 98**.

89 Correspondence on withdrawal of infantry from Newcastle, 9–17 October 1822, **Documents 347–50**.

pretence of quelling a riot when no riot was intended nor effected by keelmen'.[90] No evidence has been found to support the claim that keelmen were killed when the military were deployed against them in the strikes of 1744 and 1750, to which this complaint may refer, though the fatality by the shooting in 1740 was never reported to the government nor mentioned in the brief drawn up for prosecution of the rioters. In 1794, the keelmen complained that 'horse and foot were employed to chase and affright women and children and no regard paid to guilty or innocent', as if they had intended 'to turn the world upside down' – probably an allusion to events in France.[91] One man (not a keelman) was killed in 1819 when marines fired at a stone- throwing mob in North Shields, and another man (again not a keelman) was wounded by marines who (after publicised warnings) fired at stone-throwers in 1822. Apart from these isolated incidents, the military, despite considerable provocation by the keelmen, generally exercised admirable restraint and averted bloodshed.[92]

Bound keelmen who went on strike were liable to short terms of imprisonment, but in 1822 their employers, much to the irritation of some of the magistrates, showed reluctance in executing warrants issued for breach of contract.[93] Sentences passed on those guilty of assaults and violence during strikes were lenient by the standards of the day. The keelmen's employers and the magistrates were wary of alienating this workforce, so important to the economy of the region, by harsh sentences. The authorities were probably well aware that some of the keelmen's complaints, especially against overmeasure, were justified.

After failing to force restriction on loadings by spout in the 'long stop' of 1822, the keelmen resolved to open a public subscription to seek, by recourse to law, the removal of the spout staithes as obstructions to the free navigation of the river. At the fourth attempt, the

---

90   Keelmen's Resolutions, 5 January 1770, **Document 147**.

91   Address to the Public, 9 August 1794, **Document 207**. More than 100 special constables were enrolled at this 'peculiar crisis', *Newcastle Courant*, 19 and 26 July 1794.

92   Joseph Bulmer to Viscount Sidmouth, 15 October 1819; Minutes made in the Mayor's Chamber, 15 October, **Documents 310–11**; *Tyne Mercury*, 19 October 1819, **Document 313**; Handbill, 22 November 1822; *Newcastle Chronicle*, 23 November 1822, **Documents 397–8**; *Tyne Mercury*, 26 November 1822, **Document 402**.

93   *Tyne Mercury*, 5 and 12 November 1822, **Documents 387, 390**; *Durham County Advertiser*, 2 November 1822, **Document 387**, n. 1; Minutes of meeting of the Magistrates, 14 November 1822, **Document 393**.

keelmen's attorney obtained a bill of indictment on that ground against two staithes erected by Messrs Russell near Wallsend.[94] Henry Brougham was briefed for the keelmen and James Scarlett, KC, for the defence.[95] The case, *Rex v Russell*, was tried on 11 March 1824 before Mr Justice Bayley and a special jury at York, since a jury in Newcastle or Northumberland would probably have included coal owners or those associated with them.[96] Brougham argued that the staithes, erected by the coal owners for their private profit, seriously restricted the navigation and were of no benefit to the public. The sole question at issue was whether these structures constituted a public nuisance, and, anticipating a contention from the opposite side, he emphasised that the motives behind the prosecution were irrelevant. He called seventeen witnesses who testified as to the restriction of the navigation and accidents that had in consequence occurred.

Scarlett contended that the question was whether the public gained more than what was lost by the obstruction of the right of passage. The staithes promoted the trade of Newcastle and provided the London market with coal of a superior quality to the broken-up product from the keels. Therefore, they were not a nuisance in point of law. The best witnesses, Scarlett argued, would have been the local ship-owners, if they had suffered any disadvantage, but Brougham had called only one of them. The evidence that had not been called was of equal importance to that presented to the court. The Corporation of Newcastle, with an interest in a flourishing coal trade, had allowed these staithes, and the County of Northumberland had raised no objection against them. The prosecution had been brought to increase the number of keels, and he enlarged on the disastrous consequences that would ensue if the keelmen gained control of the local trade and the London market. He spoke with great force and called no witnesses.

In summing up, the judge stressed the potential benefit to the public as opposed to private profit that might result from the

---

94 NEIMME, Bell Collection, III, fol. 7, Applications to Newcastle Sessions, Morpeth Sessions and Newcastle Assizes failed, but succeeded at the Northumberland Sessions, 1823.

95 See Michael Lobban, 'Brougham, Henry Peter, First Baron Brougham and Vaux (1778–1868)', *Oxford Dictionary of National Biography*; Brougham was Lord Chancellor 1830–4; G.F.R. Barker, revised by Elisabeth A. Cawthon, 'James Scarlett, first Baron Abinger (1769–1844)', *Oxford Dictionary of National Biography*; Scarlett was Attorney General 1827–8 and 1829–30.

96 Michael Lobban, 'Bayley, Sir John, 1st Bart. (1763–1841)', *Oxford Dictionary of National Biography*; Bayley was appointed judge of King's Bench in 1808 and of the Exchequer, 1830–4.

restriction of the navigation, and instructed the jury to consider whether that benefit offset the prejudice that individuals suffered by curtailment of their right of passage. The proceedings lasted twelve hours, but in about three minutes the jury returned a verdict for the defendant.[97] Brougham immediately indicated that he would apply to the Court of King's Bench to set aside the verdict and enter it for the Crown on the grounds of misdirection by the judge. The case came before three judges of that court in Hilary term 1826. Brougham and his colleagues argued that it was totally unprecedented to justify the obstruction of a public right by alleging a collateral benefit – in this case better quality and cheaper coal for the consumer. Scarlett contended that the judge was entitled to point out the benefits to commerce, and his charge to the jury was correct in point of law. His observation about advantages to the London consumer was an illustration, not a direction.[98] The judges did not give their opinion until 26 May 1827, when the Lord Chief Justice, Lord Tenterden,[99] stated that he thought the verdict had been unduly influenced by the judge's remarks on public benefit and would therefore prefer the case to be tried again, but, as his colleagues considered that the verdict should stand, the rule for setting it aside had to be discharged.

Although the keelmen had lost and had to pay cost of suit, it had been proved, and even admitted by the defendants, that the staithes caused an obstruction, and in view of this and Lord Tenterden's remarks, counsel advised the keelmen to seek another trial. The case was tried again in August 1828 before Baron Hullock and a special jury at Carlisle Assizes.[100] Brougham and Scarlett again led on opposite sides and both repeated their former arguments with slight variations. Brougham again called numerous witnesses and Scarlett none. The judge dismissed many of the points on which Scarlett had placed great emphasis, particularly about benefit to the public, but he agreed that many more shipowners, who would have been the greatest sufferers from any obstruction, should have been brought to

---

97 *English Reports*, 108, pp. 568–9; *Durham Chronicle*, 14 August 1824, *Tyne Mercury*, 17 August 1824.

98 *English Reports*, 108, pp. 560–73.

99 Michael Lobban, 'Charles Abbott, First Baron Tenterden (1762–1832)', *Oxford Dictionary of National Biography*.

100 G.P.R. Barker, revised by Sinéad Agnew, 'Hullock, Sir John (1767-1829)', *Oxford Dictionary of National Biography*. Hullock was Baron of the Exchequer from 1823. The proceedings are reported in the *Tyne Mercury*, 19 August 1828, and the *Durham Chronicle*, 23 August 1828.

give evidence. It appeared that until recently no complaint had been made against the staithes, and he asked the jury to consider whether this acquiescence did not infer that they were not regarded as a serious obstacle. In the absence of evidence that he thought would have been most proper, he left it to the jury to decide whether the staithes obstructed the navigation to such an extent as to constitute a nuisance in law.

The jury retired for four hours, after which they produced a written verdict: that the navigation had been obstructed as described in the indictment, 'but that the trade of the town and port of Newcastle has notwithstanding increased'. After much dispute between counsel, the judge asked the jury whether they meant this as a special verdict to be left to the superior court to decide whether it was one of guilt or acquittal under the indictment. To this they assented, and the judge therefore accepted the verdict in that form.

On 24 May 1830, the case again came before the Court of King's Bench and counsel argued their respective interpretations of the verdict before Lord Chief Justice Tenterden. The matter had become further complicated by the death of Baron Hullock, and while Brougham and his colleague, Sir Cresswell Cresswell,[101] contended that a settlement could be made from Hullock's notes, Scarlett declared that this would be 'wild and visionary'. Lord Tenterden agreed that it would be 'utterly impossible' to settle from this source and favoured a new trial, but Brougham, concerned at the 'enormous' expense already incurred, called for an attempt to achieve an out of court settlement. This was at length agreed, and on Brougham's suggestion the papers were given to Mr Justice Bayley, the judge in the first trial. On 8 June, after hearing counsels' arguments, he declared that both sides had gone too far, and settled the matter by concluding that the verdict was consonant with that returned in the first trial.[102]

The failure, after more than eight years of litigation, to obtain removal of the spout staithes from the river meant that the keelmen's

---

101 Joshua S. Getzler, 'Cresswell, Sir Cresswell [formerly Cresswell Easterby] (1793–1863)', *Oxford Dictionary of National Biography*. Cresswell was a leader of the northern circuit, later King's Counsel and judge.

102 NCL, J. Bell, *Collections relative to the River Tyne: its Trade and the Conservancy thereof*, III, pp. 64–7; *Proceedings at Law in the Case of the King versus Russell and others relative to the Coal Staiths erected at Wallsend on the River Tyne* (Newcastle, 1830). The judgement in this case was not regarded as a good precedent in future cases of a similar nature. Its authority was 'much doubted' in 1836, *English Reports*, 111, p. 838, overruled in 1873, and disapproved in 1873–4, *ibid.*, 108, p. 560.

employment below Newcastle bridge continued to fall into a decline, hastened by the increasing use of steam-powered tugs to tow large ships to and from these staithes, a procedure which also impacted on the above-bridge men who would otherwise have loaded these colliers. The rapid development of railways after 1825, enabling the transport of coal from the pit-head to the spouts and drops, was a further blow to the keelmen. Their progressive decline, especially from the 1840s onwards, is indicated by the accounts of their Charity, which show the amount they contributed by the tide. During the 1830s their contributions amounted to between £800 and £1000, but in 1840 they fell to £620, to £571 in 1845, to £360 in 1849, and to £281 in 1852,[103] a year in which the stewards of the keelmen's hospital, which received nothing from this source, remarked on the 'decay in the keelmen's trade'.[104] Matthias Dunn, author of a book on the winning and working of collieries published that year, observed that the number of keels had become 'quite inconsiderable', a large proportion of the coal being delivered to the ships by railway.[105] Even so, some collieries continued to use keels. In 1854, it was estimated that keels still transported about one seventh of the coal exported from the Tyne,[106] but the opening of the Northumberland Dock on the north side of the river in 1857 and the Tyne Dock on the south side two years later further threatened the keelmen's employment. With 'exceptional coal-shipping facilities' these docks could discharge the equivalent of a keel-load of coal into a ship in a few minutes and 1000 tons in less than two and a half hours.[107] The dredging of the river, begun in the 1860s, enabled large ships to access these docks. In 1868, an official in one of the above-bridge concerns noted 'the rapid manner in which the shipment of coals by keels is falling off'.[108] In 1876, the opening of the swing bridge

---

103 NEIMME, WAT 1/20, Accounts of the Charity, 1827–42; for 1845 and 1849, D/70; for 1852, *Gateshead Observer*, 18 March 1854.

104 TWA 394/49, Petition of the Stewards of the Keelmen's Hospital, 1 September 1852, **Document 421**.

105 Matthias Dunn, *A Treatise on the Winning and Working of Collieries* (Newcastle and London, 1852), p. 130.

106 *Gateshead Observer*, 1 April 1854, Report of evidence given to a committee of the House of Commons. It was also said that the keelmen were 'very considerably decreased and are still decreasing'.

107 R.W. Johnson, *The Making of the Tyne, A Record of Fifty Years' Progress* (Newcastle, 1895), pp. 80, 82, 298; J. Guthrie, *The River Tyne, its History and Resources* (Newcastle, 1880), p. 114.

108 DCRO, NCB/1/Sc/631 (74), J. Nanson to R. Simpson, 9 April 1868.

to replace the Tyne bridge, which had hitherto prevented the colliers proceeding further up the river, was the final blow to the keelmen.

'It seems to me', an observer declared in 1889, 'that the time is not far distant when keelmen will be numbered with things of the past.' If keels were needed at all they were towed to and from the ships by steam boats,[109] and another writer did not regard strings of craft dragged up and down river in this manner as true Tyne keels.[110] His hope that a 'genuine old caulker-built eight chaldron keel' should be preserved in a museum was not realised, and not a single specimen of these craft has survived. Steam power both on land and water played a considerable part in rendering the keelmen redundant. Like many workers both before and after them, they were forced to yield to technical innovation, and so this body of men, once 'the very sinews of the coal trade',[111] gradually disappeared, and are now remembered only by the hospital building and a few folk songs.

109 John McKay, 'Keels and Keelmen', *Newcastle Weekly Chronicle Supplement*, 9 November 1889.
110 J.I. Nicholson, in *ibid.*
111 *Tyne Mercury*, 31 May 1803.

EDITORIAL METHOD

All abbreviations have been expanded; punctuation, where necessary, has been provided, and excessive capitalization modernized. The original spellings have been retained. If a writer appears to have omitted a word, or words have been lost through damage of the manuscript, the omission has been supplied in square brackets. An occasional uncertain reading has also been indicated by a question mark in brackets. Most documents have been reproduced in full, but in some cases, especially in newspaper reports, irrelevant matter or needless repetition has been left out as indicated by a number of dots ….

Almost all the documents bear dates and have been arranged in chronological order. The documents are numbered for convenience. The archival reference number is given in square brackets after the document's heading, and the location of documents (discussed in the preface) may be found in the bibliography.

THE DOCUMENTS

EARLY YEARS

1. Report from Newcastle c. 1638 [TNA, SP 16/408 f. 96]

There is in Newcastle upon Tyne of keelmen, watermen, and other labourers, above 1800 able men, the most of them being Scottish men and Borderers which came out of the Tynedale and Reddesdale. By reason of the stop of trade occasioned by cross winds this year, they have wanted employment and are thereby in great necessity, having most of them great charge of wives and children. And unless they have employment they must be relieved by the charity of others, the inhabitants of the town, many of whom are so poor that they are scarce able to maintain themselves, or else we doubt that in regard to their great necessity and rude condition, they will be in danger to assemble themselves and make an uproar in the town, as they did of late.[1]

---

[1]   This probably refers to a tumult in the spring of 1633, which was started by some apprentices but soon involved the whole working population. Secretary of State Sir John Coke rebuked the magistrates for failing to take sufficiently vigorous action against the rioters and suggested that the real cause of the disorder was not, as had been represented, the construction of a lime kiln on the local drying ground, but the inhabitants' desire for a change in their government. *Calendar of State Papers, Domestic, Charles I, 1631–33*, 11 and 26 March 1633, pp. 567, 585; *Addenda*, 1625–49, p. 453. The keelmen's 'necessity and rude condition' was cited by George Dawson, a customs official, who in 1653 suggested that one or two hundred keelmen might be impressed into the navy, but on seeing that they had 'nothing but what they have on their backs and no means of procuring clothes', he concluded that 'such nasty creatures on board would do more harm than good', Dawson to the Admiralty, 12 and 14 May 1653, *Calendar of State Papers, Domestic, Commonwealth*, 1652–3, pp. 324, 330.

2. Mercurius Politicus, 22–31 August 1654: From Newcastle, August 21. [University of Durham, Special Collections, The Earl Grey Papers, Miscellaneous Books, GRE/v/Misc.6, ff. 255–7]

We have had a great stop of trade by our keel-mens pretence of too small wages from their masters; they al[l] as one man stood together, and would neither worke themselves, nor suffer others, though our Major used all possible means to satisfie them; whereupon he made a Proclamation, but all was to no purpose. And now though a Company of foot, and a Troop of Horse be drawn into Town, yet they continue in their obstinacie, notwithstanding that some of their leading men have been apprehended. The Justices intend to meet, and try if they can compaese the busines.

3. Copy report of an adjustment of the keelmen's wages, 22 August 1654[1] [Durham University Library, Special Collections, GRE/V/Misc/6 pp. 255–7]

The Town and County of Newcastle upon Tyne: At a meeting of the Mayor and Justices of the Peace of the said Town and County in the Guildhall for the said Town, the two and twentieth day of August in the year of our Lord 1654:

Whereas of late diverse ships and other vessells tradeing to this Port for coles do not come so high up the River of Tyne as formerly they have done to cast their ballast and take in their loadeing of coles, or some part thereof, which of late hath putt the skippers of keeles and their keelmen, which labour continually upon the said River, to much more hard labour and hazard of their lives by carrying their loadened keeles much oftner to Shields than formerly, by reason whereof the said skippers and keelmen have not, nor do receive, such sufficient recompence to support themselves and familyes as the said labour and hazard requires, whereupon the said skippers and keelmen haveing peticoned us concerning the same as a great grievance not able to be born by them thereby desireing their wages or dues may be augmented and considered accordingly, we therefore the Maior and Justices of Peace of the said Town and County, takeing the aforesaid peticon into present consid[er]acon, thinking it not fitt to defer the same lest some obstruccon might happen in the coletrade, and for avoiding further inconveniences likely thereupon to ensue, do think fitt that for the time to come it shall and may be lawfull to and for the said skippers and keelmen to demand, receive, and take of the masters of ships and other vessells tradeing to this Port for coles these rates, wages or dues in such manner and form as hereafter is menconed and sett down (that is to say): of the master of all such ships and other vessells as cast all their ballast at sea and take in their loadeing of coles at Shields, of the master of all such ships and other vessells as are unfitt to come up the River, but cast their ballast into keeles at Shields and take in their loading of coles there, and the masters of all such ships and other vessells that cast their ballast below a place in the River of Tyne called the Pace[2] and take in their loading of coles there, the skippers and keelmen in every such case shall demand receive and take of the master of every such ship or vessell the summe of three shillings for every keele of coles over and above the ten shillings and four pence they formerly took and received for their wages or dues, meate, drinking money and loaders, and shall demand and take for every lying tide of any ship or other vessell above the Pace the summe of twelve pence, and for every lying tide[3] of any ship or vessell below the Pace the summe of two shillings and sixpence, and no more. Provided always, and it is to be understood, that whatsoever ship or other vessell shall cast their ballast att any shoar above the Pace and there take in so many coales as with conveniency and safety to the ship they may go down withall below the Pace, shall only pay their former usuall wages or dues to the skippers and keelmen and be exempted and freed from the three shillings a keele laid upon such ships and other vessells as cast their ballast below the Pace; and in case any skipper or keelemen whatsoever shall under any pretence neglect to go down to any ship or vessell being thereunto appointed by their fitters shall, upon complaint thereof made, forfeit the owners' wages and suffer such other punishment as the Mayor or Justices of the Peace of the said Town and County shall think fitt. Provided likewise that neither the present skippers or keelmen or any other that shall succeed them in their work shall now, or at any time hereafter, take, bring away, conceale or hide in their hurrocke or any other part of their keeles, any quantity of coles whatsoever from aboard any ship or other vessell without the licence or consent of the master or masters of such ship or vessell, upon the paine or penalty of the forfeiture of all their wages or dues upon just complaint thereof made to the Mayor or Justices of the Peace of the Town and County.

---

[1]   Original not found. The volume from which this copy is taken contains transcripts of various documents relating to local history evidently made by an antiquarian in the early eighteenth century.

[2]   The Pace was a point several miles from the mouth of the river. Below the Pace involved greater difficulty and danger to the keels and their crew.

[3] Lying tide, *i.e.* when through no fault of their own the keelmen were obliged to remain idle. Compensation for this was a frequent cause of dispute.

4. The magistrates of Newcastle to [the Secretary of State?], 24 March 1659/60 [TWA 394/1]

Sir,

Not knowing but ere this some misinformation or causlesse complainte may become before the Counsell of State against us in some things pertaineing to the coale trade, wee thought it necessary to give you an account of all the passages thereof, which wee desire may be communicated to the Counsell of State as you see cause; Sir, this day sennit the 17th instant, the skippers of keeles and keelemen being assembled together in a tumultuous manner, and encouraged thereunto, as wee thinke, by some masters of shipps now in this Porte and tradeinge hither for coales, did by combinacon among them draw their keeles above the Bridge to stopp the passage of all keeles and boates to go up and downe the River, where they continued untill Monday after, and then presented unto us their grevance by way of petition desireinge to be releaved, which wee tooke into consideracon, and the next day fully answered, upon which they promised to remove their keeles and to free the River without obstruction of trade, but, the next day being Wednesday, the keeles were not removed, soe, as wee did imagine, the [ship] masters were not satisfied in some particuler ends and aimes and had beene tamperinge with the skippers and keelemen to stand upon some other termes; whereupon, upon Thursday wee caused a Proclemation to be solemnly made and posted it upp in severall places commaunding all skippers of keeles and keelemen in the names of the Keepers &c forthwith to remove their keeles from above the Bridge to their usuall place of mooreing and then to departe to their owne houses or dwellings, or otherwise to follow their imployment in the keeles upon the termes and condicons lately ordered and appointed by the Magistrates of this towne in answere to their petition, upon paine of imprisonment and of being proceeded against as disturbers of the publique peace, all which did not prevaile with them, soe, as towards the eveninge, wee went to them, and the Sheriffe with us, where wee endeavoured as much as in us lay to give them satisfaccon and to perswade them to remove their keeles to their usuall place of mooreinge, but they, being at least five hundred men in number, insteed thereof fell twelve score yeards higher in the River, and there blocked it upp againe. Wee hereupon, feareinge least sume greate prejudice might happne to trade and not knowing what other inconvenience might ensue, yesterday beinge Fryday the 23th instant, together with Mr Sheriffe and some assistance went alonge to suppresse theire unlawfull assembly, which was accordingly done, soe as the skippers and keelemen the same day fell peaceably to labour in theire keeles, and will, wee hope, continue without any further disturbance to the peace and quiet of this place.

Sir, Mr Maier at present is under some indispotion of body and is not able to write, yet wee hope hee is of the mending hand. Wee desire to heare from you if any thinge happne before the Counsell of State relateing to this busines of the keelemen: with our due respects to yourselfe wee remain

your assured loueinge friends

Robert Shafto, deputie Mayor, Geo: Dawson, Mar: Milbanke, Christo: Nicolson, John Emerson[1]

---

[1] These are original signatures. The letter was evidently not sent. Perhaps it was realised that the Commonwealth was coming to an end.

5. Petition of the Keelmen, February 1677/8[1] [TWA 394/57]

To the Right Worshipfull Sir Ralph Carr, knight, Maior, Sir Robert Shaftoe, knight, Serjeant att Law, Recorder, the Worshipfull the Alderman Michaell Blackett, Esq. Sheriffe, and the rest of the Common Councell of the Towne of Newcastle upon Tine.

The humble petition and addresses of the Skippers and Keelmen of and belonging to the same Towne:

Humbly sheweth that the keeles dues usually paid and given for casting of coals aboard of shipps in the several ratches of this River are onely as are followeth (vizt) for every keel of coales cast aboard of any vessell above the Bournes mouth 6s: 4d, and betwixt the Bourns mouth and the lower end of Bykar Shoare 7s: 4d, and in Dents hole 7s: 10d, and from thence to the lower end of the Bill Ratch 8s: 4d; and for every keel laid aboard of any shipp casting ballast att any of the shoares below the Pace 13s: 4d, and onely for shipps casting their ballast on any of the shoars above the Pace 10s: 4d.

That the said severall dues are s[oe] little as that your peticoners and their familyes are not able to subsist thereon, and their imployment for these diverse yeares last past hath been much abated by the slackness of trade, and whereas your peticoners had formerly paid and allow[ed] unto them for every lying tyde aboard of any vessell above the Pace 12d, and for every lying tide below the Pace 2s: 6d, which said dutyes for lying tides hath been of late detained from them and refused to be payed by masters of shipps; and it is not onely a great hindrance and prejudice to your peticoners but to all trades and professions of this Towne, by reason of shipps casting their ballast soe frequently att the lower shoars they gett their coals aboard without coming higher up, and comeing to Sheiles furnish themselves commonly there with provisions and what things they stand in need of.

Your peticoners' humble request to your worshipps therefore is that, the premisses considered, your worshipps would be pleased to grant order for the augmenting of their dues that they may have tenn shillings 4d for every keel cast aboard of any shipp or vessell at the Bill, and 13s: 4d for every keel cast aboard of any shipp below the Pace, without having respect where the ballast was cast or to the greatness or smalness of the shipp, seeing your peticoners' labour is the same, and alsoe that there may be allowed unto them the usuall dues formerly paid for lying tydes, and the other dues be continued or augmented as by your worshipps shall be ordered and [think?] fitt. And as in duty bound your peticoners shall dayly pray &c.

Endorsed: Keelmens' peticon about their dues to the Common Councell, Sir Ralph Carr Mayor, Michael Blackett, Esq., Sheriffe, February 1677.

---

[1]   A very fragile document, some words or letters lost.

6. Petition of the Keelmen to the Magistrates, January 1679/80.
[TWA 394/1]

To the Right Worshipfull George Morton, Esqr, Maier, Sir Robert Shaftoe, Knight, Serieant att Law, Recorder, and the rest of his Majesties Justices of the peace att this present Quarter Sessions held for the Towne and County of Newcastle upon Tine assembled:

The humble petition and addresses of the Skippers and Keilmen within this Towne and County of Newcastle upon Tine:

Humbly sheweth that your petitioners are poor workemen who take great pains and earne their liveings by hard labour, whose dues for their labour are soe small that they and their families cannot subsist therewith; and, as their dues are now regulated, they finde it a great losse and greivance unto them when shipps take in the greatest part (if not all) of their loadeing att Sheeles, for that shipps casting their ballast att Hebron or Wilcom Lee, they haveing there taken in a keil or two of coales, doe comonly goe downe to Sheeles to load the rest of their loadeing, and there those shipps pay but 10s:4d dues, whereas other shipps that have cast ballast at Jarrow Shoare and take in their loadeing att Sheeles pay 13s:4d dues for each keel, your poor petitioners' labour is all the same att Sheeles, wheresoever the shipps cast their ballast, and there dues for such a tide being 3s. less for a shipp casting ballast att Hebron or Wilcom Lee then for a shipp casting att Jarrow, they humbly conceive is inconsistent with reason and equity which they humbly committ to your worshipps' judgements and consideracon.

There humble request therefor is: that the premises considered, your worshipps would be pleased to grant order that from henceforth their dues for casting aboard of any shipp or shipps, small or great, loadeing betwixt the Bill Point and the Pace may be 10s: 4d for each keel, and that for every keel casting aboard of any shipp or vessell below the Pace in this River the dues may be 13s:4d, without respect where there ballast was cast, seeing your petitioners' labour is the same; by this meanes shipps would be brought higher upp the River to load, which would not tend onely to your petitioners' advantage but to the benefitt of the inhabitants and tradesmen of Newcastle, whereas now many shipps are furnished with provisions and necessaries att Sheils; and for other places of the River they desire the dues may be continued as they are, but, in ordering of the premisses, they humbly submitt and referr themselves to your worshipps' judgements and discretion, and as in duty bound your petitioners shall duly pray &c.

7. Added below the above, but written in a different hand, ?January 1679/80 [TWA 394/1]

Att a generall Quarter Sessions of the Peace held the 14th January 1679, it's ordered that the keelmen's petecon be copeed and delivered to the Hostmen's Company and if they return noe answer and that speedel[y] the request is to be granted.

Jenison

8. Petition of the keelmen on their proposed charity, c. 1699[1] [TWA 394/43]

To the Governor, Stewards and Fellowship of Hoastmen in Newcastle: The Humble Petition of the Skippers and Keelmen of the Keeles and Coale Boates in the River of Tyne.
Humbly shew

That your petitioners are sensible of the pincheing wante and extremities which they and their familyes often groane under for lack of a due provision for them [and] are content and willing, for releife of themselves, and binding their children apprentices to trades and callings, and to succour aged skippers and keelmen past their worke, that fower pence for every keele or keele boate carrying 6,7 or 8 chalder shall be deducted and kept of[f] their dues and wages by every fitter and hoastman for every tide they make, and for every keele or keel boate carrying a less number of chalders, three pence, and for every keel or keel-boate carrying ballast or any merchandizes, four pence, to be paid by the said fitters or hoastmen respectively unto the stewards of this Company for the time being, to be by them distributed for the uses intents and purposes aforesaid.

Your petitioners therefore humbly pray that the said Governour, Stewards and Fellowshipp would take the premises into their consideration and make such orders and rules from time to time for the better settling and governing the said Charity as they shall thinke most meet and convenient. And your petitioners shall ever pray &c.

James Sanderson (signed), Robertt Young (mark), William Vickers (mark), Robertt Morton (mark), James Marshall (mark), Thomas Callan (mark), James Robson (mark), Patrick Willson (signed), Hugh Liddle (mark), Anthony Grantt (mark)

---

[1]   Parchment, *endorsed*: 'The first peticon of the Skippers and Keelmen of Newcastle to the Hoastmen's Company there desireing them to consider of proper methods for settling and governing the 4^d per tide allowed by them out of their wages for the releif of those that are not able to work.'

9. William Carr, MP Newcastle, 1690–1710, to Lyonel Moor, Collector of the Keelmen's Charity, 11 December 1705 [TWA, Cotesworth Papers CJ/3/1]

Dear Sir,

Sir William Blackett's continued weakness before his death, and the hopes of his being better, put a stop to the dispatch of the poor keelmen's affair would have had[1], but as it was his constant desire, and almost his last, that such a work might go forward, I send you their petition, which you gave me, that it may be signed by a convenient number of 'em and that it may be returned forthwith, because I would have no time lost in promoteing so good a work.[2] Pray let me have it as soon as possible you can, that no blame may lie at the door of

Your affectionate Friend and Servant,
William Carr

---

[1]   Blackett, MP for Newcastle 1685–7, 1689–90, 1695–1700, 1705, was regarded as the keelmen's 'constant benefactor and friend' ('The case of the poor Skippers and Keelmen', Dendy, F.W., ed., *Extracts from the Records of the Hostmen's Company of Newcastle upon Tyne*, Surtees Society, cv, 1901, pp. 172–4).

[2]   A petition of the skippers and keelmen praying for leave to bring in a bill to confirm and make more effectual their Charity was presented to the Commons, 16 January 1705/6. Leave was given, and William Carr, Sir Robert Eden and Sir

William Bowes were ordered to prepare the bill, but the session ended before it could be brought before the House (*Journals of the House of Commons*, XV, p. 90).

10. Petition to the Magistrates [probably late 17th or early 18th Century] [TWA 394/1]

To The Worship Major, Shirrife and Aldermen of this Town and County humbly Greetting:

Gentlemen,

Wee presume to inform your Worships what our demands is which wee hoope is reasonable and legall which wee hoope yow will grant your answer in this our pettion, and your pettioners as wee ever are bound shall pray.

Wee desire that every Hostsman shall pay ore cause to be payed to each skipper of his imployment good and suffcent moneys that is passible in this Kingdom, either large old moneys ore new[1], and that every week['s] worke our moneys may be payed one Fryday without delay, and also that every Hostsman shall not cause any pann boats ore lightners[2] to lay any coalls aboard of any ship ore ships within this harbour.

Lykewise wee desire, which is as great a hindreance as any thing, that caire may be taken of our marketts, for wee have althings att double raits because theire is such liberty given to the forstallers of our marketts by littleness of bread and hooksters bying other commoditys, theirefor wee humbly beegg that some speedy course may be taken, that all things may be quallyfyed.

Luke Hunter, John Young, Mr Cramlington's worke

Lykwise wee desire that wee may have recompence for our lying tyds [and that noe Hostsman may baill any maister for wee are many times at great loosse upon that acount.[3]]

[1]   This may relate to the great re-coinage of 1695–6, see C.H.V. Sutherland, *English Coinage 600-1900* (London, 1982), p. 177.

[2]   Pann boats were those employed in the salt trade and if allowed to carry coal would threaten the keelmen's livelihood.

[3]   The words in brackets were crossed out. It is not clear whether the complaint about lying tides and the part crossed out was peculiar to those employed by Cramlington or whether Hunter and Young were authors of the whole petition.

11. Common Council Book, 1699–1718 [TWA, MD.NC/2/3, ff. 105 verso–106]

27 March 1705. Skippers and Keelemen formerly petitioned about their wages and moneys due and payable to them from the masters, shippers and others, which being referred to a committee, Thomas

Wasse, Esq., Mayor, Sir William Blacket, Bart., Sir Ralph Carr, George Whinfeild and Robert Edon, Esqrs and aldermen, reported that they had considered the contents of the skippers' and keelemen's petition to them referred and conceived:

1st That for the better payment of the wages, the severall fitters of this Towne and County shall every Satarday morning pay their respective skippers and keelemen sufficient markett money in part payment of such wages as shall be then due to such skippers and keelemen, and within the space of ten dayes after every such Satarday, shall account with, satisfy and pay their said skippers and keelemen all such summe and summes of money as shall rest due to them over and above such markett money as aforesaid.

2ndly That in case any keele shall be imprest to goe down to Sheilds to any ship in hazard or distress, there shall be paid to the skipper and his men, by the person impressing the same, the severall summes following, vizt: For being impressed, the summe of one shilling; for rowing or carrying downe the said keele to Sheilds, the summe of five shillings; for taking out and loading of a keele of coales or ballast or other goods out off and from any ship or vessell and putting the same into any other ship or vessell at Sheilds aforesaid, or elsewhere as they shall be ordered, the further summe of eight shillings and four pence.

3rdly If att any other place or places in the Ryver, that then such skippers and keelemen shall be paid for carrying downe the keele and taking out of coles, ballast or other goods and unloading the same again after the rates above sett forth in proporcon and according to [the] severall ratches of the river.

4thly That after such keele shall be impressed, there shall be paid by the master of the ship or vessell for each lying tyde above a certain place in the river called the Pace the summe of one shilling, and for each lying tyde below the Pace the summe of two shillings.

5thly That if any keel be sent downe to Sheilds loaden with coles and the master of the shipp or vessell to whom they are sent shall refuse to receive the same, and that thereupon the said keele shall be ordered up with her loading by the fitter, that then there shall be paid to the skipper and keelemen of such keele, after the first lying tide, the summe of two shillings for each lying tide then after and before such order shall be given or sent them; provided they give notice of such refusall to their respective fitter within six hours after their going on board such shipp, and the summe of five shillings for bringing up the said keele with her loading aforesaid, and in case the skipper and keelemen of such keele shall be ordered, after their coming backe with the said loading, to goe downe with the same to Sheilds, and shall cast or lay her loading of coales on board the ship or vessell to which the fitter or his servants shall order, that then there shall be further paid to the skipper and keelemen the sum of thirteen shillings and four pence, and if such coals shall be so laid or cast on board such shipp or vessell att any other places in the River of Tyne, that then such skipper and keelemen shall be paid for casting the same in proporcon and according to the severall ratches of the River.

6th That there shall be alsoe paid and satisfied to them by their respective fitters the summe of thirteen shillings and four pence for eight chaldrons of ballast which shall by their fitter's order be taken out of any shipp or vessell and brought and delivered att the ballast key, and soe in proporcon for a lesser quantity of ballast as is paid them for coles.

7th That there shall be likewise paid to the said skippers and keelemen owners' wages[1] in proporcon to the chaldrons of coales loaded or putt on board.

8th That if any keele be sent to Sheilds and the shipp or vessell to which she is sent cannott take in all the coales, that then such skipper shall give immediate notice thereof to the fitter, and in case the coales remaining shall by the fitter's order be cast on board any other shipp, that then there shall be paid to the said skipper and his men, over and above the usuall wages of thirteen shillings and fourpence, the further summe of two shillings and eight pence, which makes double coales dues – all which they submitted to the Common Councell.

On reading the said report it's ordered that the report be confirmed in the matter and clauses aforesaid, but those two, number 2 and 4 what concernes impressing of keeles, are to be considered off and referred to the judgement and determinacon of Sir Robert Shaftoe, Sergeant att Law.[2]

---

[1]   Owners' wages were an allowance paid by the coal owners, mainly for the keelmen's beer.

[2]   By 1710 these terms were causing discontent amongst the keelmen. Some had evidently approved them at the time, but the 'generality' regarded them as 'clancularly done', *i.e.* clandestinely. See minutes of the keelmen's grievances, contained in **Document 12**, below.

DOCUMENTS CONCERNING THE KEELMEN'S STRIKE OF JUNE–JULY 1710

12. An account of events leading to the keelmen's strike,[1] probably by an informant (whose identity is unknown) of William Cotesworth [TWA, Cotesworth Papers CJ 3/6]

In the beginning of March 1709/10 several of the keelmen complaining of many abuses which they conceived they had from Mr [Timothy] Tully [their steward] and some of the fitters concerning the due payment and use made of their Hospital grotes, desired me to acquaint the Governor of the Oastman's Company and Mr Henry Liddell with some particular articles in Mr Tully's accounts which they said they know to be false, and prayed that they might have the remainder of his accounts given in to be examined for their further satisfaccion, which I communicated according to their desire on the 3d of March.

From that time to the beginning of May, the keelmen importuned the Governor and Majestrates by complaints and petitions to redress them by causing Mr Tully, and who else were concerned, to do them right, and with all to establish Mr John Carr [or Kerr] their steward. [At] a Oastman Company meeting, a committee of them was appointed to examine their business who met several times; and about the beginning of their meetings I writ a letter for some of the keelmen, on behalf of the rest, to the committee as an instruction in their affairs (copie whereof follows):

To the Gent[lemen] of the Committee

Tuesday May 9th 1710

Worthy Gent[lemen],

We render humble thanks that you are pleased to spend your time and labour in order to dow us and the rest of the keelmen justice, and humbly prays that you'l be pleased to endeavour to learne what money the keelmen have paid to the several fitters (whereof yourselves are a great part) and also to learne how much of it the fitters have paid out and to whome. This being that part of our affairs wherein we are altogether weak, as well as the principle matter in hand, we hope for ourselves and on the behalfe of the rest of the keelmen that you (Worthy Sirs) will make this your first endeavours. And since such long confused business is very troublesome, if you please, we will order a clerk (one of the Oastmen's Company) as well as Mr Carr to attend and assist as you are pleased to direct.

With all humility &c

Walter Noble, William Crake, James Scott, Robert Halliburton

At this time many of the keelmen made personal applications to the Committee, signifying their intention concerning the receipt and payment of their money (Vizt.) Mr John Carr should receive it of the fitters, and pay it to such workmen as would make oath that they did really deserve and want somuch from the keelmen for worke &c. This they urged because they conceived that Mr Tully and the workmen contrived false bills to wrong them of their money. Hereupon the Committee promised that Mr Carr should receive all their money and pay it to them that gave such assurance of the truth of their demands as the keelmen required. But contrary to this promise to the keelmen, the Committee either received themselves *.... to be paid to Mr Tully, and amongst them paid a great part of what...* to the workmen who was not willing to swear to their bills, and Mr Carr had no other power there than to look on. The keelmen hearing of this, in a rage and disorderly manner, drew together and went to the Committee and discharged them from paying the rest of their money except the persons demanding gave such satisfaction as they had required, offering that, upon such satisfaction being given, they would raise as much money as would clear them of debt, and required that the money left should be given up to Mr Carr for their use. But the Committee left that money at the Coffee House untill the first or second Monday following, on which the Oastmen's Company met, when it was expected by the keelmen that it would be ordered that who had a demand should be swore before authority and Mr Carr established according to their desire. But contrarywise, the money was privately paid by the said Committee, and the keelmen given to understand that Mr Tully should continue receiving and paying until they, the keelmen, were out of debt, which the keelmen doubted would be endless, for they perceived that Mr Tully was contracting new debts &c. Also, the Committee denyed them Mr Tully's accounts, which strengthened their jealousy of being cheated in the latter accounts. Several of the fitters have from time to time paid most part of what was left in their hand, either at their pleasure, or at the desire and to the use of some particular keelmen, whereby their Hospital stock is exhausted, contrary to the intention of the generality of them.

Between the time of their distorbing the Committee, as above, and the Oastmen's Company meeting (as 'twas sade) to settle the keelmen's affairs, upon the report of the Committee &c the keelmen appeared in great numbers upon the Garthheads (field nigh Sandgate) which I, hearing of, was going there, but one who was reconed of the heads of them, met me and .....* better or more reasonable sort of the keelmen could do in persuading the rest could not keep them any longer from rising because of such matters as I have above mentioned; and further that Mr Grey and Mr Atkinson was in danger of loosing their lives in case the mischievous party met with them that day, wherefore, to prevent mischiefe, I went to acquaint Mr Grey and Mr Atkinson.[2] I heard that Mr Atkinson was out of Towne and Mr Grey was busy, wherefore I acquainted him with the keelmen's rage by writing. Mr Grey desired me to tell them that he would dow them any good service but would not meddle with their money. I told them that, and anything else to quiet them, and at the Oastmen's meeting, which I mentioned above, Mr Grey was pleased to publish my note to the whole Company which seemed[?] like to have set the keelmen upon me. So that, according to the keelmen's acknowledgment, I can truely say that what is mentioned in the premises was the only occasion of all the disorders of the keelmen, and if these matters be not taken care of, I dout that ere long they will be in disorder againe.

Then several distorbances happened, as the women going to Town and seeking Mr Poyon, on a false report raised, which report, I was told, was first spoak in the company of Mr Cramlington. Their seeking Mr Grey at his home and the office &c for paying away the remainder of their money....* Carr asked them what they insisted upon, and they said that they had given a paper of their grievances to one of the Majestrates, and would repete them, which I writ down in order to be given by Mr Carr to the Majestrates, the keelmen declaring never to work till they were redressed therein. The grievances are as followeth:

Minutes of the Keelmen's Greivances, taken the same day that Proclamation was made in the Sandgate concerning the Keelmen.

When they go down to a ship that will not take them in, the fitters will but pay them 5s. 0d. for that tide instead of 13s. 4d., and out of this 5s. 0d. the keelmen pays 12d. for the cann [of beer] and loaders.

When they are sent down for ballast, with a warrant, if they get less than 8 chaldrons the fitter will pay them but what he pleases, perhaps 6s. 8d. or 10s. 0d., whereas it is known and provable that they ought and used to have 13s. 4d. if they get but 1 or 2 chaldrons, because it costs them a tide.

They are obliged by several fitters' servants to spend in drink, or they will stop some of their money for it, and sometime for trash liquor (for which they must leave as well as the money for it), although they have but one or two tides to receive.

They used to have 2s. 6d. for lying tides, when a ship will not take them in, and now they get nothing.

When they go to a wreck, the due is 12d. when they are prest,[3] 5s. 0d. at going on bord.

Also below the Pace, 2s. 6d. each lying tide, and 5s. 0d. each slung tide;[4] above the Pace 2s. 6d. each slung tide, and 12d. each lying tide.

The fitters have paid a great part of their Hospital grotes to some particular men contrary to the general intention.

Some part of these dues are lessened and so not wholly paid by some of the fitters, and some of them wholly denied by all.

Several of them, vizt. that for bringing back a loaden keel (the keelmen say) was reduced from 13s. 4d. to 5s. 0d., and that for ballast to be what the fitters please, about 4 years ago by an Act of the Common Council,[5] who, as some of them say, had the concurrence of some of the keelmen, which the generality of the keelmen say was 'clancularly done'[6] and therefore will not worke till they are righted therein, as well as have assurance of their due in the other articles, and several other things by the said Act, as taking off Owners' Wages for coals brought back, which is a full tide to them &c.

During the keelmen's being thus in disorder, some of them in the name of about 400 more of the principle keelmen, desired me to acquaint the Majestrates with the above wrongs and that they promised that, upon their having them redressed, they would go to work, notwithstanding several of the H.B. keelmen[7] pretended to have the Contract broak, which I writ and gave it to one of the Majestrates who promised that morning to shew it to the rest.

About this time I heard George Mason, who serves Mr John Watson, say these were but baubles (wee being then on the Key talking among the keelmen) and advised them to insist upon something worth their while to have the Contract broke. I told him and them they would not get it done, and therefore it was folly for them to offer it, and he sade I could not tell what they [ought to?] do.

Also, during the disorders, ships came in and the keelmen then pretended they were wronged of their turnes in the worke, as well as their greivances before mentioned, so that by rage and disorder they were in, occasioned by what has been mentioned, some men being like to loss their worke, and [by?] the advice of several fitters, a great part of the keelmen would neither work nor suffer such as were willing to worke. Some of the chief keelmen that stopped the keels were James Scott, Rowland Thompson, John Grant, Samuel

Underhill, and many more. The keelmen say that [?] Lancelot Cramlington told them that who blamed them, he woud say it on their face that the keelmen was on the right of it, and that the Contract was a knavish thing. Fra[ncis] Armorer told them they were in the right to break the Contract, and he would not be the man that should bid them go to worke. Mr Swaddell encouraged them at first to stop work.....* Some keelmen told me that 6 of them would oath it (as they expressed it) that Andrew Dick was one, if not the first, that bid them stopp the keeles. Those that told me of Mr Dick could not stay with me till I took their names, because it happened to be when many of them was treating with the Colonel on the Garthheads, and seeing them and me together drew about, and we dorst not say any more then. I know them by sight and perhaps may fall [in] with them againe.

Grant was instrumental to raising the mobb when they went to Alderman White's house and Mr Wilkinson's and several places in Towne, whereupon the Trained Bands was a second time raised. Many ships went away without coales by reason the keelmen would not work, or some would not suffer the rest to. Several shipmasters gave the keelmen money and persuaded them to stand out as long as they could.

The keelmen daily threatening this place, notwithstanding the Trained Bands (for some of the Trained Bands encouraged them), Regular Companys was brought against them; and due inquiry being made of the cause of their stopp, they declared that they only wanted right concerning their wages, and upon assuring them that they should be wronged no more, they went to work again.

As to proving the premises, I have not yet got that point completed, but expect to have it done every day.

Saturday 5 August 1710

Yesterday, being in Sandgate, I perceived that the keelmen doubt that the fitters intend to pay their Hospital money otherwise than they intend, and not to Mr Carr; wherefore Mr Carr will go to the fitters this day and demand it, and if he be refused their money, I am confident they will be more inraged than ever and work will be stopped till their money be paid to Mr Carr. I signify this that mischeife may be prevented.

I believe everything mentioned here of the fitters incouraging the former mischeif may be proved, except that of Andrew Dick, which I cannot yet hear any confirmation of.

---

[1]   Much of this document is printed by Francis Mander, 'The Tyneside Keelmen's Strike of 1710: Some Unpublished Documents', *Gateshead and District Local History*

Society, Bulletin, No. 1, 1969). The document is damaged in several places and the parts lost are indicated thus: *....

2   Edward Grey and Charles Atkinson were stewards of the Hostmen's Company. Grey had formerly managed the Keelmen's Charity.

3   'Prest', *i.e.* Impressed.

4   'Slung tides': those in which the keelmen were at work.

5   For the terms of the Act of the Common Council, 27 March 1705, see **Document 11**, above.

6   'Clancularly', secretly, clandestinely.

7   This seems to refer to the keelmen from one staith.

13. Petition of the Keelmen to the Magistrates, 1710 [TWA 394/57]

To the Right Worshippfull George Whinefeild Esqr Mayor and to the Worshippfull the Aldermen and the Recorder and Sherrife of this Towne and Corporation, Greetting.

The Humble Petition of all the Skippers and Keelmen in the River of Tine.

Gentlemen, These are humbly to shew your worshipps that whereas the Coallowners and Fitters hath contracted ore combined more like to raise the coalls in this River to the great prejeduce and hinderance of the coall traide, which great loose and damnage wee poor men are nott able to comprehend as to the great loss of her Majestyes revenous and also to the great lose of traide in this Towne and about it by the great hinderance of poor laboursome men that workes as miners in pitts and carriagemen imployed in the coall traide, but wee that are keellmen cann give a little nearer relation of our owne lose for wee may and dare declaire that it lost every skipper and men imployed in eatch keell above twelfe pounds for eatch keell or keellboat belonging to the River, and is like to lose a great deall more if some speedy course be nott taken for the represeing of soe hard and weighty a matter, for if this Contract ore Combination goe one they are like to breake all traids hear and to bring this whole contry to rueine, all which rightly considered and weighed is very hard to be born.[1]

2dly Gentlemen, wee desire that you will be pleased to grant and alow us the former uses and costomes of the River, vidzt: That if any keell or keell boat goe downe aboard of any ship or vessell within this harbour to cast coals, and if the ship be nott ready ore will nott take in the coals soe that they must lye with the coals, that then the skipper and men may have two shillings and sixpence for every lyeing tyd below a certaine place in the River cald the Pacce and above the Pacce one shilling for every lyeing tyd, and if in case the ship be over loaden and cannott take in the coals so that the skiper and men may have thirteenth shillings and four pence for comeing up loaden from Sheilds, and from other ratches in the River acording as the dues is stated, and if in case the skipper and men cast the one halfe ore lese ore more aboard of one ship that then they may have dues and owners wages acording to the ratch of the River, and if sent aboard with the remainer to another ship that then they shall have boats dues payed acordingly.

3dly That if any keell ore keellboat take out any ballast out of any ship ore vessell, if it be one, two, or three or four chaldron of ballast clearing the ship or vessell, that then the skiper and men shall have thirteenth shillings and four pence as the former use and costome of the River.

4dly That if any keell or keellboat being imprest down to any wrake, that then the skiper and men shall have one shilling for being imprest and five shillings for roweing down the keell or keellboat, and two shilllings and sixpence for every lyeing tyd, and five shillings for every slung tyd below the Pacce, and one shilling for every lyeing tyd and two shillings and sixpence for every slung tyd above the Pacce, and if in case that any keell take out any coals from any wrake that and cast them aboard of the same ore any other ship, that then the men shall have 13s 4d ore acording to the dues of the ratch.

5dly That noe Fitter shall imploy any pann boats or wherryes to carry downe ore cast any coalls aboard of any ship or ships within this harbour, nor take out any ballast out of any ship ore vessell in this harbour, which if they doe to forfeitt the dues to the keellmens Hospitall.

6dly That theire may be bear alowed us aboard of every ship as formerly, ore else one shilling and eight pence alowed for bear, for the seamen aboard of severall vessells gathereth all the grounds of theire drunke out bear and puts in one caske and gives us poor workemen to drinke, if never soe hott, which is the death and rueine of many poor man.

7dly That Mr John Carr [Kerr] may be established steward and collettor of our Charryty moneyes and that he may have the receipts of Mr Timo[thy] Tullyes acount and also the receipts of Mr Tobias Blackesons acount and what Mr William Cramlington left with him.

All which wee, your humble petitioners, hopes your Worshipps will be pleased to take into your serious consideration and to grant us your Worshipps asistance in this our humble request, which wee hope will seem to your Worshipps both reasonable and legall, and to breake that strong Combination, and then all to worke as soon as God send any.[2] No more stop.

God save Queen Ann

[1]   The contract for regulating the vend reduced the keelmen's employment and that of other workers in the coal trade. Another version of the above petition (TWA 394/3) includes most of the above points though in a different order and with some additions and differences. The amount lost to each keel and its men by the contract is stated 'at ore above tenn pounds, and now our poor famalyes being in a very poor [condition?]' the petitioners think fit to make it known to the magistrates that 'some course may be taken with all expedition' about it. In calling for John Carr [Kerr] to be appointed as their steward, the petitioners demand 'that he may give in his bound to two senior Aldermen, and that a just acount may be given', and that the workmen [on the hospital] may be brought 'before your Worshipps to declaire what is dew to them, and, as for idle drinkeing, wee will nott alowe nothing of it'. They hope that the magistrates will consider the premisses and 'give your Worshipps asignments to the same, but we humbly desire your Worshipps wil be pleased to cause the same to be drawne in forme in parcement for wee are not capable to do it'.

[2]   Coal shipments from the Tyne were being stopped by a combination of shipmasters to detain the fleet of about 700 sail at Harwich in order to raise the price at London.

14. Affidavit of John Reasley, of this Town and County of Newcastle upon Tyne, yeoman, this 9th June 1710 [TWA 394/3]

Deposeth that yesterday he heard Luke Nesbitt and John Watson with severall other keelmen, whose names this deponent knows not, swear severall oathes and said that if Mr William Cotesworth of Gateshead came to any steath with a keel to load or goe down they would make him that he should not be able to go home again on his feet, and that if they should catch him they would putt him in Sandgate stocks.

Jurat coram Richard Ridley   John Reasley

15. Common Council Book, 1699–1718 [TWA, MD/NC/2/3 f. 179]

Keelmen's Riot

Att a Common Councell held the tenth day of June 1710: Whereas great numbers of Keelmen imployed in the coal trade upon the River Tyne and others did on the....day of this instant June meet and assemble themselves together in a riotous and tumultuous manner and insulted several persons, stopped the navigation in the said River, and refused to work themselves or to permitt any others to load shipps with coals or to unload and bring up any goods or merchandizes in keels to the said Town, and have extorted bonds from severall persons not to load any shipps with coales, soe that severall coal ships intended to be loaded in this River have been forced to goe away unloaden, and the said rioters have also threatned to pull down houses and to comitt other great disorders unless their greviances be redressed, the cheif whereof they alledge to be a contract made by the Coalowners upon this River whereby many of them and their familyes are reduced to great necessities for want of imployment; for the suppressing of which tumults and riots her Majesty's Justices of the Peace and the Sheriffe of the said Town went to the said rioters and caused Proclamacon to be made for the keeping of Her Majesty's peace, but were opposed in a hostile manner, and the Deputy Lieutenants have caused the Militia [to be raised], and all other endeavours in their power have been used for suppressing the said riot and for preserving the publick peace and opening the trade and navigacon of the River, which have prove ineffectuall. The said tumults and disorders yett continuing to the totall destruccon of her Majesty's dutys and customs ariseing from the coal trade of this River, the diminucon of the coal trade of this Nation to the great damage of this Corporacon and the Freemen and Inhabitants thereof, it is therefore ordered that an humble petition be presented to her Majesty that her Majesty will be pleased to grant us such assistance as may effectually supress the said tumults and riotts and open the trade of this River, and that her Majesty will also be pleased to take into her royall consideracon such unlawfull contracts and combinacons as have been made tending to the destruccon or diminucon of the coal trade, and to give such releife in the premises as her Majesty in her great wisdom shall think fitt.

[f. 180] *The above, with some verbal alterations, was addressed* 'To the Queen's Most Excellent Majesty: The humble petition of the Mayor, Aldermen and Common Council of the Town and County of Newcastle upon Tyne', *ending* 'Given under our Common Seal this 10th day of June in the 9th year of your Majesty's most glorious reigne'.

16. Nicholas Ridley, Deputy Mayor, to H. Boyle, principal Secretary of State, 23 June 1710 [TNA, SP 34/12/101]

Newcastle, 23 June 1710

Sir,

In obedience to her Majesties commands signified to us by your Honour's letter,[1] wee have kept up and shall continue our militia and thereby hope to preserve the Town from the insults of the rioters, but cannot expect to make the navigacon of the River free. The keelmen are in number about sixteen hundred; our militia consists but of eight companys in the whole, raw and undisciplined; if wee should make an attempt upon the rioters with them and be repulsed wee are afraid it would be of very ill consequence....We think that eight companyse of regular troops with our own forces may be able to disperse and suppress the rioters and free the navigacon. The contents of your Honour's letter hath been made known to them but they persist in their former resolucions.

Your most humble and obedient Servant,

Nicholas Ridley, Deputy Mayor

[1]   On 17 June 1710, Boyle had ordered the Mayor to keep him informed of the keelmen's behaviour, and report to the government if the magistrates failed to persuade them to return to work 'to the end that...her Majesty may give immediate orders to the Lord Lieutenant of the County [Northumberland] to raise the militia' and also send troops (TNA, SP 44/109).

17. Jonathan Roddam, Mayor, to Sir John Delaval, Commander of the Northumberland militia, 6 July 1710 [TNa, SP 34/12/120]

Sir,

The early intimacon you gave us of the direccons you received for raising your militia and assisting us to suppress the rioters here, if they came into your County, was very seasonable, for which we return our thanks.[1] We expect all or most of the regular forces tomorrow; as soon as they come, we shall consult with the Commanding Officer to take the most proper method for opening the trade and preventing any further mischiefs. We cannot think it reasonable to putt the County of Northumberland to the charges of keeping up the militia without an absolute necessity, and therefore only desire the favour of you att present, upon the discharge of the militia, to order them to be ready upon your first orders, and that you will also recommend itt to the Justices of the Peace to issue out their warrants for apprehending such persons who shall come as vagrants, for we are very apprehensive that many Scotch young fellows, who come hither to work att the keels for the summer only, will upon sight of the regular forces make their escape into your County.

Your most humble and obedient Servant,

Jonathan Roddam, Mayor

[1]   Robert Lisle and [?] Ogle informed the magistrates that in obedience to the Queen's commands they had arranged that the Northumberland Militia be summonsed to meet on Morpeth Common, 1 July 1710 (TNA, SP 34/12/114).

18. Affidavit of John Grant, skipper, concerning violence during the keelmen's strike [TWA 394/3]

Newcastle upon Tyne

John Grant, Skipper, deposeth this 10th July 1710 that about seven weeks agoe as he with three men, Richard Flint, Thomas Dixon and James Fortune, were goeing with their keel up this River to Stella Staith for fire coal for one Mr Gerrard Robson, Swordbearer, one James Lashley, Andrew Donnisson, James Nesmith and William Armstrong, skippers, and William Richardson, keelman, did in a riotous and tumultuous manner and by force and violence, with about thirty men more in number, whose names he knows not, stop and hinder this deponent and his said men in goeing up the said River and brought the said keel back, and some of them tooke away this deponent's hook and threatned to doe this deponent and his said men an injury in case they offered to goe up the River, soe that this deponent was forced to leave his said keel.

John Grant

Jurat coram Jonathan Roddam, Mayor

19. Further affidavit of John Grant concerning violence by women during the strike [TWA 394/3]

Newcastle upon Tyne

John Grant this 10th July 1710 deposeth that about three weeks agoe, as this deponent with Thomas Dixon and John Dunn were goeing to take their keel from the Fest in order to take some leed from the key and putt the same on board a shipp then lying at Sheilds (whereof Henry Jenkins is master), Jane (wife of James Clerke, keelman), Mary Marshall, widdow, Jane (the wife of John Gentleman), Flucker, wife of Alexander Flucker, and Clerke, wife of David Clerke, with about a hundred more women, whose names this deponent knows not, haveing sticks and clubbs in their hands, in a riotous and tumultuous manner did obstruct and hinder this deponent and his said men from carrying the said keel from the Fest in order to carry the said leed, and threatned to kill this deponent and his said men if they offered to take away the said keel; and afterwards the said persons went, as he has heard, to the house of Matthew White Esq and John Wilkinson in this Towne and used severall threatning expressions there.

John Grant

Jurat coram Jonathan Roddam, Mayor

20. Affidavit of William Cragg, keelman [TWA 394/3]

Newcastle upon Tyne

William Cragg, keelman on Mr Simpson's Work, this 10th July 1710 deposeth that about a month since, as this deponent was mowering his keel, one David Clerke, William Trumble and Bartholomew Hall with severall other keelmen to the number of fifty or thereabouts, whose names this deponent knows not, came violently to this deponent and took him and one Thomas Varey his skipper of[f] the key where they were standeing…and carried them by force to Sandgate Stocks where they detained them and would not lett them goe about their lawfull occasions and bussinesse.

William Cragg

Jurat coram Jonathan Roddam, Mayor

21. Jonathan Roddam to Secretary of State, 11 July 1710 [TNA, SP 34/12/126]

Sir,

Six Companies of the Earl of Hay's Regiment have arrived. We have used all methods as well before as since to oblige the keelmen to goe to work, but hitherto we have not been able to doe it, for they abscond and goe from their houses. We have secured some of them and hope to take more of those rioters. Today we have examined and considered some of their complaints, which relates to their wages which they would have encreased beyond what has been paid them these thirty years, with severall extravagant demands not in our power to grant them. We have given them under our hands that they shall have their just and usual wages, and all other reasonable demands soe far as it is in our power to grant, yet this will not prevail with them to goe to work. We shall continue our utmost endeavours to open the trade of the Ryver, and soe far as by law we can, we shall enquire into and settle the differences between the keelmen and the fitters, to whom they are bound, wherein we desire to have the advice and assistance of the Judges of Assize for our better directions.[1]

Your most humble and obedient Servant,
Jonathan Roddam, Mayor

[1]　On 21 July Roddam informed the Secretary of State that the remainder of Hay's regiment had arrived, and 'We have with the officers laboured very much to oblige the keelmen to goe to worke, and with great difficulty prevailed with them to goe and thereby cleared the navigacon of the Ryver' (TNA, SP 34/12/144).

22. An Account of the Dues and Owners' Wages of the Several Ratches from Stella to New Key and down the River to Sheeles.[1] *Endorsed,* **'1710, The Agreement signed by the Magistrates and Fitters in Newcastle about the Keelmen's Wages'** [TWA 394/3]

	[KEEL] DUES		OWNERS' WAGES		TOTALS	
	s.	d.	s.	d.	s.	d.
Stella to New Key	6	4	3	8	10	0
Blaydon to New Key	6	4	3	4	9	8
Lemington to New Key	6	4	3	0	9	4
Denton to New Key	6	4	2	8	9	0
Scottswood to New Key	6	4	2	4	8	8
Stella below the Burn	6	8	3	8	10	4
Blaydon below the Burn	6	8	3	4	10	0
Lemington below the Burn	6	8	3	0	9	8
Denton below the Burn	6	8	2	8	9	4
Scottswood below the Burn	6	8	2	4	9	0
Stella to Snowdens Hole or Dents Hole	7	6	3	8	11	2
Blaydon to Snowdens Hole or Dents Hole	7	6	3	4	10	10
Lemington to Snowdens Hole or Dents Hole	7	6	3	0	10	6
Denton to Snowdens Hole or Dents Hole	7	6	2	8	10	2
Scottswood to Snowdens Hole or Dents Hole	7	6	2	4	9	10
Stella to St Anthonyes	7	8	3	8	11	4
Blaydon to St Anthonyes	7	8	3	4	11	0
Lemington to St Anthonyes	7	8	3	0	10	8
Denton to St Anthonyes	7	8	2	8	10	4
Scottswood to St Anthonyes	7	8	2	4	10	0
Stella to Billlratch	9	0	3	8	12	8

Blaydon to Billratch	9	0	3	4	12	4
Lemington to Billratch	9	0	3	0	12	0
Denton to Billratch	9	0	2	8	11	8
Scottswood to Billratch	9	0	2	4	11	4
Stella below the Pace	11	8	3	8	15	4
Blaydon below the Pace	11	8	3	4	15	0
Lemington below the Pace	11	8	3	0	14	8
Denton below the Pace	11	8	2	8	14	4
Scottswood below the Pace	11	8	2	4	14	0
Stella to Shields	13	4	3	8	17	0
Blaydon to Shields	13	4	3	4	16	8
Lemington to Shields	13	4	3	0	16	4
Denton to Shields	13	4	2	8	16	0
Scottswood to Shields	13	4	2	4	15	8

Ballast Dues: Taking out the ballast from any shipp or vessell by warrant and clearing her, 13s. 4d.

If any keele or boate be imprest for any wrack, the skipper and men to receive one shilling, five shillings for rowing down the keele or boate, for every lyeing tyde two shillings and six pence below the Pace, above the Pace one shilling; for every slung tyde below the Pace five shillings, above the Pace two shillings and six pence, and in case any coales be taken out of the said wrack, to be paid in proportion to the wages in the ratches.

Noe fitter to imploy pann boates; whoever shall doe the same shall forfeit the dues to the Hospitall.

Lastly, if any fitter shall order down a keel of coals to Shields or any other ratch, and the ship that the skipper is ordered for be loaden, or the master will not take him in, then upon the skippers comeing or sending up one of his men to the said fitter and his having no other shipp to cast him on the next tide, he the said skipper bringing the said coals home unbroken shall be paid full dues according to the ratch the ship lyes in.

Parchment, signed and sealed by the magistrates: Jonathan Roddam, Mayor, Matthew White, Robert Fenwick, William Ellison, Matthew Fetherstonhaugh, Henry Dalston, junior, and the following fitters: Charles Atkinson, John Simpson, Francis Amorer, James

Rawlin, Garratt Starkin, Robert Walthsey?, Lancelott Cramlington, James Morton, John Watson, Forster Muschampe, Joseph Colpitts, Thomas Allan, junior, Ellis Archbald?, Andrew Dick, Robert Blackeston, John Maddison, Thomas Allan, George Iley, Lyon Colpitts, and John….[*Surname lost.*]

[1]   These rates were by the keel, not for each member of the crew. Owners' wages were allowances made by the coal owners mainly for the keelmen's beer. They probably received little in cash from these allowances. After a strike against the overloading of the keels in 1744, some additional clauses were added to the above settlement, especially that no keel was to be obliged to take in more than the King's Measure, *i.e.* eight Newcastle chaldrons. Also, for shifting a ship from the shore, one shilling per keel was granted, and if the usual quantity of beer was not given to the crew, when casting into a ship, they were to have 1s. 4d. This settlement was known as 'The Articles of 1744'. Further clauses were added in 1791–2, see below, **Documents 195** and **199**.

DANIEL DEFOE AND THE KEELMEN

23. *A Review of the State of the British Nation*, **vol. VIII, Number 139, 12 February 1712, pp. 559–60**

But I must reserve a little part of this *Review* to speak a word or two to a case now before the House of Commons, the cheat of which, I believe, few understand, and many will wonder at when they hear of it, being so notorious in its kind, but gilded over with a specious pretence of charity and Christianity, carried on by magistracy, and concealed from the authority they apply to. This relates to a Bill for settling the Keel-Men's Hospital at Newcastle. And as I have no gain to make by speaking, nor any other end, but meer charity to the poor, sense of liberty and detecting a horrid plot upon near two thousand innocent families, as well upon trade, I speak with more freedom; and as to the truth of what I say, I am ready to vouch every word of it.

The Keel-Men of Newcastle are a sett of poor, laborious, hard working men, that take as much pains for their bread, and get it at as much hazard, as most men in this Nation; their business is to fetch coals in large boats, like lighters, from the *steths*, or wharfs, and carry them to the ships in the River Tyne, who bring them to London – and without their labour, the coal trade could not be carried on.

The plot upon them is not only to rob, but to enslave them, and the enslaving them, will, in consequence, make an absolute monopoly of the coal trade again; a thing, which the last Parliament, and the last

Ministry struggled hard with before, and which this very Parliament overthrew in their last session, but is now to be revived, under a secret and unheard of conspiracy against law, against reason, against English liberty, against right, and against charity; I say this with the more freedom, because they expect that the Parliament shall be drawn in to do their work for them, and the poor innocent and injured men having none to sollicit, none to undertake their cause, neither money nor friends; the specious outside may deceive a Parliament of any thing but angels; I doubt not the Parliament will resent their being thus imposed upon, when they shall hear the truth of it; and I only wish the House of Commons, whose ears are always open to justice and right, would find out some method to have the poor men free from the threatenings and wheedlings that have been used to extort a petition from them, represent their own case to them, and then they would see the thing to be quite different from what is laid before them.

I shall give the true state of the case in my next.

24. *A Review of the State of the British Nation*, vol. VIII, Number 140, 14 February 1712, pp. 563–4

In my last, I entered a little into the case of the poor Keel-Men of Newcastle; a case now depending before the House of Commons, but represented to that honourable House in so different a shape from what it really bears, that I could not but lay open so much of it, which I esteem to be falsly covered, and which I believe will appear the blackest design that has ever been seen of the kind in this Nation; and let them stand clear that are concerned in it.

First I shall state their case in brief, and then make some just remarks upon it.

The poor men have for some years past, by a voluntary agreement among themselves, raised and paid a little constant payment of one peny per tide out of their labour, when they are in work, in order to make a common stock, for the support of their own poor, burying their dead, providing for the widows and orphans of such as perish in the River, as many of them frequently do, and feeding the ancient disabled poor among them, as they come to want it.

With this money, they have built a very noble hospital, the finest and handsomest of its kind in this Nation to be sure, if not in the world, and which, as I have been told, cost above 2000£ building; a very good testimony what great things a little good husbandry may do.

For want of authority to manage this matter, and of power and unity among themselves to direct and govern this Charity, they have run into great mischiefs; their Stewards, their Receivers and Managers have embezelled the money, cheated the common stock, starved the poor, and there is no way to bring them to account but by obtaining a Charter of Incorporation, whereby the poor men may be empowered to direct their own Charity, and to call to account those that cheat them.

To obtain this, they petitioned her Majesty for a Charter, which petition was signed by above one thousand of their names, and being presented to the Queen in Council, was on the 10th of April last, referred to the Attorney General, to enquire into, and consider of.

The Hoast-Men and Fitters of Newcastle, eminent and famous for their late combinations with the Lighter-Men of London, for engrossing the Coal-Trade, and whose said combinations were, but the last session of this present Parliament, suppressed by a Law, finding it very necessary to have the governing power, not only of the poor Keel-Men's money, but of the Keel-Men themselves, in order to restore the projected practice of engrossing the coals, had for many years endeavoured to get the disposition of this Charity into their hands; and had used infinite frauds and corrupt dealings, to bring the poor men to consent to it, but in vain.

But finding it was now like to come to a period, and that if this new Charter were obtained, not only many of them should be called to an account for embezelling, and fraudulently keeping back the poor's money, by which several of them have been perfectly starved, and have perished for meer want of bread: BUT their farther designs of getting the absolute command of the Keel-Men, and thereby of the whole Coal Trade, as above, would be overthrown and disappointed; these Hoast-Men and Fitters bring in the Magistrates of Newcastle to join with them, many of themselves being also Magistrates, to enter a Caveat against the said Charter, at the Attorney General's, pretending that the majority of the Keel-Men had signed a petition against it, and had resolved to apply to the Parliament, to have the government of the said Hospital and Charity committed to them.

The truth of this sham, the horrid and barbarous methods made use of, to draw off the poor men from their first petition; how they prevailed with a few, and how few; and what they are now doing to procure more; this black story I leave to our next, when I shall also give you the petition itself.

Mean time, I only recommend it to the consideration of all whom it may concern, whether it can be likely the poor Keel-Men should willingly petition to be under the government and direction of those, who are the very men that have oppressed them, and who they desire nothing more, than sufficient power, to call to an account for the injuries they have already received from them.

25. *A Review of the State of the British Nation*, vol. VIII, Number 141, 16 February 1712, pp. 565–8

Pray Gentlemen, allow me one *Review* for an act of charity, in behalf of the poor under an oppression that I believe no Christian man can read without detestation.

In the last part of this Discourse, I introduced the case of the poor Keel-Men of Newcastle, and their oppressors, the Magistrates, Hoast-Men, and Fitters at Newcastle, and I promised there to give the Petition which they presented with their Case to her Majesty, and as it expresses their case very fully, it may serve for an abridgment of the present affair; the Petition is as follows.

To the QUEEN'S most Excellent Majesty

The humble Petition of the poor Skippers and Keel-Men employed in working of Keels, and carrying Coals for the loading of ships in the River Tyne, in the County of Northumberland, and in behalf of themselves, and of all the said Keel-Men and their numerous families Humbly Sheweth,

That your petitioners being in number above one thousand five hundred men, and their families, considering the many hazards and dangers of their employment, and other accidents which frequently bring them, or their widows and children to poverty and distress (the burthen of which would be too great for the parishes wherein they live to support), have voluntarily, and of their own accord, agreed out of their day-labour to pay and contribute the sum of one penny per tide for each man, as often as the said man worked in the said River; which said sum is, and has been duly paid for near twelve years past, into one common stock, for the relief of such of their number as have been, or shall be poor, aged, or disabled, and the widows and children of such.

And whereas your petitioners have suffered great loss and inconvenience by the persons entrusted with the said money, by mis-application, embezzlements, insolvencies, and other disasters by which your petitioners have been greatly injured, their poor miserably starved, their Hospital which they have built at their own charge entirely neglected, and the charitable design of their said contribution in danger of being ruined and destroyed.

Your petitioners therefore most humbly pray your Majesty to take their sad and deplorable condition into your royal consideration, and that your Majesty would be graciously pleased to concurr in the settling and confirming their said charitable contribution by encorporating your petitioners into a body, by the name of the Governour and Society of the Skippers and Keel Men of the River of Tyne; with such powers for collecting and receiving the said contribution, for the naming and choosing of officers, and for the duly applying the money to the uses for which it is contributed; as to your Majesty in your great wisdom shall seem meet.

And your petitioners shall ever pray, &c.

John Ker, Steward of the Keel-Men's Hospital, John Hodgson, Alexander Forbes, Keel-Men

A True Copy, Christopher Musgrave

This Petition being presented to the Queen in Council, was referred by the Council to the Attorney General, as appears by the following copy from the books of the Council.

Upon reading this day at the Board the humble Petition of the poor Skippers and Keel-Men, employed in the working of keels, and carrying of coals for the loading of ships in the River of Tyne, in the County of Northumberland, in behalf of themselves and of all the said Keel-Men and their numerous families, praying to be incorporated into a body, the better to enable them to collect, receive, and dispose of the charitable contributions raised among themselves, as a common stock for the relief of their poor. It is ordered by her Majesty in Council, that it be, and is hereby referred to Mr. Attorney-General to consider of the said Petition, and the Case thereunto annexed and to report his opinion to her Majesty at this Board, what is fit to be done thereupon.

Christopher Musgrave

While the Petition lies before the Attorney General to be considered, behold a Caveat is entered by the Magistrates of Newcastle, and when they come to be heard, they alledge, that the Keel-Men have changed their minds, and have signed another Petition to the Parliament, that their Hospital may be under the direction and government of the said Magistrates of Newcastle.

Now tho' it is something surprizing, that men should petition to have their hands tyed when they were free, and that they should desire to have the direction of their own Charity taken from them, that so, instead of preserving their own votes, in appointing who should or should not be relieved by their own money, they should desire that they may be left to the mercy of the Magistrates, who contributed not a groat themselves, and to the Hoast-Men and Fitters, who have many ways injured and oppressed them, and to come perhaps on their knees to them, for admittance into their own Hospital; this was indeed surprizing, but when I received the copy of a Petition from Newcastle, signed by some of the same poor men who were forced in to sign the other, it was no more a mystery to me; and I here publish it that it may no more be a mystery to the rest of the world, the original, as I hear, will suddenly be laid before the Parliament.

To the Knights, Citizens, and Burgesses and Commissioners, in Parliament Assembled:

The humble Petition of the Skippers and Keel-Men of Newcastle and parts adjacent, being employed in working keels for the carrying of coals on the River Tyne,

Humbly sheweth,

That your Petitioners, together with several hundred other skippers and keel-men as above, did join in a most humble Petition to her Majesty, representing our sad and deplorable condition, with respect to our poor, for whom provision had been made by us, from a certain voluntary contribution for their subsistence, in case of age, poverty, or disaster; which said provision is sunk and decayed, and rendered useless for want of a regular settlement, management and direction thereof; so that our poor and disabled brethren and their widows and children are miserably unprovided for, perish and starve, notwithstanding our having built a large and convenient Hospital, and having contributed very large summs of money every year for relief; for remedy whereof, we and our said brethren, as above, did humbly petition her Majesty, as aforesaid to grant her royal Charter of Incorporation, in order to empower us to choose, nominate, and appoint out of our own numbers, such proper officers to manage, inspect, and direct our said voluntary contribution and Hospital, as that our poor might be regularly provided for, and the misery and ruin now they are exposed to, be prevented, as by our said Petition hereunto annexed may appear.

And that her Majesty having heard the said Petition, was graciously pleased to refer the same to the Attorney General to consider thereof, and report his opinion thereof, and of what was fit to be done therein; which said petition lies still before her Majesty's said Attorney General. The Magistrates and Aldermen of Newcastle having desired to be heard before the said report should be made, alledging, that they had a petition from us the said Skippers and Keel-Men, wherein we desired, that the government and direction of our said Contribution-Charity and poor, might be committed to the said Mayor, Aldermen, and Magistrates of Newcastle.

Now your petitioners humbly represent to this honourable House, that true it is, that we your underwritten petitioners were, by great promises of favour, but especially by threats of being turned out of our keels, and left destitute of our employments, prevailed with by our masters and employers, the Hoast-Men and Fitters, who are also many of the Magistrates of Newcastle; to sign a petition, not daring to do otherways, for fear of losing our employment, as abovesaid; but we humbly represent to this honourable House, that as we are but a few of the great body of the said Skippers and Keel-Men, who had subscribed the said former Petition, and that our circumstances obliged us to this base retracting of our former Petition, and that at the same time we declared to the said Hoast-Men and Fitters &c that their desire of obtaining the said government and direction of our Charity and Hospital was most unjust, and with design to oppress, influence and rule the whole body of Skippers and Keel-Men, with respect to their rates and preference in their labour, and that we should declare the same to the Parliament, if ever they offered to petition for the said government &c.

We therefore your poor petitioners, humbly crave leave to retract the said petition, as being forcibly, unjustly, and with unlawful design, extorted from us; and most humbly implore this honourable House, to take the sad and deplorable condition of the said Skippers and Keel-Men into your consideration; and that this honourable House would become intercessors to her Majesty on their behalf, that their said Charter of Incorporation may pass according to the prayer of their aforesaid Petition, and that the direction and government of their own Charity, which they spare out of their dayly labour, may be left to themselves, who only can have a legal, just claim to the disposal thereof, and for want whereof, their poor are now reduced to inexpressible misery.

And your petitioners as in duty bound, shall ever pray, &c.

I shall make some remarks of this in my next; I conclude with saying this only, that I wonder how any men who had acted thus, could appear in the face of a British Parliament.

26. *A Review of the State of the British Nation*, vol. VIII, Number 142, 19 February 1712, p. 569

My last was as distressed a case, I think, as ever came before an English or British Parliament, and I could dwell longer upon it, but that opportunity will offer to make it more publick, and sufficiently expose the people guilty of so great and scandalous an oppression, I mean the poor Keel-Men's case of Newcastle.

I shall only add now, that as trade is concerned in this cause, all the trading-men in this part of England are embarked against it; for if the Hoast-Men and Fitters of Newcastle carry this point, in vain have all the steps been taken to prevent combinations of Fitters, Lighter Men, &c. in the coal-trade; for if once they get the Keel-Men at their mercy, it shall for ever be in their power to put what price upon their coals they please, and the City of London in particular shall pay a larger tax to them than ever they yet paid for the building of churches, or are ever like to do.

I pass however from this for the present to some other cases before us in trade….

27. Daniel Defoe to Robert Harley, Earl of Oxford, 14 February 1711/12 [*The Letters of Daniel Defoe*, George Harris Healey, ed. (Oxford, 1955), p. 369, letter 183]

My Lord,

I reproach my Self with The Answer I gave your Ldpp when you were pleased to Ask me if I had any Thing Perticular to Offer, Because I Fully purposed to have Represented a Perticular Case of the Poor keel men of New Castle, which I Once Offred formerly[1] to your Ldpp, and who are Now like to have the Governmt and Maunagemt of Their own Charity Subjected to The Fitters and Magistrates; by which a New foundation also will be Lay'd to Influence and enslave The Poor Men, and Thereby Again Make a Monopoly of the Coal Trade.

There is So Much Justice and Charity in The Case That I Perswade my Self your Ldpp will be pleased with Appearing in behalf of a Thousand Families of poor and Injured Men, who None but God and your Ldpp can Now Deliver; if your Ldpp pleases to give me Leav I would Gladly Lay an Abstract of The Case before you; it being in a Few days to pass the house of Commons.

[*The rest of the letter concerns matters not relevant to the above and ends (p. 371):* 'I am May it Please your Ldpp your Ldpps Most Humble and Obedient Servt.']

---

[1]   Writing to Harley on 19 June 1711, Defoe had promised to lay before him 'something Relateing to The Poor keel men of New Castle whose Oppressions Seem Reserved for your Ldpps hand to put an End to' (p. 332, letter 165). The editor incorrectly states that the Commons decided in favour of the keelmen (p. 332 n.). In fact, they passed the magistrates' bill to which Defoe was so strongly opposed, but it was rejected by the Lords.

28. Printed paper [*damaged in places*] [TWA Cotesworth Papers CJ3/13]

The Keelmen's representation to the Magistrates of Newcastle, a true State of their Case, and an Account of the Reasons [why they] have applied themselves to Her Majesty for a Charter of Encorporation for management of their Hospital.

The Magistrates of Newcastle Having appeared in public to oppose the poor Keelmen's petition and entered a caveat with the Attorney General against their charter, and their agents having raised several reports against the reasonableness of the Keelmen's request, the poor Keelmen, desiring the world may judge of the[ir] actions according to truth and justice, humbly represent to the said Magistrates their Case as follows, appealing to their own justice and consciences [to accept?] the truth and reasonableness of every part of this Representation.

1. They represent that the money contributed is entirely and indisputably their own, a meer collection of charity out of their own labour, and there can be no just pretence made by any in the world why, according to the right of free Britains, they should not have the power of directing and disposing what is their own.

2. As it is their own property, so the contribution is voluntary and free, nor has any man or body of men any right to demand it of them or oblige them to pay it but by their own free consent, and therefore they cannot be compelled to pay it, so they ought not to be compelled to pay it into such hands, or leave it to be directed by such people as they do not approve.

3. All men will allow the poor Keelmen work hard enough for their money and can ill spare it as any men, and therefore they have good reason to consider that it be trusted with such as shall rightly and impartially apply it to the uses for which it is given, which, as is too manifest, has not hitherto been done, they having now no power to sue any man for the injuries and embezzlements they have suffered.

4. The Town of Newcastle are real gainers by the Charity of the Keelmen, as it takes off the burthen of the poor families of Keelmen from the parishes where they dwell, which, if this Contribution cease, they are bound by Law to provide for, and must do it; and therefore it seems very wonderful if the Magistrates of Newcastle should go about to put an end to it.

5. The Keelmen desire to be subject to the Magistrates in every just and legal thing, but they humbly conceive they ought not to leave it to the Magistrates how their own money shall be

bestowed but are themselves the only rightful judges which of their families want relief, and when and in what manner they should be relieved.

6. If the Magistrates are made governors of the Hospital, then the poor Keelmen who shall want relief, and their families, must lie at the mercy of the said Magistrates and must sue to the Magistrates for the said relief; whereas, by right of their contribution, they have a legal claim to the relief they shall want and may demand it as their due. Nor ought it to be left in the breast of the Magistrates to judge whether they shall be relieved or no, by which many poor families, who may have paid their contribution several years to support others, may perish and be starved themselves because the Magistrates may not think fit to relieve them, though it be out of their own money.

7. They represent that it cannot easily be conceived why the Magistrates of Newcastle should seek by force to have the government of the Keelmen's Hospital, unless it were that they desire to have some greater influence upon, and power over, the Keelmen than their office of Magistrates, or by the Law, they can legally have.

8. The Magistrates of Newcastle being oftimes Fitters or Hoastmen as well as Magistrates, by consequence the employers of the Keelmen, it cannot be reasonable they should have the government of the Keelmen's Charity, which power they may then employ to awe and over-rule the poor Keelmen, either in their work, or in their Charity as they please, excluding them from the Charity, if they refuse to be imposed upon in their labour, or refusing them employment if they do not submit to be imposed upon in their Charity.

For these reasons, and not from any disrespect to the Magistrates of Newcastle, they have applyed themselves to Her Majesty's clemency, beseeching Her Majesty to enable them to manage their own Contribution, that they may have relief from it in their distress, which was the true and just intent and meaning of the first Contribution, and they hope it can be no offence to the Magistrates that this matter may be settled as Her Majesty shall think fit.

They unanimously claim as their right, and as one man resolve, that if they cannot obtain such power by reason of the opposition of the said Magistrates, they will no more contribute or pay one penny to the said publick stock, or any other of like nature, as they have done, leaving themselves and their poor to God's mercy and the Parish provision as the Law directs.

Lastly, to prevent the vain and idle reports raised by their enemies against the poor Keelmen's proceedings, as that this Application is not by their consent, that a majority are for having the government put into the hands of the Magistrates, and that they seek an illegal and unreasonable power, and the like, they have hereunder published their humble petition to Her Majesty[1] with the heads of the Charter they petition for, whereby men may see they seek nothing but the just power of disposing their own Charity, which, as it was never denied to any people in the Nation before, they have no doubt, depending on Her Majesty's goodness and justice will not be denied to them now, notwithstanding all the unjust allegations and pretences of their opposers.

And they farther represent that to this petition they have subscribed above one thousand of their hands, and the rest are ready to subscribe the same, if required, declaring that all pretences to a majority of hands on behalf of the Magistrates being governors must be vain and frivolous.

[1]   The petition to the Queen was printed by Defoe in volume VIII of his *Review*, No. 141, 16 February 1712, see above, **Document 25**. The language and some of the arguments in the above representation are similar to those used by Defoe in his other publications in support of the keelmen.

CORRESPONDENCE AND DOCUMENTS CONCERNING THE MAGISTRATES' BILL TO CONTROL THE KEELMEN'S CHARITY

29. 'Reasons to be offered against the Keelmen's having any grant for Incorporacon unless under the government of the Mayor and Aldermen of Newcastle only, or some of them' [*Draft with many alterations.*] [TWA 394/3]

1.   A part of the land belonging to the M[ayor] and Bur[gesses] of Newcastle on which the Keelmen's Hospitall was built is by lease demised in trust for advancing this Charity to the Governor and Stewards of the Company of Hoastmen in the said Town, and by their good management and care, and by the order and direccon of the said M[ayor] and Aldermen, the said Hospitall was erected and a good foundation laid for mantenance of the poor skippers and keelmen and their widows and children.

2.   But some turbulent Skippers and Keelmen, designing wholly to hinder the good intencon of the said Charity and to get

the charity moneys into their hands and to waist at their own pleasures, have for some years obstructed the collecting of the said Charity by any person appointed by the Mayor and Aldermen of Newcastle, and the said money has been ever since misapplyed and great part thereof spent in drinking at their extravagant meetings; other sumes of money charged *....for to be laid out*.... which was never done, and what remained was kept as a fund and was.*..in support of such as were guilty of great *...[*words illegible and part crossed out, probably because the substance is repeated in 3 below.]

3. Of this the Corporation of Newcastle have found the ill effects and they are the only sufferers on these occacons and particularly in the mutiny which the Skippers and Keelmen made Anno 1710, when the trade and navigation was soe long stopt, and a considerable summ of the money that should have been employed in releiving of their poor was spent extravagantly upon those riotors who were committed to goal and to protect and support them in opposition to the Law therefore.

4. Itt is much to be feared that if they have the money in their disposall they will frequently raise mutinies and tumults in the Town and thereby stopp and hinder the navigacon and trade of the said Ryver.

5. The Skippers and Keilmen doe all inhabit within the Town of Newcastle and the liberties thereof, during the time of their working in the keeles, the government whereof is in the Mayor and Burgesses, and if any incorporacon should be made of the Keelmen it would be very inconvenient for country Gents to be concerned.

6. The Skippers and Keelmen have no interest in any of the keeles and lighters or in their tackle but they are only day labourers and hired yearly to the fitters and Oastmen in Newcastle, and a great number of them come yearly from North Brittain and worke at the keels in the summer season but retorne back in the winter, and when such of them as are inhabitants dy, their wives [and] children are a very great charge to the Town, and no contribucon given towards their support from any of the neighbouring collierys.

If these reasons may not be sufficient for the preventing the incorporating of the skippers and keelmen, Mr Justice Powell[1] and Mr Baron Price[2], who were judges of our Assizes after the last tumults, can give a further account, they having inquired into the said mutinies by the Queen's command.

They were so insolent in their behavior that when the Magistrates of Newcastle went amongst them to preserve the publiq peace they were assaulted and their officers beaten, their windows broken, their persons publiqly affronted in the streets. The Keelmen's wives in great numbers went into corn shops, threatned to take it away unless they might be supplyed without moneys.

Their number is 1500 or thereabouts and most of them persons without any sense of religion or manners, and if they should be made an Independent Corporacon and get moneys into their hands, it will be impossible for the Magistrates to preserve the publiq[ue] peace, and by such a power lodged in the Skippers and Keelmen the whole trade of the River Tyne will be in their power.

[1] Stuart Handley, 'Powell, Sir John (1645–1713)', *Oxford Dictionary of National Biography*.
[2] Stuart Handley, 'Price, Robert (1655–1733)', *Oxford Dictionary of National Biography*. Price was Baron of the Exchequer.

30. Copy petition of 813 Keelmen to the Magistrates requesting them to obtain an Act of Parliament to settle the Charity, 4 June 1710 [TWA 394/5]

To the Right Worshipful William Ellison, Esq., Mayor, and the Aldermen of the Towne of Newcastle upon Tyne.

Wee the Skippers and Keelmen employed in the coal trade in the River of Tyne whose names are heretoe sett and subscribed, on behalfe of ourselves and the skippers and keelmen employed in the said River, being very sensible of the great loss and damage which wee have sustained for severall yeares past by the late Receivers appointed for the collecting of our charity money by the misapplication thereof by the said Receivers and by a party of turbulent and factious skippers and keelmen, who have waisted and spent the same and not applied the said moneys as was intended for the releif and support of the poor decayed keelmen, their widdowes and children, which are in the Hospitall that was built by the said keelmen att their own charge, and for the preventing of any tumults, riotts or troubles for the future which may arise by such ill persons, wee doe earnestly desire your worshipps to procure us an Act of Parliament soe as the said Hospitall may be governed by the Right Worshippfull the Mayor for the time being, with the help and assistance of five severall Aldermen, and that the Twenty Men, which are choosen and elected out of the ninety and nine, may have the liberty of representeing such objects of charity as are to be putt into the said Hospitall; particularly for the electing of a Steward, wee humbly desire the right worshippfull the Mayor for the time being, with five several Aldermen, to make choice of such a person that can give good security, soe as your Worshipp call him to an account once every year, or as often as your worshipps shall see occasion. This is the humble and hearty request of, honoured Sirs, Your obliged servants.

Endorsed: 4 June 1710, subscribed by eight hundred and thirteen persons.

Further endorsement: 31 October 1711 [to] William Wrightson. Copy of the Keelmen's petition signed, 4 June 1710, by 813 persons, William Ellison, Esq.

31. Drafts [Matthew Fetherstonhaugh] to Nevile Ridley in Newcastle, 2 November 1711 [TWA 394/3]

Mr Ridley,

I have inclosed sent you an affidavit about the keelmen's signing the lists, as also some reasons against the skippers and keelmen being incorporated which wee hope may sufficiently answer what was expected from us.[1] I think it strange that I had not the favour of an answer from you, though you were pleased to send it elsewhere; if there be anything else necessary let us know it. I do not doubt your care herein and with Mr Carr's assistance, to whom pray give my most humble service.[2] We have noe further occasion for Mr Waite; you will advise with Mr Carr and our Counsell whatt more [is] to be done by us and comunicate their thoughts and what is acted in this affair to your humble servant.

Written underneath:

Mr Ridley,

Inclosed is the affidavit which should be sent per next [post] shall send your answer per next. 2 November 1711

Y[ours]

Communicate all to Mr Carr and let nothing be wanting for the best of Councill and of any money, advise and it shall be remitted.

Endorsed: 2 November 1711. Letters to Mr Ridley about the keelemen's business.

---

[1] For draft of reasons against the keelmen's being incorporated, see **Document 29** above.

[2] William Carr had been MP for Newcastle, 1690–1710, but continued to seek justice for the keelmen. See Carr to Matthew White, 23 February 1711/12, footnote, and Nevile Ridley to Matthew Fetherstonhaugh, same date (**Documents 48** and **49** below).

32. Affidavit concerning the signing of the petition of 813 keelmen requesting the magistrates to obtain an Act of Parliament to control the Charity[1] [TWA 394/7]

John Rotherford, William Mathews, Heugh Engleish and John Dunn of the Towne and County of Newcastle upon Tyne, yeomen, make oath severally that they were present at and did see the severall skippers and keelmen (whose names are set and subscribed to the annexed petition) set and subscribe their marks or names, or directed and consented that their names should be set and writ to the said annexed petition, and they say that the same was done freely and voluntarily at the desire and request of the said skippers and keelmen. Signed by John Dunn and Hugh Ingliss; Rotherford and Mathew with a mark.

Jurat…coram Matthew Fetherstonhaugh, 31 October 1711

The above affidavit was copied on 31 October 1711 and the original returned to Mr [Nevile] Ridley, 2 November 1711.

[1] See **Document 30**, above

33. Nevile Ridley to Matthew Fetherstonhaugh, 3 November 1711 [TWA 394/4]

Sir,

By Mr Carr's direction I send you the coppie of the intended Bill and what papers else may be of use to you, a coppie of the petition and order of Councill thereon and the petitioners' case. Mr Ord, pray hasten up what you are advised to offer to the Attorney Generall, wee being called upon, and if posable lett me receive your commands by the 12th instant. I am, Sir,

Your most obedient and most humble Servant,

Nevile Ridley

34. Ridley to Matthew Fetherstonhaugh, now Mayor of Newcastle, 6 November 1711 [TWA 394/3]

Right Worshipfull,

Last post brought me yours with the keelmen's petition and reasons against their being incorporated save under the Magistrates, and a pacquett of affidavits which I have waited upon Mr Carr with, and tomorrow evening wee attend Mr Lutwitch.[1]

By last post I sent the last amended Bill and draught of a petition in order to conform them to the keelmen's last petition, and then sent 4 of the 9 keelmen's accounts, wee having nothing to prove them by,

but hopes you may gett some affidavitts to shew their good mannag-
ment of their Charrity money which I wish may be returned with
them by next post, for I do not expect they will admit any thing but
what will be proved against them. I ask your pardon in not writing
you the post before I left Town, and you may depend upon my care
in this affaire, for I am with great duty and resspect,

Your most Obedient Servant,
Nevile Ridley

---

[1] J.M. Rigg, revised by Robert Brown, 'Lutwyche, Thomas (1675–1734)', *Oxford Dictionary of National Biography*. Lutwyche was a barrister and MP for Appleby, 1710–15.

35. Affidavit concerning the stoppage of salt pann boats during the keelmen's strike [TWA 394/3]

Newcastle upon Tyne

William Varey of the Towne and County of Newcastle upon Tyne,
Notary Publique, maketh oath that in or about the month of June,
anno 1710, the skippers and keilmen in Newcastle aforesaid concerned
in the tumults then raised by the keelmen aforesaid stopt the pann
boats and other lighters in the said River of Tyne and would not suffer
them to goe upp and downe the said River without giveing a Bond
or Covenant to the Steward or Clerke belonging to the said keelmen,
one Mr John Kerr, and particularly this deponent remembers that one
Samuel Underhill and George Dunshire, two keelmen dureing the
time of the said tumults, came with one Mr Harle of South Sheilds
in the County of Durham, whose pann they had stopt, and caused
the said Mr Harle to give a Covenant under his hande and seal unto
the said John Kerr their Clerk and Steward, under a certain penalty
therein named, not to cast any coales on board on any shipp or shipps
in the River of Tyne, and afterwards dureing the said tumults, the said
keelmen came and severall other saltpann owners of the South and
North Sheelds, who had and imployed severall pann boats in the said
River (viz^d Mr John Cay, Mr John Richardson and Mr Michael? Hall),
and caused either of them or their skippers of their severall boats to
give the like Covenant to the said John Kerr under the like penalty not
to cast coals on board of any shipp or shipps in the said River of Tyne,
and this deponent can the better depose the same for that either he or
his clerk drew the said Covenant.

William Varey

Jurat octo die Novemb^r anno domini 1711 coram me Matthew
Fetherstonhaugh

36. Draft Affidavit concerning methods used by John Kerr, Steward of the Keelmen's Hospital, to secure signatures to a petition. Endorsed 10 November 1711 [TWA 394/3]

David Gibson of the Town and County of Newcastle upon Tyne and Walter Ormston of the said Town, keelmen, two persons placed in the Keelmen's Hospitall in Newcastle aforesaid by the twenty men to inspect and governe the other poor keelmen and widows of keelmen in the said Hospitall, severally make oath that, in or about December last, James Scott, Robert Alliburton, James Drydon, Walter Noble and William Crake, skippers in Newcastle aforesaid, with severall other skippers and keelmen, whose names these deponents cannot now remember, to the number of eighty or thereabouts, with Mr John Kerr, the Steward or Clerk to the skippers and keelmen in Newcastle aforesaid, came to these deponents and the other poor keelmen in the said Hospitall and showed to them a paper to be signed, which the said Mr Kerr and James Scott and the other skippers and keelmen said was for the getting an Act of Parliament for the making them freemen, and that they would not have any occasion for Protections[1] for the future, or words to that effect, and threatened these deponents and the said other keelmen in the said Hospitall that if they did not signe the said paper they should not live any longer in the said Hospitall, whereupon these deponents and the said other keelmen were forced to signe the said paper, and the deponents further say that they were present when the said paper was signed by severall other skippers and keelmen to whom the said Mr Kerr and James Scott and others declared in words much to the same purpose as they did to these deponents, and say that they see a great many persons signe the said paper who were strangers and foreigners and noe skippers and keelmen or inhabitants in the said Town, and these deponents likewise say that severall young women and children have been of late putt into the said Hospitall, who raise disturbances and committ great disorders there, and that neither these deponents nor any other poor people placed in the said Hospitall to their knowledge have had any subsistance from the stewards or other managers of the said Hospitall or other charity for these 12 months last past, neither have they had any coals for firing, as they used to have, but are forced to go abegging; and these deponents say that while the said Hospitall was managed and governed by the Magistrates of Newcastle aforesaid, they, these deponents, had paid to them quarterly the summ of ten shillings apeice towards their relief, but have not received any since Martinmas 1710, during which time the said Hospitall and Charity have been managed and governed by the said John Kerr and some skippers and keelmen. And these deponents say they have heard and beleive that some shortt time before signing the aforesaid paper one Daniel Deffoe was in the Town of Newcastle [and] promised to procure an Act for making them all freemen of Newcastle, and that he for that purpose then and since has received above a hundred pounds moneys belonging to the said Hospitall.[2]

---

[1] Protections against impressment into the navy.
[2] Defoe evidently claimed that he had received only £40[?] and was 'much more out of pockett by that service', Nevile Ridley to Matthew Fetherstonhaugh, 27 March 1712, **Document 52**, below.

37. Draft affidavit concerning misapplication of the funds of the keelmen's charity [TWA 394/5]

Timothy Tully of the Town and County of Newcastle upon Tyne, merchant, maketh oath that he was concerned as Steward or Receiver for the Keelmen's Hospitall in Newcastle for the space of four years ending about January 1709, and during that time there was waistfully spent by the skippers and keelmen in drink in severall alehouses in this Town the summ of one hundred and eighty pounds and upwards, and saith that £120 or thereabouts, part of the said summ was paid and discharged out[?] of the moneys of the said Keelmen's Hospitall, and the rest remaines yet unpaid, as he believes. T.T.

Jurat coram Matthew Fetherstonhaugh, Mayor, 10 November 1711

Written under the above: **Draft letter Fetherstonhaugh to Nevile Ridley, 10 November 1711**

Dear Sir,

I have inclosed sent you an affidavit of what moneys has been expended and waisted by the keelmen as far as we can at present be informed, and another affidavit about Mr John Kerr their present Steward, a sixth presbyterians, acting to get their paper signed which hope will be of good service. You'l please to communicate these likewise to my brother Carr and Mr Wrightson[1] whom I doubt not you have seen ere this. Prey push this business as forward as you can that the Attorney General's report may be obtained, for there can be no expectation of the keelmen's consent to a Bill in Parliament till they be disappointed in this, and give us timely notice of everything that happens that we may govern ourselves accordingly.

I am your humble Servant

---

[1] William Wrightson, MP for Newcastle, 1710–22.

38. Nevile Ridley to Fetherstonhaugh, 15 November 1711 [TWA 394/3]

Right Worshipfull,

I have your commands of the 10ᵗʰ with 2 affidavits, and have been with your rebellious keelmen's sollicetor to see when he will attend Mr Attorney [General]. He told me [he] had received directions to wait for further orders, so believes their Charter [of Incorporation] is at an end. I will watch them so as they shall not surprize us by any trick now wee had no business before Mr Attorney but to prevent theire being incorporated, so you may proceed in your Bill and the sooner you begin the better, that time may be to remove any objection and to finde satisfactory profes if required. Mr Wrightson is your humble servant.

I am with great Duty and Respect, Sir,

Your most Obedient humble Servant,
Nevile Ridley

39. Copy of the Magistrates' petition to the House of Commons concerning the Keelmen's Charity, 21 December 1711 [TWA 394/3]

To the Honourable the Knights, Citizens and Burgesses in Parliament assembled, the Humble Petition of the Maior and Aldermen of the Town and County of Newcastle upon Tyne.

That the Skippers and Keelmen imployed in coaltrade upon the River of Tyne to the intent that some provision might be made for poor aged and disabled skippers and keelmen, and for the widdows and children of skippers and keelmen, did severall years since voluntarily consent and agree that there should be from time to time for ever deducted and kept out of their severall wages due to them the summe of four pence per tide for every keel or coal boat imployed in carrying six or more water chaldrons of coales or ballast, or any quantityes or numbers of lead and deals or other goods or merchandizes (manure and fire coales not exported out of the said River only excepted), and for every keel or coal boat carrying less than six water chaldrons of coales or ballast (fire coales not exported out of the said River only excepted) three pence for every tyde. And in pursuance of the said voluntary agreement and contribution, the summes afore mentioned were for some time collected and applyed towards the building a large and convenient Hospitall for the poor aged and disabled skippers and keelmen, and the widdows of skippers and keelmen, which is well nigh finished, and towards the maintenance and support of other poor aged and disabled skippers and keelmen, their widdows and children, inhabiting in Newcastle upon Tyne aforesaid not placed in the said Hospitall. But of late, great part of the said Charity being not duly collected or misapplyed, and the said skippers and keelmen, being sensible thereof, did request and desired us to use our best endeavours for the procureing an Act of Parliament to be passed for settling the said Hospitall and perpetuating the said Charity, and for the better collecting and receiving thereof, to be forever applyed toward the purposes aforesaid, and to the intent therefore that the said voluntary and charitable contributions may be established and made perpetuall, and that the Hospitall and Charity aforesaid may be under a good and orderly government and inspection, your petitioners most humbly pray that leave may be given to bring a Bill into this honourable House for settling the said Hospitall and perpetuating the said Charity to the good ends for which the same were intended, and your petitioners shall ever pray &c.[1]

Signed by Matthew Fetherstonhaugh, Mayor, M. White, Thomas Wasse, Joseph Atkinson, W. Ramsey, R. Fenwicke, Jonathan Roddam, William Ellison, H. Reay, Richard Ridley.

[1] On 18 January 1711/12, the Commons ordered that leave should be given and that WilliamWrightson, Sir William Blackett and Sir Robert Eden should prepare and bring in the Bill, *Journals of the House of Commons*, XVII, p.31. The Bill was read a third time and passed on 29 March and sent to the Lords, p. 160.

40. William Carr to Fetherstonhaugh, 19 January 1711/12 [TWA 394/4]

You will, I presume, Dear Sir, by this post receive from your Members [of Parliament] an account of the progress of the keelmen's Bill to which this morning at Westminster I was doing the best service I could among some old friends and acquaintance. Mr Ferrier, one of the Yarmouth members,[1] attacked me after a friendly manner about it, being possessed with an opinion that the Bill will tend to enhance [the] price of coals by establishing a rate of two and a half percent upon the keelmen's labour. I endeavoured to satisfy him to the contrary, allegeing that though the contribution of the groats had continued divers years had in the least appeared hitherto no such effect, and that, if the Charity were not settled by Parliament, the collection nevertheless would continue, but with this difference, that the money would be squandered away and made use of when they saw fitt to mentain tumults to the stop of all trade in that River, which I thought would affect Yarmouth as much as any place. There will, I guess, be a debate upon the 2nd reading of the Bill, but I hope your Representatives will be sufficiently able to answer any objections that can arrise against the comittment of it; besides, t'would be very hard not to commit a Bill of that nature. I will do all I can possibly to help the Bill forward, and begg you'll give my best service to Mr Recorder, my brethren, &c, and believe that I am, Dear Sir,

Your most faithfull humble Servant,
William Carr

I dined this day with Lord Scarborough who drank your health.

<hr>

[1] Richard Ferrier, 'A very sensible understanding merchant', MP for Great Yarmouth, 1708–15 (E. Cruickshanks, S. Handley and D.W. Hayton, *History of Parliament, The Commons, 1690–1715*, III, pp. 1026–7).

41. Carr to [Fetherstonhaugh], 22 January 1711/12 [TWA 394/3]

I troubled you with a long letter, Deare Sir, by the last post, and therefore shall not repeat any part of it in this, but must acquaint you that I find the objection is very industrously spread especially among the great consumers of coals. They have likewise found great partiality in the Bill by exempting the keel dues for coals brought to Newcastle &c from bearing a part in the contributions. I have endeavoured to satisfie as many as I have mett with that much the greatest part of the inhabitants, and I hope I am right, are supplyed with coals not by water but land carriage, and as the wages of the keelmen are proportioned to their labour, t'would be a hardship upon the fellows to deny their choice of what part of their wages shall contribute, and what not, since the money when due is all their own. Another cavil is that the Charity is confined to the reliefe only of the skippers, keelmen, &c inhabiting within the libertys of Newcastle. Such an objection is best answered by banter, and therefore I ventered to ask wether it could be thought reasonable that the keelmen of Sunderland River should be supported by the charitable contributions of those at Newcastle, and for any other I never knew or heard of any but such as were inhabitants as above; but besides, the Bill carrys an answer to the objection, if I mistake not. I am sorry it is to have a 2nd reading on Thursday next, because I am fully perswaded giveing so short a day was not intended in favour of it. The order of that day will most probably make a full House, which could be no disadvantage to the Bill if there be time to set Gentlemen right which are sett wrong. I shall do all I can without doors, and I hope your Representatives will not be wanting within. If the Bill be committed upon the 2nd reading, as I hope it will, for, as I hinted in my last, t'would be very harsh to reject so reasonable a Bill upon a 2nd reading, especially since the faults, if it contained any, may be mended in the Committee if it be comitted. I say then there will time, before the Committee by the orders of the House can proceed upon it, for informing your worthy Members in some matters which at present probably may not be known to them, and yet necessary, since I hope objections are raised to be made use of at the Committee. I should think it were not amiss, with submission to yours and my brethrens' judgments, that they should be acquainted, if they know it not already, with how much money the Hospital has already cost, which must be lost if the Charity fall to the ground, and likewise the number of people are or can be mentained if the Charity be settled under a good government, and the difference in the wages betwixt place and place may be of use to be known to them. The Town's benefaction to the keelmen and their children in the Chappel and school may probably on occasion be made good use of, for perhaps had it not been for the good received from them they would never have entered upon so good a work. I was talking to Mr Ridley this day of some other matters relating to this affair, which I hope he will hint to these Gentlemen, because probably I may not meet with the favour of their conversation. I will not omitt being at Westminster tomorrow and Thursday in order to do all the service I can, being to Yourself, Mr Recorder, and my brethren,

a very faithfull, Dearest, humble Servant,
William Carr

42. Nevile Ridley to Fetherstonhaugh, 22 January 1711/12 [TWA 394/4]

Sir,

The Voats of Saturday last will tell you how your Bill hath proceeded, and I presume Mr Carr writt you last for what past between him and Mr Farrier, Member for Yarmouth, whom I have waited on since, and findes that he, with much zeal, persists in his opinion that making this Charrity of 4^d and 3^d per tide obligatory will be an incumbrance upon the cole traide, to which wee have replied that the payment hath for 12 years past made no alterrations in their wages, so by consequence can have no effect upon the cole traid. Another objection is the Charrity being confined to the keelmen and skippers inhabitants in Newcastle; next the voluntary duty not extending to coles brought to the Town, and I presume, as he hath time, will object to all the Bill. Mr Carr is now preparing some replies to be made to these objections, to be printed if occation.

Wee did not expect any opposition from those concerned in the consumption of coles, believing the Bill to be much for the advancement of that traid by preventing riotts and interruption to the traid by those mutaneers, but Mr Farrier is active in throwing out the Bill and applys to all Members where cole is imported and prepossesses them of the ill consequences of this Bill, and wee are as active in truly informing them.

I wish you can get the Collector of the coast duty to write to Mr Gibson, who is concerned here for the Duke of Richmond and Earl of Peterburra, what his sense is of the Bill as to their duty, which will influence his Grace to use his interest in both houses. I am told the riott in 1710 was 1000£ out of the way of those the farmers.

If any of your Town be coming up lett them be fully informed of the present condition of the Hospitall, what number placed there, and what relief they have received and when last paid, for our affidavits sent to that purpose cannot be used at a committee.

All Members I have yett discoursed [with] looks upon the governing part to be properly place[d] in the Magistrates. Your Members is diligent in your service and I hope successe may attend it. Mr Swadle is in Town; tomorrow I hope to see him, he being a fitter may do us service.

I am your most obedient humble Servant,
Nevile Ridley

43. Earl of Sussex to Matthew Fetherstonhaugh, 22 January 1711/12 [TWA 394/4]

Sir,

I received your letter of 11th which did not come to my hands till the 19th by reason it was directed for me at Windsor when I was in London. I shall be very glad to do you any kindness in particular and to your brethren the Aldermen in general when it is in my power for the civility you all shewed me when I was last in Newcastle, which I desire you to acquaint them with, and that as soon as the Bill you mention comes to the House of Lords I will use all my endeavours to forward its despatch. And you may assure yourselfe that in this and all other occasions you will always find me ready to serve you and your Corporation, being in all sincerity

Your affectionate humble Servant,
Sussex

44. William Carr to Matthew White, 24 January 1711/12 [TWA 394/4]

I wrote, Dear Brother, by the last post, and that before to Mr Mayor who, Mr Ridley tells me, he believes is out of Town, and therefore you have the trouble of this. The Keelmen's Bill was read a 2[d] time this day and committed without any debate. Besides the objections mentioned in mine to Mr Mayor which were raised against the Bill, they had found out a knocking one yesterday, viz. that arbitrary methods had been used to procure the hands of keelmen to a former petition by refuseing to give their Protections [against impressment into the navy] out unless they signed it. This [was] told to Mr Cross, the Member for Westminster, by a gentleman that came lately from the North, and he had told it to Mr Ferrier, who yesterday gave it all the air he could. I had an opportunity of talking to him and Mr Cross together yesterday, and told them this must be a mistake grounded upon the Mayor's, that then was, requiring security from some mutineers for their good behaviour as persons not fitt to be protected without it,[1] and that the complaint of their being refused came not from themselves but [from] some that went after that in an odd manner to demand them of the Mayor when he was going to church on a State Holy Day. Cross was well satisfied seemingly with what I said, but the other, who is inveteratly against the Bill, will do all he can in the Committee to obstruct its passing, and no doubt will introduce or make use of a petition, which that northern gentleman told Mr Cross was coming up from the keelmen against the Bill. I had a good deal of talk yesterday, and this too, with Mr Wrightson upon this affair, and will continue to do all I can in favour of it. My Lord Scarbrough was so kind upon my sending a letter this morning to desire Lord Lumley's being at the House early, to come himself too, and was in the lobby of the House of Commons soliciting his friends in favour of the Bill and took printed copys of it to distribute. Pray let no time be lost in sending up an account of these matters I hinted in my last, and of anything else you may think proper. I will, if there be the least occasion, constantly attend the Committee, haveing, as well as I could in so short a time, earnestly recommended to the favour of all my acquaintance the reasonableness and necessity of the Bill. I shall add no more than my service to Mr Recorder and my brethren, and that I am, Dear Sir,

Yours entirely, William Carr

---

[1] The Mayor, Robert Fenwick, explained that he had withheld protections from some keelmen involved in a dangerous riot in 1708 to obtain security for their good behaviour and to stop a 'misapply'd charity', 19 March 1708/9, Durham Cathedral Library, Additional Manuscript 97. See also Fewster, *The Keelmen of Tyneside*, p. 26.

45. Nevile Ridley to [one of the Magistrates], 24 January 1711/12 [TWA 394/4]

Sir,

I percieve by yours that Mr Mayor is not in Towne so I send these to acquaint you and your Brethren that this day your Bill was red and committed, and mett with no opposition though much threatned by Mr Clavering. He talks much of petitions coming up against it, and loudly talks of Mr Fenwick (when Mayor) would not deliver the Protections unless the keelmen petitioned for this Bill, which they refused, and was forced to apply by a frende to the Lord High Admirall for them.[1] Mr Carr made a smart returne, saying the[y] demanded their Protections upon a Feast day, and, being denied, took that way to have them. Lord Scarbrough came into the Lobbie at the Commons and ingaged severall Members, and Mr Carr is very diligent. Mr Swaddell gives a good account as to the continuance of the [keelmen's] wages, and that this Charrity made no alteration in them; he talks of going home, but wee shall stay him untill the Committee be over. We paid fees of comittment £28. 15s. 4d., and must pay double that in the Lords' House, so computes wee shall want £100 upon that account. Mr Farrier continues in his obstinate oppinion but none yett joynes with him. Mr Gibson waits for a letter from their [the keelmen's] Collecter which will influance severall Members. Certainly this Bill will be an advantage to the cole traid. All Members of the sea Ports is of the Committee. Severall I have ingaged to attend it and questions not but sett the London Members right.

No signature; endorsed: 24 Jan. 1711 Mr Nevile Ridley's letter about the Keelmen's Bill.

[1] The Clavering family's business had suffered when the keelmen refused to work without protections, which accounts for the Claverings' anger against Robert Fenwick.

46. Nevile Ridley to Fetherstonhaugh, 21 February 1711/12 [TWA 394/4]

Sir,

In obedience to your commands I delivered yours to Mr Fortiscue, and upon recieving yours of the 16th I waited upon Mr Wrightson and am sorry to finde your directions to him which hath at present putt a stopp to your Bill (which was to have been reported this day) and if he pursue them will certainly loos it, for by the common rules in Parliament no Bill can be altered by any way than an amendment in the Committee, and that agreed by the House, or an amendment in the House. Now what your fitters proposes is to most Members so unreasonable that I am confident none would move for it. The parragrave they complain on is so essentially a part of the Bill that it will pass neither House without it, and it seems your fitters is concious of what the Review complains on, or they never would be desireous to be exempted from doing the keelmen justice so. I wish their petition had come up, and where can they be injured by that penalty, unless they detain the poor men's money ? – for the Directors by the Bill is to make them just allowances, and what they have paid the keelmen, or the treasurer by them appointed, ought to be allowed them, and only answerable for what shall be detained by them, which in reason and concience they ought to pay. I prest Mr Wrightson to pursue the usuall method in Parliament and to proceed, but he looks upon your commands an injunction upon him and waits your further orders. So Mr Review hath a fair oportunity to clogg the Bill with petitions and have it recommitted.

As to the keels carrying less than 6 chaldron of coles, by all the petitions sent up they are to be charged at 3^d per tide; this may be altered in the House by an amendment, but how will that agree with the preamble of your Bill where it's recited at 3^d?; and the keelmen by their petition to the Queen in Council say that for 12 years past there hath been duly paid 1^d per tide for each man so imployed, unless you are satisfyed, and so it must be laid before the House, that such keel is wrought by two men only, so chargable 2^d.

In the lease[1] an agreement and petition is recited. I wish such petition could be found; it would be satisfactory to the Lords seeing an alterration is to be made in the duty and in the enacting part. I wish these matters of fact had been truly stated before the Bill [was] brought in, and what the fitters complaines on, if it had been omitted, would have been by order of the House incerted. A noble Lord who is most concerned for the Bill told me it was unjust to think of leaving out that parragrave, for without it the Bill would be lame and ineffectuall. The pennalty is only double the money remaining in their hands, so no crime, no punnishment – why should they be against it? I hope your next will incourage your Members to proceed, and that your fitters will be content, seeing the Governors and Directors hath not power to injure them if they pay what shall only be remaining in their hands.

I am with humble duty, Sir,

Your most obedient humble Servant,

Nevile Ridley

---

[1] Presumably the lease of the ground on which the hospital was built.

47. William Carr to Fetherstonhaugh, 21 February 1711/12 [TWA 394/4]

Lincoln's Inn, 21 February 1711/12

I had the favour of yours, Dear Sir, which I hope left you well after your late journey. You have undoubtedly had an account, and from better hands, of the Keelmen's Bill haveing passed the Committee. I was yesterday, and that before, at Westminster speaking to divers of my friends and acquaintance in favour of it that, I dare say, would attend the Report from the Committee, if they knew when that would be. If Mr Ferrier and his friends prove no greater opposers of the Bill in the House than he was at the Committee, I hope 'twill easily pass the Commons, for, to do him justice, I found none there, in my poor opinion, that gave it better assistance than he did. I shall continue to do the best service I am capable of, not only while it remains with the Commons, but after it goes to the Lords, where I wish your evidence of the matters sett forth in the Bill may be as full as that House requires, but I presume Mr Ridley and Mr Douglass will acquaint you with what they conceive may be wanting, and therefore I shall conclude with my best service to Mr Recorder, my Brethren and Mr Sherife, and with assureing you that I am very truly, Dear Sir,

Your most affectionate and faithfull humble Servant,

William Carr

Mr Douglass, my sisters and self were to wait on good Mrs Mayeres [?] the last week, but were not so happy as to find her at home.

48. William Carr to Matthew White, 23 February 1711/12 [TWA 394/4]

Lincoln's Inn, 23 February 1711/12

I am, Dear Brother, indebted to you for the favour of yours. Being this day at Westminster, I was pretty much surprized at a letter Mr Wrightson shewed me from Mr Mayor relating to the Keelmen's Bill, because, had not the Bill passed the Committee, what seems to be desired now could not well have been procured. I protest I always thought that matters had been so well conce[r]ted among us at Newcastle that no opposition could have come from any folks there, and why the fitters were not made easie by being acquainted with the Bill long since seems unaccountable to me. That they should be less charitable now than they have been 12 years last past in the collection of this Charity is odd, and why they should be against giveing an account of that money is more so. Had they not better account with their neighbours and friends than be called to do it before the

Barrons in the Exchequer, which [they] would have been almost a years since, My Lord President having directed the Attorney General to exhibit a bill upon the complaint the keelmen then made of their money not being brought to account by the fitters, but I put a stop to it at that time.[1] I should be glad to know the meaning of this, for really I believe there will not be many can think the leaving out that clause reasonable, could it be done, without confounding the whole Bill, and in a parliamentary method.

My best service to your good fireside.

I am, Dear Sir, your own William Carr

[1] Carr promised that a bill would be brought in to do the keelmen justice and so prevailed upon the Council to countermand the order. Even after his defeat in the Newcastle election of 1710, Carr regarded himself as 'obliged to see it done' (see next item).

49. Nevile Ridley to Matthew Fetherstonhaugh, 23 February 1711/12 [TWA 394/4]

Sir,

I have yours of the 19th and Mr Wrightson tells me the 2 packetts came safe and will be of use should we proceed upon our Bill which waits your order as I mentioned in my last.

Mr Wait has been with me having the Fitters' petition to be heard by their councill at the Barr of the House against the Bill. I told him what directions I had received from you, and wished he could putt the amendment made upon the Report (which to me seems imposable). I gave him a coppie of the Bill so he may proceed as he shall be advised.

Now admit the Fitters could gett that parragrave expunged, they will be in a worse condition, for instead of being accomptable to the intended Governors and Directors they will then be lyable to a suit in the Exchequer; for by an order of Councill in August 1710, Sir James Mountague, then Attorney Generall, had direction to file an English Bill in the Exchequer against them to sett forth their reciepts and payments.*...Mr Carr being present prevailed with their Lordshipps to countermand their directions, assuring them due care would be taken by a Bill in Parliament to do the keelmen justice, and he looks upon himselfe obliged to see it don. But if the Legislative Power before whom it is shall think fitt to overlook them and pass by such an oppretion so much complained on, it must be submitted to. Mr Wait expects further instructions from his clyents. It's pitty so good a Bill should be lost in screening the Fitters, for it's impossible it should pass as they desire it. They may, when it's to be reported, try the inclination of the House by moving for an amendment, which wee shall not oppose. By this delay wee loos time, and Mr Douglas talks his stay will not be long, so I wish a speedy order herein, and am, Sir,

Your most dutyfull and obedient humble Servant,

Nevile Ridley

*Five words illegible

50. Nevile Ridley to Matthew White, 1 March 1711/12 [TWA 394/4]

Sir,

I am favioured with yours and have waited upon Mr Mayer who is well. Mr Wrightson will proceed in reporting your Bill which had been don this day, had not the House been taken up in agreeing to the Representation to the Queen which is finished. Mr Kerr[1] is very humble and told Mr Wrightson he had no objection to the Bill save the small number of Directors and wished some more were aded and espetially your Members. Wee are for pasing it as now agreed in the Committee.

The Fitters' petition is not presented and I believe when offered may be rejected, for it carries an ill face.

I am, Sir, Your most Faithfull Servant,

Nevile Ridley

[1] John Kerr, the keelmen's steward.

51. Nevile Ridley to Richard Ridley, 13 March 1711/12 [TWA 394/4]

Sir,

You may think it straing I have not for 3 posts writt you or any of your brethren concerning your Bill which wants a 3^d reading, and 2 petitions wait to meet it. They are frevilous and not worth regarding, but time may make them considerable. Sir William Blackett is pleased not to be in the House though I have writt him a pressing letter to attend (which he had), but business or pleasure prevents him. I am told he is tomorrow for Newmarkett. Mr Wrightson is unwilling to move for a Reading in [Sir William's] absence, which indeed may occation his frindes to decline the interest he essposed. I am confident he is really hearty for the Bill, but believes it's not in hazard, so thinks it not to be feared. Could I have the faviour of seeing him, am confident he would recommend it to his frindes and then wee shall not fear it. Young gent[lemen] will minde their pleasures, and I protest that's all I can think of it. Mr Wrightson is constantly in the House and is ready to do what may be most for its service. He believes Sir William will not long be absent, but if he go to Newmarkett wee must do without him.

Yours N.R.

I have great assurance Sir William will not leave London untill your Bill be sent to the Lords. Ker is [not?] to be believed in writing of his hopes of success, no mony can serve so ill a cause. Though our enimies may conclude otherwise, tomorrow is no day for privatt business, but upon Satterday wee will if posable press it forward, and question not its success. I have ingaged all my frindes in it and only [need our?] Members to give it countenance.

52. Nevile Ridley to Matthew Fetherstonhaugh, 27 March 1712
[TWA 394/4]

Sir,

I hope these may finde you safe at home. I have nothing to acquaint you but that wee are perparing to encounter Mr Kerr on Satterday. We are at a loss for want of testimony to the condition of [the] Hospitall, so must interrogate Kerr. Mr Carr and Mr Wrightson is very zealous for the Bill and I do not doubt its success, though Daniell Defoe spairs no pains, having writt Mr Wrightson how much he is a looser by that service, having only received £40[?] being much more out of pockett.

I am your most obedient Servant,

Nevile Ridley

53. The Case of Charles Atkinson, John Johnson, John Simpson, and great numbers of the Trading Hoastmen, commonly called Fitters, of the Town and County of Newcastle upon Tyne [Lincolns Inn Tracts, M.P., 102, f. 86]

That there is, and for several years hath been a voluntary contribution made by the skippers and keelmen, imployed by them and other Hoastmen and Fitters in Newcastle aforesaid, about the delivering, loading of coals aboard of the ships in the River Tyne, out of their wages, for certain charitable uses, which was begun and continued in a great measure by the encouragement given by the Hoastmen and others concerned in the coal trade at Newcastle, to the good inclinations of their servants, the said skippers and keelmen to so pious a work.

That there being now depending, in this honourable House, a Bill for the settling and better regulating the said Charitable Contribution under the title of a Bill *For Erecting a Corporation for the speedy finishing the Hospital and Establishing, Perpetuating and Management of the Charity of the Skippers and Keelmen of the Town and County of Newcastle upon Tyne*, there are some clauses in the said Bill, which, the said Hoastmen humbly conceive, will subject them and other Hoastmen and Fitters (if the said Bill be passed into a law) to the payment of the said Contribution, in some cases, out of their own proper monies, and to the penalties for the non-payment thereof, and of other the sums to be paid by them, inpursuance of the said Bill.

That although they have, from time to time, paid and applied the money received or retained by them out of the wages of the said skippers and keelmen, for making the said contribution with the privity, and by the direction of the governing part of the said skippers and keelmen, from the beginning of the said contribution, which was about twelve years since, yet now, by this Bill, the said Hoastmen are to be liable to an examination and account, not only for the sums they shall receive or retain, but also for the sums they have received or retained, out of and from the wages of the skippers and keelmen for the purpose aforesaid, and to be examined upon oath concerning the same.

Wherefore, and for as much as it will be a great inconvenience and hindrance to the said Hoastmen in their trade and business, and seems to be unreasonable that they should in any case be in danger of being obliged to answer the said contribution out of their proper money, and should be subject to account and to an examination upon oath concerning the said contribution, as well for so long time past as for the time to come, and also to be subject to penalties in such cases as are mentioned in the said Bill, and which are to be levied in such summary way as is appointed by the Bill, all which is out of the common method ordinarily used in cases relating to wages owing by masters to servants, and will be a considerable disadvantage and prejudice to them in the management of their trades.

The said Hoastmen humbly pray that they may be heard by their Council at the Bar of this House against the said clauses contained in the said Bill, before the same do pass into a Law.[1]

---

[1] On 18 March 1712, the Commons ordered that the petition of 25 Hostmen against clauses in the Bill which might be 'injurious and very prejudicial' to them should be heard by their Counsel at the Bar of the House on the third reading of the Bill, *Journals of the House of Commons*, XVII, p. 141.

54. Copy of the Keelmen's Petition against the Magistrates' Bill
[TWA 394/57]

To the Honourable the Commons of Great Britain in Parliament Assembled

The humble Petition of John Kerr, Steward of the Keelmen's Hospitall at Newcastle, and 891 of the said Keelmen in behalfe of themselves and the whole Body of the said Keelmen and of their numerous Familyes

Most humbly sheweth

That your petitioners by our own voluntary contribution have for many yeares past raised a considerable summe of money out of our daly labour, for a charitable mentanieng and relieving the distreses of such of us as through age, infirmity or disaster become unable to worke, and our widdowes and children, by which the Town of Newcastle and the parishes adjacent are and have been equally secured from the charge of our said poor.

That your petitioners out of our foresaid charitable contribution have built and errected a large and commodious Hospitall for the receiving and entertaining our said poor which has cost us above £3000 starling.

That your petitioners having by our agreement consented to leave our said contribution, being one penny per tide per each man, in the hands of the Fitters and Hoastmen of Newcastle, who are our employers and paymasters, having no better way to collect the same, great summs of our said charitable contribution have been sunk and imbezelled or otherwise detained from us upon frivilous and trifling occations by our said employers and other persons intrusted by us, who refuse to account with your petitioners, knowing that your petitioners, being not incorporated, could not sue for the same but by a multitude of writts and by process in all our names separally.

For this reason your petitioners about 9 months since presented our most humble petition to the Queen, beseeching her Majesty wee might be incorporated into a body with powers given for the governing and directing and mannaging our said Charity, for the calling such persons to account who have detained any of our said money in their hands, and for the choosing out of our own number such officers, stewards, governors &c yearly as wee thought fitt for the governing the whole affaires of our said Hospitall and Charity, and for the calling such officers to account as there may be occation.

That her Majesty having refered the consideration of the said petition to Mr Attorney Generall before whom it still lyes, the

Magesstrates and Hoastmen of Newcastle entered a cavett at the said Attorney Generall's office against the said petition, and have since applied themselves to this honourable House in order for their privat ends to gett into their own management, government and direction our said Hospitall and the Charity money so contributed by us as aforesaid for the reliefe of our poor.

That the pretence they the said Magestrates have for this is that they have 800 hands of the keelmen, your present petitioners, signing our consents and request that the said Magestrates should have the continued government of the said Charity as aforfesaid. Albeit your petitioners are well assured they have no such numbers, or near the same, but true it is that they have obtained the hands of about 200 men, being such of us the keelmen aforesaid, who by threats of loosing our keels, of starving our familyes, and being turned out of our employment, and [by] such other unjust usage and corrupt practices, they have prevailed upon and drawn us to signe the said petition, almost every one of whom, having since reflected on the said usage, have declared the same and the force putt on them, have revoaked the said petition, and have vollantaryly signed the present petition, so that your petitioners are above 20 to one against them in majority.

Also your petitioners finde that in the Bill which the Magestrates and their Agent have obtained to be brought into the House not only established themselves perpetuall governors of the Hospitall and Charity of your petitioners, but also, in order to perpetuate their government to themselves, have turned our charitable volantary contribution into compultion and tax upon us, whereas by law wee are not held bound to keep the said poor but the parishes are to keep and support them. Wherefore your petitioners humbly hope that, as they made the said Charity their choice, so they have a right to preserve it in their choice to continue the said Charity or not as the occation of it may continue.

Wherefore your poor petitioners most humbly beseech this honourable House to take their sad and deplorable condition into your consideration and not suffer the Bill now depending in your honourable House to pass into a law. And your petitioners shall ever pray

The above copy, which appears to be in the handwriting of Nevile Ridley, bears the following note:

This petition is in severall sheets pined together, the first only signed by Kerr, Helleburton and Mins upon clean[?] paper; the rest seems to have been some old lists. They give it out as sent up by Sir Gilbert Ellett [Elliot]. Wee much question whether ever this petition was sent to be signed. I wish it could be detected which pray endeviour.

This and the Hoastmen's petition is to be heard at the barr of the House (and Councill to be there) upon Satterday 29th instant, so see what objections can be made against this petition and sent in due time. Mr Ferrier is much Mr Kerr's humble servant and is proud of this petition. Had not the Fitters occationed delay wee had had none of this trouble. Mr Douglas can do me justice: I was against delaying the Bill, and did pres to forward it, for what the Fitters requested was not to be regarded.

55. 'The CASE of the Poor Skippers and Keel-men of Newcastle, Truly Stated: With Some Remarks on a printed Paper, called and pretended to be their Case' [1712]. [British Library 8223 E 9 (32)]

So much falshood and so many mistakes are contained in a printed paper, pretended to be *The Case of the Poor Skippers and Keel-men of Newcastle*, that one who knows little of these poor men, their condition and circumstance, from what is there suggested, would readily apprehend nothing less to be designed by the BILL now depending, than oppression of them, and the misapplication of their Charity. In compassion therefore to these poor labouring people, who may be sufferers through what hath lately been offered as their *Case* by a Mercinary Writer, well acquainted with some instances of the wasting and misapplying their money collected for better ends;[1] what follows, on their behalf, is humbly offered with strict truth, well supported by undeniable evidence ready to be produced.

The Skippers and Keel-men employed on the River Tyne are in number about 1600, very few of which, if any, during the season of their employment, live without the liberties of Newcastle, from which place they and their families have always received great benevolence, and many charities.

The Corporation, many years since, at its own expence, erected a Chapel, and established therein reading of prayers, preaching and catechizing, for the benefit of them, their wives and children, the latter of which are taught *gratis* by Schol-Masters appointed, and very liberally rewarded, by the Town for that service.

These and many other great kindnesses, constantly shewn them by the Town, such as yearly cloathing many of their poor of all ages, and relieving more with other charities, their own being very insufficient for supporting the number of those that want, induced them, as some of the better sort of them have owned, to think of doing somewhat for themselves; in order to which, they resolved upon making such deductions out of their wages, as are mentioned in the *Bill*, to be applyed towards building of an Hospital; and in the year 1699 did petition the Corporation for ground on which to build the same.

The Town very readily complyed with their petition, granting them ground; and the deductions, according to their agreement, were made and continued till the year 1704; in which time was collected and disbursed, in the building, and other charitable uses, the sum of £ 2350 3s. 10d, the management at that time being under the Magistrates of Newcastle, assisted by the Governor and two Wardens of the Hoastmen's Company.

Soon after this, some turbulent-spirited persons among the Skippers and Keel-men, desirous of having the money into their own hands, raised divers ill-grounded clamours against the two Wardens, who had received and payed their money, without any reward for their trouble: upon which being weary of that service, quitted it, passing their accounts to the intire satisfaction of the late Sir William Blackett, named in that Paper,[2] and the other Magistrates of that Corporation.

Another person was appointed for that service, who continued one year in it, having in that time received between 3 and £400, applying the same to the uses for which it was collected: but this proving a disappointment to some ill-designing men among them, who could not be satisfyed unless they had the fingering of the money, in order to dispose of it at their pleasure, they appointed a Steward, or Clerk, who better pleased them.

In some time after, the wiser and honester sort of them, weary of this management, and being truly sensible of the great misapplication made of their charitable contributions, the greatest part of which was consumed in riotting, drunkenness, and other unnecessary expences, did petition the Mayor of Newcastle, and Governor of the Hoastmen's Company, to use their endeavours towards procuring an Act of Parliament for perpetuating and settling their Charity.

The Mayor and Governor did accordingly petition the House of Commons, and obtained leave for the bringing in a Bill for that end; but that session of Parliament being too near an end to pass the Bill into an Act, nothing was then done.

The same ill management continuing, and the wants of the poor in the Hospital encreasing, whereby they were reduced to a starving condition, and common repairs, &c. wanting, the greatest part of the Skippers and Keel-men, in compassion to themselves and their poor, did the last year renew their petition to the Magistrates of Newcastle, praying them to procure an Act of Parliament for settling their Charity, and the government of their Hospital, who accordingly did petition for leave to bring in the *Bill* now depending.

The Stater of their *pretended Case* can tell, if he pleases, how much money was shamefully squeezed out of these poor deluded people towards obtaining a Charter of Incorporation, and how little was done for them, after they had parted with their money.

It is very falsly sugested that the Petition of these poor men was obtained by any undue practices: one of the worthy Representatives in Parliament for that Town having good reason to believe the contrary from what he knows attested upon the oaths of some of them.

He is likewise very unlucky in so confidently affirming that their Petition to Her Majesty was signed by above a thousand of them. It is now remaining with Mr. Attorney-General, to whom it was referred, and is only signed by Ker their Steward, and two other persons.

The *Bill*, as it now stands, will effectually cure most of the mischiefs he complains of, and, for the future, prevent many such tumultuous riots as have frequently been raised and continued, by the misapplication of that Charity-Money.[3] The truth of which would appear, from the account of money squandered away in June and July 1710, in supporting these men who now oppose this *Bill*, in a tumult then raised, to the entire stop of the Coal-Trade, and could not be suppressed by any other means than Her Majesty's being pleased to order the Lord Hay's Regiment from Hull to Newcastle.

---

[1] An obvious reference to Daniel Defoe, who was believed, with good reason, to be the author of the *Case of the Poor Skippers and Keelmen*, printed in Dendy, *Records of the Hostmen's Company*, pp. 172–4. Dendy, who evidently did not realise that Defoe was the author, inserted this undated document, and a *Farther Case*, pp. 175–7, which can also be attributed to Defoe (being closely associated with what appeared in his *Review*), between material relating to 1707 and 1709, but both items should have been placed at the end of 1711 or beginning of 1712, having been drawn up to circulate among MPs who were about to deal with the Magistrates' Bill to regulate the Keelmen's Charity at that time. See John Robert Moore, *A Checklist of the Writings of Daniel Defoe* (Bloomington, 1960), pp. 94–5, and Furbank and Owens, *A Critical Bibliography of Daniel Defoe* (London, 1998), p. 121. Defoe had supported the keelmen in an earlier publication. Referring to Defoe in a letter to William Cotesworth of 4 December 1710, the coal owner Henry Liddell asked: 'What sort of spiritt possesses that man, who seems by the print of which he is suspected to be the author to encourage, modestly speaking, a refractoriness among that sort of people?' Some two weeks earlier, Liddell, probably referring to a ballad, 'The Keelmen's Lamentation', then being sold in Newcastle, stated that it 'plainly tends to the keeping up of a turbulent spirit among the poor thoughtless crew', J.M. Ellis, ed., *Letters of Henry Liddell to William Cotesworth*, 21

November and 4 December 1710 (Surtees Society, CXCVII, 1987), pp. 11 and 13. Likewise, Thomas Barr of Newcastle, yeoman, declared that the ballad, printed and sold by Joseph Button of Gateshead, tended to 'stirr up the said keelmen to riots and tumults', Deposition, 20 June 1710 (TWA, Cotesworth Papers, CJ/3/4). Button was a friend and correspondent of Defoe who, in view of Henry Liddell's comments above, may have been the author of the ballad. About Button see Richard Welford, 'Early Newcastle Typography 1639–1800', *Archaeologia Aeliana*, 3rd series, III (1907), pp. 16–17. No copy of the ballad has been found.

[2] Blackett is described in the keelmen's *Case* as their 'constant benefactor and friend', Dendy, pp. 172–4.

[3] The Bill passed the Commons but was defeated at the third reading in the Lords.

56. *Endorsed*: **Petition of the Skippers and Keelmen of Newcastle to Ralph Reed Esqr, Mayor, to procure an Act of Parliament, 1716** [TWA 394/6]

To the Right Worshipfull Ralph Reed, Esqr (Mayor), the Recorder and Aldermen of Newcastle upon Tine, the Petition of the Skippers and Keelmen imployed in the River of Tine:

Humbly sheweth that the Hospitall lately erected by the keelmen of this River being in all probability agoeing to decay without some immediate repair, although it was not onely designed for the releife of decayed keelmen and their widdows but alsoe a means to prevent such necessiated people from being troublesome to the Corporation, soe that your petitioners are very unwilling such a costly structure which was soe piously designed should entirely be lost, your petitioners humbly crave your Worshipp's consent that the same may be encouraged, they haveing noe designe to affront or disobleige your Worshipps, they onely crave that they may have their common and accustomed dues and wages, and that the money to be collected be applyed to good uses which they doe not doubt but your Worshipps will comply to; and as you see encouragement in this affair, hopes an Act of Parliament may be obtained for the settlement of it.

Your petitioners therefore humbly crave your consideration of the premises and that you'l please to grant that the Right Worshipfull the Mayor for the time being and his successors, the Mayors of Newcastle, be governers of this Society, and that the money to be collected bee reposed in their own box, and alsoe that the Steward or Stewards, by your petitioners yearly to be chosen, shall be obleiged to produce a just account once a year of all receipts and disbursements of the money that shall be collected for this use, and that no charity money or other disbursments be made or given without the consent of such a certaine number of the most just and eminent men (to be chosen out of this Society) as you the Governer shall think fitt.

And they alsoe further pray that a new subscription may be by them taken from the hands of all such keelmen as are desireous to have the benefitt hereof, and that the subscription and such other orders and lawes for the carrying on of this affair may be ordered by your judgments. And your Petitioners as in duty bound shall pray &c.

THE STRIKE OF THE KEELMEN OF NEWCASTLE IN CONJUNCTION WITH THOSE OF SUNDERLAND, 1719

57. *Endorsed*: **'The first[1] Remonstrance and Demand of the Keelmen of Newcastle upon their Combination not to work till their wages were increased'** [c. May 1719] [TWA 394/7]

Whereas we the Keelmen of the River of Tyne hath been oppressed so long with great measure and a contracte among the [ship]maisters and fitters that we are not able to maintain our selfs and familys without we have ane advancement and addition of our wages:

First our request is to have four shill[ings] every tyde besides what wee have had formerly.

2nd That when there comes half a dozen or half a scors of ships to this port, the fitters' men must have ther keells to load them so that another man cannot gett a tyd amongst them, therefor[e] we desir to have redress of this.[2]

3rd That we have our lying tyds as formerly was the custom of this River.

4th That we going down with a keell of coalls and the ship be load and cannot take them in and we bring them home again, to have 13 shill[ings] and 4 pence as formerly.[3] We have a great many more greiveances then thos but we will mention no mor at this tym, but without this be granted we cannott goe to work.

[1] Though this document is endorsed as the first remonstrance of 1719, discontent had been apparent the previous year. Writing to William Cotesworth, on 4 May 1718, George Liddell attributed the slowing down of the trade to the high price the agents at London had put on coal there, 'so that all our staithes are now full and our keelmen presented a petition to the Mayor and were ready for a mutiny, but that care was taken by the Magistrates and fitters. If they do not lower their price they must break of course, for, as all staiths are full, the whole country would be in a rebellion if ships should not be dispatched as soon as they come in.' (TWA, The Cotesworth Papers, CP/1/45).

[2] This obscurely worded complaint refers to the practice known as 'fitt tides' whereby the fitters' servants, without their masters' knowledge, appropriated the keels to their own use, and paid the keelmen less than the normal rate. Some

keelmen gave money to the fitters' servants in order to be so employed. See the fitters' answer, and the keelmen's second remonstrance, below.
[3] The keelmen had made this claim in 1710 and the wage settlement after the strike that year seemed to grant them full dues for this contingency.

58. [*draft with some alterations*]. 'The Answer of the Fitters in Newcastle upon Tyne to a Paper in the name of the Keelmen in the River of Tyne'[1] [TWA 394/57]

To the first: They answer and say that the wages now paid to the said keelmen are the same that have been paid time out of mind and were alwaises thought very great wages and (as they the said fitters humbly conceive) if increased will probably be a greater burthen upon the cole trade than the same will bear. And as to the measure, they, the said fitters, take it to be no more than has been heretofore given, but if any staithes do give more than they should, they, the said fitters, desire some method may be thought upon to prevent the same, though the said keelmen being bound to serve them for one year from Christmas last ought, as they the said fitters think, to have taken some other method to gett any thing which they call a greivance redressed.

To the second: That they, the said fitters, do not allow or permitt their servants to take or receive any money of the keelmen for going fitt tydes, and if their servants do receive any such money it is at the desire and request of the said keelmen, for they, the said fitters, do alwaies discourage their servants from such practises, the same being very much to the disadvantage of the said fitters and they will to their utmost endeavour to prevent their servants from doing the like for the future.

To the third: That the sums to be paid to the said keelmen for lying tydes were setled by the Magistrates of this Town some time ago,[2] and they, the said fitters, have never refused, but alwaies paid, the said keelmen according thereto and are willing to continue so to do.

To the fourth: That the sums to be paid for a keel of coles going down to Sheilds when the ship the keel was designed for is loaden was setled at the time abovemenconed and have been also constantly paid by the said fitters who are not desireous to alter the same.

If they, the said keelmen, will particularly mencon any thing else which they call greivances imposed upon them by the said fitters, they, the said fitters, hope to be able fully to answer the same, but do not really know of any other, though at the conclusion of the said paper it is menconed that they have many more.

[1] The document bears no signatures.

[2] This probably refers to the magistrates' decision on the keelmen's wages, 27 March 1705 (see above, **Document 11**), and to the settlement of 1710 (**Document 22**, above).

59. The Magistrates of Newcastle to James Craggs, Secretary of State, 16 May 1719 [TNA, SP 43/57]

Sir,

The keelmen here upon the River Tyne did about fourteen days ago enter into a Combination with those at Sunderland upon the River Weare that they will not go to work in their keels without a great increase of their wages, although they have bound themselves to the Fitters for certain wages for a year ending at Christmas next, which are duely paid them, and they insist upon other exorbitant demands which if not complyed with they refuse to work. Wee who are Justices of the Peace for this Corporation sent to those (who as we apprehended governed the rest), but some kept out of the way and others refused to come. They have committed no riotous act except stopping a keel which attempted to pass.

We have read the Proclamation against riots and arrested some who we observed to be abusive and most active and committed them to prison. We have not proceeded against them with rigour in hope of persuading them to return quickly to work, but should they remain obstinate we desire that the military be ordered to our assistance because the keelmen are too numerous for our Townsmen to suppress. Many of them come out of Scotland whose names we cannot discover.

We do believe that the Combination amongst them is made with a view to their private interest only, without any design of disturbing the publick peace of the nation.

We are, Sir, Your humble and obedient Servants,
J. Cuthbert, William Ellison, H. Reay, Richard Ridley, Edward Johnson, Ralph Reed, Francis Rudston, James Green

60. John Makepeace to Gilbert Spearman, Whitsunday [17 May] 1719 [University of Durham Archives and Special Collections, Shafto Papers, 494]

Sir,

On Tuesday the 5th Instant the Keelmen both at Newcastle and on this River [Wear] entered into a Combination, nor will they allow the Fitters to employ any other persons to unload the keels, for on Friday last, being at Sunderland, I see the Fitters goe into their own keeles and carryed them to the ship sides in order to cast the coales, but the Keelmen immediately pursued them in a light keel and brought these loaden back to the same place whear they were before moored, upon which the Proclamation was redd so they dispersed, but immediately after assembled together. Mr Hedworth[1] has been twice at Sunderland to accomodate thir difference but without success, for the Menn not only insist upon three shillings advance each tyde but that the Keelmen's demands at Newcastle be likewise complyed with, for several [ship] masters to be despatched offered to give it at this time, but they were so farr from embraceing it that they had the impudence to demand bond from them and all masters they load to submitt to this imposition, so I see noe prospect of a speady agrement. This misfortune has put noe small dificulty upon me, for on Friday last, notwithstanding I was favoured with Mr Peareth's company and went amongst all our Dealeres, yet could not be supplyed with above forty five pounds eight shillings, as the several discouragements of a Contract, Imbargo, cross winds and now, the most fatall of these, mutinous Keelmen, has hindred the trade and frustrated my expectationes insomuch that I have not been enabled to pay the Duty nor please the workmen; yet the latter are pritty easy, and I think will keep close to their work as they have noe keels to load nor other business to divert them.

I am sorry to be the author of ill newes but don't question but Mr Peirson would acquaint you with Mr Greenwell's death which sad accidant has been a great concerne to me, and though ther's noe trade at present, yet wee must hope when it does begin it will be very brisk, so if you have another person to recommend in his place I shall be ready to receive him, but if at this time you'd please to allow Mr Peareth the election, ther's one Anthony Carrock recommended by him and every way qualified for that station, having been conversant with this same business and perfectly acquainted with all our Keelmen which may be of singular use this year, as the other Coale Owners have engaged the Fitters to a quantity, so a stranger's officiateing may be of ill consequence to us, but I humbly submit this to your superior judgment and shall punctually obey your commands in that and all other respects. I have a relation of my own very much accomplished, yet could wish to oblige Mr Peareth in this matter.

I shall pursue the sinking with the utmost celerity but hope I cannot be censured for its not being already begun, as wee labour under these discouragements in wanting money and even the trade from which wee should be supplyed. I faithfully assure you so soon as I am enabled I'le carry it briskly forward having nothing more at heart.

The ginn at the Hope Pitt is now fixed and will begin coale work next week. I have nothing further to add save that I crave leave to subscribe myself with a tender of my most humble service to Madam Spearman (and with great respect to you both), Sir,

Your most Faithfull and Obedient Servant,

John Makepeace

[1] Hedworth was one of the County Durham magistrates.

61. Extract from a letter from Mr Robinson, Collector of Sunderland, 15 May 1719 [TNA, SP 35/16/62(1)]

The keelmen continue to put an entire stop to our Trade. They are now assembled in a tumultuous manner and will not work themselves but hinder others that would, on pretence their accustomed wages are too small, and making such extravagant demands as all concerned with the Trade think not fitt to be complyed with. They are about 800 in number so that the civill power is not able to curb them. The Proclamation against Riots was this day read before them, but they shewed no regard thereto but continue in a great body in a riotous and dangerous manner.

62. Copy of the Warrant issued out for apprehending severall keelmen upon their combinacon not to work till their wages were increased [TWA 394/7]

Whereas the skippers and keelmen employed in the cole trade in the River of Tyne have entered into a combinacon and refused to work, and whereas severall of the said skippers and keelmen have frequently riotously and tumultuously assembled [them]selves together for hindring and preventing such persons from working in the said employment as were willing so to do, to the disturbance of the publick peace, and for continueing of the said combinacon and supporting themselves therein have collected severall sums of money, and whereas we are credibly informed that Archibald Hope, – Dixon, – Pearson and – Halliburton are the cheif and principall promoters, encouragers, aiders and abettors of the said combinacon, disturbances and tumultuous assemblies, these are therefore in His Majesty's name strictly to charge and command you and every of you forthwith upon sight hereof to made diligent search and enquiry for the said Hope, Dixon, Pearson and Halliburton and them bring before us, His Majesty's Justices of the Peace for this Town and County, or one of us, to answer the premisses and be farther dealt with according to Law and Justice.

63. Secretary of State James Craggs to the Magistrates of Newcastle, 21 May 1719 [TWA 394/7]

Gentlemen,

Though you will receive from Mr De la Faye, Secretary to the Lords Justices [of the Regency], such directions as are thought necessary with regard to the riotous proceedings of the keelmen in your neighbourhood, I cannot omit acquainting you that your zeal and vigilance on this occasion for His Majesty's service and the publick peace are very acceptable to the Lords Justices and will be represented in the best manner to His Majesty.

I am, Gentlemen,
Your most humble servant,
J. Craggs

64. Charles De la Faye, Secretary to the Lords Justices of the Regency, 'to the Mayor and other Magistrates of Newcastle and to every or any of them', 21 May 1719 [TWA 394/7]

Gentlemen,

Mr Secretary Craggs has received your letter of the 16th instant giving an account of a rising of the Keelmen in your Town and neighbourhood under pretence of their wages being too small, and has laid it before the Lords Justices, who ordered me to return you their thanks for your care and diligence in sending up this account and using your endeavours to suppress the tumult. The assistance which the officers of the troops quartered in your Town have given you is very much to be commended, and though all subjects are obliged to assist the magistrates in the due execution of the laws and in preserving peace, yet that the military officers may have no scruple in this respect, their Excellencies directed the Secretary at War to write to them to that purpose.[1] Their Excellencies have ordered the Informations to be put into the hands of the King's Sollicitor, that care may be taken for prosecuting the rioters with effect, and I am to desire that whatever further Informations you take may be sent up to be laid before their Excellencies.[2] I am likewise commanded to signify to you their Excellencies' further directions that such of the rioters as have been seized or may be apprehended, which it is taken for granted will be as many as you can secure, be kept in safe custody in order to be brought to tryal, and particular care taken that they do not escape.

I am, Gentlemen, your most humble servant,

Ch. Delafay

[1] The efforts of the military were not entirely successful. Writing to the Secretary of State to request military assistance on 6 May 1738, the magistrates pointed out that the Commanding Officer must have power to act in Northumberland and Durham as well as in Newcastle, otherwise 'the end of their march may be fruitless as happened about 20 years ago upon the like occasion, when a military force was sent to aid the civil magistrates, notwithstanding which for want of the above mentioned power many of the principal offenders escaped by flying into these Countys' (TNA, SP 44/130/343–4).

[2] The Solicitor to the Treasury asked for 'the Christian names of some of the offenders who are mentioned in the informations only by their surnames, an account of those taken up, by what warrants and in what gaols confined, the original paper, if it could be had, of their combination drawn up by one Flower, the accustomed wages paid to the keelmen and skippers and what advance they respectively demand' (Delafaye to the magistrates, 30 May 1719, TWA 394/7).

65. Copy letter William Cotesworth and George Liddell to Sir Henry Liddell, 24 May 1719 [TWA, Cotesworth Papers, CJ 3/8–12]

Dear Sir,

We presume you will be told before this reach you what application has been made to the Lords Justices by the Town of Newcastle and Mr Hedworth to send directions to the military power at this place to assist the civil magistrates in quieting what has been called the Keelmen's Rebellion in both rivers, and the Lords Justices have accordingly given orders for the civil magistrates to be assisted. Yesterday, about 5 in the evening Mr Robarts, the King's Messenger, arrived here with Mr Treby's directions to Colonel Cholmly to march to Sunderland which he did this morning to assist the magistrates in that river, and the same messenger brought orders to Colonel Kirk to assist the magistrates in this Town.

We understand that it has been represented the disturbance the keelmen have given at this time is in favour of the rebellion now on foot against the State the more readyly to prevaile for the assistance of the military power.[1] If it prove true that any have so done, we think our selfes bound to set that matter in a right light and to pray that the Lord Justices may be told what is the truth, that the keelmen in this river have not at any time in our memory shewn any disaffection to the present Happy Settlement, but on the contrary have always expressed a hearty zeal for King George and his Government, and on the rejoicing that was by countenance made on the King's first landing, were very usefull in protecting us against the insults that were made upon us in our innocent mirth at a tavern in our market place in Newcastle, where a town mob pulled down our bonfire and threw some of the materials as they were burning in at the windows where we were drinking the King's health. That the keelmen in both rivers have very imprudently and unjustly as well as illegally, and that in concert with each other, put a stop to the coal trade of both rivers is very true, and have by violence hindered some very small number from working, but it is chiefly on pretence that they cannot subsist their families without an encrease of their wages by reason of the agreement the masters and owners of ships are come to to contract their time of trade into less compass. We have taken great pains to bring the men to the labour they bound themselves to last Christmas by fair means, but the violence the magistrates used at first by comitting them to jayle has so exasperated them that all our gentle methods have failed, though we did yesterday, at a meeting the keelmen desired at Pratts, in conjunction with a few of the cheife fitters and some of the most considerable [ship]masters, agree and promise to redress all their grievances and to comply with every thing except an encrease of their wages, and we also recommended it to them to perform the agreement they had at present subsisting, and next Christmas, if they did not like the terms then, not to hire themselves, but nothing we could say would take any effect, so that we must now waite to see the issue of the military power and the poor men's better consideration of the kindness we have shewn them. We were desireous you should be fully apprized of this whole proceeding in hopes you will take an early opportunity of comunicating it where you shall judge proper. W.C.

Endorsed: The copy of a letter I writ, and Mr Liddell only signed, in both our names to Sir Harry and sent by Mr Robarts, the King's Messenger, who brought Mr Trebys orders to Colonel Chalmly and Colonel Kirk at the instance of the magistrates and Mr Hedworth to repell force by force on the poor keelmen of both rivers for refusing to worke without an increase of wages, the 24 May 1719.

---

[1] This probably alludes to what John Hedworth had written to the Secretary of State, to request troops to protect Sunderland, 15 May 1719: '…for though I cannot yet call it a rebellion, yet as so great a number as eight hundred men upon the Were, and two thousand upon the Tine are above the reach of the Civil power, it is uncertain how long such a body made desperate by their obstinacy and poverty may contain themselves within any legal bounds.' He believed that the 'rising' was 'calculated with a further view to distress the City of London by putting an entire stop to the coal trade at a most dangerous time, if it had not pleased God to have disappointed our enemeys…I really apprehend that they now want only a leader to hurry them into the most violent extreams' (TNA, SP 43/57).

66. Copy of Mr Treby's letter to Colonel Cholmley [TWA, Cotesworth Papers, CJ 3/8–12]

It is the Lords Justices' directions that you cause the several companies belonging to H.M. Regiment of Foot under your command at Newcastle upon Tyne to march immediately from thence to Sunderland and remain untill farther order and be aiding and assisting to the civil magistrates in suppressing any tumults or insurrections that may happen there and to repell force with force in case the said civil magistrates shall find it necessary, wherein the civil magistrates and all others concerned are to be aiding and assisting unto providing quarters, impressing carriages, and other wise as there shall be occasion. Given at Whitehall, 21 May 1719.

67. *Endorsed*: **The second Remonstrance and Demand of the Keelmen of Newcastle upon their Combinacon not to work till their wages were increased** [TWA 394/7]

Right Worshipfulls,

Whereas we the skippers and keelmen belonging to the River of Tyne, being so much oprest by reason of the long Contrak made by our respective fitters and masters of ships and others, in so much that we are not able to subsist and maintain our selves and familys, our wages being so low and the Measure so great, therefor our request is by a generale consent of all and every of our Sosiety of Keelmen that fore the time to come we shall have for every keell of coals load[ed] at any staith and cast on any ship or veshell, we shall have an Adition, or advancement of four shillins per tyd, and fore every four chalder two shill per tyd, as also for every keell of coals load[ed] at any staith and taken down the forsaid river and brought up again uncast our full dwes that formerly we used to have, viz 13sh & 4d for every keel load as aforsaid and not cast. Further, if any of our forsaid fitters shall cause any keell aboard on any ship or veshell and that forsaid ship or veshell cannot take in all the forsaid keell but shall hapen to leave 3 or 4 chalder less or more, ore any part thereof, we shall not be abridged any of our wages; as also for every lying tyd what formerly use[d] to be given, not to be abridged as of laite we have been; as also for every keell of balaise taken out of any foresaid ship or veshele, if it bear a balise warrant, our full dues as formerly, viz 13s & 4d; as also fore the fitters' men haveing five grots for every tyd that is served them by any keell or boat out of his master's employment, taken of[f] and come in to the skipper that so serves such tyds; as also that no fitters' men shall have any keels stird fore them but to live upon their own selliry; upon the account they gett men to stir keels and boats thatt is not capable of ther labour, whereby the forsaid skipers are objected against, as also men's lives being endangered by there not being cappable of ther labour; and we being opprest by the fitters' men and abused at the staith beyond all reason; as also that every on[e] of our forsaid Soscety of Keelmen that is now in close prison, and women besid, shall be released and sett at liberty, and all old feeds and enmityis taken away; as also for every ship shifting of[f] the Keys, on[e] shill[ing] a keel; and bear to drink in time of heaveing the coals, or sixteen pence for every keell instead thereof. This is what we have all consented to with a generall consent, without any objection at all.

68. Another version of the above with some variations and additions, especially the following:[1] [TWA, Cotesworth Papers, CJ 3/8–12]

That every one of us has agreed that in case any of our respective Fitters make any objection against any thing herein mentioned and take any advantage at any of our forsaid Socyiety of Keellmen and discharg that person or persons so accused from his imployment, that in that and such like cases we have agreed that no keell shall move from his place till that person or persons… so objected against be restored to his former station unless a mor lawfull reason cane be shewed.

[1] There is no call for the release of prisoners in this version.

69. The Magistrates of Newcastle to the Secretary of State, 30 May 1719 [TNA, SP 43/57]

Sir,

Since our last, several of the Keelmen on behalf of themselves and brethren appeared before us complaining of some grievances from the Fitters (who were likewise present) which were adjusted by us to all their satisfactions. On these occasions wee pressed on them their duty to his Majesty's Government and the hazards they were in by continuing to stop the Trade and navigation of this River in so tumultuous and riotous a manner, and therefore urged them to work according to their bonds, whereupon some hundreds of them assembled together and after their Deputys had reported to them what passed with us, they by a vast majority sent us word they would not work till they had additional wages of four shillings per tide, which annually in this Port would amount to Six or Seven Thousand Pounds, a burthen too great for the Coal Trade to bear as we apprehend, so we are at a loss what to do. In the meanwhile we have issued out warrants against such of the Keelmen as by informations appear to be the Ring-leaders and chief abettors of the tumult.

We are informed that two tenders are coming to Sunderland and Newcastle and wish to know whether the Commanding Officer has directions to impress such Keelmen as shall be most active and leading amongst them in this Port. We also ask permission to protect those Keelmen willing to work, which we hope will be an effectual way to put an end to the Combination amongst them.[1]

Your humble obedient Servants, Cuthbert, H. Reay, Richard Ridley, Edward Johnson, Ralph Reed, F. Rudston

[1] Orders had already been issued to Captain Delaval, Commander of *The Gosport*, at Inverness, to proceed to Sunderland and apply to the magistrates there and at Newcastle to 'receive from them such Keelmen as they shall have to send on board you for his Majesty's service', 22 May 1719. These orders were cancelled on 3 June, Delaval being ordered 'not to impress…any of the Keelmen of Sunderland and Newcastle who the magistrates of those places, or Mr Hedworth, or any other Justice of the Peace…shall inform you have submitted, and are willing to return to their work' (*The Delaval Papers*, ed. John Robinson, Newcastle, n.d., p. 144).

70. *Endorsed*: **The third Remonstrance and demand of the Keelmen of Newcastle upon their Combinacon not to work 'till their wages were increased** [TWA 394/7]

To His Majesties Justice[s] of the Peace of Newcastle upon Tine and pleise your Worships, we are desirous and [to?] further incourage business, provided we had the King['s] Measure, and likewise a keel of coales which are boarded upon a ship, finding the ship are load[ed], we expect as formerly thirteen shillings and four pence, and likewise for breaking a bulk of coales we desire as formerly full dewes and owners' wages. All Ballast tides by warrants we expect as formerly thirteen shillings and four pence, and likewise for each lying tide, according to ancient custome, two shillings and six pence, and each keel shifting a shipp of[f] the shore we expect as formerly a shilling; further, whilst we are casting, failing beer, we expect one shilling and four pence; and likewise no served tides for fitter or fitter's man, also no stured keels, excepting old men and widdowes, and if in case a keel should goe on board of two shipps accordingly we expect keel and boates dewes; notwithstanding the prisoners must be relieved.

71. Thomas Armstrong to Cotesworth, 3 June 1719 [TWA, Cotesworth Papers, CJ 3/10]

Sir,

Two dayes past I have been in a busey place perswadeing to get the Keelmen to goe to work, and yesterday we came to the following resolutions:

1. That all the keels goe to the several staiths and load as the King's measure is,[1] as well to please the owner as the [ship] master.
2. That all the prisoners be released upon recognizance, their charge[s] to be referred to the Magistrates [to] ease them as well they can.[2]
3. That lying tides be paid them.
4. In case a keel loaden goes down the river and the ship hapens to be gone to sea, the full dues be paid, or if half be cast in a ship, full dues be paid.
5. That shifting a ship from the key or dike when the Keelmen assist to receive one shilling.
6. Small drink: if none given by the [ship]master at the casting, 16d. to be allowed by the fitter, but that is as fitter or master pleases.

[1] That is eight Newcastle chaldrons to the keel. In a separate note it is stated that 'the keelmen agree to carry the same quantity of coals in their keels that the Sunderland men carry in their keels' (Cotesworth Papers, CJ 3/8–12).
[2] The following, found apart, seems to relate to the negotiations to which Thomas Armstrong refers: 'That on finishing this agreement, all offences given by any skipper or keelman or by their wifes or any other person in their favour shall be released and that such person either men or women as are now in jayle on account of the present stop of the keels and of the trade of the River shall be immediately discharged' (Cotesworth Papers, CJ 3/8–12).

72. The Magistrates of Newcastle to the Secretary of State Craggs, 4 June 1719 [TNA, SP 43/61]

Sir,

…We have apprehended and committed to prison two of the Keelmen who were esteemed the most active and whose example and authority did very much influence the rest which had so good an effect that afterwards application was made to us by a considerable number of them who offered for themselves and the rest to go quietly to work if we would discharge those whom we had committed to prison. We said that we had express orders to the contrary, but we promised them if they would go to work first and behave themselves as they ought to do, we would endeavour to interceed on their behalfs to their Excellencies [the Lord Justices of the Regency] that all prosecutions against them may be staid; and thereupon, after consultation with their fellows, they submitted, and yesterday they went chearfully to work and promise not to trangress for the future. We therefore ask that, since no capital charge is involved, the men and women against whom no particular information as to their guilt of any riotous act has been made should be discharged from prison, providing they give sureties for their appearance at the next general Quarter Sessions, and to discharge out of prison such of them as have been most busy and active upon their giving security for their good behaviour and to appear at the next Assizes, because the authority of the Judges will be a much greater terrour to them than any thing we can do, and by this means they may be enabled to support their families who (as we are credibly informed) are by their obstinacy reduced to very great necessitys.

We have had powerful assistance from the soldiers whose officers on all occasions supplied sufficient men to put the Law into execution.

Your humble obedient Servants,

Cuthbert, Richard Ridley, Edward Johnson, Ralph Reed, F. Rudston

73. J. Craggs to the Magistrates of Newcastle, 9 June 1719 [TWA 394/7]

Gentlemen,

I am obliged to you for the kind sence you expressed of my endeavours to serve you in the disturbance lately happened amongst the keelmen. Mr Delafaye will signify to you the Lords Justices' orders which are agreeable to your request, as he is the proper person to lay every thing before them and to receive their commands. I refer myself to him and am truly,

Gentlemen, Your most humble Servant,

J. Craggs

74. Charles De la Faye to the Magistrates of Newcastle, 9 June 1719 [TWA 394/7]

Gentlemen,

The Lords Justices being informed by your letter to Mr Secretary Craggs that the Keelmen are now in a great measure appeased and returned to their labour and that you are of opinion the releasing those under confinement would be a means of quieting them, their Excellencies approve of what you propose: that they should be let out upon bail, the ring-leaders and most mutinous to appear at the next Assizes, and the rest to appear at the next Quarter Sessions for which you will give the proper directions.[1]

I am, Gentlemen, Your most humble Servant,
Ch. Delafaye

[1] In another letter of 9 June 1719 Delafaye declared: 'The Lords Justices are tender of those poor people who are the best, if not, I fear, the only well affected mob in England' (TNA, SP 43/61).

75. De la Faye to John Hedworth and Anthony Ettrick on the conclusion of the Sunderland strike, 16 June 1719 [TNA, SP 44/281/62–3]

Gentlemen,

…Their Excellencies recommend it to you to enquire whether these poor people have not just ground to complain of oppression from their masters the Fitters, particularly in those matters you mention about cloathing and other necessarys being imposed upon them in lieu of money for their wages, and to do them right, and as far as the law enables you to prevent any injustice being done them.[1]

The prisoners are to be discharged and on appearing at the Assizes will meet with the indulgence you promised them.

I am, Gentlemen, Your most humble Servant,
Ch. Delafaye

[1] On 4 June 1719, Matthew Fetherstonhaugh and William Ellison, two of the magistrates of Newcastle, were called before the Lords Justices and questioned on the same matter. They denied that the [Newcastle] keelmen were being obliged to do more work or were paid less wages than constantly had been the case, and they affirmed that the wages were paid weekly in ready money (TNA, SP 43/61).

76. Hedworth to Delafaye, 23 June 1719 [TNA, SP 35/16/139]

Sir,

According to your directions of 16 instant, Ettricke and I released the 4 keelmen upon security to appear at the next Assizes, and that the Mayor of Durham, Mr Brabin took bail for Flower the school-master, as soon as we were gone out of Town, though we had before shewed him your letter; so that now I despair of any further discovery or information about this matter.

I will go to Sunderland tomorrow to forward the petition you so kindly advise in behalf of the poor people and am persuaded nothing can conduce more to keep the rest in quietness at their work than an entire discharge of them.

As to the oppressions they pretend to lye under about cloathing and other necessarys, I made the strictest inquiry before I sent the account of their rising, and could never find more cause than what was transmitted to you, and I dare say it could not be expected that so few grievances should have happened to a body of 800 men in four years, the space of time referred to in these examinations. However, the Fitters have faithfully promised for the future not to impose necessaries or houses upon them for the future. The latter is truly a grievance, but the former can hardly be avoided from the nature of trade, which must as well be carried on by Truck as with ready money, because the masters of ships generally bring corn the first voyage of the year and oblige the Fitters to take it in discount for their loading of coals. …

I am, Sir, your humble obedient servant,

John Hedworth

77. De la Faye to the Magistrates of Newcastle, 2 July 1719 [TWA 394/7]

Gentlemen,

I am to return you my thanks for the favour of your letter of 21 past and the notice you were pleased to take of my readiness to serve you, which, if it could in any way contribute to render your care effectual for suppressing the late tumult of the Keelmen, can not but give me great satisfaction. As I believe you do not desire to punish those who were imprisoned, I intimated to Mr Fetherston[haugh] that it were convenient they should by some proper hand be perswaded to petition the Lords Justices for a stop to any proceedings against them, acknowledging their offence and expressing their repentance, the effect of which petition they might hope to obtain through your intercession. I gave the same hint to Mr Hedworth, who has sent up a petition of the like nature from those which the Justices there had seized, which petition their Excellencies readily granted.

I am, Gentlemen,

Your most humble servant,

Ch Delafaye

78. John Hedworth to [De la Faye], 12 July 1719 [TNA, SP 35/17/26]

Sir,

I am very sensible of the great trouble you have had about the affair of the Keelmen, yet I cannot avoid adding this letter for my own justification on to the Judges, when they come the Circuit, because as you have not mentioned anything particular in your last letters about Flower the school master,[1] they may think me negligent in not having matters prepared against the Assizes for his prosecution, towards which I applyed to Mr Anto. Ettricke to give security for his appearance to give evidence against him according to his information formerly sent up, but he absolutely refused, and I did not care to commit a man of his temper and knowledge in the law without positive directions from their Excellencies. But indeed I hope Flower is intended to be included in the favour granted to the poor Keelmen, as a fresh instance of their Excellencies' clemency, and which, I doubt not, will have a very good effect upon the common people, who now in general repent of their error and own themselves to have been in the wrong.

You are desired to cause the orders for their stopping proceedings against the Keelmen to be directed to the Attorney General of this County, because it is a County Palatine, though no doubt you will be much better informed of the proper method of doing it than by

Your most humble servant,

John Hedworth

---

[1] Richard Flower, a schoolmaster of Bishopwearmouth, had instigated the Sunderland keelmen to strike and had drawn up Articles of Combination with the keelmen of Newcastle; see Hedworth's letter to De la Faye of 26 July 1719 (**Document 81**, below).

79. De la Faye to the Magistrates of Newcastle, 21 July 1719 [TWA 394/7]

Gentlemen,

I have received by the hands of Mr Fetherston[haugh] your letter of 17th instant whereby you are so charitable to interceed with the Lords Justices for a stop to the proceedings against Thomas Dixon and other Keelmen who were apprehended upon the late riot in your parts and are now under bail to appear, some at the Assizes and others at the Quarter Sessions. Orders will be given to Attorney General to stop any prosecution of these poor men, since they are sensible and repenting of their crime, and you will be pleased to put off any proceedings against them.

I am, Gentlemen,

Your most humble Servant,

Ch. Delafaye

80. Hedworth to Delafaye, 26 July 1719 [TNA, SP 35/17/46]

Sir,

I am favoured with yours concerning Flower the schoolmaster[1] whom I had recommended to the mercy of the Lords Justices with no other view but that the Mayor of Durham having taken him bound only to the Sessions, and a strong party being formed to discharge him, I was willing his enlargement should be wholely oweing to their Excellencies' goodness, and not to a vote of our bench; but contrary to my expectation he was continued over to the Assizes by the majority of one voice. I could never obtain any further information about the Articles of Combination than what has already been sent up. How far the Magistrates of Newcastle may be able to contribute to the discovery I can make no conjecture. I am persuaded they will use their endeavours upon the least intimation from you.

I am Your humble obedient servant,

John Hedworth

[1] Despite Hedworth's plea of 12 July on behalf of Richard Flower [see above, **Document 78**], Delafaye informed Hedworth that the Lords Justices called for Flower to be punished with the 'utmost severity'. Delafaye therefore asked whether Hedworth could obtain from the keelmen 'a copy of this Flower's draught of the Articles of Combination so as to fix it upon him; it would be very usefull towards carrying on that prosecution' (23 July 1719, TNA, SP 44/281/164–5), but Hedworth had already pointed out that the Mayor of Durham had released Flower on bail 'so that now I despair of any further discovery or information about this matter', 23 June, SP 35/16/139, as he reiterated in the letter above. Presumably, the intended prosecution against Flower collapsed through lack of evidence.

ANOTHER ATTEMPT TO REVIVE THE CHARITY

81. Draft petition of the Keelmen to the Mayor [c. February 1722/3]. *Endorsed on a separate cover*: Petitions of the keelmen about their Charity in order to have it under the management of the Magistrates, William Ellison, Esq. Mayor[1] [TWA 394/10]

To the Right Worshipfull &c

Wee the Skippers and Keelmen employed in the coal trade in the River of Tyne whose names are hereto sett and subscribed being very sensible of the great loss and damage which wee have sustained for severall years past by the misapplicacon of the Charity money given by us out of our wages for the releif and support of the poor decayed keelmen their widdows and children which are in the Hospitall, and of the many inconveniencies which wee suffer and have suffered for want of an Act of Parliament for setling the said Charity and governing the said Hospitall, which we formerly desired your worships to obtain for us, but afterwards opposed, being induced and perswaded thereto by some keelmen and othrs,[2] who waisted and spent the said Charity and did not applie the same as was intended, whereby the said Hospitall is not yett finished, but that part already built will go to decay without immediate repair, and the people placed therein are in very great want. Wee do therefore earnestly desire your Worships to procure us an Act of Parliament so as the said Hospitall may be governed by you and your successors, with the help and assistance of the Governour of the Hoastmen's Company for the time being, and that such a certain number as you think fitt to be chosen and elected from amongst us may have the liberty of representing such objects of charity as are to be putt into the said Hospitall, and also of seeing and peruseing once a year the accounts of all moneys received and paid for the said Charity, and also of nameing yearly three or four persons fitt to be stewards or overseers of the said Hospitall, out of which number one to be appointed by your Worships for that service, and also that all the money received on this account be put into a strong box or hutch to be kept in the said Hospitall and locked with as many keys as you think proper, one whereof to be kept by the Steward appointed as aforesaid, and as for all other matters or things which shall be necessary or proper to be inserted in the said Act for setling the said Charity and governing the said Hospitall wee humbly desire they may be inserted in such manner and form as to your judgments shall seem meet. This is the humble and hearty request of us who as in duty bound shall ever pray &c.

---

[1] Some of the wording is identical with that of the petition to Ellison when he was Mayor in 1710, see above **Document 30**. The Hostmen considered the petition on 18 February 1722/3 and unanimously agreed to forward 'so good a work', but on 20 March they resolved that the Charity should be 'solely under the management and direction of this Fraternity' (Dendy, pp. 188–9). There had been much discussion and 'a good deal of battleing' between Richard Ridley, Governor of the Hostmen's Company and a magistrate, who wanted the magistrates to control the Charity, and other members of the Hostmen's Company, especially Charles Atkinson and Jack Johnson, 'who bore briskly up to him'. The Hostmen prevailed, but, George Liddell remarked, 'I think it will come to little, for I fancy as the Magistrates have not carryed it, they will not push it forward...' (Liddell to William Cotesworth, 22 March 1722/3, TWA, Cotesworth Papers, CP 1/90). Eventually, as Liddell predicted, nothing

resulted. See Fewster, *The Keelmen of Tyneside*, pp. 40–2. The keelmen would have preferred government by the magistrates (see next item).

[2] 'A party of turbulent and factious skippers' *crossed out*.

82. Petition to the Mayor, 26 March 1723 [TWA 394/57]

To the right Worshippfull William Ellison, Esqr, Mayor

The application of Adam Craggs concerning the Keelmen's Grotes[1] and Hospitall, vizt:

That the Fitters would have the Governours of the Hoastman's Company to be the Governours of the said Hospitall &c.

That the Keelmen in generall (as he this Supplicant dares say) would have your Worshipp and your Successors to governe the same.

That he and the rest of your Supplicants, his brethren in conjuncon with him, prays that your Worshipp will please to aid them herein, as may seem best in your Worshipp's great and singular wisdom, prudence, charity and judgement may seem most meet, and your petitconers shall as in duty bound ever pray &c.

[1] The four pence per tide the men subscribed to their Charity.

OBJECTIONS TO A PROPOSAL BY THE SHIPMASTERS TO DELAY THE START OF THE COAL TRADE

83. George Liddell to Henry Ellison, 14 January 1728/9 [TWA, Ellison Papers, A32/21]

…But what I had like to forget, and is very materiall: what must become of the poor keelmen? They are a sort of unthinking people that spend their money as fast, nay generally before they get it. They gave over work the beginning of November, and many of them had not then a shilling before hand. They live upon their credit, and a little labouring work, till they get their binding money at Christmas. That money goes to their creditors, and then they borrow of their fitters to buy provisions, and have credit with the runners for a little drink, and so they put of[f] till trade begins, which is generally about Candlemas [2 February]. Now if they are not to begin till about Lady Day [25 March], half of them will be starved, for as their time of working will be so much shorter, trades people will not trust them, their being no prospect of being repaid. Not only so, but the keeles must suffer greatly by being so long unused.…

THE KEELMEN'S STRIKE, MAY 1738[1]

84. Petition of skippers employed by Henry Atkinson to the Magistrates, 3 May 1738. *Endorsed*: **Keelmen's Demands delivered to the Fitters, 4 May 1738** [TWA 394/9]

To the Right Worshipfull Mayor, or any of the Worshipfull Aldermen of Newcastle upon Tyne, this Representation and Petition most truely, humbly and earnestly shews and craves That whereas we hereto subscribeing some of us at present are, and some of us formerly were, skippers to Mr Henry Attchenson, fitter, and all us want fire coal which covenant and common practice obliges our said master and fitter, and all fitters in the coal trade belonging to this River, to give to their skippers, and some of us subscribers want of our said master and fitter our due fire coal for one year, some for 2, some for 3, some for 5, and some of us for six years, and we cannot procure the same of him, we being poor men and not able to sue for justice at Law; it is therefor most humbly and earnestly begged your Worship would cause justice be done to us in the case by causeing us [to] get either our said due fire coal immediatly, or the due value thereof in money, especially considering our most melancholly necessitous circumstances at present, we and our wives and families being at the point of starving for want of the necessary supplies of life by reason of the want of busyness, and trade in our busyness haveing been worse this winter than ever was known in the memory of any now alive, and continues so to be, to our utter undoing and ruine. Your granting that our just petition will be ane act of both justice and mercy done to us and our suffering and starving families, and in so doing expect the divine blessing and dayly prayers of Your Worships most indigent, suffering and starving and much injured Petitioners,

George Smith, Luke Hutchison [mark], John Small, Richard Robertson [mark], John Law, John Coulson, Walter Brass, John Blaier, Thomas Thompson [mark], he subscribeing in the name and stead of Patrick Bell ane orphan child, son of James Bell, deceased, who was a skipper in the said Work and wanted his fire coal, he the said Thomas haveing been the bound man of the said James Bell and having now the charge of his poor helpless orphan.

---

[1] On 2 May there was a meeting of the magistrates and keelmen employed by 30 fitters. Most of the keelmen appeared willing to work, though Thomas Carr, employed by John Simpson, declared that he would not work 'save upon terms' (TWA 394/9), endorsed 'Minutes at a meeting about and with some of

the keelmen on account of their stopping keels upon the River', 2 May 1738. The meeting failed to end the strike.

85. Petition of Francis Simpson's Keelmen, 4 May 1738 [TWA 394/9]

To Mr Francis Simpson of the Town and County of Newcastle, Being the humble petition of the skippers and rest of your men imployed in your severall keels belonging to your imploy:

First, We are imposed on by the pan keeles in taking ballast out of ships for under wages which is not their right so to do, that being a branch of our business.

2ndly, In going to Sheilds or any other part of the River and the ship not taking in the said coals but [we] must bring them home again, instead of having 13s.4d we are paid with 5 shillings.

3rdly, In going to Sheilds or any other part of the River we are obliged according to the Rights of the River to lye one tide, but what tides we lye more we ought to have 2s.6d each tide where we never receive any thing.

4thly, In going aboard of a ship lying at any key as Jarrow, Willington &c, and whatever keels cast on the said ship before she come from the key, our due is 1shilling each which we don't receive.

5thly, In going on board of ship or ships severall times where we ought to have beer or 1s. 4d allowed in lew of beer we don't receive any thing.

6thly, In making in coals at staith dykes severall times to further business, instead of being paid money for the said work we are obliged to take drink at 4d a quart when we would rather have ready money.

7thly, In going down to Sheilds or any other place on board of a ship and the said ship cannot take in the coals, in sending a man for orders his due is 1 shilling which we have not.

Now leaving this to your judicious sentiments in hopes of a favourable answer, we remain your most humble, most obliged and obedient servants to command. [*Not signed.*]

86. Petition of Thomas Waters' Keelmen, 5 May 1738 [TWA 394/9]

To Mr Peter Carter in the Town and County of Newcastle upon Tyne, being the humble petition of the skippers and other the men belonging to the imploy of Mr Thomas Waters.

Humbly sheweth that we your said servants, having suffered wrong this considerable time by- past by masters of ships and others, we therefore hope you'l take it into consideration while we declare our case in the manner following:

First that you would take it into consideration of our being very much wronged by the pann keels taking ballast out of ships for under wages which is not their right so to do, that being a branch of our business.

2nd, In going down with a keel of coals, or 4 chaldrons or any other quantity, to Sheilds or any other part of the River we are obliged to lye one tyde according to the rights of the River, but whatever tydes we lye more we ought to have 2s.6d each when we do not receive any thing.

3rd, In going on board of a ship lying at Jarrow, Willington Key, &c, as many keels [of ballast] as the said ship shall cast before she come of[f] from the Key shall pay 1shilling for every keel.

4th, In going on board of ship or ship[s] severall times where we ought to have beer or 1s.4d allowed in lew of the said beer we don't receive any thing.

5th, In making in coals at staith dykes severall times to further business, instead of having money for the said work we are oblidged to take drink at 4 pence a quart where we would rather have ready money.

6th, In taking down a keel of coals, or 4 chaldrons or any other quantity, to a ship at Sheilds, or any other part of the River, and the said ship not taking in the said coals but we are oblidged to bring them home again, instead of having 13s.4d for 8 chaldrons, and the rest according in order, we receive but 5 shillings and sometimes nothing at all.

7th In going down to Sheilds, or any other part of the River, and the said ship cannot take in the said coals, in sending a man home for orders his due is 1 shilling which we have not.
Sir,

Leaving this to your judicious sentiments, we rest in hopes of a favourable answer and remain, Sir, your most humble, most obliged and obedient servants to command &c.

87. Representation by Joseph Smith's Keelmen [n.d.] [TWA 394/57]

To Joseph Smith

Most onerable Master, after wiching a good frie tred that everey pour man may live, this is to lett yow know what the stop is for; it is becaus that the work is not right pearted, for ther is sum that gettes to mutch and ther is otheres fitt to sterve, so yow most endover, and other gentelmen fitters that his thes pour men servantes under them, to sie to gett them work that they may live, other wayes yow most suport them with muny till sutch tim they gett work, but we do hop yow will sie the work better perted, that every pour man may live; lickwayes the stop is for our rightes which is deu to us, and that is for every tid we lay loded doun the watter and is not taking in on bord of sutch shipes as yow or yowr servantes is plised to order us, yow most pay to us two shilinges and sixpence, or if yow or your servantes order us to any ship that is laying at the kie kasting her balest and if we do cast ther yow most pay to us on shillon for the shiftting her, lickwayes if at any tim yow or your servantes order us to go to any ship that is over loded and so can not tak the coles in [and] we send hom a man to aquant yow with it, yow most pay to that man on shilon and 13[s]:4[d] for our dues, lickwayes yow most pay us sixtinpence for our bier or order the [ship] masteres to pay it to us befor we begin to kast, and as for our faier coll[1] we most have them acording to the custom of the River; we hop that yow wil sie us righted at the steth, for the steth men his got a fachon now that when we make in any coles, the which we are forest to sum times by your servants, they wil give us nothing but drink for it, but we do insist upon reddey muny, lickways the sixpences we pay for the spowt it does loses us many tied and disapoints the shipes that your servantes is sencobel of,[2] so we do disair them to be don away; and for the pan men, they tak our brid from us by taking balest out of shipes at ounder wadges, and lickwayes by taking fitt tides,[3] so that we stop them till ther masteres give us a bound of ther handes that they wil do so no mor, especting yow will sie us righted in al this, and hopes that his onerabel wirshep the mair and alder men wil tak our pertes in all this, for if ther be any defeck in any of al thes dues beloning to us ther will be nothing but stoping so far as we do hier, so master, we hop in this we have not ofended yow.

[1] Fire coal.
[2] If the keel was loaded by spout instead of by hand the staithman received sixpence from the keelmen. For the abuse of this system see the third article of the keelmen's representation of 1750 (**Document 116**, below).
[3] About 'fitt tides' see the keelmen's first remonstrance, 1719 (**Document 57**, note 1, above).

88. Representation by William Selby's Skippers and men, 5 May 1738, *Endorsed*: **'Paper containing Keilmen's greevances delivered by severall Skippers and Keelmen to William Carre Esq. Mayor, at the Mayor's House, 6th May 1738'** [TWA 394/9]

To the right Worshipfull the Mair and Eldermen of Newcastle, that whereas we who arr skipers and men bound in the river of tine hav of a long time peacably and quitly lyn under many impositons by shipmasters in gererall and some others which we arr unwilling annie longer to undergo, and, seeing this disturbanc hath hapned, we disir to have some ashourance of better yousage for the time to come.

The partiqulars of our griveances ar thees: first if we should ly oneboard of anie ship some days together their is no satisfaction for that time lost; if we stage a keell of coals when the shipe is at the keey ther is nothing for that; as for beer to drink we have all ways werrie littill and often non, so our disir is that our masters may be layd wnder ane obligation to satsisfe us in thees things when complaint is made to them that we arr wronged, becaus self intrest hath so hardned the shipmasters' harts that we neither have nor cann get anie justice doon us by them; as for our fier coal yearly, which some have quit laid aside and others lyke to do the same, we disir that our masters may be oblidged to give them to us as formerly; as for the steath men's opresions they arr so great we cannot bear with them, as six pence for the spowt for three or four waggons and some tims les, and often losing our tide staying one them, this we disir to be intirly laid aside; and for makein the coals no satisfaction for it, who reaps the benefite we knou not, but we bear the opresion. We also disir that thees men that ar bound to serve the salt pans may be laid under ane obliggeation that they shall neither carrie coals on board of anie shipe nor take ballas out of them, thees demands beeng so just and reasonabl that we expect that we shall have ashurance given us that we shall be satisfied in them, which will be a means to appease tumults and caus every man yeld unto their masters deu obedence when ther wrongs arr redressed. And as for going one board of anie shipe when she is overloadn and a man be sent hom for orders he shall have one shiling for his pains, and if we bring them hom thirteen shilings and fourpence and eight shilings for four chalder; thees things we requir as being just.

89. Copy of a paper delivered to John Finlason, Skipper, in [Richard Smith's] Work to communicate to the Keelmen unlawfully assembled, 5 May 1738 [TWA 394/9]

The Magistrates of this Corporation do hereby signifye to the Keelmen assembled that if they will go peaceably to work the severall complaints delivered to their Fitters in writing shall be fully considered and justice done therein, but that whilst they continue together in the present tumultuous manner it is not agreeable to the laws of this Realm for the said Magistrates to do as the said keelmen seem to insist upon.

90. Petition of the Keelmen, 9 May 1738, *Endorsed*: **'Remonstrance delivered by Keelmen in Mayor's Chamber to the Mayor and Aldermen,**[1] **9 May 1738'.** [TWA 394/9]

Newcastle upon Tyne: To the Right Worshipfull William Carr, Mayor and Worshipfull Aldermen, the most Humble Petition of the Keelmen of the said Corporation:

Sheweth: That your petitioners is deprived of our ancient dues settled by your Worships' predicessors in anno 1710, and since that time by the Combination of the Coalowners and Hoastmen is deprived of working at all times that ships required coales. Not only our fire coales is by many of the Hoastmen keept of[f] us, but 12d for shifting tydes, one and foure pence for beer, two shilling and sixpence for lying tydes, sixpence at the spoots to the Steathman, the pann boats allowed, contrary to a former order signed by the Magestrates, to lay ballest ashore from ships and to lay coales aboard of any ship. Also thirteen shilling and foure pence for a keel load of coale brought from Sheilds to Newcastle; the said Hoastmen obliges us to load others at the steath to the no small ditrement of your petitioners. Another imposs[it]ion the Hoastmen puts upon us they'll upon a Saturday evening send us to Sheild[s] and obliges us to cast the coales which wee cannot get cast untill the Lord's Day is come one. This and the other matters wee submitt to your Worships' judicious judgments, praying that all minoplyes in trade combinations and privet contracts may be set aside, seeing they are so ditrementall to some thousands of his Majestyes loyall subjects and only for the interest of a sett of men that preffers a privet intrest before a publick good.

Wee your petitioners, knowing your worships has learned the sublime leassons of Christianity, hopes you'll not suffer us any longer to labour under a barbarity abhored by Jewes, Turks, and

Infidales: our wifes and children are all inocent persons in the case, and yet the cruilty of Coallowner and Hoastment is such they would sterve them. Your worships obliging the Hoastmen to give us a bond to pay our ancent dues is humbly desired. Wee are and all along have given them a bond and performed our part; without they be tyde to us they have no regarde to honour and honesty. The decission and finall determination is by all of us most humbly submitted to your worshipps and as in duty bound will for you ever pray &c

[*In another hand*]: This paper was drawn by John Blair as Mungo Glendinning saies.

[1] The Mayor, William Carre, five aldermen and 19 fitters attended the meeting.

91. Copy Affidavit concerning the above Remonstrance [TWA 394/9]

Newcastle upon Tyne: John Higgins, Skipper in Mr William Selby's Work, Richard Brewhouse, Skipper in Mr Henry Atkinson's Work, and John Berkley, Skipper in Mr William Johnson's Work, jointly and severally make oath as followeth:

And first the said John Higgins, for himself, observing that a paper writing drawn by John Blair[1] was expressed in terms too rigorous, he the said John Blair answered to this or the like effect: 'What need you be afraid of such expressions to the Magistrates of Newcastle upon Tyne when the like have been delivered to the King and Parliament'; and all these deponents say that the paper so drawn as aforesaid by the said John Blair was delivered this day to William Carre Esquire, Mayor, and severall of the Aldermen of the said Town of Newcastle upon Tyne assembled in that part of the Guildhall of the said Town usually called the Mayor's Chamber, and that the expressions and contents of the said paper would, as these deponents verily believe, have been altered by the joynt and unanimous consent of all the skippers and keelmen who were present at the time when it was drawn up as aforesaid, if the said John Blair had not hindered and prevented the same as aforesaid; and all these deponents further say that the said John Blair was directed at the time abovementioned to write nothing in the said paper writing but what was contained in a parchment writing now produced relating to the wages of the skippers and keelmen in the River Tyne.[2]

Taken and sworn at the Town of Newcastle upon Tyne this ninth day of May 1738, before William Carre, Mayor.

[1] Blair was one of the signatories of the petition of the skippers employed by Henry Atkinson (see above, **Document 85**) and some of its language is similar

to that of the above remonstrance. Shortly after the strike, William Scott, one of the fitters, commented that the keelmen had amongst them 'a villainous fellow ....who wrote for them; he did not spare the C[oa]l O[wne]rs, but the keelmen by some informations made before the Magistrates cleared themselves of what these gentlemen were charged with, but what this scribe will say for himself when he's called on I cannot tell, but as yet it would not be prudent of the Magistrates to give him any trouble' (Scott to George Bowes, 12 May 1738, Durham County Record Office, D/ST/C1/3/42 (2), reproduced by permission of Lord Strathmore and DCRO in Fewster, *The Keelmen of Tyneside*, p. 83).

2 This was the wages settlement of 1710, see above (**Document 22**). The magistrates believed that some of the keelmen were willing to return to work but were afraid of being ill-treated by the others. They thought that 'a little military force may not only conduce to His Majesty's peace but remove the present obstruction to Trade'. They added that the Commanding Officer must have power to act in Northumberland and Durham, otherwise 'the end of their march may be fruitless as happened about 20 years ago, upon the like occasion' (TNA, SP 44/130/343–4). William Scott was instrumental in breaking the strike before the military arrived by urging those willing to work to make the attempt (Fewster, *The Keelmen of Tyneside*, p. 85).

THE RIOT OF 1740 IN NEWCASTLE

92. Matthew Ridley's Account [NA, ZRI 27/8]

The winter of 1739 was very severe, a hard frost continuing for 3 months [and] a great drought followed, which occasioned a scarcity of all grain, so that wheat was sold in the markets at 10 to 11 or 12 shillings per boll (2 Winchester bushells), rye at 8 s. and oats 4s.6 to 5s. The poor labouring people about Newcastle, especially in the coal works, were in great distress, although a considerable advance had been made in their wages. Some turbulent spirits among those of the collieries upon the River Wear in the Bishoprick of Durham stired up a number of the rest upon the suggestion that great quantities of corn were lodged in granaries belonging to the corn merchants of Newcastle and was intended to be kept up with a view to sell at a great advanced price. They gathered a body of 3 or 4 hundred men women and children and came to Newcastle and demanded corn at a low rate on Thursday the 19th of June 1740, and threatned, if their demands were not complied with, they would take the corn out of the granaries by force. The Magistrates of Newcastle sent for the corn merchants, and representing the present distress of the people, recommended to them to come into some reasonable method of easing their present complaints, upon which the Town merchants confessed to deliver the corn in their granaries at the price it actually cost them, and they produced the invoices of the several parcels to confirm the truth of the same, but this was not sufficient. The people before mentioned then broke into several granaries and took away a considerable quantity of corn. Elated with this success, they marched in triumph about the streets of Newcastle, huzzaing and blowing horns, and were most of them well armed with cudgels. In this situation the Town was on the Thursday, the inhabitants were under great uneasiness and apprehended with reason that it would encourage these unruly people to go great lengths if some immediate stop was not put to their proceedings. On Friday the 20th the Magistrates resolved to summon the several inhabitants to Watch and Ward according to ancient custom in times of danger, and accordingly issued out the Mayor's precept to the several Wards to return proper persons to go upon guard for defence of the Town against seven o'Clock the next morning, and spoke to the gentlemen concerned in the coal trade to collect all the persons they could against the time before mentioned and to meet at that hour at the Forth. Mr R[idley] immediately sent to the workmen employed under him, and appointed them to meet him in the Shield Field at six the next morning, where appeared sixty men well mounted, and above three hundred on foot well provided with good oaken cudgels. Every man put a green bough into his hat and marched regularly by the outskirts of the Town to the Forth. When they came thither, the place was empty, so they proceeded to the Mayor's house where was a number of men of those that had been summoned, and the arms of the Train bands were put into their hands. The Magistrates appointed officers, and a certain number was detached to guard each gate, and the body of men brought in by Mr R[idley] was fixed as the main guard on the middle of the Sandhill. The rioters (for so they ought to be called) upon seeing a sufficient force to quell them, presently laid down their weapons and seemed as idle spectators, except a few that were unwilling to drop their powers were a little unruly and were seized and committed to prison. A watch was continued at the gates that night, and all was quiet. The inhabitants in their turns came chearfully to the defence of the Town and were ranged into companies, and the officers of the Train Bands were placed over them. Alderman Nicholas Fenwick attended Saturday night as Deputy Lieutenant, and all was quiet. Sunday night Alderman Ridley attended as Deputy Lieutenant, a proper guard was placed at each Avenue and he visited the posts every three hours, and there was no disturbance. Monday night Alderman Collingwood attended as Deputy Lieutenant , proper guards were set, and all remained quiet. Tuesday night Alderman Nicholas Fenwick was

again upon guard as Deputy Lieutenant. Several of the Merchants'
Company, when they met to fix upon some persons to serve Watch
and Ward agreeable to the Mayor's precept, voluntarily offered to
attend in person if the Governor would head them, which he readily
accepted, but first went to Mr Mayor to acquaint him with what had
been proposed, and desired his opinion of the matter. He said it was
very well and they might guard in the day on Wednesday and the
other inhabitants should come on in the evening. The Merchants and
some other young gentlemen who offered themselves as volunteers
met according to appointment 7 o'Clock at the Guildhall and were
compleatly armed and well dressed, and from thence marched round
the Town to shew the inhabitants there was a guard ready to protect
them. At 12 o'Clock they returned to the Sandhill, and Mr R[idley],
who commanded the company, sent the first Lieutenant, Mr William
Greenville to the Deputy Lieutenant, Alderman Nicholas Fenwick,
to desire his orders what post they should go to. He immediately
came himself, and said they might for the present depart, and attend
at two o'Clock to deliver some meal at a low price. They did so
and delivered it to the poor people from the Exchange. The Town
still remained quiet, and the inhabitants were gathered together
according to the Mayor's precept the day before and expected to be
placed as a guard, but Mr Mayor had thought proper to go into the
Country, upon some differences that had arisen between him and
the Corn Merchants, so there was no authority to set on the guard,
and the Town was left naked that night. About two on Thursday
morning a great number [of] colliers, wagoners, smiths and other
common workmen came along the bridge, released the prisoners and
proceeded in great order through the Town with bagpipes playing,
drum beating, and dirty clothes fixed upon sticks by way of colours
flying. They then increased to some thousands and were in possession of the principal streets of the Town.

The Magistrates met at the Guildhall and scarce knew what to
do; the inhabitants could not be raised again, for the rioters would
intercept the arms. An expedient was thought of which might be
successful: a ship laden with rye was lying near the key, and it
had been given out among the people, by way of keeping up their
warmth, that this ship with the corn was to fall down the River
and sail away; therefore, if that corn could be delivered, it would
appease the people, and during the time of their taking it, a guard
might be raised. Upon this, Mr R[idley] went among the rioters
and proposed to deliver this corn, if any of them to the number of
30 would undertake to be a guard that it should not be imbezzled,

but the whole paid for at the low price agreed upon, which was six shillings a boll for rye. Two of the leading men among them thought this a fair proposal, and undertook to get a sufficient guard, but in an hour's time returned and told Mr R[idley] *that the people were all mad and they could not get them to hear reason so they would leav them,*[1] which they accordingly did.

While this was transacting, about 20 or 30 of the principal inhabitants with some young gentlemen that was of the Company that did duty the day before (which afterwards by way of ridicule was stiled 'the White Stocking Regiment') offered themselves a voluntary guard to deliver this ship of rye, and with a good deal of difficulty about 20 muskets were conveyed by stealth into the Guildhall. As soon as the arms were charged which was all with powder only, except 3 or 4 which happened to have a charge of partridge shot, they desired Mr R[idley] to lead them down, which he did. As soon as they stepped on the Sandhill, the rioters surrounded them and knocked down the gentleman that were in the rear, upon which Mr R[idley] seized the rioters' drum that an alarm might not be made, and retreated as well as they could up the stairs to the Guildhall again, but in the scuffle several of the gentlemen discharged their pieces, and the ringleader of the rioters was killed upon the spot. This served them with a fair pretence to execute their favorite prospect, viz the seizing the Town's treasury in which was about £1500, but this could not instantly be done without attempting something against the Magistrates; so with great violence they assaulted the Guildhall where they were assembled, broke all the windows, and at last forced their way into the Hall, upon which Mr R[idley] went among them and drew them down to the Sandhill again, and led them to the ship before mentioned and assured them that he would not stir till all the corn was delivered. Some seemed to be satisfied with this, but in ten minutes they witdrew one after another and left him almost alone in the ship. They had indeed more tempting game in view for they broke into the Hutch and took out fifteen hundred pounds. They tore and destroyed most of the records, and broke down every thing that was ornamental, two very fine capital pictures of King Charles 2nd and James 2nd, the first by Sir Peter Lily, the other by his disciple Ryley. They tore all but the faces, and afterwards safely conducted the Magistrates to their own houses in a kind of mock triumph. Mr R[idley] seeing now the true design of the people, and that they were not to be brought to reason, complied with the earnest sollicitation of a few friends that were in the ship with him and stept into a boat which carried him safe to the glasshouses, where he mounted a horse and went to his house at Heaton. He had not been there five minutes till several messages came that he was killed, and that the rioters were coming immediately to attack the house and plunder and burn it, upon which to ease the minds of the family he removed with all but one servant to Mr White's house at Blagdon, and summoned a number of his own workmen to guard Heaton House. The rioters flushed with the success mentioned before now forshed a scheme to support themselves in their power, and were for putting in practice the old levelling principles, and had gone so far as to mark several houses to be pulled down, burnt or plundered, which would too certainly have been carried into execution, if two companies of Major General Howard's Regiment, who were upon their march to Stockton, had not upon the request of the Magistrates of Newcastle made a speedy march from Alnwick that day and came into the Town about 5 o'Clock. They were commanded by Captain Marmaduke Sowle, Lieutenant Charles Fielding and Ensign Hewett. When they were come near St Nicholas Church, word was brought that the rioters in number about a thousand were coming up the Side with great fury, most of them armed. Captain Sowle upon this ordered his men to halt, and immediately load their musquets and fix their bayonets, which was done in the face of the rioters, and had a great effect, for they were now convinced that the soldiers had power to fire upon them, which they before imagined could not be done since the affair of Captain Porteous at Edinburgh.[2] This circumstance, and the appearance of the soldiers drawn up in order, although there were not above 150 men in the whole, struck such a damp upon the spirits of the rioters that they fled with the utmost precipitation. Several were seized and committed to prison. The Town was in a very little time quiet; Captain Sowle placed his main guard at the Sandill, and with the assistance of the Train Bands, who were then immediately raised, proper guards were set at the several gates, till all apprehensions of the inhabitants should be over. Thus ended the riot at Newcastle on the 26th of June 1740, a day for ever memorable at that place, and which ought to be observed by every inhabitant with particular regard and due thankfulness for God's signal providence in preserving every thing that was dear and valuable to them from instant destruction.[3]

The Corporation of Newcastle made Captain Sowle a compliment of his Freedom in a gold box of 50 guineas value, [and] also presented Mr Fielding with a handsom piece of plate, and Mr Hewet with a gold watch.

[1] Emphasis in original document.

[2] Captain John Porteous, who had allegedly ordered his men to fire on a mob at Edinburgh, was tried for murder and condemned to death. Although reprieved, he was lynched by a mob; see K.J. Logue, 'Porteous, John (c. 1695–1736)', *Oxford Dictionary of National Biography*. The case had serious implications for magistrates faced with riotous mobs. Alderman Ridley strenuously denied the allegation that he had given the order to fire, *Newcastle Courant*, 28 June 1740.

[3] For a modern account of the riot, see Joyce Ellis, 'Urban Conflict and Popular Violence: The Guildhall Riots of 1740 in Newcastle upon Tyne', *International Review of Social History*, XXV (1980), pp. 332–49.

93. Cuthbert Fenwick, Mayor to the Duke of Newcastle, 20 June 1740 [TNA, SP 36/51/127–9]

May it please your Grace,

The pitmen yesterday assembled in very great numbers on pretence of the high price of corn broke open the granaries of several corn merchants, forcing into houses of divers other persons, stopping corn carriages and seizing and carrying off great quantities of corn. The crowd was manifestly too strong for myself and brethren, the Magistrates, to control and we could only have recourse to persuasion and arguments with the chief of them to disperse and return to work, but all in vain till the merchants proposed to sell on next market day (tomorrow) wheat at 4 shillings, rye at 3 shillings and oats at 1 shilling and 6 pence per Winchester bushell, considerably under the prime cost. The leaders promised to disperse and return the corn that was taken, but are neither gone to work or dispersed nor return the corn as promised. They want an increase in wages from the coal owners, from hence we are under great fear…of a want of coals for keeping our Keelmen employed and supplying the ships with coals, the consequence whereof is of greatest moment, for they on wanting work will be too apt to joyn those rioters, which will make a most formidable body not to be restrained by any civil authority as hath in these parts been experienced.

We therefore beg that a military force may be sent, and must warn that without authority to the Commanding Officer to act under the Justices of the Peace of Northumberland and County Durham as well as of Newcastle the end of their march may be frustrated as has happened heretofore on the like occasion.[1]

I am, your Grace's most obedient and most humble Servant,

Cuthbert Fenwick

[1] This refers to the strike of 1719, see above, footnote 1 to letter De la Faye to the Magistrates, 21 May 1719, p. 69.

94. Fenwick to Duke of Newcastle, 27 June 1740 [TNA, SP 36/51/198–9]

May it please your Grace,

The riotous behaviour of the pitmen has yet continued and what we then [20 June] apprehended is also come to pass. The Keelmen have thrown up their work upon the River, [and] come into the Town in terrible numbers, armed with all sorts of weapons, insulting all the inhabitants and threatening them with entire destruction. Myself and brethren, the Magistrates, have used our utmost endeavours by arguments, submissions and at length by raising the Posse of the Town, either to appease the rioters or to defend ourselves and the people of the place 'till we should be favoured by your Grace with an order for soldiers to protect us. Yesterday morning the rioters were so resolute and audacious as to attack the Guildhall of the Town where myself and other Magistrates were assembled for keeping the peace, which soon proved impossible.[1] Stones flew in among us from without through the windows like cannon shot from which our lives were in hazard every moment, and at length the mob broke in upon us in the most terrible outrage. They spared our lives indeed, but obliged us to quit the place, then fell to plundering and destroying all about them. The several benches of justice were immediately and entirely demolished. The Town Clerk's office was broke open and all the books, deeds and records of the Town and its courts thrown out of the windows amongst the mob without doors where they were trodden under foot, torn and most of them lost and the rest defaced and made useless. The Hutch was forced and plundered of about £1400; many accounts and receipts were destroyed. The Guildhall, a large and beautiful fabric was rendered almost a perfect ruin. After this the rioters divided into several bodies of great numbers, terrifying the whole Town all day, and in the evening besett a person's house threatening to burn or pull it down, when very fortunately 3 Companies of Major General Howard's Regiment came into Town upon their march from Berwick, by whose good care and conduct we have been delivered from the plunder and mischief there was so great a reason to apprehend, Captain Sowle offers all assistance in his power, either by keeping guard or otherwise, consistant with his orders, to obey the call of the Justices of the Peace of County Durham, but has not sufficient number of men (in case he had particular orders on our behalf) to quell the mob, which, though discouraged, are not yet dispersed. We therefore beg an order for soldiers to march to assist us with all convenient speed.[2]

I am your Grace's most obedient and most humble servant,

Cuthbert Fenwick, Mayor

[1] The Mayor fails to mention that the attack on the Guildhall was provoked by the shooting that killed one of the rioters and wounded others.

[2] In reply, the Lords Justices ordered by express three more companies of General Howard's Regiment to march forthwith to Newcastle, to be soon followed by two more companies. The Commanding Officer of the troops quartered in Newcastle was to be ordered to assist the civil magistrates there and in County Durham and Northumberland in suppressing riots and preserving the public peace (TWA 394/10, Secretary of the Lords Justices to Fenwick, 1 July 1740).

95. Alderman Matthew Ridley to the Earl of Carlisle, July 1740
[Historical Manuscripts Commission, *Carlisle*, p. 195]

The villainous riot that has lately happened at Newcastle has without doubt reached Yorkshire ere this – I mean the news of it – for I pray that you may never see or feel the like of it. They have destroyed all that they could possibly lay hold of, that belonging to the Corporation, and have robbed the Treasury of £12,000.[1] They had not begun with private property when a party of General Howard's Regiment marched into town, upon which the mob (which chiefly consisted of keelmen) surrendered or fled. The prisons are full of them, so we hope peace will continue, especially as all the men concerned in the collieries are gone to work.

[1] The actual sum stolen was £1,200, or according to other accounts, £1,300, £1,400, £1,500.

THE KEELMEN'S PART IN THE RIOT

96. Brief for the King against the Rioters [TWA 394/56]

…About break of day the Keelmen in general by instigation of one another made a stop in their work upon the River, and about 6 or 7 of them went to Mr Crowley's Works and required his workmen (commonly called Crowley's Crew) to come to Newcastle that day and join in their designs.[1] Early that morning a letter was taken up in the street directed to the Magistrates, threatening them in case the rioters were opposed, which letter was wrote in better terms than rioters were apprehended to be capable of. And about 9 aClock that morning, a great number of keelmen appeared upon the Sandhill and remained there some hours with clubs and staves, horns blowing, a drum beating and colours flying, and though the

Magistrates used many endeavours to appease the tumult, yet all was in vain, and at length the rioters actually attacked the Guildhall, threw stones of large size into the same through the windows with prodigious force so as one gentleman therein was actually knocked down, and the Magistrates and others there were in danger of their lives from stones flying in upon them every moment, and having ordered the doors to be shut as their only hope of their security against the rioters, yet were the same forcibly broke open by the said rioters and the Magistrates all insulted and obliged to quit the place, not without imminent danger of some grevious harm to their persons if not death itself. The Mayor particularly was aimed at sitting upon the Bench by a large stone thrown by a villain from the other end of the room with such force as broke the board on the back of the bench and missed the Mayor's head not an inch, even graizing on his wigg. And now they fell to breaking down the windows, benches, pictures and everything within the Guildhall and all places thereto adjacent, and more especially the Town Clerk's office, and destroyed all books, papers, writings and every-thing therein, throwing all out of the windows into the street, and after this they proceeded to a room or chamber under the Guildhall where a large chest stands that the publick money is actually kept in called the Town's Hutch and broke open the same room and also the chest and plundered the same of about 1300£ or upwards, and having got into their possession a great many firelocks by them taken into the Guildhall, they, after the aforesaid violences and plunders, continued in the said Town, threatning to pull down or burn diverse houses, going in great bodies through the streets armed with gunn barrells besides clubs and other terrible weapons, and exacting money from the inhabitants everywhere with oaths threats and menaces in case of refusall, as they had before done, till about nine aClock that night, when some soldiers coming into the said Town, the same was most happily delivered from the outrages and barbarities that were too reasonably apprehended would have been committed the night ensuing.

---

[1] Crowley's crew were iron workers at Swalwell. The keelmen urged them to assist in seizing corn still in Newcastle before it was 'shipped off in the night', leaving them starved for want of bread. David Levine and Keith Wrightson, *The Making of an Industrial Society – Whickham 1560-1765* (Oxford, 1991), p. 386.

CENSUS OF KEELMEN AFTER THE RIOT OF 1740

97. Letter from the Magistrates to the Fitters, 16 July 1740 [TWA 394/10]

Sir,

You are desired to return to us as soon as may be an exact list of all Skippers with their respective men that executed the last usual bond taken by you with an account of the time they have respectively been in Town and the place they respectively came from and were born or settled in before they came to this Town, and if they have quitted your service to mark upon such list the day of leaving the same or as nigh the time as you can be informed.[1]

Wee are Your humble Servants

[1] The fitters who responded to this request did so with a variety of details and in various formats. The following tables include all the information each provided. Only a proportion of the keelmen are included in the total of 594 men named here, and only some of the fitters are represented by the thirteen returns. In 1738, 30 fitters attended a meeting with the magistrates and keelmen (TWA 394/9). In 1750, 823 keelmen were bound to 21 fitters, counting partnerships as one, see below, **Document 122**. Many of the keelmen were natives of Scotland. See Harry D. Watson, 'Newcastle Keelmen in the 18th Century: the Scottish Connection', *Journal of Northumberland and Durham Family History Society*, vol. 13, no. 3 (1988), with an appendix identifying and locating many of the place names. The article does not include all the thirteen returns.

98. List of the Keelmen that were at Xmas [1739], and now are in Henry Atkinson's Work [TWA 394/57]

Skipper's Names with their respective men	Time of their being in Town	Where they came from	Where born or settled	The time of going, of those who have left the work
James Bone, Skipper	Born in Town			
James Young, Bound	Born in Town			
Robt. Arklay, Bound	Born in Town			
Thomas Willson	Many years			June 28

James Robinson	2 months	Denny	Denny	
John Blair, Skipper	28 years	Middle Lothian	Middle Lothian	
John Chaplain, Bound	12 years	St. Andrews	St Andrews	
Peter Atkinson, Bound	14 years	Leighton	Caldstream	
John Portus	22 years	Newton in Scotland	Musslebrough	
Robt. Adams, Skipper	26 years	Long Houghton	Newcastle	
John Laing, Bound	16 years	Elgan a Murray	Elgan a Murray	
John Yull, Bound	14 years	Falkirk	Campsey	
Alexander Moor	7 years	Falkirk	Falkirk	
James Hempseed, Skipper	Born in Newcastle			May 31st
John Finlason, now Skipper	22 years	Musslebrough	Musslebrough	
David Turner, Bound	Born in Newcastle			May 31st
Geo. Gordon, Bound	4 years	Kinghorn	Kinghorn	
William Manners	4 years	Trenent	Trenent	
Alexander Brison	9 years	Trenent	Fenton	
John Coulson, Skipper	Born in Newcastle		Fenton	
James Sharp, Bound	Gateshead	Gateshead	Gateshead	
James McCallister, Bound	12 years	Alloway	Alloway	
2 boys [no details]				

Walter Brass, Skipper	27 years	Long Leviston	Long Leviston	
Thomas Bruce, Bound	16 years	Linlithgo	Linlithgo	
John Dougall, Bound	24 years	Bothkennar	Bothkennar	
William Johnson	7 years	Bothkennar	Bothkennar	
James Temple, Skipper	22 years	Painston	Painston	
Thomas Hogg, Bound	10 years	Whittingham	Whittingham	
Thomas Coulson, Bound				July 6th about one o Clock in the morning
Geo. Brotherston	18 years	Long Netherie	Long Netherie	
Stephen Gothard, Skipper	28 years	Fourforth, Yorkshire	Fourforth, Yorkshire	
Andrew Paterson, Bound				June 1st
John Kahown, Bound				Sometime in March
Geo. Viccars	14 years	Sterling	Menstrea	
John Kennedy	18 years	Melross	Newcastle	
James Straughan	15 years	Aberdeen		

99. Mr Charles Atkinson's Keelmen [TWA 394/12]

Bond dated Xmas 1739			
Skippers & Mens Names	How long they have been in Newcastle	Where born or came from before they came to Newcastle	When they quitted this service
David Simpson, Skipper	Sixteen years	Redderney, Shire of Fife	

Thomas Turnbull	Sixteen years	Dundee, Shire of Angis	
John Robertson	Fourteen years	Dalckeith, Shire of Bamph	
David Dogg, Skipper	Forty years	Arbroth, in Scotland	
Thomas Marshall			Gone in another keel of Mr Atkinsons
Henry Rutherford	Eighteen months	Couris, in the Shire of Perth	
George Beveridge, Skipper	Thirty two years	Born in Dumfarmlin in Scotland	
James Drysdell			Gone to Mr Ridleys two months agoe
John Fotheringall	Seven years	Born at Saton, last from Edinburgh	
Archbald Good Ale, Skipper	Seventeen years	Liberton…near Edinburgh	
Samuel Hay	ten years	Crail in the Shire of Fife	
William Burnett			Prest at Shields in the month of March
John Reneson Skipper	Sixty years	Newcastle, All Saints Parish	
Thomas Bruce	Twenty years	Dunfarmlin, Shire of Fife	
Thomas Morrison	Thirty years	Gateshead	
Edward Steel, Skipper	Twenty one years	Newton, near Edenburgh	
Andrew Ruddie	Twenty two years	Kirkaldy, Shire of Fife	
Thomas Thompson	Twenty years	Spicer? Lane, All Saints Parish	
James Youelle	Eighteen years	Sandgate, All Saints Parish	
George Dixon, Skipper	Forty two years	Born in Sandgate	

Robert Portis	Nineteen years	St Andrews, in Fife Parish	
William Anderson			In William Scotts Worke
Andrew Penny			In John Bakers Worke
Mathew Carr, Skipper	Twelve years	Stella, Riton Parish	
William Sheel	Ten years	Dunce, Shire of Mars	
James Dixon			Gone in another keel of Mr Atkinsons
David Waddell, Skipper	Nineteen years	Gladsmoore, East Lowden	
Robert Primrose	Eleven years	Couris, in the Shire of Perth	
John Forthingham			Gone to Mr Ridleys work a month agoe
Robert Clark, Skipper	Nineteen years	Preston Panns, Scotland	
William Anderson			Gone to William Scotts worke
John Cohound	Three years	Kirkaldy, Shire of Fife	
Cuthbert Norman			Gone to sea, six weeks agoe
Richard Williamson, Skipper	Fourteen years	Bladon, the Parish of Riton	
Robert Portis	Thirty years	St Andrews, Shire of Fife	
William Gardner			Goes in another keel of Mr Atkinsons
Andrew English, Skipper	Eighteen years	Kirkaldey, Shire of Fife	
George Bell	Twenty five years	Craile, Shire of Fife	

Andrew Coventry	Eighteen years	Kirkaldy, Shire of Fife	
John Howey	Twenty years	Seaton, East Lowden	
John Stracron, Skipper	Thirty six years	Sandgate, Parish of All Saints	
Thomas Holmes	Seven years	Wakefield in Yorkshire	
John Cowey	Four years	Falkirk, Shire of Sterling	
William Alexander, Skipper	Forty years	Pandon, All Saints Parish	
James Haston?	Sixteen years	Easterheals, from Edenburo last	
John Wilson	Seven years	Weelsburn, Parish Dumfarmin	
William Miller, Skipper	Thirty two years	Sandgate, All Saints Parish	
John Jemeson	Nineteen years	Burnt Island, Parish of Fife	
Robert Gray	Three years	Glascow	
Rowland Rogers, Skipper	Twenty seven years	Sandgate, Parish of All Saints	
John Hanby	Nineteen years	Sandgate, Parish of All Saints	
Henry Bewhanin			Bound to sea three weeks since
Francis Maners			Bound to sea three weeks since
John Clark, Skipper	Twenty seven years	Sandgate, Parish of All Saints	
John Gilphillan	Ten years	Elphiston, Shire of Sterling	
Thomas Trumbell	Twenty years	Sandgate, Parish of All Saints	
Robert Duff, Skipper	Twenty three years	Sandgate, Parish of All Saints	
William Robeson			Prest[1] at Shields in the month of March

Thomas Liddell	Fifty years	Wathnowls, Parish of All Saints	
Andrew Nockles, Skipper	Eighteen years	Torrie Panns, Shire of Fife	
John Nockles	Thirteen years	Torrie Panns, Shire of Fife	
William Stewart			Gone to Mr Johnsons Work
William Lock, Skipper	Seventeen years	Kirkgunnock, Shire of Sterling	
Andrew Ker	Seventeen years	Dunneepace, Shire of Sterling	
John Liddell	Three years	Both Kenner, Shire of Sterling	
John Cram, Skipper	Nineteen years	Dumblain, Shire of Perth	
James Gardner	Sixteen years	Torry, Shire of Fife	
Alexander Wilson	Twelve years	Cowris, Shire of Perth	
William Brown, Skipper	Eight years	Barlow, Parish of Riton	
Bartholomew Morrison	Twelve Years	Fawkirk, Shire of Sterling	
John King			Gone to Mr Ridleys Work
William Douglass, Skipper	Fifty years	Mindrim, near Wooler	
James Bewhanin	Forty three years	Kingcarn, in Shire of Perth	
Robert Yoner	Eighteen years	Parish Fawkirk, Sterling	

[1] 'Prest', *i.e.* impressed into the navy.

100. Skippers and Men bound to William Johnson, Fitter, 1740
[TWA 394/11]

Skippers and men's names	While in Town	Place of Nativity	When absent
George Sowden	36 years	Shire of Aire	
John Kenny	21 years	Shire of Sterling	
John Gallbreath	4 years	Shire of Berwick	
John Mannoughton, junior	24 years	Sandgate	
John Mannoughton, senior	50 years	Dunkell	
John Mills	16 years	Shire of Mayrin	
James Greenfield	24 years	Dallkeith	
David Wood	28 years	Thurlestone	
William Roye	24 years	Sandgate	
Richard Robson	41 years	Pandon	
James Archbald	4 years	Mayling	
William Dure	4 [years]	Kingcairne	about 4 months
Thomas Purviss	39 years	Unse Burne	
George Hunter	36 years	Pan Kallkin	
James Bell	21 years	Dundass	
John Nicholls	46 years	Gateshead	
James Thompson	6 years	St Andrews	
Stephen Nicholls	19 years	Gateshead	
John Crookshanke	36 years	Sandgate	
Thomas Crookshanke	18 months	Currey	
Andrew Crookshanke	2 years	Currey	
John Barckley	19 years	Johns Haven	
William Lisshman	13 years	Writes Housess	
Thomas Chillton	25 years	Railwood nigh Gateshead	
John Watson	26 years	Sandgate	
Allexander Gibb	28 years	Sandgate	
Robert Coventree	17 years	Kirk Cadey	
Alexander Lumsdell	26 years	Sandgate	

Joseph Willson	2 years	Unseburne	
Michale Johnson	17 years	Sandgate	
Henry Brown	14 years	Nether Witton	
Archibald Willson	17 years	Sterlingshire	
John Drysdell	18 years	Coal Ross	
Henry Nicholls	43 years	Gateshead	
Charles Miller	40 years	Sandgate	
James Forrest	18 years	Samuel Stone	
David Watson	24 years	Sandgate	
Francis Watson	20 years	Sandgate	
Andrew Richardson	16 years	Norham	
Alexander Banke	16 years	Cassellogle	
Thomas Moorhead	18 years	Fawkirke	
Donkin Mackfarland	4 years	Kingcairne	Absent about 4 months

101. Skippers and Men Bound to John Robinson, January 1739/40 [TWA 394/11]

Skippers' and Men's Names	Time in Newcastle	Where Born	When absent
John Look	24 years	Gorgunnok	
William Taylor		Newcastle	
Thomas Wattson	16 years	Hexam	
Mungo Glendning	25 years	Gillmoortown	
Thomas Phillip			Left the work in April
John Turner			Left the work in April
Robert Smith		Newcastle	
James Reay	18 years	Torry	
James Gibson	14 years	Sproustown	
David Baxter	30 years	Courass	
George Young			Left the work in May
Peter Mackenkie			Left the work in June
Andrew Meine	19 years	Colin Town	
William Robinson			Left the work in April
William Sofley			Left the work in April

John Robinson		Newcastle	
William Dixon	30 years	Dalkeith	
James Stirk			Left the work in June
James Caverhill	29 years	Jedbrugh	
James Bowerhill	17 years	Earlstown	
Thomas Young			Left the work in June
Thomas Hamilton		Newcastle	
Richard Brown			Left the work in March
John Elder			Left in April
Joseph Allen		Newcastle	
Thomas Allen		Newcastle	
George Scott			Left the work in June
John Blakey		Newcastle	
William Eddie	15 years	Elfistown	
George Reed	18 years	Elfistown	

102. A List of the Skippers and their Bound Men that executed the Bond for 1740 in the Service of John Vonholte [TWA 394/11]

Men's Names	When came to Town	Where from, Born or Settled	When left my Service
Thomas Heweth, Skipper	1688	Sandgate	
George Heweth, Boundman	1718	Sandgate	
John Simson, Boundman	1734	Erbroth	Left June 10th
John Matfin, Skipper	1715	Newcastle	
Thomas Matfin, Boundman	1717	Newcastle	
Joseph Dunn, Skipper	1708	Sandgate	
William Wadle, Skipper	1717	Middle Lowden	
Archbald Gillchriste, Boundman	1728	Mack Mirra, East Lowden	
Alexander Lockert, Boundman	1732	Wascarse, Fawkirk	
James Henderson, Skipper	1704	Sandgate	

George Simson, Boundman	1720	Cooris in Pearth
John Chrystie, Boundman	1729	Kinghorne
Archbald Burrell, Skipper	1690	Sandgate
George Rebeccah	1680	Cranstone, Aberdeen
James Feargrief	1730	Tranant in East Lowdon
William Christie, Skipper	1723	Crowden Parish, Aberdeen
Andrew Morrow	1733	Ellon Parish, Aberdeen
William Weare	1736	Low Howeth, All Saints Parish
John Keedy, Skipper	1721	Kingsbarnes, Enstroth in Fifie
Andrew Mochren	1738	Moor Evenside, Sterling
George HayayHay	1735	St Andrews, Fifie
William Thomson	1696	Newcastle
Archbald Ronlson	1737	Chrighton
Andrew Criech	1735	Toory in Fife

103. Skippers and Keelmen in Francis Amorer's Employment, 1740 [TWA 394/12]

Names	Time in Newcastle	Where Born
James Miller, Skipper, aged 48	44 years	In Decath
Andrew Brass, Bondman, aged 42	19 years	In the Orkenys
Thomas Filp	No details	
William Melvin, Skipper, aged 48	30 years	In Fife
John Smith, Bondman, aged 34		In Newcastle
Andrew Ramsey, Bondman, aged 40	20 years	In Fife
John Thompson, Skipper, aged 62	45 years	In Conhard?
Henry Wilson, Bondman, aged 40	15 years	In Falkirk
John Cooper, Bondman, aged 17		In Newcastle

John Aukey, Skipper, Aged 51	26 years	In Falkirk
James Aukey, Bondman, aged 23		In Newcastle
John Aukey, junior, Bondman, aged 19		In Newcastle
Luke Martin, Skipper, aged 30		In Newcastle
Joseph Wilson, Bondman, aged 25		In Newcastle
James Donkin, Bondman, aged 28		In Newcastle
Andrew Batty, Skipper, aged 52	21 years	In Fife
David Dingwell, Bondman, aged 25	7 years	In Fife
Jacob Volance, Bondman, aged 28	6 years	In Ternent
Cuthbert Fissher, Skipper, aged 39		In Newcastle
Cuthbert Johnson, Bondman		In Newcastle
Michael Huntley, Skipper		In Newcastle
George Smith, Bondman	[No details]	

104. A List of the Keelmen bound in Mrs Jane Watson's Work, 1740 [TWA 394/11]

Names	Time lived in or about Newcastle	Place of Birth	When left
Archibald Cuningham	19 years	Harrington in the Shire of East Lowden	
Thomas Peacock	18 years	Kingkarne in the Shire of Pearth	
Robert Hardey			Took on to be a Mearine May 2[d] 1740
William Robinson	4 years	Kittle Naked in the Parish of West Kirk and Shire of Midell Lowden	
John Gibson	43 years in Gateshead	Gateshead, County Durham	
Robert Bainbridge	27 years in Gateshead	Gateshead	
Joseph Stot	24 years in Gateshead	Gateshead	

Samuel Ellot	22 years in Pipewell Gate	Gateshead	
Thomas Moss	29 years in Gateshead	Gateshead	
Robert Dick	7 years in Pipewell Gate	Swalwell, County Durham	
James Addison	26 years	Parish of All Saints, Newcastle	
John Morrison	8 years	Kinggorn, Fifeshire	
James Smart	9 years	Garbit Hill in the Shire of Dumbarton	
John Lawson	8 years in Gateshead	Ryton, County Durham	
John Purvis	10 years	Harrinton in the Shire of East Lowden	
Nicholas Sheavell	12 years in Gateshead	Ryton	
Jarrard Cristey	26 years in Gateshead	Westward Parish in Cumberland	
John Johnson	9 years	Coours in the Shire of Pearth	
Andrew Kenity			Left the work June 20
James Gelton	6 years	Trophen in the Shire of Linlisko	
Francis Blakey	19 years	Longnewton in Twedale	
George Cristey	24 years	Parish of All Saints	
James Strian	18 years	Parish of All Saints	
Robert Colvell	24 years	Parish of Torey in the Shire of Fife	
David Potter	5 years	Cooper in the Shire of Fife	
Andrew Shearer	10 years	Couruss in the Shire of Pearth	
James Blakey	19 years	Clarkinton in the Shire of East Lowden	

John Hudson	12 years	Peath Head in the Shire of Fife	
Thomas Clark			Impressed into His Majesty's service, March 25th 1740
George Davison	20 years	Kingkarne in the Shire of Pearth	
Daniel Thomson	18 years	Ile of Arron in the Shire of Bought	
James Gib			Absent since the 26th of June
Alexander Mason	22 years	Gillbra, Parish of Federass, Aberdeen	

105. Messrs. Simpson's Keelmen [TWA 394/11]

Men's Names that were Bound	Where Born	When they left the Work
James Flint, senior, aged 52	In Sandgate	
James Flint, junior, aged 22	In Sandgate	
Henry Flint, aged 25	In Sandgate	
Andrew Turner, aged 36	In Wark, Northumberland	
Archibald Hunter, aged 24	In Preston Pans in East Lowden	
William Black, aged 40	In Moram nigh Edinburgh	
John Oliver, junior, aged 28	In Sandgate	
John Simmeril, aged 23	In Sandgate	
Alexander Hume, aged 25		Went to Mr John Robinson junior's work, May 23rd or thereabouts
William Simpson, aged 52	In Edinburgh	

Alexander Callender, aged 35	In Sterlin	Gone the 5th of March
William Gillchrist, aged 37	In Noram upon Tweed	Gone May last
Thomas Graham, aged 37	In Sandgate	
John Smith		Prest in April last
George Clark		Prest in April last
Patrick Thomson, aged 22	In Sandgate	
Archibald Thomson, aged 29	In Sandgate	
James Mills, Aged 39	In Stonehive in Kennif parish	
William Hamen, aged 28	In Shore side below Sandgate	
James Thomson, aged 22	In Salton nigh Edinburgh	
John Knocks, aged 30	In Edinburgh	
Andrew Morrow, aged 34	In West Farna Mill	
James M'harbour, aged 32	In Luttery in Fife	
David Wishart, aged 38	In Linkes of Arnet	
George Rotherford, aged 26	In Sandgate	
Thomas Grey, aged 28	In Stoneaway	
Arthur Grey, aged 20		Went to Mr Ridley's Work July 4th or thereabouts
Francis Hopkirk, aged 26	In Sandgate	
John Anderson, aged 26	In Brogsburn in the Parish of Carin	
Alexander Lapsley, Aged 35	In Leathkoe nigh Edinburgh	

Ralph Dixon, aged 27	In North Shields		Not bound
Alexander Willson, aged 30	In Fife		Not bound
Robert Damsten, aged 39	In the Shire of Mairnes nigh Montross		Not bound
William Morris, aged 62	In Fife		
James Broomfield, aged 33	In Hume in the Shire of Berwick		With F. Hopkirk
Archibald Reynoldson			Went from his skipper in April last
John Williamson, aged 50	In Plain in the Shire of Sterlin	16 years	
Robert Williamson, aged 18,	In Plain in the Shire of Sterlin	14 years	
James Sheilds, aged 50	In Kelsoe upon Tweed	17 years	Gone last February
John Ross, aged 46	Bervey nigh Montross	30 years	
James Cockram, aged 32	In Lufroe nigh Edinburgh	12 years	
Arthur Byrn			Not bound
Thomas Adams, aged 46	In Abercorn	28 years	
Thomas Knockles, aged 28	In Allaway	7 years	
John Blair, aged 22	In Allaway	3 years	
Matthew Reed, aged 35	In Pandan		
Robert Mitchel, aged 46	In Morton nigh Edinburgh	23 years	
Thomas Thomson, Aged 40	In Buckhaven	16 years	Bound with William Tailor? deceased
Henry Miller			Was not with his skipper this year; received a wound in the late tumult

John Oliver, senior, aged 53	In Cornwell	50 years	
James Oliver, aged 27	In Sandgate		
John Pigg, aged 36			Went to Mr Holts work, June 20
Thomas Archibald, aged 37	In Clackmannin in the Shire of Sterlin	19 years	
David Henderson, aged 32	In Torwood in the Shire of Sterlin	10 years	
William Fairly, aged 22	In North Crile? in Fife	8 years	Gone the 18th of June
Thomas Rotherford, aged 29	In Sandgate		
John Lundy, aged 20	In Sandgate		
Matthew Goodwilly	In Bruntisland in Fife	18 years	
Thomas Anderson, aged 40	In Lemmington in Newburn Parish	10 years in Swalwell	Gone May
Alexander Miller, aged 24	In Murrevenside	4 years	
Nicholas Carn, aged 56	Scotswood in St John's Parish	30 years in Swalwell	
A. Anderson, aged 80	In Largye in Aberdeen	45 years	
Samuel Gibson	In Gateshead		
Thomas Carr	In Newcastle		With Mr Williamson
Michael Smith, aged 52	In Gosfort	50 years	
John White, aged 50	In Kircaldy	20 years	
William Willson, aged 46			Went to Mr Hudspeths work the latter end of May last
William Liddell, aged 40	In Plain Mellar in the West	22 years in Dents hole, nigh Newcastle	

John Curry, aged 50	In Dentshole nigh Newcastle		
Francis Marshal, aged 44	In Arvou in the Shire of Sterlin	20 years	
Robert Fulthorp, aged 40	In Jarrow	22 years in Swalwell	
William Stephenson, aged 27	In Swalwell in Whickham Parish		
Thomas Fulthorp, aged 44	Jarrow	22 years in Swalwell	
John Gibson, aged 19	In Gateshead		
Thomas Robinson			Went to Mr John Smith's Work, June 24th or nigh that time
John Curry			Took on to be a Marine
John Dixon			Deceased
John Tonathy, aged 19	In Sandgate		With John Gibson
Alexander Morro			Went off lately
Men that were Protected[1] and not Bound			
John Donkin, aged 34	Born at Duddingstone, nigh Edinburgh	18 years	
James Bruce, aged 35			Went to Mr Airey's Work, May 17th, or thereabouts
George Young, aged 47	In Seton, nigh Edinburgh	16 years	With Mr Reed
John Small, aged 37	In Millfield, nigh Dundee	16 years	
William Bairns, aged 45	In St Giles in the Fields, London	25 years comes the 4 of November	

Alexander Russell, aged 37	Went to Mr Ridley's Work May 10 or thereabouts
Alexander Myers, aged 50	Not well since June 24; was with W. Morris
David Cairns, aged 40	Wounded in the late Tumult but left June 11

[1] Protected from impressment.

106. A List of Mr Thomas Airey's Skippers and Keellmen who executed the Bond, and also of the fourth Man,[1] with an Account of the Time they have been Here, and where they came from [TWA 394/57]

Names	Time in Newcastle	Came from	When they left the work
John Leviston, Skipper	16 years	Preston Pans	
James Brewis, 1st Man	16 years	Near Edinburgh	
William Ward, 2nd Man		Born here	
John Read, 4th Man	6 months	Near Berwick	
William Curry, Skipper		Born here	
Thomas Ushey, 1st Man		Born here	
William Leaton, 2nd Man		Born here	
William Norwood, 4th Man	15 years	Near Belfast in Ireland	
Henry Dog, Skipper	13 years	Near Edinburgh	
William Allaburton, 1st Man			Prest
John Hutcheson, 2nd Man			Left his skipper in May
George Allen, 4th Man	21 years	Falkirk	
James Adamson, Skipper	14 years	Near Edinburgh	

John Adamson, 1st Man	40 years	Near Edinburgh	
John Adamson, 2nd Man		Born here	
Hugh Adamson, 4th Man		Born here	
Thomas Scott, Skipper		Born here	
John Rogers, 1st Man	24 years	Near Edinburgh	
Thomas Scott, junior, 2nd Man		Born here	
William Cooper, 4th Man		Born here	
Edward Curry, Skipper		Born here	
William Watson, 1st Man	11years	East Lothian	
Andrew Higgie, 2nd Man			Left his skipper 28th July
Robert Liddell, 4th Man	----	Falkirk	
William Bailey, Skipper	21 years	East Lothian	
William Simpson, 1st Man	13 years	Near Dundee	
John Bailey, 2nd Man	17 years	East Lothian	
John Hay, 4th Man		Born here	
Hugh Drisdle, Skipper	20 years	Near Leith	
William Hay, 1st Man			Prest
George Hay, 2nd Man			Prest
John Ward, 4th Man	20 years	Prestin Pans	
Thomas Guttery, Skipper		Born here	
James Smith, 1st Man	15 years	Prestin Pans	
Archbald Willson, 2nd man	14 years	Falkirk	
John Farguson, 4th Man		Born here	
John Masterton, Skipper		Born here	
James Gray, 1st Man	14 years	Haddington	
William Robson, 2nd Man		Born here	
John Penman, 4th Man		Born here	
John Nichols, Skipper	30 years	Prestin Pans	

Thomas Portis, 1st Man		Born here	
James Cooke, 2nd Man			Left his skipper 25th July
James Nichols, 4th Man		Born here	
Robert Hambleton, Skipper		Born here	
John Richey, 1st Man		Born here	
James Meak, 2nd Man		Born here	
John Simpson, 4th Man		Born here	
Robert Masterton, Skipper	38 years	Recores	
George Fair, 1st Man	15 years	Near York	
Stephen Burnett, 2nd Man		Born here	
James Farguson, 4th Man		Born here	
Thomas Dixon, Skipper		Born here	
Thomas Coldwalls, 1st Man	16 years	Near Edinburgh	
James Brady, 2nd Man	[No details]		
Luke Wandless, 4th Man		Born here	
Adam Dog, Skipper	14 years	Near Edinburgh	
Andrew Sunter, 1st Man			Prest
Andrew Donelson, 2nd Man			Prest
George Ridley, 4th Man		Born here	
William Shepard, Skipper	14 years	Montrose	
Alexander Watson, 1st Man			Prest
James Hambleton, 2nd Man			Kild in the Tumult
Robert Bryson, 4th Man	9 years	Perth	
James Walker, Skipper	20 years	Haddington	
Alexander Mills, 1st Man	4 years	Montrose	
Andrew Dickey, 2nd Man	18 years	Kelsey	

William Graham, 4th Man	3 years	Falkirk	
Robert White, Skipper	30 years	Edinburgh	
James Thompson, 1st Man	16 years	Near Alnwick	
John Nish, 2nd Man	14 years	[no details]	
James Wreight	20 years	Edinburgh	
Alexander Horn, Skipper			Prest
William Young, 1st Man	3 years	Falkirk	
James Graham, 2nd Man		Born here	
Andrew Millar, 4th Man			Left his skipper and has not got one of his Room

[1] The crew of a keel generally consisted of a skipper, two men and a boy or another man. In this case the fourth member of the crew was a man who was not bound

107. A List of John Baker's Skippers and Boundmen [TWA 394/11]

Names	Where Born	When Absent
George Miller, Skipper	Parish of Crith, Fifeshire	
John King, Boundman		Absent before the ryott
Robert Fethe, Boundman		Absent before the ryott
William Roy, Skipper	Sandgate, Parish of All Saints	
John Roy, Boundman	Sandgate	
George Thompson, Boundman	Aberlady	
Benjamin Trumble, Skipper	Sandgate	
Alexander Tillace, Boundman	Killronker	
William Ray, Boundman	Aberbrothneck	
Robert Lundy, Skipper	Sandgate	
Alexander Porteus, Boundman		Absent before the riott
John Lamb, Boundman		Absent before the riott
Robert Shade, Skipper	Sandgate	

Robert Hume, Boundman	Sandgate	
Henry Bolton, Boundman	Morpeth	
James Lundy, Skipper	Sandgate	
Andrew Cristall, Boundman	Seaton	
Thomas Alexander, Boundman	Sandgate	
Ralph Browell, Skipper	Newcastle	
Matthew Forster, Boundman	Sandgate	
James Porteus, Boundman	Sandgate	
David Dure, Skipper	Newcastle	
Andrew Walker, Boundman		Absent before the riott
William Begger, Boundman		Absent before riott

108. A List of Joseph Ord's Keelmen [TWA 394/12]

Names	Where Born	When Absent
Patrick Smith	Parish of Torry in Fieff, Scotland	
Matthew Lowrey	Parish of Torry	Absent before riot
David Sinclair	Parish of All Saints, Newcastle	
Martin Bainbridge	of Whickham, County Durham	
James Barley	of Whickham	
Ralph Cole	of Whickham	
Matthew Reay	All Saints, Newcastle	
William Petree	All Saints, Newcastle	
Thomas Naisbeth	All Saints, Newcastle	Absent before riot
Thomas Bainbridge	of Whickham	
William Lawson	of Whickham	
Edward Coats	of Whickham	
John Wilthew	of Ryton	
Thomas Maddison	of Whickham	
Robert Cole	Gateshead	
William Brass	Leveston, Scotland	

Andrew Brass	All Saints, Newcastle	
Joseph Rutherford	All Saints, Newcastle	Absent before riot
William Archer	Whickham	
Thomas Sankster	Gateshead	
William Johnson	Gateshead	
John Richey	Fawkirk, Scotland	
Andrew Richey	Fawkirk, Scotland	
James Richey	Burlestones, Scotland	
William Loggen	of Trenent, Scotland	
William Thompson	All Saints, Newcastle	
Alexander Buckannan	of Weems, Scotland	

109. A List of the Skippers and their Bond and Free Men in the Imployment of Mr Samuel Sheilds for this present year 1740
[TWA 394/12]

Skippers	Bondmen	Free Men	When Left Work
Robert Watson	William Willson, George Carns	Thomas Hutton	
John Tennant	Robert Blakey, James Moody, James Rogers	George Smith	George Smith gone off the day after the ryott, and shipt himself at Sunderland
James Scotland	William Robson, Richard Manuel	Thomas Trail	Thomas Trail gone off to Scotland the day after the ryott
Joseph Davison	John Davison		
	Thomas Wardale	Richard Moorhead	
William Scott	Peter Blackett	George Scott	
	Joseph Cook		
Robert Manuel	Thomas Adams		
	John Stirk		

Benjamin Dickinson	John Dickinson	Robert Willson
	John Cuningham	
Henry Waugh	Philip Bone	
	James Narne	
John Henderson	William Orrick, jnr.	Edward James
	John Rutlash	
William Hedley	Robert Blenkinsopp	Henry Rutlict
	William Hall	
Thomas Scotland	George Scotland	Isaac Airsbell
	Alexander Marchell	
John Adamson	James Adamson	Christopher Swan
	Robert Willson	
Alexander Lea	Robert Wardale	William Turnbull
	Andrew Willson	
Charles Hall	John Donnison	Alexander Scott
	William Hall	

110. An Account of the Skippers and Boundmen belonging to Thomas Binks, 1740 [TWA 394/11]

Skippers	Boundmen	Absentees
James Tennant	John Dykes, Charles Allen, John Ormston	
William Gregg	David Cooper, John Christy, Peter Nocks	
Robert Croudes	James Hutton, Thomas Croudess, George Ridley	
John Nelson	John Paull, Richard Wake, Robert Jackson	James Burn absent from John Nelson

John Tosh	Alexander Brown, Alexander Hall, John Rosebrough	Andrew Eunion absent from John Tosh
David Tennant	Henry Bewhanan, Geo. Fotheringame, Henry Curry	William Cooper absent from David Tennant
William Bewhanan	George Walker, John Sharp, David May	
James Watson		Absent from his keel and his bondman George Taft

111. A List of Skippers and Men bound to John Hearst for the Year 1740 [TWA 394/11]

Skippers	Place of Abode	Boundmen[1]
William Methuen, now with me	Gateshead	John Craggs, with me
		Thomas Haswell, gone
William Wilson, now with me	Sandgate	Thomas Wilson, with me
		John Wilson, with me
Robert Turnbull, now with me	Sandgate	George Paterson, gone
		John Hay, gone
John Pye, dead		John Lowry, with me
		John Jackson, with me
John Dixon, a Marine		James Marshall, gone
		John Alexander, gone
Robert Hardy, now with me	Sandgate	
Alexander Caldcleugh, now with me	Sandgate	Collin Henderson, with me
		John Holiday, with me
Isaac Brown, now with me	Sandgate	Isaac Archbald, gone
		John Ferguson, gone
Mathew Grahame, now with me	Sandgate	Nicholas Foster, gone
		John Christy, gone
William Livinston, in Dixon's place, gone		Thomas Ferguson, with me
		John Bruce, Marine
To the best of my knowledge, John Hearst		

[1] No information as to where they lived.

THE KEELMEN'S STRIKE OF 1744

112. M.A. Richardson, *The Local Historian's Table Book, Historical Division, volume I* (Newcastle, 1841), pp. 412–13

July 27 The keelmen of the river Tyne refused to work, and would let no keel pass down the river in consequence of the fitters loading the keels with ten chaldrons of coals instead of eight, which was the statute measure. They were in such a state of insubordination that the Riot Act was read by order of Ralph Sowerby, Esq., Mayor of Newcastle, and four companies of soldiers were sent to Sandgate to keep the peace. During this affray, Walter Blackett, Esq. M.P. and Alderman of Newcastle (afterwards Sir Walter Blackett, Bart.) received a cut on the head by a keelman. Matters in dispute were at length adjusted, and the keelmen resumed their labours.[1]

[1] This is the only account of the strike that has been found. After the strike, a document known as 'The Articles of 1744' was drawn up on 4 August and signed by eight magistrates and 24 fitters. It was copied in 1792 by Andrew Mitchell in his *Address to the Keelmen* (see below, **Document 199**). It reiterated the wages established in 1710 (see above, **Document 22**) with the additional provisions that 'no keel shall be obliged to take in more than the king's measure', *i.e.* eight Newcastle chaldrons; that a shilling was to be paid to the crew of a keel who had to cast on board a ship lying on shore 'to shift her'; and that if a shipmaster refused to give the keelmen the usual quantity of beer when they loaded his vessel they were to receive 1s. 4d.

Recently, what appears to be part of the original document has come to light, but it has remained in private hands.

THE KEELMEN'S STRIKE OF 1750

113. William Brown of Throckley, colliery engineer,[1] to Carlisle Spedding at Whitehaven, 30 April 1750 [NEIMME Letter Book, Brown/1, pp. 4–7]

Dear Sir,

Having an opportunity per the Revd Enashead, our Vicar at Newburn, to send this safely to Carlisle, from which doubt not but will come safe to hand, embraced the opportunity.

At present bussiness especially that part appertaining the Coale Trade in our River is in a bad situation, such as one has not been seen the last century, occationed as follows vizt: In my last of 13 January[2] I hinted to you the nature of a Regulation then subsisting amongst the principal Coale Owners, which Regulation in a great measure was overturned as soon as ships durst look out to sea; there was a great many meetings amongst the Owners but could not agree, nor did they all together fall out, so that in fact nothing was fixed on as to a new Regulation, in consequence that every Owner began to undersell another, though not in price fair but in giving extraordinary measure of coales (vizt) 9 or 10 chalders of coales instead of 8, and received no more for them then for 8. This sort of dealing began to lie hard upon the Keelmen so that they could scarce keep the keel above water, and labouring under severall greiveances before, they on the 19 of March last made an intire stop so as not a man of them would go, nor suffer any elce to go up or down the river with a keel to carry coales [not?] excepting the glasshouses and salt pans.[3] The Fitters and Owners seemed at first to laugh at such a stop, and thought in two or three weeks the Keelmen would be glad to go to work again on their own accords, and thought the want of cash to subsist on would bring them too, but experience has shewed the contrary, for their is no more likelyhood of their going to work then the first moment. The Keelmen putting up printed bills in the publique places of the Town shewing wherein they are greaved and the terms they require to go to work upon, and the Fitters answers their bills by the same method, but is not likely to come to a point or agreement.

Last Friday [24 April], the Fitters sent twixt 20 and 30 of the principal Keelmen to joal being bound servants, in order to frigth the rest, but to no purpose; it was thought that the rable part of the Keelmen would [have] endeavoured to resqued their going to joal and raised a mobb or riot so as a military force might have been turned upon them and obliged them to work, which the magistrites have called into Town for fear of a great disturbance, but instead of that they are allowed to go with the utmost cevillity whatever before some hindreds of the Keelmen who offered to go themselves to jail if required and did and has since the stop behaved very civilly in a word, though looks with a bad face.

Trade is intirely stagnated. Cash grows scarce, especily with the Coale Owners; nothing is heard but complaints [not?] excepting dealers in Town especially the Butchers. The River looks dejected, or rather deserted, nothing is seen but a few wherrys going up and down instead of the keels to the number of 5 or six hundred; the Harbour is full of ships, but empty ones, that indeed that part of craft is not at all uneasie at the stop, fire coals at London was so low that, if the keels had not stopt, the masters of ship would [have] been obliged to laid by their ships or employed them in other branches of business. Indeed the prices of coals begins to rise pretty fast now, and that will make the ship masters uneasie if does not get loaded soon. Sunderland, by the by, makes a fine sett out and would [have] done much more, but the wind has been against them verry much. How matters will be compremised is not yet known, time only will shew that; so much for the coal Trade which is the suport of all brenches here so consequently of Trade in generall.

We have nothing that's new in the engineering way….

I am, dear Sir, your obliged humble Servant,

William Brown

---

[1] For further information on Brown see Les Turnbull, *The World of William Brown, Railways – Steam Engines – Coalmines* (NEIMME, 2016).

[2] In his letter to Spedding of 13 January 1749/50, Brown describes the Regulation as 'a sort of agreement entered into by most and the powerfull Gentlemen in the Coale Trade by which they oblige themselves not to sell their coales under such prices as is therein mentioned, and also that they are not to exceed the vend of [a] certain quantity, as also that they take their turns as to vend alternately, one after another, and to vend a certain quantity each turn, till the year determines, and in case one or more gentlemen has vended the quantity assigned him [a] considerable time before the year determines, he or they must throw his or their Dealers upon such of the gentlemen concerned as is short and has not vended the quantity assigned them. This is what we term the Contract, and has been the three years past inviolably and justly observed, notwithstanding the express accounts to the contrary, and what is more, there is no obligation in force to oblige them to it more then their word and promises one to another, and the stronger obligation (viz), self interest, for by this Regulation there is as much profit arises at the vending ten thousand chalders as their is at thirty when there is a fighting trade, for when that is the case, one owner undersells another so that some sells cheaper then they work, and then the ship masters makes a fine time; and their has been two meetings of the gentlemen in order to settle the aid regulation for 3 years more, but has not yett agreed. Mr Humble of Newcastle is the only person that will not come into such measures, relying on the great quantity he works….' (Letter Book, pp 1–2).

[3] Brown twice omits 'not' before 'excepting' when the sense suggests that it should be inserted. The case for the prosecution set out below [**Document 115**] states that the keelmen prevented coal being delivered to glasshouses and salt works and other manufactories.

114. William Brown to Carlisle Spedding, 12 July 1750 [NEIMME Letter Book, Brown/1, pp. 9–11]

Dear Sir,

…In my last of the 30th of April, which I hope came safe to hand, I gave you an account of the combination among the Keelmen so far as that day. In a day or two more, the [ship]masters then in the Harbour sent their sailors to work the keels up the river, and being assisted per pittmen and waggonmen down, got loaded, so from an intance or two of this the rest took the hint and the Keelmen went to work by degrees and are now verry quiet.

Immediately after the stop of the keels, the principal Coale Owners begun to drop their prices of coales and is now under selling one another. Some of them has lowered their prices 5s. per chald[ron], and its belived will go lower. The prices before this hapned was about 13s. per chald[ron]. The trade in our River is mostly between Lord Ravensworth and partners, comonly known by the name of the Grand Allies, and Lord Windsar and Simpsons, but the latter has rather the better of the former, their coales being rather better. In short, trade never had [so] bad appearance in my time as it has at present. How long it may continue is uncertain, though it is generaly belived the Owners will come to a new Regulation in a little time....

I am, Sir, your obliged humble Servant,
William Brown

115. The King Against the Keelmen Rioters: Case for the Prosecution [TWA 394/24]

The coals which are vended at the Port of Newcastle upon Tyne are conveyed by keels from the staiths to the ships; each of the keels employed in conveying the coals has a Skipper and 3 or 4 Keelmen who navigate the keel, and these Skippers and Keelmen for the most part are hired servants to Fitters and are bound by articles to the Fitter under whom they are employed at certain rates or wages for the space of one year, and are bound by the Fitter at Christmas annually to serve to Christmas again, and the work which they are to perform, as also the wages or rates they are to be paid for the same, are partly agreed upon and settled between them and the Fitter at the time of hiring or binding, and every Skipper of a keel has given him by his Fitter or master 20 shillings or more for his own and his men's use as a gratuity.

On the 19th March 1749/50 a number of the Skippers and Keelmen employed in the coal works at Newcastle thought proper to desist working or following their employment though bound or hired for a year as aforesaid from Christmas 1749 to Christmas 1750. Those Keelmen, not choosing to work themselves or suffering others to work who were inclined to do so, in a riotous manner assembled on the River Tyne and New Key in Newcastle on the said 19th March and there stopt and prevented all keels from passing and repassing on the River and coals from being cast on board of ships, and to compleat this undertaking several parties of them on the 20th and 21st March assembled in the like manner and went to Shields and there boarded several keels lying there belonging to several Fitters in Newcastle and broke open the hurricks or cabbins of the said keels and broke and destroyed all the shovells, ponvies, hurrick or cabbin stores and other utensils and work gear belonging to those keels, and then returned in great triumph to Newcastle; by which outragious proceedings that great and valuable branch of trade was stopt and obstructed, and those rioters became sole masters of the River and navigation thereof to the impoverishment of many familys and others employed in that service, and the preventing many ships being loaded with coals and other merchandize bound for London and forreign parts, and many of the outward bound ships were obliged for want of coals to proceed in their ballast to their respective ports, and other ships bound to London went to other ports to load, and some detained in the harbour for 7 or 8 weeks for want of coals, nor would they permit a vessell to be loaden with coals on his Majestyse account bound for the use of the garrison of Gibraltar, or permit any coals to be carried for the use of the glass-houses, salt works, engines and other manufactorys carried on in the River of Tyne, or for the use of a private family, and the whole Town and the neighbouring County were all this time in the greatest consternacon for the consequence of their outragious proceedings.

The Magistrates of the Town published orders for all the idle people to go to work at the call of their respective masters, and in their said orders promised their protection and security for all their just rights and demands, but all was to no purpose, and they continued in such a riotous behaviour that there is the greatest reason to believe nothing but the presence of the military force prevented them from plundering the Town. Some of the Skippers were committed by the Magistrates upon proper informacons and convictions to the House of Correction upon the late Act of Parliament, but this had no effect to make them return to their duty, and they still refusing to work, and there being a great demand as well at home as abroad for coals and for the benefit of trade, it was thought prudent and adviseable to procure sailors, waggon men, labourers and others to carry on the business instead of the Keelmen, which was done accordingly for some days, and the Keelmen, perceiving that their business would be done without their assistance, they on the 4th May last, between the hours of 1 and 2 o'Clock in the afternoon, riotously assembled together to the number of 1000 and upwards at a place called Sandgate Shore near Newcastle, and there manned keels and boats and lay in the middle of the River and stopt all laden keels navigated by masters of ships, sailors &c and brought them to anchor, and barbarously beat and abused the sailors &c employed in such keels and prevented them going on board their vessells, and broke and destroyed and threw into the River the work gear belonging to the keels, and by force and violence took a Skipper out of one of those keels which belonged to Mr Alderman Sowerby and Mr Colepits and greatly beat and abused them and threw the Skipper, one William Cole, into the River, who narrowly escaped being drowned; and they continued assembled as aforesaid for near 2 hours when the Magistrates with the military force were obliged and did march to disperse them on the shore side, whilst an armed power was employed against them on the River, and the trade by that means was open for that day and untill the [7th May] when they thought proper to return to their work.

Informacons being made against some of the most notorious rioters, it is thought proper for examples sake and the safety and peace of the Town and the neighbouring Countys to prosecute some of the offenders, and it is hoped that the Court will inflict exemplary punishments on such as shall be found guilty.

116. The keelmen's Explanation of their Grievances [TWA 394/19]

We the Skippers and Keelmen on the River of Tyne being informed that many of the grievances mentioned in our former Representation[1] are hardly understood even by the gentlemen Coal Owners themselves, or any body else except we who are the sufferours and such as are the gainers by the practices complained off, we do therefore begg leave to make some explanations of our grievances. We would not be understood to complain of all the Gentlemen Fitters, for there are severall of them who have not laid any hardships upon us but are rather willing to hear and redress our grievances, if they could prevail on the rest to be unaninous therein.

As to the first of our grievances touching the over measure, the Gentlemen Fitters have proposed a remedy much worse than the distemper, namely that if any keel be too deep laden the same is to be brought to the key and looked upon by the King's inspector. Now it is submitted whether this be practicable, for though we are liable to a visite from him, he is not subject to answer the call either of us or our masters; however, the King's measure is so self evident and plain by the mark or nail on each keel that it is impossible for us or any person to err in the observation of it.[2]

As to the second article of our Representation touching the consined Can-houses, there are a variety of hardships included in this grievance:

1st. Every five shillings of market money we receive there is 3d. stopped from each of us.

2nd. If we pay but one keel of borrowed coals to any other fitter than our own immediate master, there is 3d. taken off the skipper for that.

3rd. We are obliged to spend more of our money than we can afford in waiting at these houses for orders, and if we refuse to wait or slow in drinking we are abused and threatened by the Can-house keepers, who are all the fitters' servants, to be turned out of our keels, and as this rank of our masters (for we have many degrees of masters), as we are informed have no other wages but the benefit of these Can-houses, they make it as considerable a perquasite as possible, for which reason we have not the same liquor as the other customers, but a certain other liquor is brewed for us, which they call 'savage beer' or 'beer for savages', at the same time doing us the honour to take the gentleman's price for it.

As to the 3rd article of our Representation, touching the spout sixpences, there is one shilling of our money which is allowed by the coal owners to each keel each tide, which shilling is sunk in the following manner: we are obliged to fill two quarts of bad drink for one sixpence and we must carry the other sixpence to the steath for two loaders to help us, but the steathmen to engross this perquasite to themselves oblige us to ly at the steath a whole day for the luire of this dear sixpence, and then we are forced to goe down to Shields in dark and stormy nights to the danger of our lives, beside the loss of our tides, so that to gain them six pence we often lose 13s.4d., and the steathmen themselves have often times acknowledged that they made £50 a year by this perquasite, and, say they, who but savages would complain of this.

As to the 4th article of our Representation, it needs no other explanation than this, that the ship-masters instead of giving us good beer to the value of 1s.4d. or the money, sometimes order their servants to give us a small quantity of stuff, sometimes sowr and sometimes yeast which, if we venture to drink it, is ready to kill us [and] has killed some of us, on account of our being over heated with hard labour.

As to the 5th article of our Representation, the necessity of our money being paid on a Saturday morning appears from this: that when our payment is delayed till it's late, we or our wifes must go to market at a very great disadvantage both with regard to the quality and price of provisions, and sometimes there is nothing left in the market for us.

As to the 6th article of our Representation, can anything be more moderate than our demand of a shilling for a man to travel from Shields and back for and with fresh orders? It is just three farthings a mile.

Now with respect to our going down to Shields after 12 O'clock upon Saturdays, it is a considerable loss to us, because ships are not always ready, being frequently at the ballast key when we come there, and the fitters often send great numbers of keels to finish ships on that day because they will not allow us for lying tides on Sundays, as on other days, although we are both kept from our familys and likewise from publick worship which is our desire to attend however we may be deriaded for it.

As to the stirred keels, this grievance has creeped upon us in the following manner: the skipper of each keel is intitled to twenty pence more wages than the other men, but the fitters to engross this perquasite likewise to themselves make a practice of enticeing a common man to stirr keels for their benefit for a groat extraordinary, so that the fitters have sixteen pence each of these stirred keels, and to such a hight some of them have carried this practice that they have [a] stirred keel for each child, and such as have no children make a perquasite of stirred keels for the benefit and according to the number of their horses and doggs. Now as these perquasites is the right and property of the skippers only, we cannot help looking upon it as a very great encroachment upon us and a great discouragement to such as spend their lives and labours to enrich those that oppress us. We may venture to affirm that there is two thirds of all the keels in the River employed as stirred keels.[3]

As to the shilling we demand for shifting a ship from the key, we earn it very hard, for when a ship lyes aground alongside of the key we have a stage to hang with roaps and two of our men must stand in the keel's hold and throw the coals to other two of our men who stand on the stage who throw them into the ship's hold, and when we are denyed payment (which is often the case), we only receive our holliday title of savages.

As to our fire coals, though the fitters agree it's our due to have a caldron yearly for each keel, yet many of us do not receive it.

Lastly, the making in of coals and helping of barrows is a great imposition on us, for when we labour hard to come home to our respective steaths we are often weared, and yet we are not allowed time to take the least refreshment, but must at the demand of fitters' men and steathmen directly go and make in coals and help barrows, which is no part of our duty as keelmen.

Upon the whole when what is above represented is duely weighed and considered, we hope the just part of mankind will be of opinion that all our grievances ought to be redressed, and such methods taken to adjust and settle our demands as to prevent any necessity of further complaints, so that the coal trade may be carried on with quietness and expedition, to accomplish which our laborious endeavours shall never be wanting.[4]

[1] This first representation has not been found.

[2] 'The King's inspector', *i.e.* of customs. 'The King's measure' was the normal keel load of eight Newcastle chaldrons. Although a greatly overloaded keel would be obvious to all, there were circumstances where the nature of the load was less clear (see Introduction, n. 72, above p. xxxi).

[3] 'Stirred' is an obsolete form of 'steered'. The skipper steered the keel with a huge oar. The fitters charged the ship masters with the keelmen's wages and could therefore gain by retaining sixteen pence of what was normally due to the skipper by 'enticing' a 'common man' to steer the keel, a practice which could endanger the lives of the crew when such men were not 'capable of their labour' (second Remonstrance of the Keelmen, 1719, see above, **Document 67**).

[4] It seems that the document was printed, as is implied by a question asked to Edward Mosley, one of the fitters, when giving evidence to a committee of the House of Commons in 1770: 'Do you remember any printed paper containing explanations of grievances any time about 20 years ago that was delivered by the keelmen to their masters?' (TWA 394/29). The reference to the 'just part of mankind' also implies that the keelmen expected their paper to circulate beyond their masters. According to William Brown, the keelmen displayed 'printed bills in the public places of the Town showing wherein they are greaved and the terms they require to go to work' (see his letter to C. Spedding, 30 April 1750, above, **Document 112**). The magistrates evidently barred the keelmen from publishing their case in the newspapers (see the Keelmen's Case, **Document 120**, below).

117. Order of the Magistrates, 21 April 1750 [TWA 394/25]

We the Mayor, Recorder and Aldermen of the Town and County of Newcastle upon Tyne having taken into our consideration the great prejudice done to the publick by the stop lately put to the Coal Trade, and that by means thereof many poor families are likely to be reduced to the utmost necessity, do think fit to make publick this our Order, and we do hereby order and strictly charge all Skippers and Keellmen within the limits of our jurisdiction immediately to go to work in their several employments, and we do hereby further declare that upon compliance with this our Order by the said Skippers and Keellmen we will rigorously enforce an obedience and compliance by all masters and employers of such Skippers and Keellmen to and with the several regulations and agreements made and entered into by them in the year of our Lord 1744.

Given under our hands this 21st day of April 1750, Robert Sorsbie, Mayor, Christopher Fawcett, Recorder, Edward Collingwood, Ralph Sowerby, Cuthbert Smith, John Stephenson, Nathaniel Clayton, Matthew Ridley, William Peareth.

118. Robert Sorsbie, Mayor, to the Duke of Bedford, Secretary of State, 30 April 1750 [TNA, SP 36/112/141–2]

My Lord Duke,

The keelmen employed on the River Tyne in carrying coals on board the ships have for these six weeks by past refused to work under a pretence of some grievances. The Magistrates of this Town sent for the men and their masters and redressed their just complaints immediately, but the men would not go to work without having their wages advanced, which were very extravagant demands and could not be complied with. The men have remained idle without doing any mischief, and we are proceeding upon the Act of the 20th of his present Majesty[1] and have committed sixteen of the offenders to prison, and shall go on in the same way and hope to bring the men to their duty.

I think it my duty to acquaint your Grace of this, and particularly of an affair that happened on Friday, which we did not get information of until late on Saturday evening, upon which we issued the Proclamation which I take the liberty to inclose to your Grace. We are using all the endeavours we can to find out the persons and shall leave nothing that is in our power undone to get to the bottom of the affair, and shall be glad to receive your Grace's directions in what you think proper. There are six companies of the Earl of Ancram's Regiment quartered in the Town under the command of Major Rufane who is ready to assist the civil power in case of necessity.[2]

A person who calls himself Herdman, and pretends to be a lawyer of Edinburgh, has been extremely instrumental in advising and spiriting up the keelmen, but at present he conceals himself in the neighbourhood of the Town and out of the limits of our jurisdiction. However, we hope to apprehend him soon. I am, with the greatest regard,

Your Grace's most obedient, humble servant,
Robert Sorsbie, Mayor.

---

[1] The Act 20 George II cap. XIX specifically included the keelmen and empowered

magistrates to commit servants found guilty of misdemeanour or ill behaviour to the House of Correction for a period not exceeding one month.

² On information from Sir Walter Blackett 'some time before His Majesty had left England' that there was 'some uneasiness brewing amongst the keelmen', the Secretary at War had ordered six companies of Lord Ancram's Regiment that were dispersed in different places to be drawn up and kept together at Newcastle, and 'it is hoped the insurrection will be put an immediate stop to and the authors of it brought to speedy justice' (R.N. Aldworth and R. Leveson Gower to Mr Stone, 4 May 1750, TNA, SP 44/318/12–14).

119. Proclamation, 28 April 1750 [*Enclosure*, TNA, SP 36/112/143]

Newcastle upon Tyne: Information upon oath having been made this day before five of His Majesty's Justices of the Peace for the said Town, that yesterday, between the hours of twelve and one o'Clock at noon, several persons, to the Informant unknown and who appeared by their habits to be keelmen (and who as the Informant verily believes were keelmen), were seen in one of Elswick Fields near this Town; and that one of the said persons, in company with about five others, stood upon a stile and said: *I proclaim Prince* CHARLES *King of England France and Ireland, Defender of the Faith*; and let every one of my way of thinking say *Amen*, or used words to the like effect. And that thereupon several of the other persons, to the number of four at least, immediately rose up and said *Amen*.

The Corporation of Newcastle hereby promise a Reward of one Hundred Pounds to any person or persons who shall discover the person making the said proclamation, or any of the persons saying *Amen* as aforesaid, to be paid by the Town Clerk upon the Conviction of the said offender or offenders.

By order of the Magistrates
Cuthbertson

120. The Keelmen's Case [TWA 394/19]

We the poor persecuted and oppressed keelmen of Tyne River having first represented our grievances to the worthy Magistrates of this Town and County and afterwards explained them, do now in obedience to your commands come to attend your Court, but certainly under the greatest disadvantages, awed by the dignity of offices and superiour fortunes, as well as unable to argue with gentlemen of more generous education, nor will (we believe) any gentleman that professes the Law here chuse to incurr the resentment of our opponents (made formidable by the sweat of our brows) by appearing to speak in our behalf.

The Contract or Articles in 1744 now insisted on was broke only by our various taskmasters without regarding the injustice done to us and dishonour done to your Worships who then vouchased to be their guarrantees. If it was a Contract it was mutually binding, and if it is no tye upon those who signed it, it can never be interpreted an obligation upon us who did not sign it; and if our being hired for a year is insisted on, we affirm the covenants of that hireing are likewise broke by our taskmasters. Indeed, nothing is more plain than their intention to starve us into a compliance with what hardships they resolve to impose on us, and how far these may extend, after the Laws of Justice have already been by them openly trangressed, is hard to determine.

The other hardships not mentioned in the Articles in 1744 and now complained of do in justice and reason call for and are intitled to redress as well as the others, though we have been denied the liberty to explain and publish them in opposition to that so much contended one of the press; nor are we allowed in that manner to vindicat ourselves against the false aspersions which were assigned for the cause of the Government sending troops by forced marches against innocent oppressed men.

As we act from the first principle of nature, self preservation, so we doubt not of finding some of both power and influence sufficient to support our just claim, as well as to represent it in a true and publick light in which we hope this Court will be found to have acted with impartiality, honour and justice, for we are determined, rather than have a hand in our own ruin, to apply to the Courts of Earth and Heaven where we shall either find or not need advocates. This is the sense of all of us, and we will continue unanimous in it; and as the honour of this Court can never allow a stumbling block to be laid in the way of our ignorance, so we are resolved not to intrapt ourselves by entring upon arguments beyond what is here contained.[1]

God save King George [*added in a different hand*][2]
Archbald Hunter, Peter Herret, Walter Pateson, James Tennent, James Abercrumby, James Greenfield, James Veitch, James Richey, Patrick Gib, Patrick Bell, George Wilson, John Cristel, John Shad, Michael Smith, Robert Croudas, Mark Edgar, Alexander Carclough, John Clark, George Millar, James Stephenson.[3]

[1] This was the work of Mungo Herdman, the lawyer of Edinburgh, who could not represent the keelmen in person because he was liable to arrest on suspicion of high treason. William Dollar, who was 'writer or scrivener for the keelmen at the request and by the direction of Mr Herdman', was reported to be surprised that the magistrates had not sought to arrest him as well (Information of Joseph Dixon, Sergeant at Mace, 27 April 1750, TWA 394/26).

[2] Presumably added to counter the 'false aspersons' that the keelmen were disaffected.

[3] Almost all these men, each employed by a different fitter, were subsequently prosecuted by their respective employers for breach of the terms of their bond, and on conviction on 26 April were sentenced to hard labour for a month in the House of Correction. Most of them were, however, discharged on 7 May (TWA 394/24, 25).

121. Handbill with the names of 823 keelmen issued during the keelmen's strike by the following fitters: John and Francis Simpson, Sowerby and Colpitts, Thomas Airey, Edward Humble, Matthew Bell, John Baker, Thomas Waters, John Robinson, Salkeld Robinson, Johnson and Hedley, William Jefferson, Ann Hudspith, Elizabeth Atkinson, Elizabeth Ord, John Vonholte, Thomas Binks, Robert Shortridge, William Scott, Henry Atkinson, Moseley and Watson, Nicholas Fairless [NCL: J. Bell, *Collections relative to the River Tyne: its Trade and the Conservancy thereof*, vol. I, f. 12]

Newcastle, 28 April 1750

Sir,

Above is a List of the Keelmen which are bound to us; and we desire that you will not employ any one of them in any Work or Service whatsoever; for if you do, we shall call upon you for such a Satisfaction as the Law will give us.[1]

[1] See also copy of letter from the Mayor to Lord... 7 May 1750, **Document 126**, below.

122. R.N. Aldworth to Robert Sorsbie, 3 May 1750 [TNA, SP 44/318/10–11]

Sir,

In the absence of the Duke of Bedford I have received your letter of 30 April inclosing a proclamation which you have ordered to be published on account of the late riots and treasonable practices which have happened in your neighbourhood, and on laying them this morning before the Lords of the Regency I received their Excellencies' directions to acquaint you with their entire approbation of your zeal and activity as well as those of the Justices of the Peace who have acted with you upon this occasion, and to inform you that for the more easy discovery and conviction of the persons concerned in these riots, their Excellencies have ordered an advert to be published in the Gazette promising His Majesty's pardon to any person or persons concerned (except such as actually proclaimed the Pretender as mentioned in your proclamation) who shall discover any of his or their accomplices, and likewise a reward of £100 over and above what has been offered by your Corporation to be paid upon conviction of any such offender.

I am your obedient humble servant, R.N. Aldworth

123. R.N. Aldworth to Robert Sorsbie, 3 May 1750 [TNA, SP 44/318/11–12]

Sir,

As it appears from your letter that one – Herdman…has been very instrumental in stirring up the keelmen to sedition, His Grace the Duke of Bedford will send a messenger to you as soon as possible with his warrant for the apprehending of the said Herdman, and the messenger will be directed to apply to you for instructions and assistance.

I am your obedient humble servant,
R.N. Aldworth

124. Duke of Bedford's Warrant to Richard Lucas, one of His Majesty's Messengers in Ordinary [TNA, SP 44/85/183–4]

These are in His Majesty's name to authorize and require you forthwith to repair to Newcastle upon Tyne, and, taking a constable to your assistance, to make strict and diligent search for [Mungo] Herdman, of whom you shall have notice and, him having found, you are to seize and apprehend upon suspicion of High Treason, and to bring him together with his papers in safe custody before me to be examined concerning the premises and further dealt with according to law. In due execution whereof all Mayors, Sheriffs, Justices of the Peace, constables and other His Majesty's officers, civil and military…are to be aiding. Given at Whitehall, 4 May 1750

125. The Mayor's Warrant to Mr Thomas Aubone and all others his Majesty's officers for this Town and County for the arrest of Herdman [TWA 394/24]

Newcastle upon Tyne. These in his Majesty's name to authorise and require you and every of you to whom this warrant is directed immediately to make diligent search for Mungo Herdman in all places within the Town and County of Newcastle upon Tyne where you shall suspect the said Herdman to be concealed, and him to bring before me, or some other of his Majesty's Justices of the Peace for the said Town and County, to answer several informations against him for High Crimes and Misdemeanours, and in case of resistance you are hereby authorised to break open doors and search for the said Herdman and all papers belonging or suspected to belong to him, and then to bring before me or some other Justice of the Peace as aforesaid forthwith, and for so doing this shall be your warrant.[1]

Given under my hand and seal this 6th day of May 1750.

Robert Sorsbie, Mayor

[1] The search for Herdman was extended to County Durham, Sorsbie's warrant being endorsed by Revd William Lamb, one of the magistrates for that county. Although the search at an inn and then at a private house proved fruitless, the constables believed that certain persons who had obstructed the search knew where Herdman was and had helped him to escape (Information of Thomas Aubone and others, 9 May 1750, TWA 394/24).

126. Copy letter from the Mayor to Lord ?, 7 May 1750 [*The Lord is not named and the letter may not have been sent as the strike had ended.*] [TWA 394/25]

My Lord,

The great outrages which of late have been committed by the Keelmen of this Town, and the informations which have been made against several of them for crimes of the highest nature, call upon all the Magistrates of this Town to use their utmost diligence in finding out the offenders. I therefore make no doubt of your Lordship's excuse for the trouble I give you by this letter. We are informed that several keelmen, who ought to be employed in carrying keels down the River, are now at work as labourers or otherwise in your Lordship's service, and considering what has happened lately in the Town and neighbourhood, I dare to say you will readily comply with the request of the Magistrates of this Town and immediately order a list of the names of all persons who have been employed as keelmen and are now employed in any kind of work under your Lordship to be sent to, my Lord,

Your Lordship's most obedient humble servant,

Robert Sorsbie, Mayor

127. *Newcastle Courant*, 18–25 August 1750

At the Assizes last week, Thomas Gibson, John Coats, Benjamin Tate, James Stephenson, James Wanley and Michael Petree, keelmen, were severally indicted for riots and other misdemeanors during the late stop of the coal trade, and, being convicted thereof, the two first were ordered to be imprisoned for three months and to enter it security for their good behaviour for three years, the others to be imprisoned for one month and to give the like security.

THE KEELMEN'S STRIKE OF 1768 AND ATTEMPTS BY THOMAS HARVEY, AN ATTORNEY, TO OBTAIN AN ACT OF PARLIAMENT TO ESTABLISH THEIR SOCIETY AND CHARITY AND LIMIT THE KEEL-LOAD

128. Petition of the Keelmen, 29 March 1768 [TWA 394/29]

To the Right Worshipfull Maior,

We the Keelmen belonging to the River Tine under the gentlemen Fitters and Coal Owners desire to humbley submitt ourselves as bond servants, we being for some time very heavily oprest with Over Measure which we are not able to subsist with. We have this day all meet in the Garth Heads in Sandgate and Castle, and we all with one voice desire no other terms then King's Measure, which is eight chaldron, and with one consent we are all willing to serve our Masters upon thess terms so never to be oprest no more.

Wherass, Your Worship, we who belong to this River under the Gentlemen above mentioned desires this requist: as their is keils at Sheilds that desstress us very much by taking in three kells of ballast for two, and namly, when we are ordered for a ship that cannot stand without her ballast, we are oprest by casting to extremety for this ballast that is in the said ship, and when we have steffened the ship according to order, thess kells that belongs to Shields come and shares us out of it. We all desire that your Worship would take it to consideration and right us according to our opression and perti-culerly to lay thesse pan keels of[f] in Shields. We are your humble servants, the bond Keelmen in this River Tine.

129. Resolution of a Meeting of the Mayor and Aldermen, 29 March 1768 [TWA 394/29]

Present: Edward Mosley, Mayor, John Simpson, William Peareth, Matthew Bell, Aubone Surtees, J. E. Blackett and John Baker, Aldermen

On an inquiry into the complaints of the Keelmen employed in the River Tyne, resolved that for the time to come no more than the King's Measure shall be put into any kell at one time. [*Endorsed*: 29 March 1768, Keelmen's complaint redressed and went to work again the 31st.][1]

[1] At a meeting of the fitters, each accompanied by one of their skippers, held on 29 March it was agreed 'that for the time to come no keelman or keelmen are to take in more coals at one time than the King's Measure' (TWA 394/29).

130. The Keelmen to the Right Worshipfull the Mayor [*c.* 29 April 1768] [TWA 394/29]

Please your Worship, we the Skippers and bondmen servants under the Fitters and Coalowners in Newcastle upon Tyne as we have made our applications to your Worship concerning our great oppression, and have been righted by your Worship to the great satisfaction of every Skipper and man in whom it does concern in this River Tyne, now we all meet together in submission to the Worshipfull Mayor and Magistraites humbly makes our redress for George Turnbull's pardon and Charles Miller's.[1] This done, wee the whole Skippers and men belonging to the River Tyne are joined together in prayer for your peace and tranquility.

[1] Turnbull and Millar had been arrested and were to be tried at the Assizes for involvement in an assault on Henry Robson, a keelman who had refused to contribute to the recently established fund for an application to Parliament, and was also accused of navigating an overloaded keel. He was seized by a mob of 50 or more, carried on a pole through the streets, beaten, severely wounded, and put in fear of his life (Warrant for the arrest of William Calbreath and several others also involved, and notes by E. Mosley, TWA 394/29).

131. Matthew Ridley to George Ward, 29 April 1768 [NA, ZRI 38/2, Matthew Ridley's Letter Book, 1767–77, pp. 44–5]

To George Ward

Newcastle, 29 April 1768

…At present there is a total stop to the trade here by some of the Keelmen refusing to work and those that are well inclined from working unless they will come in to pay so much per keel to Mr Harvey, an Attorney, for business that *is to be done* for them, as he expresses it in his receit. If these men remain quiet, their lying idle will not be of much damage, but it is scarce to be expected that they will long remain without work or without mischief. They now make a point to have some that are in custody for beating and ill using of their brethren discharged and they will go to work, but I presume the Magistrates will not comply with a demand of that kind. A few days must determine peace or war with 'em.

132. Copy note from George Turnbull and Charles Millar to the Keelmen, 30 April 1768 [TWA 394/29]

This is to acquaint all Keelmen that as it has happened that we are at present confined in Newgate, we are very sorry that the consequence of it should have occasion to give such a general concern as that no keels to go to work, but if it should be on our account, we desire and hope that no person will stay any longer at home from work, for it will give little satisfaction for people to distress theirselves and families for us, so that in going to work you will greatly oblige your well wishing friends, George Turnbull, Charles Millar.

133. Draft Advertisement for Discovering Riotous Keelmen, 29 April 1768 [TWA 394/29]

Whereas some men yesterday going down the River in a keel with coals to be shipt at Shields were forcibly opposed, stopped and obstructed by several disorderly, ill-designing persons, unlawfully and riotously assembled. In order therefore that the offenders may be detected and brought to justice, whoever shall discover one or more of them by Information on oath before the Right Worshipfull the Mayor shall be intitled to a reward of five guineas to be paid by the Town Clerk upon conviction. And notice is hereby given that all persons who shall hereafter commit or be found parties in any offences of the like nature, or other disturbances of the public peace in this Town, will be prosecuted and punished with the utmost rigour of Law.[1]

And all persons who have not wherewith to maintain themselves and their families and live idle, neglecting their respective employments, and refusing to go to work for the usual and common wages, will be apprehended as idle and disorderly persons, and such of them as shall be found to have gained legal settlements in this place will be committed to the House of Correction to be kept at hard labour, and such as are not legally settled here will be punished as vagrants and as such sent to the places of their respective settlements.

By Order
Gibson

---

[1] This was published in the *Newcastle Courant*, 7 May 1768, omitting the second paragraph.

134. The *Newcastle Courant*, 7 May 1768 (Thomas Harvey's Justification for aiding the Keelmen)

The late disorderly proceedings of some of the keelmen having engaged the attention of the Mayor and the rest of the Magistrates of this Corporation, and Mr Harvey's conduct having been exceedingly misrepresented, this method is taken of informing the public that the above gentleman solemnly declares that he did not at any time advise, promote, or encourage any stop amongst the keelmen, much less any unlawful or riotous obstruction of the coal trade. The very surmise of his being capable of entertaining such a thought, much more of his having aided, abetted, promoted, or encouraged proceedings so contrary to the laws of his country, so opposite to the respect due to the Magistracy, and destructive of the peace of the community, affects him in the most sensible manner. The large quantity of coal conveyed by the keelmen above the King's Measure, and contrary to the regulations of the dues in this respect, was the occasion of the keelmen presenting a request to several of the magistrates and gentlemen concerned in the coal trade, craving a redress of their grievances. "Mr Harvey declares he was then an utter stranger to the contents of these requests, that they were drawn up by he knows not who, without his knowledge or privacy. But finding several gentlemen had subscribed their names to these papers, and thereby acknowledged the reasonableness of the keelmen's complaints, and consequently had thereby virtually promised that the causes of their complaint should be removed, he could not reasonably apprehend his giving any offence by promising the keelmen that in case they would *return to their business*, he would consider their case, and use his endeavours to settle them under such regulations as would establish good order and peaceable behaviour amongst them, remove the occasion of their complaints, and tend to the good of the coal trade in general, as far as a *Certainty of Measure* would effect so salutary an end". This is all Mr Harvey undertook in behalf of the keelmen, and thinks himself justified in so doing both by the nature of the case, the uprightness of his intentions, and the example of the gentlemen who subscribed the keelmen's requests. He only begs leave to add, that the stop made by the keelmen on Monday 25 April to compel some of their brethren to pay their pecuniary contributions, was without his knowledge, and that it ceased on the same day by eleven o'Clock in the morning. As to any subsequent stops, obstructions &c, he equally disowns his being privy, consenting to, or encouraging the same, and hopes that justice will be done him, as to believe the declaration of his abhorrence of all such riotous and illegal proceedings to be sincere.

135. Copy 'intended Advertizement' [by Edward Mosley] about Harvey, 14 May 1768 ('not executed') [TWA 394/29]

As Mr Harvey is pleased to publish in the *Newcastle Courant* his apprehensions of being misrepresented to the publick with respect to the Keelmen, [I] hope notwithstanding what he has done have produced so very disagreable effects, that his sencibility, good will, and feeling for the general concern and laws of his Country may be true as he represents, yet [I] cannot conceive what service he can be of to the Keelmen, who are under so good regulations, and perhaps are the best paid labouring people in the Kingdom, for to stir them up with vain expectations of being serviceable to them upon any occasion of their grievances in the coal trade. When it is certainly known, the Magistrates are always ready, and do redress them upon their first just complaint. That their late grievances were properly so settled as soon as communicated, and acknowledged by themselves to the Mayor in the name of the skippers and men employed in the River that every man of them were greatly satisfied and thankfull.

That what Mr Harvey observes with respect to the pecuniary contribution to be paid him by the Keelmen, the stop made on that account the 25th April [I] believe might be without his knowledge, but that the stop ceased on the same day at 11 a clock in the morning cannot be true; therefore [I] must beg leave to explain myself as follows: that the stop made by the Keelmen on Monday the 25th April continued to Monday the 2nd May following. [I] apprehend Mr Harvey may mean the tumult only made on that day, if so he is right and he must know, if not, everybody else did, that the tumult was quashed as soon as it was well known, and the people became very peaceable and quiet, but during the week the sensible part of the Keelmen, willing and disireous to work, durst not under pretence of running a risk of danger from the mob, who are indeed a very worthless few, and it's very amazing that such numbers, who know so much better, can suffer themselves to be so shamefully imposed upon.

That on Thursday the 28th April an attempt was made (unknown to the Magistrates, otherwise they would [have] been protected), to carry a loaded keel down the river which was stopped by the way by some people, to discover any of whom, the Mayor, that instant, offered a reward, either for that or any other future attempt or offence on the like occasion, and that on Monday the 2nd May all the Keelmen went to their respective employments with great satisfaction and cheerfulness, and have ever since behaved very well.

Upon the Mayor asking some keelmen why the work of the River was stopped on Monday the 25th April, he was told that some of their brethren had not paid Mr Harvey the money that other Works had done, and that some men had said that untill such payment was made by every concern no keel should go to work, and as a further pretence they vented their rage upon one of those unfortunate men who had not paid, ahangeing him with a further fault for taking in too much measure one day in his keel, which upon examination was found not to be true.

136. Notes concerning the examination of a keelman [TWA 394/29]

Saturday morning the 23rd July 1768, Gilbert Miller, keelman, being carried before Alderman Peareth for creating some disturbance at the quay about buying a penny worth of herring out of a coble there, on his being spoke to by the Alderman, he said he hoped we should have a warr on before Monday next. The Alderman ordered him to the Tower for examination, and, on his being brought to the Mayor's Chamber about an hour afterward and being asked what he meant by the aforesaid expression about a warr, he said that his expression was that he hoped there would be a warr in a month, or by that day month, but that he meant nothing more by it than it would make a scarcity of keelmen.

Being asked some questions about Mr Harvey, he said Mr Harvey had prepared a large parchment writing for the keelmen, that some hundreds of them, and he for one, had signed it, and that all the rest of the keelmen, ballastmen and panmen on the River Tyne were to sign it, and everyone that signed paid a half a penny for the woman that cleaned the room; that by this parchment they had all agreed not to carry more than the King's Measure, and that the men of every keel should pay a fine of 15 shillings every time they carried too large measure, and that every man commencing [work as a] keelman should pay 20 shillings on his first entry into any keel, and that three keelmen in every Fitter's employment were appointed to receive these payments which were to go towards composing a fund.[1]

[1] A note under the above states that 'a north countryman named Colin Hutt [was] taken into Mr Lamb's work as a keelman on Saturday the [23rd] July who conformed to pay Mr Harvey, an attorney who has undertaken to do some sort of business for them, which they will not divulge or pretend to know little or nothing of, 20 shillings for leave to work in the keels, to be applyd to some certain fund, as likewise 3s. 4d. for Harvey's fee'.

137. William Cramlington (Fitter) to Edward Mosley, Mayor, 3 August 1768 [TWA 394/29]

Dear Sir,

I have used my endeavours to come at the contents of the contract Harvey has drawn amongst the Keelmen, but he has enjoined them so strongly to secrecy that I can come at few particulars. All I can learn is that they themselves are to be judges when their keel is load and not to be subject to any controul from the offputter or Fitter's servant, and that, if any keel take in more than what may be adjudged proper measure by them, each man on board such keel to be subject to a fine of 5 shillings, and that no person is to be permitted to go at the keels untill he has paid the sum of twenty shillings for his admittance into the hands of Mr Harvey for certain purposes. This is the cheif of what has yet transpired, but am told there is a great number of other articles. If I get further intelligence it shall be at your service. I am in haste, Sir,

Your most obedient humble servant,
William Cramlington

138. E[dward] M[osley] to Mr Recorder, 28 August 1768 [TWA 394/29]

Dear Sir,

I have enclosed copies of what has passed concerning Welch[1] as also what is hatching between Harvey and the keelmen for your speculation. I do apprehend they mean not to be bound any more to their several Works nor be under the direction of the fitters' men as usual. They are remarkably secrett and nothing transpires they can help. I keep a watchfull eye over them, keep them up to their duty, and don't suffer the least imposition neither upon us, nor amongst themselves, which am sure the considerate part amongst them are very sensible of...[*requests return of the papers when finished with*].

I am &c, E.M.

[1] It is not known to what this refers.

139. Affidavit concerning stoppage of a keel on 5 September 1768 [TWA 394/29]

I, John Hymers of Stella in the County of Durham, Keelman and Skipper in the employment of Matthew Waters Esqr, make information on oath that on the 5th day of September last my men and me (when on our passage to Newcastle with our keel loaded with coals)

were forceably stopped, boarded and detained above the space of half an hour in that part of the River Tyne opposite Whitefield Staith by John Wilkinson, Archbald Ellison, John Buttler, William Crooks, John Olliver, senior, John Olliver, junior, Anthony Minican and John Watson, Keelmen in the employment of George Silvertop Esqr, and that they there examined the marks of my keel on both ends and sides, and the wind blowing then high, they removed her out of the due course of the River into a more still corner or creek where they examined her a second time, when all in the said keel, notwithstanding such additional weight and the movement of the keel and water, which rendered the ascertaining the just quantity of coals in her an impossibility, yet they all declared her to be too much measure, and one of them threatened to throw one of my men overboard for the same, and all of them swore that they would inform Mr Harvey of us and we should be fined for breaking through his Bond, and further that they would at all times watch mine and the other keels belonging to the said Matthew Waters Esqr., and if they could find the least hold on any of us we should be punished by themselves as well as by Mr Harvey, with many other threatening words of the like nature; and notwithstanding, I verily believe my keel was not more than her just measure at that time. I have ever since been affraid of being detained by some of them in like manner, and would on that account rather go from the staith with too little than too much measure at any time when the roughness of the water prevents a certainty.

John Hymers [mark]

Newcastle, 14 October 1768
Sworn before me, Edward Mosley

140. Note concerning the above incident [TWA 394/29]

Monday 5 September 1768, Mr Thomas Yellowley, agent or servant to Matthew Waters, Esqr acquainted Mr Mosley that a keel was stopped of his master's by Mr Silvertop's keelmen on the River Tyne under pretence of having on board too much measure, and a stick was produced marked of how much over measure, which stick they carried or sent to Mr Harvey and ordered the men not to cast, for that they would make them pay the fine. Upon application to the Collector of His Majesty's Customs, he with one Mr Armstrong and Mr Summers, two Custom House Officers, went and examined the said keel and found her to be no more than proper measure.

141. Copy letter Thomas Harvey to John Baker, Mayor, 23 November 1768, responding to the news that the magistrates and fitters had decided to prepare heads of a bill to establish a Charity for the keelmen [TWA 394/29]

Sir,

There was a meeting of the representatives of the keelmen on 21st Instant when I communicated the contents of your two letters. I am desired to return you thanks in their name for the intelligence of their masters' intention to prepare Heads of a Bill. None of them were acquainted with the services their masters have premeditated on this account. They flatter themselves the resolutions taken by the keelmen of establishing and collecting a fund &c in the manner I before mentioned will not frustrate nor abate the good intentions of their masters towards them, but be esteemed essentially necessary previous to a parliamentary sanction being obtained, because a fund will be increasing in the time of preparation and application for a Bill. Satisfied of this, they proceeded on the buissiness they mett upon, and in order to oblige every keelman to contribute his part, it was unanimously resolved that if any keelman shall bind himself in any contract between his master and him without the two covenants I mentioned being inserted, each keelman is liable to pay a considerable sum of money; and they propose this resolution shall take place at the next binding of the keelmen, presuming, from what you have been pleased to communicate, the above resolutions will meet with your patronage and of their masters in general.

I am your humble and obedient servant,

Thomas Harvey

The two covenants above mentioned are:

1st A covenant that the keelmen will permitt their masters to deduct one half penny for every chalder of coals waterborn in keels from their wages to raise a fund &c.

2nd A covenant from their masters to pay that money from time to time to such person as the keelmen shall apppoint.

N.B. The keelmen are not to bind before their respective representatives are bound without incurring a penalty. (Copy taken from a board put up in Sandgate, 9 December 1768.)

142. Thomas Harvey to the Keelmen, 27 December 1768 [TWA 394/29]

You had an undoubted right to make terms with your several masters at your binding in order for the re-establishing of your

Hospital and a fund &c, but since your masters have, contrary to all expectation, shewn themselves so averse to collecting the halfpenny a chalder, and that many keelmen have submitted to bind themselves under the old terms, I think it would be very hard upon the rest of the keelmen, although a great many, to sustain a total loss of their employments for the sake of such undeserving men as have not understanding nor integrity to know and act for the good of themselves and families. Therefore I recommend an observation of peaceable good behaviour among all, and that no disturbance nor riots may arise to the prejudice of yourselves nor coal trade, and that every keelman shall bind himself to such Fitter and in such manner as he pleases without regard to the two covenants heretofore requested to be inserted in the bonds, and after binding is finished, that the two representatives may take down and deliver to me the names of all such persons as intend to become members of the Hospital and to contribute thereto.

I am your Friend and Servant, Thomas Harvey

Ask your masters to promise you to retain the halfpenny a chalder in their hands for 2 or 3 months until I can get a Deed of Settlement prepared to appoint other persons, but, if they refuse, pay no regard to such refusal. T.H.

143. Copy Edward Mosley to Matthew Ridley (MP Newcastle 1747–74), 4 January [1769] [TWA 394/29]

Dear Sir,

Nothing but the setling my annual affairs as usual on 31 December would have prevented me answering the honour of your last of 27th [December] sooner.

I did imagine you had been apprized of the two articles required by the keelmen at their binding, viz. to retain halfpenny [per chalder] from their wages and to pay the same to whom they should appoint, but I find that you was only told the first, and yet, if that had taken place without Act of Parliament, the keelmen upon any future pretended stop might take it into their heads to demand the money to answer a bad purpose, and who in that case could refuse the delivering up the part of [their] wages detained in our hands, or the Hostmen's Company either, without a parliamentary sanction. The moment Harvey gave leave for the keelmen to bind, I sent a copy of his letter to Sir Walter Blackett[1] for your speculations, from which you will see how much they are under his directions, and so much power in such a hand may be attended with difficulty to the trade, and some time or other [with] very bad consequences. As to my part, I tould our men, when they begged and prayed to be bound and taken into favour again, that I never would consent to any proposition whatsoever that came from Harvey, that they ought to have confidence in their masters who were much better known than the stranger they confided in, and who, from his present unfortunate circumstances, might be tempted to make them believe he could do great things for them when at the same time he could do them no service;[2] that if they meant we should apply to Parliament, it must come from themselves at their own earnest request, in which case it would be properly gone upon and not otherwise entered upon….

Should not the Mayor for the time being be joined with the Governor and Stewards of the Hostmen's Company &c, and a skipper out of each work, to examine the accounts and certify their approbation, or, on second thought, perhaps he had better not, because in case of differences he may then be consulted.

I have the pleasure to write you the keels are all at work, and the men in appearance seem to be very well satisfied, but they are very artfull and must be watched. Now and then when they are in their cupps am told they cry out 'Harvey and Liberty' and let drop some more unwarrantable expressions. However, as nothing is required of them but their duty to perform, shall take care to have it complied with, and as I presume no body will desire any favour or anything from them but what is right, I think there can be no great difficulty in managing them, nor can there be any thing to fear from what they pretend to do in any of their ungarded expressions. A committee of five trading brethren, amongst whom Mr Waters is one, are appointed to consider and draw up, with Mr Fawcett's advice,[3] the heads of such a Bill as you and Sir Walter will take the trouble to apply for, after being approved of by the keelmen themselves.

I hope there is no fear of Sir Matthew's succeeding against Ayre.[4] I should be very sorry of a chance of his so doing. However, be it as it may, Sir Matthew has acquitted himself with so much credit as must turn out much to his honour and reputation; he has our good wishes, and am, with the compliments of the season to your good family,

Your obedient obliged servant,
E.M.

[1] Blackett was MP for Newcastle 1734–77.

[2] There is no further mention of Harvey's 'unfortunate circumstances'. Perhaps he was in financial difficulties. Mosley showed the Justices of Assize some minutes he had written about recent events, and 'the Honourable Justice Gold [? Sir

Charles Gould, 1726–1806] said that Harvey seemed to be an artful and dangerous person, or words to that purpose' (TWA 394/29).

[3] Christopher Fawcett was Recorder of Newcastle, 1746–53, 1769–94.

[4] This refers to the petition of Francis Eyre against Sir Matthew White Ridley, who had been returned in the Morpeth election of 1768, see Joseph Fewster, ed., *Morpeth Electoral Correspondence 1766-1776*, Surtees Society, 221, pp. 137–48.

144. The unanimous Resolution of the Keelmen of Newcastle upon Tyne on the Heads of a Bill proposed to them by their Masters [*endorsed* 23 January 1769] [TWA 394/29]

The Keelmen having agreed to a Deed of Settlement (which they intend to have established by an Act of Parliament) for a future provision &c more agreeable to themselves and better calculated for the speedy and impartial relief of their brethren and under all circumstances than the proposed Heads, they do therefore decline giving any assent to the proposed Heads being made a publick Act.[1]

[1] No copy of the 'heads' has been found, but the following, suggested by Mosley, may indicate their contents: 'Minutes offered for consideration on forming an Act of Parliament for relief of the keelmen &c.' A general Court of at least 32 governors of whom the Mayor, Recorder, Sheriff of Newcastle, the Governor and Stewards of the Hostmen's Company, the Governor and 2 senior Wardens of the Merchants' Company and the Master of Trinity House to be ten. If desired a skipper to be appointed out of each Fitter's Work to elect a fourth part of the Governors with qualifications of £500 personal estate. The keelmen may recommend servants and officers, subject to the approval of a general Court, with salaries not exceeding…. The keelmen may appoint committees to audit accounts. To consider whether the collection to be general upon keels or upon such as only lay coals on ships. The Governors to be empowered to lay out money to establish a workhouse &c and employ the poor therein, and have power to reduce the collection of 4d. per keel, or suspend the payment altogether if necessary (TWA 394/30).

145. The Keelmen's Resolutions as sent to Mr Hedley by Mr Harvey, 5 January 1770 [TWA 394/29]

The answer of the trading brethren of Hoastmen of Newcastle upon Tyne, dated the 20th December last, having been attentively considered by the Governors of the Keelmen's Society at a general meeting, it was resolved and agreed that the answer to the Keelmen's petition and Deed of Settlement, containing a disapproving thereof in general terms and no reason assigned or particular objections made to any article therein, which the Keelmen hoped would have been done in order that the premises or any part might, if necessary and agreed to on further consideration, be altered, amended, or explained by an Act for that purpose, and that the future quiet and relief of the Keelmen in the premisses, so much sought after and required, is not treated by the Hoastmen in their answer with that respect and attention due to such useful and laborious men as the nature of their case deserves, and some of the persons concerned in the vend of coals have used many endeavours to prevent or discountenance the said Keelmen's payments and contributions towards the support of their said Society, and others have discovered th greatest aversion thereto and have informed the collectors in their employments to desist or quit their service.

In regard to the repeated offer of their masters to obtain such an Act for the Keelmen as was proposed to them last year, it was resolved and agreed the several articles following be communicated to the Hoastmen for reasons against committing the absolute superintendancy conduct and management of their contributions to the Hoastmen as designed by the heads of a Bill:

1st The Keelmen had approved the draft of their Deed of Settlement before the said heads of a Bill were presented to them by their masters.

2nd Although the said heads had been a long time in meditation without any previous consultation with any of the Keelmen thereupon, when the said heads were delivered for the Keelmen's approbation, no more than one printed copy of the said heads was delivered amongst the men in each fitter's Work, but an answer was required in so weighty a matter within 24 hours.

3rd The Keelmen returned an answer to the said heads, within the limited time, that they had agreed to the said Deed of Settlemen which they looked upon more agreeable to themselves, and bette calculated for the speedy and impartial relief of their brethren unde all circumstances than the proposed heads, but would have beer very willing at that time to have shown their particular reasons fo refusing their assent to the said heads being made a publick Act it time had permitted, and are willing to show many other objections to the said heads of a Bill than are herein set down, if they were requested or heard.

4th The Keelmen reflecting on the misapplication and suppression of former contributions towards the relief of Keelmen &c under the directions and management of former masters, and numberless instances of distress many of the Keelmen and their families have undergone without relief since the said suppression, and also in later times for want of the same publick relief being administered to them in their necessities as they were intitled to by the Laws of the Poor in common with others in like cases.

5th The many overtures which from time to time have been made to re-establish a future provision for poor Keelmen, their wives and children, in their necessitys and especially their late attempts – dutiful and humble requests made to their masters in this behalf which were either slighted or rejected.

6th The many oppressions Keelmen have long endured respecting over Measure conveyed by them in keels contrary to their articles under their masters' contrivance or connivance, and when they have humbly represented their grievances and used lawfull means for obtaining redress, many of them have been long imprisoned or turned out of bread with infamous characters before the expiration of their respective contracts, and the mildest ways used for subduing the Keelmen to passive obedience in respect of the said over Measure were frequent threats of turning them out of their respective employments.

Lastly, when the said oppressions became general or intolerable and the Keelmen unanimously resolved to be relieved or desist from carrying such over Measure (which was lawful for them to do), armed soldiers have been drawn up and marched against them, and several Keelmen have been killed or wounded by the military, contrary to the laws of this Kingdom, under the pretence of quelling a riot when no riot was intended nor effected by keelmen.

Received 5 January 1770 in the evening, John Hedley

146. Rough Note by Mosley [TWA 394/30]

Committee of trading fitters mett and gave notice to Mr Harvey that they were ready to meet the keelmen and appointed a day for that purpose, but neither they nor Mr Harvey appeared. However, they adjourned to a day in the following week to as little purpose. That Mr Mosley had the thanks of his keelmen for his readyness to serve them and that the heads of a Bill which was offered them would do very well, as far as they could judge of, but was not at liberty to accept of it on account of their engagement with Mr Harvey. That his men made no complaints whatever, and [he] never discouraged or interfered with them from making collections, nor never desired them to carry more than Statute Measure. That he has known and been in the Trade between 20 and 30 years and does not know of any armed soldiers being drawn up against them on account of a riot but that many …. [*rest missing*]

147. Thomas Harvey to John Hedley, Steward of the Fraternity of Hoastmen, 5 January 1770 [TWA 394/29]

Sir,

At a meeting of the Governors of the Keelmen Society the 4th of this instant January, amongst other orders and resolutions the inclosed were made, and the Petition before laid before the Keelmen's Masters has been since altered, setled and agreed to be presented as in the copy also inclosed which I present to you to be communicated to the Fraternity of Hoastmen by order of the Governors of the Keelmen Society and am, Sir,

Your humble and obedient Servant

Thomas Harvey

148. Draft petition of the Keelmen to the House of Commons
[*Endorsed*: **5 January 1770...delivered to Mr Hedly by Mr Harvey**]
[TWA 394/29]

To the Honorable the Commons of Great Britain in Parliament Assembled

The humble petition of A., B., C., D., E., F., and others whose names are hereunto subscribed being Skippers and Keelmen employed by Hoastmen or Fitters of Newcastle upon Tyne, and also Skippers and Castors employed by Fitters of Sunderland in the County Palatine of Durham, in working, navigating, unloading or delivering keels upon the Rivers Tyne and Weare on behalf of themselves and other Skippers, Keelmen and Castors so employed there,

Sheweth

That several Statutes have heretofore been made for the better maintenance of keels and keel boats in Newcastle upon Tyne and the members thereof for remedying of certain deceits, frauds and abuses to the diminution of His Majesty's Customs and to the prejudice of the buyers and sellers of coals, and particularly by a Statute made in the 6th and 7th years of the reign of his late Majesty King William the 3d it was amongst other things enacted that Commissioners should be from time to time appointed by His Majesty, his heirs and successors, for the admeasuring and marking of all keels, pan keels, pan boats and other boats and wains and carts used for the carriage of coals in Newcastle upon Tyne and the members thereof therein particularly mentioned, and that such admeasurement should be made by a dead weight of lead or iron, or otherwise as to the said Commissioners should seem meet, allowing three and fifty hundred weight to every chaldron of coals, provided that no such keel should be admeasured, marked or nailed to carry more than 10 such chaldrons at any one time.

That several regulations have for many years past and till lately been observed for the benefit of the coal trade whereby the full measure or loading of keels in the said Port of Newcastle upon Tyne and the members thereof was limited to 8 such chaldron to the keel and no more, and the rates and dues of Skippers, Keelmen and Castors have been adjusted and paid accordingly, and the same order hath for some time likewise been observed with respect to lead, stones, ballast, chalk, ashes, manure and rubbish loaded and carried in keels navigated by the said Keelmen.

That several abuses and impositions have for some time past been practiced by a greater measure having been put upon your Petitioners than is warranted by the said regulation, not only tending to the diminution of His Majesty's Customs and other duties governed by the said measure, but more especially to the great loss of your Petitioners who, notwithstanding such overmeasure, are paid after the rate of 8 chaldrons by the keel only.

That the Keelmen employed in navigating keels upon the said River Tyne being very numerous and obliged to reside in some few places near the said River and have, together with their wives and children, in cases of distress arising from sickness, age and other causes, been truly miserable for want of parochial or publick relief, and especially as to such of them as were natives of Scotland, have lately instituted a Society for the purpose of relieving poor indigent Keelmen, their wives and children, by or out of a fund to be raised from time to time by the several members thereof by stoppages out of their respective weekly wages.

But in regard such stoppages cannot be effectually made except the several Hoastmen and Fitters of Newcastle upon Tyne are armed with a proper authority for that purpose. And in regard it would tend greatly to the quiet and relief of your Petitioners in the premisses to have the measure of coals and ballast &c restrained to 8 chaldron to each keel after the rate aforesaid, and to have the said Society established and extended, as those salutary purposes cannot be effectually obtained without the aid of Parliament, your Petitioners humbly pray for relief in the premisses, and that they may be at liberty to bring in a Bill for the several purposes aforesaid.

And your Petitioners &c

149. Printed Notice, Newcastle upon Tyne, 8 January 1770 [TWA 394/31]

Notice is given that the Keelmen's Petition intended to be presented to Parliament is ready for signing by the parties, and attendance will be given for that purpose 15th, 16th and 17th days of this instant January at Mr Heaton's in the Old Custom-house Entry; and 18th, 19th and 20th days of this instant January at Mr Erwins's, the King's Head in the Low Street Sunderland. [*Copy of the petition follows, as above*, **Document 149.**]

150. Harvey to Hedley, 8 January 1770 [TWA 349/29]

Sir,

If I had been cal[le]d on to shew objections on behalf of the Keelmen to the Heads of a Bill delivered to them last year, I should [have] wait[ed] on the Gentlemen and acquaint them of many objections the Keelmen then had, and I understand still have, to the said Heads being made into a publick Act. I shall communicate your letter to me, dated this day, to such of the Governors of the Keelmen Society as shall attend at the next weekly meeting, but cannot undertake to communicate the contents thereof to the Keelmen in general.

I am, Sir,

Your humble and obedient Servant,

Thomas Harvey

151. Committee of Hoastmen's Resolutions for Mr Mosley to Transact, 6 February 1770 [TWA 394/29]

Mr Mosley, having at the request of the committee, consented to go to London on behalf of the Trading Brethren of the Hoastmen's Company to attend the Keelmen's present application to Parliament, the committee are come to the following resolutions:

1. Resolved that it is the opinion of this committee that a proper Act of Parliament for the relief and support of the Skippers and Keelmen employed in the River Tyne who by sickness or other accidental misfortunes, or by old age, shall not be able to maintain themselves and their families, and for the relief of the widows and children of such Skippers and Keelmen, would be a usefull and desirable object.

2. Resolved that the Keelmen's present application to Parliament to confirm their Deed of Settlement, so far as has come within the knowledge of this committee, is not a proper method of obtaining so usefull and desirable an object, but, on the contrary, would be very

inconvenient to the Trading Brethren and of dangerous consequences to the public.

3. Resolved that the said Edward Mosley Esqr be instructed, and he is hereby instructed, to give his assistance towards obtaining a proper Bill for the relief of Keelmen as mentioned in the first resolution.

4. Resolved that, if such a proper Bill cannot be obtained, that he do oppose the Keelmen's present application to Parliament to carry their Deed of Settlement into a Law.

152. 'Memorandums for Mr Mosley' [TWA 394/30]

To know from Mr Harvey if any and what deed, agreement or covenant is entered into by the several Keelmen on the River Tyne in order to compel the payment of a certain sum, and how much to him for every new keelman that enters into the service of any fitter in Newcastle, and, in case such new keelman refuses to pay such a sum, if the keelmen now employed on the said River are not bound by such deed or covenant not to allow such person or persons to work in their respective keels, and if any such deed tells[?] in whose hands the same is in, and to compell the same to be produced.

Mr Harvey to be called upon to know what deed or writing obligation or covenant any of the keelmen have executed to him, and particularly what writing William Nimmy hath executed to him for what consideration, and to be compelled if possible to produce same.

William Nimmy and Archibald Cram as well as all other keelmen to be discharged from all deeds, covenants, bonds &c that they may have entered into with Mr Harvey, and particularly Nimmy and Cram who are now under prosecutions at Mr Harvey's suit. Mr Harvey to discontinue those and all other prosecutions and pay costs thereof.

If the [House of Commons] committee have powers to compell the producing of deeds &c executed by keelmen, and that matter ought to be the first step to be taken if possible, and the keelmen ought likewise if possible to be discharged therefrom, as such deeds are highly injurious to the coal trade.

153. Notes by Mosley concerning Harvey's action against some keelmen [TWA 394/29]

Mr Mosley had delivered to him by Alexander Williamson, keelman, the notice as follows:

Take notice that information upon the oath of 3 persons is made that you John Turner and Andrew Galloway have each of you incurred the payment of 5s. 0d. apiece for loading your keel on the 30 instant August [1768] with coal at South Moor Staith an inch over the plate at the head and a quarter of an inch over the plate at the stern, and for navigating the said keel loaded as aforesaid, and unless you and each of you pay the said 5s. 0d. within 14 days after the delivery hereof you will be sued for the same'. Dated 31 August 1768. Signed Thomas Harvey. Directed to Alexander Williamson, skipper in the employment of Edward Mosley.

N.B. The said parties made oath, 1 September 1768, that the above keel was only loaded to her marks (to wit) half plate at the head and meeting the underside of the nail at the stern and no deeper, and on Mr Mosley's requesting them not to pay or give any attention to Mr Harvey's notice, they promised so to do.

Isabella Galloway told Mr Mosley that upon her fears of her son Andrew Galloway coming to some mischief from the threatenings of the keelmen if he did not comply with Harvey's demands for pretence of taking in over much measure, she went to Harvey, 22 September 1768, and asked what they were upon, which he gave in figures as viz:

William Williamson, skipper, and 2 others 15s. 0d.; Oaths &c, 4s. 4d.; Capias, 4s. 6d.

Total, £1. 3s. 10d.

Saturday 24 September, she went to Harvey – said she would pay if he would run it to no more charge when the men came home. Told him the Mayor had forbid her to pay anything to which he replied she might do as she pleased, but if she did not pay he would send for a London writ. Williamson and John Turner also went to Harvey on Saturday and asked why he took the above money. He replied that if it was not paid on Monday against 12 o'Clock it would be more. That on 25 September the money was paid by the under copy of account: Alexander Williamson, John Turner, Andrew Galloway, 3 fines 15s. 0d.; Information and notice, 0s. 44d.; Capias, 0s. 46d.

Total: £1. 3s. 10d. Received 25 September 1768 the above contents, Thomas Harvey.

Isabella Galloway and Alexander Williamson's informations upon oath more particularly related of the above affair.

154. Copy Mosley to the secretary of the [Hostmen's] Committee [TWA 394/30]

London 14 February 1770

Dear Sir,

This day I attended the Committee on Mr Harvey's petition which was tottaly imployed upon the Sunderland enquiry and was very ill supported for want of evidence. He alluded to persons whose names he could not recollect, which if he would please to have found out was offered the Chairman's warrant to bring them up.[1] The matter will be reported to the House and leave desired to sit again, which will be on Friday at 12 o'Clock in order to proceed upon the Newcastle affaire, and for which I hope I am sufficiently prepared, but still I would have every eclarisement the Gentlemen of the Trade can recollect, and whose orders they may be sure will be punctually observed. Sir Walter Blackett was in the chaire and a large committee present. Mr Waters desires his best compliments to the gentlemen of the committee at Newcastle, and am &c, E.M.

[1] Harvey had attempted to obtain support of the keelmen on the River Wear to limitation of the keel-load to eight chaldrons. Emissaries were sent to Sunderland to obtain signatures to the petition, without success, but a note was inserted at the bottom of the petition stating that it was 'at the particular request, and for and on behalf of upwards of four hundred skippers and castors employed upon the River Wear, who durst not, but with the greatest hazard of their respective employments under their masters the Fitters at Sunderland, be seen or known to subscribe their respective names'. Harvey was closely questioned but declined to name individuals and failed to substantiate the authenticity of the note. Moreover, the skippers and castors of Sunderland had sent a petition disassociating themselves from the intended Newcastle charity which, they alleged, would load them with an unnecessary charge for the relief of others 'with whom they have, nor desire to have, any connection'. The committee concluded that the note on the Newcastle petition was ill-founded and that such misrepresentation in a petition to Parliament was a dangerous practice and ought to be discouraged, *Journals of the House of Commons*, 32, pp. 709, 774–5.

155. Mosley to the Gentlemen of the [Hostmen's] Committee
[TWA 394/30]

London, 16 February 1770

I am sorry to write you that Mr Harvey by his extraordinary windings have got the Committee to range in other order the allegations of his Sunderland hearsay evidence, by which we have lost this day's proceedings upon the Newcastle part of the petition, and the report of what is past will not be made to the House till Monday next. Am much affraid of a long stay here, and really for the convenience of our attendance at this end of the Town with our lodgings and the good company we must consequently keep makes it very expensive, of which I assure you shall be glad to have an end of. Tomorrow shall have leave to spend in my own way in the City where I have not yet seen one of my friends. My good friend Mr Waters joyns in best compliments.

Edward Mosley

156. Mosley's notes of Evidence to be given to the House of Commons Committee includes the following comments on the keelmen [TWA 394/29]

It is the custom to bind keelmen to their work for one year, as likewise to retain servants to look after them and see they take in their measure of coals at the warfs, and, after so taken in, to order the same on board their respective ships. They are a set of men by no means to be trusted, and without someone to look after them they will never, or rarely, take in the Statute or King's measure of 53cwt to the Newcastle chaldron, which they are bound to do by their bond to their masters, and that without being well looked after, frequently imbezel and dispose of coals in their way down to Shields....

The keelmen say they will not be bound for the future, neither will they be directed by the Fitters' men what to do – that the steathmen shall put the keels of[f] when they are loaded and that they will have no more to do with Fitters' servants. Fitters – those who take the coals of the owners and provide ships to put them on board, of whose servants' business is only to see they get their measure and order them to the ships &c, and as Mr Harvey has now such an assendance over the whole body of keelmen, which is very considerable, and apprehend with the least intimation can make them do what he please, think it too much power to be trusted with him, and as the tendency of their several meetings to sign parchments the public knows not the contents of, apprehend it may be attended with dangerous consequences hereafter – as such may not Harvey be compelled to produce them? If any good meant why are not the magistrates consulted who are acknowledged even by [the keelmen] themselves to be always ready to redress their grievances.[1]

---

[1] The proceedings before the committee are recorded in *Journals of the House of Commons*, 32, 774–9. Mosley's notes in TWA 394/29 include some evidence that was not reported in the *Journals*. His claim that the magistrates were always ready to redress the keelmen's grievances is not borne out by the evidence given to the committee.

157. Copy Mosley to the secretary of the Hostmen's committee [TWA 394/29]

London, 6 March 1770

Dear Sir,

I have only time to acquaint you that I have just come at Mr Harvey's Bill[1] which has been shewn to some gentlemen of the Committee for their consideration before it is produced to the House, which suppose, if offered at all, may be on Thursday or Friday first, of which you have herewith for your remarks thereon, which desire may be transmitted as soon as possible. However, if it should be presented before your further directions come to hand, shall certainly oppose it in all its circumstances, as beleiving it agreeible to your designes. The allegations against the [Keelmen's] petition have not yet been presented, and which must be made to the House before the Bill is admitted, and are such as I apprehend will be sufficient to defeat Mr Harvey's designs. Mr Waters joyns in best compliments to the gentlemen of the Committee, and am, Sir,

Your odedient and very humble Servant,

E.M.

[1] Harvey's proposed Bill sought to establish a Society, governed by the keelmen themselves, and a fund for the relief of indigent keelmen and their dependents. It also sought to deal with the problem of overmeasure. Money collected under the original deed of settlement was to be transferred to a new fund, and the deed declared void. The keelmen were to contribute a halfpenny for each chaldron they transported. The fitters were to deduct this amount from their men's wages, and were to keep a muster roll showing the numbers of keels and keelmen, and the number of tides worked. They were to be liable to examination before the mayor and two aldermen in respect of the money collected, and any sums concealed, embezzled or misapplied were to be levied by distress. Refusal to appear or be examined would incur a fine of £10. The keelmen governors were to be empowered to sue and might themselves be sued. No keel was to be loaded beyond eight chaldrons at a time, allowing 53 hundredweights, King's measure, to each chaldron, and both the employer and the crew of any overloaded keel were to be fined and the proceeds applied to the Charity (TWA 394/29).

158. John French, Clerk of the Hostmen's Company, to Mosley, 9 March 1770 [TWA 394/30]

Sir,

At a meeting of a considerable number of the trading brethren of the Hoastmen this day I was ordered to acquaint you they unanimously approve of every step you have hitherto taken relating the affair of keelmen. The copy of Mr Harvey's intended Bill received from you has been layed before the gentlemen of the Trade and is objected to by them as a Bill by no means calculated to answer the purposes that were intended by them, but quite the contrary, and therefore desire that the whole of that Bill, if offered to the House, may be opposed in every particular, it appearing to them that the same, as it now stands, invests a power in the hands of a sett of people who ought not by any means to be trusted. The Bill will be layed before Mr Fawcett, together with the observations that have been made thereon, after which such objections (which are many) as to particular parts thereof will be forwarded to you as soon as possible; in the mean time, the Gentlemen desire you will send down a draft of a proper petition against the Bill to be signed here upon the Bill being carried into the House.

I am, Sir, Your most obedient Servant,
J. French

159. French to Lord Ravensworth, 12 March 1770 [TWA 394/30]

Sir,

I'm ordered to acquaint you that, in consequence of your and Mr Water's letters of the 8th Instant, the Keelmen have been called together by their several employers and informed that it is impossible to obtain a Bill upon their own plan, but in case they choose to have such a Bill as Parliament thinks proper, that all endeavours should be used for that purpose upon a plan of placing the direction in the hands of gentlemen who will see their Charity properly administered; to which they have all given for answer that they will abide by Mr Harvey and the plan proposed by him and no other. Mr Hedley's men were more particular in their answer and told him they had signed a petition last week which was as good as if they had given their oaths, and they will abide by Mr Harvey. What they could mean by saying it was as good as their oaths I know not, but suppose it was a petition which I hear is, or soon will be, forwarded to Mr Harvey. As it seems to be their determined resolution not to come into any measure or plan but what comes from Harvey, I'm therefore again ordered by the gentlemen here to desire that every possible opposition may be made to Mr Harvey's Bill.

I am, Sir, your most obedient Servant,
J. French

160. J. Airey to Mosley, 20 March 1770 [TWA 394/29]

Dear Sir,

I have just received your favour of the 17th and enclosed you have the [keelmen's] bonds. It is there 'King's Measure', or such as shall be ordered or directed. I fancy 'King's Measure' alone is not generally mentioned in the bonds, some no mention of the measure, as there was a Statute properly limitting the quantity for that purpose and the keels marked accordingly....

We begin the *Euston* tomorrow. This easterly wind and snow has allmost stopped all trade here for this ten days; a great number of ships load in the harbour. I have seen four of the Keelmen's bonds and they are all different. We have not got either of the small ships for France nor any new orders.

I am, Dear Sir, your much obliged and most humble Servant,

J. Airey

161. Airey to Mosley, 24 March 1770 [TWA 394/29]

Dear Sir,

Your favours of the 20 and 21 I duly received and accordingly communicated to the Committee such parts as related OM [over-measure?]. We had a meeting this morning with the Coalowners to consider what steps was necessary in case Mr Fuller went forward with his amendment to the 7th of William [III], at which meeting we got our letters, and was all very glad to hear Harvey had dropped his Bill and that Mr Fuller did not mean to propose his this sessions,[1] and all agreed that no Bill [is] much better than one disagreeable to the Keelmen. I sincerely congratulate you and Mr Waters of an end of what I should think a troublesome disagreeble service, and hope now it will not be long before we have the pleasure of seeing you. The proposed Bill for the coal heavers as mentioned by Mr Ward may do very well as the trade will be at liberty. The Undertakers we have nothing to do with. The men I fancy have been oppressed by them.

Bad tides and worse weather has allmost prevented anything been done. *Euston* only just begun. Some small ships have got away and expect others will go this tide, but no great ships, I am affraid.... Nothing from France nor any ships got down for some time, so that every body is allmost done.

I am, Dear Sir,
Your much obliged and most humble Servant,
J. Airey

[1] Evidently realising that his Bill had no chance of success, Harvey abandoned it and joined with Rose Fuller, MP for Rye, a landowner and iron-master in Sussex, who proposed to introduce a Bill dealing solely with overmeasure by amending the Act 6 & 7 William III regulating the admeasurement of keels. In a letter of 23 March 1770 (mostly about other things), Mosley declared: 'Harvey's matter seems to be over and believe he will not present his Bill..., so that Mr Waters and I shall get away the latter end of next week' (TWA 394/29).

162. Copy Mosley to Airey [TWA 394/29]

London, 27 March 1770

Dear Sir,

Your favours of 20 and 24th came duely to hand….I waited upon Mr Fuller this morning who still seems determined to bring in his Bill. I find Harvey was with him yesterday and hangs much about him, and if more matterial buissiness did not put him of[f], he said he would move for his Bill today, which if he does, don't apprehend he will succeed. Suppose it may lay upon the table for the consideration of the gentlemen in the cuntrey and perhaps taken up again afterwards, but I hope and rather think it will cease hear, though one cannot say, nor can one account for an old man's possitive humour, who has been used to a Westindian imperious life, where he was Governor for 20 years, and the assumption of which power seems not to have left him.[1]

We mean to set forward on return home on Monday 2nd July, if attending on Harvey's motions don't stop us. I shall call upon Mr Lund at York which will take us a little out of our way, but you will hear from us again. In the meantime we are with our best compliments to the gentlemen of the Committee, &c, E.M

[1] Fuller had been a member of the Council in Jamaica, where he possessed extensive estates and had held high judicial office there, but he had not been Governor of the island. Namier and Brooke, *The House of Commons, 1754-1790*, II, pp. 477–80.

163. Copy Mosley to Airey [TWA 394/29]

London 29 March 1770

Dear Sir,

I wrote on the 27th to which refer. Yesterday Mr Fuller made motion for his Bill which was seconded by Mr Mackworth,[1] a gentleman I understand to be under the influence of Lady Windsor, and who, as well as Mr Fuller, are in the interest of Mr Harvey. It was much pressed by Mr Ridley[2] and Sir Thomas Clavering[3] to have the Bill waved or at least put of[f] till it was well considered by the gentlemen in the North, but Mr Fuller will have no consideration and says he knows all about it and will have it finished this sessions, if there is time. He has deceived us, and what Mr Waters and I wrote to Newcastle would make us, I think, appear very little, if it had not been under Mr Fuller's own authority, who told us expressly that he would not hasten the Bill, but that every body concerned should have time to consider and make their objections. In consequence of his motion, he with some gentlemen named are ordered to bring it in.

This unexpected deception of course retards our return. The

difficulties naturally arising, though Harvey makes all smooth way to Mr Fuller and Mackworth, will make it impossible to be dispenced with, and therefore if not checked now, suppose must be petitioned against afterwards, but that will be better judged of when Mr Fuller is pleased to produce his Bill about the measure, which as soon as we can come at shall send you. I don't know whether Mr Waters writes tonight or not; however, I thought right to send you the above, and was with joyning his compliments to the gentlemen of the Committee, am &c

Edward Mosley

[P.S.] What makes me write in this partial manner is that everything in my evidence that materially affected Harvey was struck out of the Report by Fuller's doeings in order, as he said, that he, Harvey, might appear fair to the House, and Harvey's own evidence was allowed to be altered and framed as he pleased himself.

[1] Herbert Mackworth, MP Cardiff Boroughs, had interests in copper and coal and often spoke in the Commons on a wide range of subjects (Namier and Brooke, *The House of Commons, 1754-1790*, III, p. 91).
[2] Matthew Ridley, MP Newcastle, 1747–74.
[3] Sir Thomas Clavering, MP County Durham, 1768–90.

164. Copy Mosley to Airey, 31 March 1770 [TWA 394/29]

Dear Sir,

Nothing more yet about Mr Fuller not having communicated his Bill to the gentlemen who are ordered to carry it in, so that we must have the further mortification of staying here upon a disagreeable uncertainty….and am &c, E.M.

165. Airey to Mosley, 1 April 1770 [TWA 394/29]

Dear Sir,

Your favours of 27 and 29 past came in course but was much surprised at the latter. This Mr Fuller has behaved very ungenteely and much unlike a gentleman. Your letter which was communicated, as also Mr Water's letter of same date, to the Committee this evening, when extracts was ordered to be sent to every coal owner that they may have a meeting and act accordingly. Nothing can be done till their intention is known, but, whatever is the alteration, I am affraid it will be attended with expence and inconvenience in this country.

The Grafton has got 9 keels of Team and will be load on Wednesday… We have not got a ship for either of the small French orders. I have not time to say more but we are all much disappointed at your longer stay. Mrs Mosley is well. I am, Dear Sir,

Your much obliged, &c,

J. Airey

166. Copy Mosley to Airey, 5 April 1770 [*written below the above*] [TWA 394/29]

Dear Sir,

I perceive by your favor of the 1st that you seem to be more alarmed with Mr Fuller's proceedings than is necessary, as it will be soon enough for the gentlemen of the Trade to stirr in it when the contents of his Bill is known, which [I] will certainly forward them as soon as it appears, and which by his declaration must [be expected immediately]...

167. Copy Mosley to Airey, 6 April 1770 [TWA 394/29]

Dear Sir,

Your favour of the 3rd is just come to hand. Mr Fuller had the gentlemen today who were named with him to bring in his Bill, who found him better disposed than they expected and prevailed on him to alter it a good deal, and that, upon the whole, no body is to be fined but the keelmen themselves who take in over measure,[1] and that Harvey is to have nothing to do in it but to be left intirely for the Justice[s] to settle. That the Bill is to be brought into the House and read on Monday, and then, after a 2nd reading, to be left on the table and printed for the full consideration of the gentlemen in the countrey, when suppose it will drop, and Fuller not trouble himself more about it.[2] [I] believe he now begins to find Harvey out and would have dropped it now but that he had swore he would have a Bill.

I have...taken 50 guineas more of Mr Thallasson which expect will bring me to Newcastle, which [I] hope to see against Easter Sunday, but shall write you, and am &c,

E.M.

---

[1] In Harvey's proposed Bill, both the employer and the crew of any overloaded keel were to be fined (See footnote to **Document 157** above).
[2] Mosley was right: the Bill did not proceed beyond its second reading.

THE KEELMEN JOIN IN GENERAL INDUSTRIAL UNREST OVER THE HIGH PRICE OF CORN BUT CONTINUE THEIR STRIKE ON ACCOUNT OF A THREAT TO THEIR EMPLOYMENT, 1771

168. Matthew Ridley to George Ward, 14 June 1771 [NA, ZRI 38/2, Matthew Ridley's Letter Book, 1767–77, p. 112]

Newcastle, 14 June 1771

I am favoured with your letter of the 10th, what [was] rumoured as to the Pitmen and Keelmen stopping took place on Tuesday last [11 June]. The Pitmen assembled in great numbers proceeding from colliery to colliery stopping all work at present at the collieries on the Wear; their outcry is the high price of corn, which I am affraid at this time cannot be corrected. I should hope that all persons concerned in the Trade would be of opinion to releave the necessities of the men as far as they have it in their power, if they behave peaceably and return to their work.

The keelmen complain of loading ships directly out of the waggons by spouts without making use of keels. This has been the practice from the beginning of the colliery at Chirton and Tinmouth Moor. I have just now erected a spout at Byker for small coasting ships, as the Trade has undoubtedly a claim to be excused the expence of keel hire when they can be better dispatched without, both in saving the coals from being so much broken and also dispatched. There is no saying how long this behaviour of the workmen may continue, so no doubt the ships at London will take the advantage.

169. Aubone Surtees (Mayor) to Lord Barrington, Secretary at War, 12 June 1771 [TWA 592/1, Newcastle Corporation Letter Book, f. 112 verso]

My Lord,

On Monday last the Keelmen employed on this River assembled together and refused to go to their work and still continue in that state, and this morning the Pitmen employed in the neighbouring collieries followed their example. I am under the strongest apprehensions that all the other Pitmen in this country will join them, and, being of opinion that military aid might become necessary for the safety of this Town and the adjoining counties on the present occasion, I applied to the Commanding Officer at Tynemouth, acquainting him with the same, who told me that he had no power to bring the troops from Tynemouth hither to make any stay. I therefore take the liberty of requesting your Lordship to send an order to the Commanding Officer to march the soldiers at

Tynemouth to this Town to remain here till the present disorders have subsided, the principal cause of which it seems is the high price of corn and other provisions.

I am, my Lord, your Lordship's most obedient and most humble Servant,

A.S.

170. Surtees to Barrington, 14 June 1771 [TWA 592/1, Newcastle Corporation Letter Book, ff. 112 verso–113]

My Lord,

Since my last letter to your Lordship, the pitmen of several more collieries in this neighbourhood have ceased working and have been going in bodies from place to place among the coal works collecting the pitmen from every colliery both here and on the River Wear, and laying off the work &c they have brought several of the Wear water pitmen here. Our keelmen are still lying off, and the keelmen on the River Wear have likewise left working.

Under these circumstances it is thought advisable to be prepared with a greater military aid for our safety than Tynemouth Barracks can at present supply. I am therefore further to beg that your Lordship will be pleased to give an order to the Commanding Officer of the horse troops at York to send two or three of his troops to this Town to be aiding and assisting the civil magistrates in preserving the public peace, and that your Lordship will be pleased either to order them hither immediately to be in readiness, or when the Mayor or magistrates of this place shall send a request to the Officer for them, as shall seem most proper to your Lordship. Perhaps their presence may be of use either as a preventive or on a sudden occasion.

I am, My Lord, your Lordship's most obedient and most humble Servant,

A.S., Mayor

171. Surtees to the Duke of Northumberland, 14 June 1771[1] [TWA 592/1, Newcastle Corporation Letter Book, f. 113]

May it please your Grace,

I think it my duty to inform you that on Monday last the keelmen employed on this River assembled and refused to go to their work, and the pitmen in our neighbouring counties followed their example, and have since been going from place to place among the coal works collecting the pitmen &c of every colliery both here and on the River Wear and laying off the work, and have brought several Wear water colliers hither. Our keelmen are still lying off and the keelmen of the Wear have likewise left off working.

Under these circumstances I have written to the Secretary at War for an order to have the soldiers at Tynemouth Barracks and 2 or 3 troops of horse from York to be sent hither and assist the civil magistrates in preserving the public peace. The chief cause it seems of these disorders is the high price of corn and other provisions. I beg leave to subscribe myself, may it please your Grace, Your Grace's most obedient and most humble Servant, A.S.

[1] A similar letter was sent to Lord Ravensworth.

172. Surtees to the Duke of Northumberland, 22 June 1771[1] [TWA 592/1, Newcastle Corporation Letter Book, ff. 113 verso–114]

May it please your Grace,

On the 14th Instant I had the honour of transmitting your Grace an account of the rising of the keelmen and pitmen here, and of an application made to the Secretary of Warr for some military aid on that occasion, since which we have received two companies of Foot from Tynemouth Barracks, and advice from the Warr Office that orders have been sent to the Commanding Officer of the Dragoons at York to furnish such detachments as may be judged necessary by the magistrates of Newcastle for their assistance in the preservation of the peace.

I am glad to inform your Grace that all or most of the pitmen have settled to their work as well as the keelmen on the River Wear, but am sorry to add that the keelmen of this River are still lying off and will not go to their employments nor suffer their bussiness to be done by any others. They have not as yet proceeded to any desperate or outrageous acts, but they have forcibly obstructed and laid off several keels that were manned by a few of their well disposed brethren with other watermen and conveying coals upon the River to ships and glasshouses, and they have beat and assaulted some of the persons thus employed. And this day a body of them have gone down to Shields in order to obstruct some sailors and others, who it's said are now engaged there in the like employment. When they will settle, or to what lengths they may carry their proceedings, it is impossible to say, but at present I hope we shall not have occasion for the troops from York, though the order that has been given to the Commanding Officer there is very agreable to the Magistrates here, as an unforeseen occasion may happen, and it is not intended to send for any of those troops but in case of necessity.

I beg leave to subscribe myself, may it please your Grace, your Grace's most obedient and most humble Servant,

A.S., Mayor.

[1] A similar letter was sent to Lord Barrington, TWA 592/1, Newcastle Corporation Letter Book, ff. 114–114 verso.

173. Matthew Ridley to George Ward, 28 June 1771 [NA, ZRI 38/2, Matthew Ridley's Letter Book, 1767–77, p. 113]

….The City of London must for the present be supplied with coals from Sunderland as the Keellmen here will not go to work; many are gone to Sunderland and are employed in casting coals on board the ships there. No riots have yet happened here, but it can scarce be supposed that such a number of men can remain long idle without breaking the peace.

174. Surtees to the Duke of Northumberland, 29 June 1771 [TWA 592/1, Newcastle Corporation Letter Book, ff. 114 verso–115]

May it please your Grace,

I am honoured with and highly obliged by your Grace's letter of 26th Instant. The resolution of the Privy Councill to procure the importation of rye will, I believe, have the desired effect. Your Grace's influence and assistance which you so kindly offer for the service of this Town must upon all occasions be highly desirable and lay the Corporation under great obligations to your Grace who, I hope, will always find them gratefully acknowledged.

The moment I received intelligence of the Privy Councill's resolution, I sent an account thereof to be published in our newspapers, but two of them being then printed off it was only inserted in one. I therefore ordered hand bills of the same to be printed and distributed to assist the publication; and I had some of the keelmen with me yesterday, and from their behaviour and what passed in the conference I think the most, if not all of them, are disposed to return to their work, and though they did not promise it, I entertain strong hopes we shall see them all at the respective employments on Monday first. I beg leave to subscribe myself, May it please your Grace, Your Grace's much obliged and most odedient humble servant,

Aubone Surtees, Mayor

175. Surtees to the Duke of Northumberland, 8 July 1771 [TWA 592/1, Newcastle Corporation Letter Book, f. 115]

May it please your Grace,

I had great hopes of the honour of informing your Grace before this that our keelmen had returned to their employments, but so it is, and such are those people, that though several attempts have been made, and such means used as were judged the most prudent to effect it, 'till now they could not be brought to a sense of their duty.

This morning the majority of them went to work, and there is no doubt but the rest will follow their example. Last week the ill-disposed of 'em committed two or three riots on the River by assembling and forcibly obstructing those who had gone to their bussiness, and warrants were granted against ten of the ringleaders, one of whom as yet has only been apprehended, and he was committed to gaol. Some of the magistrates went in the keels in order to spirit and protect those who were at work.[1]

I am, may it please your Grace, Your Grace's much obliged and most obedient humble Servant,

      A.S., Mayor

---

[1] In a letter to Barrington of 9 July 1771, Surtees declared that as a result of the magistrates' action 'further disturbance gradually subsided without calling on the assistance of the military' (*ibid.*, f. 116). 'After a stop of some weeks the keelmen on the Tyne went to work again, to effect which Alderman Mosley exerted himself in a very praise-worthy manner by going down the river himself in different keels, time after time, till he got them all to work, no one attempting to insult him, though the keels had not previously been suffered to pass with such men as were willing to work. The grievance complained of by the keelmen was the erection of some new staiths near Shields, the owners thereby saving the keel dues.' M.A. Richardson, *The Local Historian's Table Book*, *Historical Division* (Newcastle, 1841–4), II, p. 194.

176. Alexander Murray: Account of the Keelmen's Hospital and Society… and an Address to Young Keelmen (Newcastle, 1781) [NEIMME, Bell Collection, XIII, ff. 511–41]

The weekly collection of the original society fell into the hands of 16 skippers who soon sunk into a profligate and abandoned use of what came under their charge, drinking immoderately, and making feasts with the money, rather than putting it to the proper uses for which it was intended. These managers were kept in countenance by the profligate part of the keelmen in spending the public money, which caused many to refuse the ordinary collection when they found that what was collected was used for such base purposes.

The scheme of collecting languished for several years, and at last the stock was parted among those who had contributed to the last when the faithful trustees had not left so much as to give every man a shilling. This makes it evident that they had spent the money as fast as it was collected.

In the year 1730 a number of those who had been contributors by paying a penny every tide agreed to form themselves into a society upon another plan and to pay an equal and stated contribution every six weeks. They formed articles to which they agreed, but they were no way calculated to bring the Society to that state of perfection which seems to be aimed at by them. About two hundred commenced this Society, who, for want of encouragement from keelmen entering, were obliged to take in members who were not keelmen to keep up such a number as was competent to support the Hospital. That honesty and care which are necessary to the thriving of such societies were wanting in this new one; so that very little was given to the distressed members, and yet hardly so much could be spared to keep the Hospital in due repair.

In the year 1770, when I was chosen Secretary, the stock was almost nothing, the building in need of every repair, not a hundred members in the Society, and of those a great number of old men, fitter to be supplied themselves than to support others.

Since 1770, above two hundred pounds have been laid out on repairs, benefits to distressed members doubled, legacies and funeral charges advanced, some hundreds laid in stock, and 240 members at present in the Society.

And now suffer me to address the young keelmen belonging to the River Tyne on a subject which, if duly considered, would tend to their own peculiar honour and advantage in the issue.

An Address to Young Keelmen

It is acknowledged on all hands that Keelmen are as useful a body of men in several respects as are in any part of Britain. Yet notwithstanding the necessity of their kind of employment to the place and nation, the hardships of their labour and the dangers which attend it, they can gain no more by it than a bare competence, sufficient to maintain themselves and their families while able to work, and though it is impossible they can save from their wages, there is no provision made for them, either local or national, to keep them from starving when disabled by age or infirmity to continue their laborious task. They cannot even obtain the benefit of a parochial settlement, though they should serve indented servants from year to year for forty or fifty years together. I do not mean here to expose this cruel kind of oeconomy but to shew what necessity there is for keelmen, while they are young, to secure some means to preserve them from starving when distress or old age shall overtake them.

Pray, think seriously, for a moment, that you are saving nothing for a time of distress, or age; you have no settlement as keelmen to depend upon. The favour of your masters is precarious, neither have they places to put you all in, when past your keel-work, what can you do but beg or starve? Look forward to the time when you cannot help yourselves, and while you have youth and health, secure a safe retreat for distress, or old age. I here present you with one at present in a thriving condition, which wants no more but the young keelmen to join with it, to render it, beyond all doubt, a sure and comfortable fund of support to all who shall need the same in any future period. It is very remarkable that young keelmen should need any other incitement to a conduct so visibly fraughted with benefit to themselves, than the bare opportunity of becoming interested in the privileges which are so happily calculated to remedy what they have more to fear, and secure what, above all things in the world, they should most ardently wish. The melancholy spectacle of their brethren in distress, and the deplorable situation of the aged and starving keelmen who have neglected the present means here recommended of joining in their youth, is sufficient caution to such as have yet health and youth to take a wiser course for the benefit of themselves and families.

But lest I should be thought tedious, I shall at this time, leave these, with many similar considerations, to the serious perusal of such as they mostly concern, and remain their friend and well-wisher,

A.M., Secretary[1]

[1] Alexander Murray, a schoolmaster, was secretary of the Hospital Society 1770–85.

UNEMPLOYMENT CAUSED BY ACTIONS OF THE SHIPOWNERS, 1787

177. *Newcastle Courant*, 24 February 1787

The Shipowners at Sunderland and Shields, on account of the slow demand for coals at different markets, at a meeting on Tuesday last resolved to laying their ships for 3 weeks as they arrive before taking any coals on board and to continue this every voyage until there may be a quicker sale at the markets.

178. *Newcastle Courant,* **3 March 1787**

The low price of coals at London having induced many of the shipowners rather to lay up their ships than continue in a trade where they were such considerable losers, this step has necessarily laid many keelmen and others employed in the coal trade off work, and those so laid off have become very tumultuous, and forcibly laid in all the collieries and other works in the neighbourhood…Surely it would be much greater wisdom in those who feel or suppose themselves injured or oppressed to have recourse to peaceable and quiet measures, rather than tumults and disorders, the one will be more likely to procure redress than the other.

179. Handbill, 1787 [NEIMME, ZD/70]

The Mayor's Chamber, 5 March 1787

The gentlemen of the Coal Trade of the River Tyne agree to support such of the keelmen as are out of employment upon condition that those who have work will immediately go to work and all behave themselves peaceably.

A committee is appointed to distribute the money for the support of them and their families, according to their necessities, and no part of this money to be returned.

The following gentlemen are appointed a committee for the above purpose: John Erasmus Blackett, Alexander Adams, Robert Lish and Jonathan Airey, Esqrs., Robert Rayne, Henry Scott, Thomas Allan, Thomas Ismay, Mr Hood, Mr Leavis.

180. *Newcastle Courant,* **10 March 1787**

The tumults among the pitmen, keelmen and others employed in the coal works, from the laudable conduct of our magistrates and those concerned in the coal trade, have entirely subsided, and [on] Thursday several ships, coal loaded, sailed from this port.

181. Example of a Keelman's Bond; Bond to Anthony Hood, Hostman, 28 December 1787[1] [NCL: J. Bell, *Collections relative to the Tyne: its Trade and the Conservancy thereof,* vol. I, f. 10]

Know all men by these presents that we John Watson, junior, Thomas Coats, John Wheatley, Matthew Coats, Stephen Parker, Edward Errington, William Spoor, Christopher Whitfield, James Sadler, Robert Storey, John Watson, senior, William Coats, Thomas Thompson, Henry Lamb, Thomas Simpson, John Mitcalf, George Turnbull, Thomas Barrett, and John Golightly, Skippers, Anthony Greener, John Swaddle, James

Farguson, William Clarke, George Robinson, William Mains, Cuthbert Brown, George Carr, John Clarke, John Storey, Roger Errington, Robert Smart, Joseph Spoor, John Spoor, John Howey, John Tulip, Joseph Watson, John Greener, John Brown, John Portous, John Watson, Taylor Coats, John Sadler, Richard Stephenson, Thomas Newton, Joseph Lister, William Smith, William Potts, George Simpson, John Nicholson, John Gansby, George Johnson, John Gibson, William Bourne, George Ling, George Golightly and Joseph Crozier, Bound Men or Shovelmen, are held and firmly bound to Anthony Hood of the Town and County of Newcastle upon Tyne, Hoastman, in the sum of Two Hundred Pounds of lawfull money of Great Britain to be paid to the said Anthony Hood or his certain attorney, his executors, administrators or assigns, to which payment well and truly to be made we bind ourselves and each and every of us by himself our and each and every of our heirs, executors and administrators jointly and severally for the whole firmly by these presents, sealed with our seals, dated the twenty eight day of December in the twenty eight year of the reign of our sovereign Lord George the Third by the grace of God of Great Britain, France and Ireland, King, Defender of the Faith, and so forth, and in the year of our Lord one Thousand Seven Hundred and Eighty Seven.

The condition of this obligation is such that whereas the above named Anthony Hood has hired and retained the above bounden John Watson, junior, Thomas Coats, John Wheatley, Matthew Coats, Stephen Parker, Edward Errington, William Spoor, Christopher Whitfield, James Sadler, Robert Storey, John Watson, senior, William Coats, Thomas Thompson, Henry Lamb, Thomas Simpson, John Mitcalf, George Turnbull, Thomas Barrett, and John Golightly, to be and go Skippers of nineteen severall keels, coal boats or lighters severally belonging to, or to be employed by, the said Anthony Hood for the term of one whole year to be reckoned from the day of the date of these presents, and has also hired and retained the above bounded Anthony Greener, John Swaddle, James Farguson, William Clarke, George Robinson, William Mains, Cuthbert Brown, George Carr, John Clarke, John Storey, Roger Errington, Robert Smart, Joseph Spoor, John Spoor, John Howey, John Tulip, Joseph Watson, John Greener, John Brown, John Portous, John Watson, Taylor Coats, John Sadler, Richard Stephenson, Thomas Newton, Joseph Lister, William Smith, William Potts, George Simpson, John Nicholson, John Gansby, George Johnson, John Gibson, William Bourne, George Ling, George Golightly and Joseph Crozier to be Bound Men or Shovelmen to serve in the working and going in the said severall keels, coal boats or lighters during one whole year from the day of the date hereof, and has given them the said Skippers to each and every of them the sum of Twenty Shillings apiece for the binding of them and their said men to the said work and service, and has lent unto the said Skippers, and to each and every of them, the like sum of Twenty Shilings, If therefore they the said Skippers and each and every of them do and shall on or before the eleventh day of June next ensuing well and truly pay or cause to be paid unto the said Anthony Hood his executors, administrators and assigns the said sum of Twenty Shillings apiece so lent and advanced to them and each and every of them as aforesaid, and also if they the said Skippers and their said men and each and every of them above particularly named do all of them honestly, diligently, truly and faithfully serve the said Anthony Hood, his under fitters, agents or assigns in working and going in the said severall keels, coal boats or lighters to such coal staith or staiths within the Rivers Tyne or Derwent, as he or they shall order, and do there load and take in such loadings and quantitys of coals of the King's measure as he or they shall direct and after so loading do cast the same on board such ship or ships or other vessells as he or they shall appoint without hiding or bringing away any of the said coals from any such ship or ships as aforesaid and do not at any time or times serve any fitt tickett or ticketts for the use of or by the appointment of any person or persons whomsoever, without the licence of the said Anthony Hood, his under fitters, agents or assigns first thereunto had and obtained, and that the said Skippers and their men or any of them shall not at any time or times consume, or embezle any of the furniture, tackle and apparell belonging to the said severall keels, coal boats or lighters but do use their and every of their endeavours to preserve the same from spoil, loss and damage, and that they and every of them do find their own work geer at their own charge and do upon demand at the end of the said year yield and deliver up the peaceable and quiet possession of the said severall keels, coal boats or lighters, with all their furniture, tacle and aparell unto the said Anthony Hood, his executors, administrators or assigns, and that the said Skippers and their said men shall and will help one another to load at the staith dyke and also will be aiding and assisting to the utmost of their power in casting their severall loadings of coals on board of any ship or ships or other vessell which they shall be appointed to ship or deliver the same on board of when two or three or more of the said keels are lying on board any ship or vessell, or otherwise shall forfeit to the said Anthony Hood for every such default the sum of Two Shillings and sixpence, and shall not take on board of the said keels nor any of them [any] prohibited goods and merchandizes whatsoever, Then this obligation to be void or else to remain in force.

Signed, sealed and delivered: 68 seals. All signed with a mark except John Howey, John Sadler, Thomas Coats, John Wheatley, William Mains, Matthew Coats, Thomas Simpson, George Simpson, William Burn (Bourne?), George Ling, Henry Lamb, Robert Sto[rey?][2]

---

[1] This is the earliest example of a keelman's bond that has been found. Another, 24 December 1819, is in NEIMME, ZD 70. Several bonds of the 1850s are in Durham County Record Office, NCB I/Sc/548, 550, 560.

[2] There are three other signatures of men whose names do not appear in the body of the bond, though some blank spaces were left, presumably for them: Rolland Treall(?), John Henderson, William Patton.

A NEW ATTEMPT TO ESTABLISH A CHARITY FOR THE KEELMEN, 1786–8

182. William Tinwell, Clerk of the Keelmen's Society, to the Worshipfull the Governor and Gentlemen of the Hostmen's Company, 11 December 1786 [TWA 394/31]

Gentlemen,

I am directed to inform you that the proposal made by the Town's Clerk concerning the intended Association of Keelmen having the Mayor of Newcastle for the time being Governor, and four of the Gentlemen of the Town Trustees, met with the immediate concurrence of the present acting Committee.[1] They also make free to lay before you how they design to proceed with the plan in future.[2]

First they beg that you will be so kind as to desire your men at binding time to appoint one of their number out of each employ to form a committee that the several articles drawn up may be submitted to their inspection and such alterations, additions, &c made as may appear to them requisite. Next they desire that leave may be granted to assemble all the keelmen before whom to lay the whole scheme for their approbation, after which it is proposed to petition Parliament for leave to bring in a Bill for the several purposes of the Association. If leave be granted, then it is hoped the several Fitters will be pleased to sign their names at the head of their men in the Bill which will then be given to the worthy Representatives of Newcastle in order to be presented to Parliament.

I have the honor to be with the utmost respect, Gentlemen,

Your most obedient and very humble Servant,
William Tinwell, Clerk of the Keelmen's Society

[1] The members of the acting committee were Mr Day, Adam Stephenson and Henry Straughan (TWA 394/30).
[2] The proposed scheme was based on the following calculations: the number of keels on the Tyne 'has been found on very good authority to amount to 355, and as each keel cast at an average 8 score tides per year this amounts to £946. 13s. 4d. at a halfpence per chalder'. It was expected that something would also be collected from keels carrying ballast, lead, stones &c to make a total of £1,000 per year (TWA 394/57).

183. Draft 'Plan of Keelmen's Institution' [TWA 394/30]

That a corporation or body politic be appointed and that it shall consist of a governor and 21 members who shall be elected and chosen annually from the Representives of the Town, [the] Mayor, Aldermen, Recorder, Sheriff and Common Council, and from the Hoastmen's Company, but that the two Members [of Parliament], the Mayor, Recorder, Sheriff, four senior Aldermen, the Governor and Stewards of the Hoastmen's Company to be ten.

That the people employed in each work shall under the hands or marks of the majority of them deliver in to the fitter at the time of binding a name of a person who shall be the delegate for that work, which delegates shall meet on the first Monday in January in each year, and the major part of them shall nominate the twelve Trustees to be elected out of the body before mentioned who shall be Trustees for one year. That the senior of such delegates shall be a chairman and shall have a casting voice. The return of the persons elected shall be made to the Mayor for the time being. That these delegates, or any of them, shall certify the proper objects of the Charity.

Fines to be mutual on the loader of the keel, if overmeasure, [and] on the keelmen navigating the vessel in case of undermeasure, a penalty to be recovered before a magistrate, who shall hear and determine. In case of any information given of a penalty ....and not supported with sufficient proof, the informer to pay all the expenses of the inquiry &c.

The Treasurer to be elected annually by them to be accountable to the Trustees and to be under their directions as to placing out money, and who shall render a monthly account of the state and application of the fund to the Mayor for the time being and such of the delegates as shall require the same. Money to be put into the public funds.

That the makings out of each ship shall be had, and if it appears that more than 15 [London chaldrons] to the keel has been made out, the surplus to be paid [for?] by the fitter overloading the keels, then 1 shilling to be paid by such fitter for each London chaldron.

184. The Scheme of the Bill for the Relief and Support of indigent Keelmen, their widows and children to be brought in this present session of Parliament. [1788] Addressed to J.E. Blackett. 'Mr Clayton [Town Clerk] called with this letter'. [TWA 394/29]

That a Body corporate be constituted which shall consist of 21 Members by the name of the President and Governors for the Relief and Support of Skippers and Keelmen employed on the River Tyne and their widows and children.

That the Members shall be elected annually, as after mentioned, of whom the Representatives in Parliament for Newcastle, the Mayor, the Recorder, the Sheriff, four senior Aldermen, the Governor and Stewards of the Hoastman's Company to be always twelve, the remaining nine to be elected out of the body of Aldermen and Common Council or the Hoastman's Company.

That the Skippers and Keelmen employed in each work shall under the hands or marks of a majority of them deliver to the Fitter at the time of binding the name of a Skipper in each work who shall be a delegate for that work, which delegates shall meet and a majority of them shall elect the 21 Trustees by writing under their hands or marks, the return to be sent to the Town Clerk for the time being who shall summon the Trustees to meet and qualify by taking an oath for the faithful discharge of the office. The Trustees so elected to have a power to provide in the present Hospital, and in any necessary additional buildings, for the objects of the Charity and to relieve them as the funds will allow.

The objects of the Charity to be pointed out by the Delegates and no other person relieved by the Trustees.

The money raised to be invested in the purchase of stock. The Fund to be raised by a stoppage of a halfpenny per chaldron.

And it is further proposed that some mode which shall be deemed most effectual shall be adopted by the Bill to prevent all Overmeasure and any grievance or oppression arising therefrom.[1]

An observation of Mr Jonathan Airey: 'No mode whatever should be introduced in this Bill in regard to Measure'.

[1] The keelmen's proposals concerning overmeasure in the earlier draft (**Document 183** above) have been dropped.

185. Draft note from the Town Clerk, informing the Fitters of a meeting relating to the Keelmen's Act [TWA 394/32]

Newcastle, 28 June 1788

Sir,

I take the liberty of apprising you that in the due execution of the Keelmen's Act[1] it will be necessary that you should appoint a time and place for the meeting of those in your employment for the election of a skipper or keelman as a steward for your Work for the year ensuing, and that such meeting should be held either on Monday next or Tuesday morning next early.[2]

Mr Mayor having fixed to be at the Chamber on Tuesday next at one o'Clock for the purpose of swearing the offputters, I am directed to beg you will be so good as to require those who are employed at your staith to attend him at that place and time, and that you will take the trouble of recommending to the steward appointed for your Work to attend also in order that he may satisfy his constitutents that the oath required by the Act has been duly administered.

I am directed also to submit to your consideration whether the staith belonging to each work will not be the properest place for assembling the keelmen.

I am, Sir, Your most faithful humble Servant,

[Nathaniel Clayton]

[1] The Act for establishing a permanent fund for the relief and support of skippers and keelmen employed on the River Tyne, who by sickness or other accidental misfortunes, or by old age, shall not be able to maintain themselves and their families, and also for the relief of the widows and children of such skippers and keelmen, passed the Commons on 23 May 1788, was agreed by the Lords on 30 May, and received the Royal Assent on 11 June. As indicated in the above letter, the men of each work were to elect one of themselves to be a steward of 'The Society of Keelmen on the River Tyne' for the ensuing year. The stewards were to elect the 21 Guardians of the Society for the year, twelve of whom were always to be the two MPs for Newcastle, the Mayor, Recorder, Sheriff, four senior aldermen, and the governor and stewards of the Hostmen's Company; the remaining nine were to be chosen from the trading brethren of the Hostmen's Company. The off-putters, who were responsible for loading the keels, were to swear that they would cause them to be fairly and justly loaded 'after the due and accustomed rate of eight chaldrons to each keel' (*Journals of the House of Commons*, 43, pp. 498, 519, 545). A copy of the Act is in TWA 394/54 and in J. Brand, *History of Newcastle*, I, p. 655.
[2] A list of the stewards elected for 1788 is in TWA 394/32.

186. An example of the offputter's Oath [TWA 394/32]

I, Robert Bowman, do swear that I will faithfully and according to the best of my skill, knowledge, and judgment, execute and perform the duty of off-putter at the staith at Walls End where I am now employed, and that I will, to the utmost of my power, cause the keels using the said staith to be fairly and justly loaded after the due and accustomed rate of eight chaldrons to each keel, without favour, partiality, malice or prejudice to any person or persons whomsoever. So help me God.

Signed: Robert Bowman

Sworn, 1 July 1788 before William Cramlington, Mayor[1]

[1] The same oath was sworn by the off-putter of 31 other staiths, between 1 and 7 July 1788. Two signed with a mark; the rest wrote their names.

187. Printed Notice, 4 July 1788 [TWA 394/32]

A Committee of the Guardians of the Society of Keelmen beg to inform you that the weekly stoppages of one halfpenny per chaldron per tide from the wages of the skippers and keelmen in your employment will commence Tomorrow in pursuance of the Keelmen's Act and the order of the Guardians; and that Mr Tinwell is appointed to collect the amount of every week's stoppages, for which purpose he will call upon each fitter on Monday next, and on every following Monday between Twelve and Two o'Clock.

The Act requires each fitter shall keep a muster roll and deliver a duplicate thereof signed by himself or his clerk to the collector of the stoppages, and as it will be expedient that all the fitters use the same kind of muster roll, and duplicate, forms of each, as approved by the Guardians, are inclosed.

188. An example of Articles submitted to the keelmen of each Work by the steward elected for that Work [TWA 394/32]

To the Keelmen in Mr Ralph Atkinson's Employ

I am desired to take your opinion of the following articles which are intended, if you approve them, to be laid before your Guardians on Monday 25 August 1788. John Wilthew, Steward [*Signed with a mark*]

1st That certificates be given the keelmen specifying when they began paying into the fund &c.

2nd That money be paid instead of the beer received from the ships loaded with coals, and that 4d of this money go into the fund.

3rd That all work done by keelmen at the several staiths be paid in money, not in drink.

4th That an inspector be appointed to see that the offputters do their duty with respect to the measure and be impowered to bring such who do not to justice for the crime of perjury.

5th That abstracts of the Act together with any regulations that may take place at present be printed and given to the people.

6th That the stewards with their clerk have a proper place to meet in, that they may transact the necessary business concerning the fund and levy fines upon such as break through the regulations of the Act, or any other regulations that may be established by the mutual consent of the Guardians and people.

7th That those who go a short tide, and receive less for it than the common full dues, may be only liable to pay one farthing per chalder.

8th That a plan be adopted to cause all those who go glasshouse tides &c to pay one half penny per chalder when they receive the common full dues, or if they receive less, as above.

[*On back of the above*] Agreable to all the Articles…excepting articles 7 and 'litere close' [latter clause?] of 8. [*Signed by 27, mostly with marks.*][1]

---

[1] There are ten other returns, four of which have objections to the seventh and eighth articles, *e.g.* 90 men in Bell's employment 'think it will be a bridge [breach?] of the Act'. Robert Taylor's keelmen queried whether the farthing per chaldron in article seven 'includes the 4 pence beer money' [see article two above]. They agreed that 'halfpence per chaldron be paid if beer money be paid'. They objected to article eight, called for payment of owners' wages 'as formerly', for abolition of spout sixpences, and for all captains of ships loaded under the spouts to pay a halfpenny per chaldron 'for the strengthe[n]ing the fund'. In some of the other returns a considerable number of keelmen appear to have been willing to contribute eight pence to the fund.

189. The Case of keelmen employed in Glass House Works, 8 July 1788 [TWA 394/32]

We whose names are hereunto subscribed being skippers of keels employed in the Glass Factories &c on the River Tyne, and not under any of the fitters, having heard that the Committee appointed to regulate the fund to be raised by the keelmen of the said River agreeable to the late Act of Parliament are determined to stipulate our subscriptions to the said fund at and after the rate of eight score tides annually, which number of tides are absolutely more than we can possibly get, which will be a great hardship upon us, as the best of our tides being no more than 10 shillings per tide, and the principal part at 9 shillings and 8 shillings per Tide. We therefore are of oppinion, and which may be proved at some of the offices, that upon an average we make no more than six score tides each keel annually, and as such are willing to pay at and after that rate, or to pay no more than we do really make, which shall be left at the different offices where we receive our pay. As witness our hands, Edward McGregor, Andrew Adams. [*Both signed with a mark.*]

190. Petition to the Guardians of the Hospital Society, incorporating the substance of the articles submitted to the keelmen in the various Works [25 August 1788] [TWA 394/43]

To the Worshipful the Guardians of the Keelmen's Hospital Society, the Petition of the Keelmen of the several works upon the River Tyne, sheweth

That your petitioners are very thankful for the favour you have done them in procuring an Act for the purpose of provinding a sustenance for their aged and distressed brothers, widows and orphans. That your petitioners think the best way of shewing their gratitude is to inform [you] of [the] real state of the people at present that so you may have an opportunity of giving full satisfaction.

That your petitioners desire that a number of certificates be printed specifying when such and such keelman commenced paying into the Fund and of consequence when he will be intitled to the benefit if in distress. That as there are constant broils about the beer which they received from ships they load with coal, and as the Majestrates, Fitters &c are so much troubled about it, your petitioners humbly desire that money be given them instead of beer, and that fourpence of this money be paid into the Fund and the remaining shillings disposed of as the keelmen please – not to be compelled to drink it upon any account – and also that what work they do at the different staiths they be paid for in money and not in drink. That your petitioners are sorry to inform you that the Measure is not still taken proper care of but that several keels are loaded far about[1] the plate; therefore your petitioners think that a person should be appointed an inspecter and to bring any offputter who does not fulfil his duty to justice to be punished for perjury. That your petitioners desire that an abstract of the Act together with the regulations you now please to make to be printed and copies thereof dispersed among the people, and that leave be granted the Stewards of the keelmen to me[e]t and transact business for the people and to fine any person who breaks through any of the article[s] of the Act, and the money arising therefrom to go into the fund. But it is always to be understood that the Stewards are to receive sanction from one or more of the Guardians before they put any of theer resolves into effect.[2] That your petitioners think it rather hard that any person who goes a short tide, and of consequence does not receive the full dues, should pay as much as they who receive the whole. It therefore appears reasonably that whoever does not receive the full dues only pay one farthing per chalder. These things your petitioners, whose names are under, lay

before you hopping you will answer theer request in every reasonably desire, and they as in duty will pray &c.

Parchment, signed by 229, mostly with a mark.

¹ Presumably 'above', not 'about', was intended. The plate marked the eight
chaldron load.
² Added in a different hand: 'the last article is superflous'.

191. Representation to the Guardians of the Keelmen's Hospital Society [1788] [TWA 394]

Gentlemen, We the Committee of the Keelmen give you in the
name of the people at large our grateful thanks for the active part you
have taken in getting the Bill for supporting aged keelmen, widows
and orphans past into law, [now] lay before you the following for
serious consideration.

First, an objection has been made since the passing of the Act,
viz. that as there are no provisions made in the Bill for the Stewards
to be present at the auditing of the accounts, either in receiving or
disbursing their money, therefore they are merely nominal. Therefore,
with all due deference, we would propose, as the only means to take
off the force of this objection, that the Stewards should have a clerk to
keep a fair account of all moneys received or disburst, by which they
will have a proper idea of the state of the fund and be able to give the
people at all times a just account of their affairs.

Another objection has been made – in the plain language of the
objectors – that as power to build a new hospital, or make a proper
addition to the present one, is entirely left to the discretion of the
Guardians, it is to be feared that too much attention will be paid to
ornament and too little to utility, as has been done in building several
edifices for similar purposes in different parts of the kingdom. The
present hospital might have been raised a story higher for the same
expence if several parts had been omitted, such as the galleries,
alleys, &c.

Secondly, we beg leave to advise from our knowledge of the people's
sentiments since the passing of the Act, our own regard to justice, and
a desire of preserving the public peace, that you will be pleased to
order the Stewards to inspect the off-putters at the several staiths to see
that justice be done to all parties, and that the offputter may be enabled
to fulfil his oath in the execution of his office; and for the preservation
of the Trade in general, we hope that you, Gentlemen, whose business
it is to see all concerned have their rights, will empower the off-putter
not to load a keel unless she swims fair.

That you would as soon as possible petition Parliament that leave may be given to have the keels weighted or measured at any time when it shall appear necessary, either at their respective staiths or at different convenient places which may be judged proper to give justice to all, on account of the strength or weakness of the water, as we can assert from long experience that it will take three parts of a chalder more to put a keel [down?] to her marks, as they are now measured, at Willington Key or the Point than at Whitefield.

That when Parliament is petitioned they should be asked that the off-putters at Sunderland be sworn for the same purpose as at Newcastle. It seems strange that these people who have so much under their charge should not have been sworn long ago, when others with far less responsibility have been, and are, sworn. And we are certain, if this be done in both places, the people will be freed from a great oppression, justice [will be done] to everyone concerned, and the public revenue greatly increased.

We think, after weighing matters with the greatest deliberation, and from hearing the fears of those concerned in the Trade of the consequences of our plan, that, if the above or such like are not carried into immediate execution, it will have a tendency to hurt our Trade, ruin the Corporation, and bring the curses of the people upon us instead of their blessings.

We also desire printed copies of the Bill, and the duty of Stewards, their clerk, and the off-putters added to it, to be bound, and each of the Stewards to have one during office, to be given by the old Stewards to the new at the time of their election.

It seems reasonable to us that any keelman belonging to the Society either up or down river who is entitled to benefit, but finds it inconvenient to dwell at the Hospital, should have his money paid without being obliged to abide there.

192. A Representation by some discontented Keelmen, 1788 [TWA 394/29]

We the undernamed Skippers and Keelmen on the River Tyne do humbly take this method for ourselves and others of petitioning the Right Worshipful the Mayor and all other Gentlemen who are our employers or have any concern in the Coal Trade:

Inprimus we beg leave to say that we are not induced to adopt this step by any fractious intentions or in the smallest degree to disturb the harmony of the Trade, but from a sensible feeling of our distressed condition according to our respective circumstances.

Secondly we beg leave to say that the manifold imperfections which have crept in amongst us since the first establishment of our wages by means of subtle selfish men, who have ever been encroaching on us till our privileges are annihilated, our interest ruined, our credit marred, ourselves made worse than the slaves in foreign countries, and lightly esteemed and scornfully reproached by all other men whose callings are of similar import, our wives poor to a proverb, our children beggars or burthensome to the contiguous Parishes – this hath ever been the case of your humble servants, and the effect of tyrannical power over injured and oppressed innocence – and the small encouragement the many stops and civil Addresses have ever met with from our employers is the moving cause that forms the basis of this petition.

Thirdly, whereas we consider ourselves wronged by some proceedings in the Trade, probably unknown to the Gentlemen who are our supreme masters, by the subtilty of their under agents that generally take more upon them than the former do, and therefore we think this the most dutiful and respectful way of knowing from our superiors their opinion upon the subjects complained of; and, moreover, in respect to the Bill that hath lately taken place by unanimous consent of Parliament for the relief of the aged, sick or disabled keelmen, we are informed that we are impowered by the said Act to name Trustees for the uses therein specified, yet as the provisions must arise from our small endeavours, which are now too little to support our families above that which is given to the weekly poor, we can see no reason why we should blindfold ourselves and crouch down under another burthen, without knowing the least lawful reason for so doing; besides, we can see no mannner of reason why any body of men whatever should be delegated with a power which we never designed, i.e. of depositing our money in some of the London banks and appropriating it to what use they please, as if our own Corporation was not competent to be intrusted therewith.

[Fourthly], Whatever might be the intention of the legislator of the said Act of having the beer at four pence per gallon from sundry houses appointed by him or any other, when we ingenuously apprehend it is only what is called 'Eight shillings Beer' and frequently sold to others at three pence, this would be the height of oppression and opening an avenue to bribery in the abstract. So in order to prevent such imposition, and shut up every avenue to bribery, we think most proper to have one shilling paid with our Tide and the other fourpence to make this permanent Fund, which will have the good effect of procuring harmony amongst us that are concerned therein and at once stop the mouths of the laity.

[Fifthly], Concerning the prevailing report that is circulating amongst us at present of having four pence more than the four pence off our beer or tide, which is one and the same thing with the four pence specified in the Act, would be an absurdity in the highest degree and entirely repugnant to the mind of every one of us, which charity bids us rather suspect it to be the suggestions of some enemies or through the ignorance of the laity and not from the sole purpose of the legislator, but be it which way it will, we can see no reason why we should be thus imposed upon by any certain body of men under any pretence whatsoever.

In the next place we humbly observe that although reading Acts of Parliament be above our sphere of employment, yet we have been given to understand that our legal wages ought to be fifteen shillings and eight pence (our beer money not included). Now how it happens that we are paid only thirteen shillings and four pence is to us really surprising, notwithstanding we have heard several reasons such as they are assigned for this treatment, but as we never gave any consent to such stoppages we consider them illegal and no way binding upon us.[1]

We would therefore humbly set forth that we have a strong presumption that many fraudulent practices prevail with respect to what is called 'Stirrd Keels' to the great hurt not only of the owners of them,[2] but in consequence thereof, of all those keelmen who do not come under such denomination. Trusting therefore, Gentlemen, that you will deign to give these our humble sentiments a due consideration and do in the premises what in your wisdom seemeth right.

'That all men is agreeable'. [*Signed, with marks, by 10 men from Whickham, 8 from Swalwell, 3 from Blaydon, 4 from Lemington, and 5 from Dunston.*]

[1] Some deductions from the keelmen's wages were abolished or reduced in 1791–2, see below, **Documents 193** and **197**.
[2] The keelmen complained about this practice in 1719 and 1750. See their Second Remonstrance, 1719 (**Document 67**) above and their petition of 1750 (**Document 120**) above.

ADJUSTMENT OF THE KEELMEN'S WAGES, 1791–2

193. Resolutions of the Coal Owners and Fitters, 26 September 1791 [*Printed*] [TWA 394/10]

At a General Meeting of the Coal Owners and Fitters[1] on the River Tyne held on Monday the 26th Day of September Inst., after much Deliberation, it was resolved by the Coal Owners and Fitters concerned in the Works below Bridge:

That as soon as the bonds, by which the keelmen are bound to their employers on their present terms expire, which will be at Christmas next, the following Regulations will be proper to be adopted, with respect to the keelmen employed in these Works.

1st. That the practice of deducting 1s. Can Money from the keelmen's dues each tide, and the payment of Spout Sixpences be abolished, and that every keelman be at liberty to supply himself with liquor wherever he pleases, and not any particular Can or Public House.

2dly, That each keel crew receive 1s. 4d. Beer Money instead of beer.

3dly, That the payments made at the staiths, called 'Making-in Money', continue as before, but shall always be made in *Money*, and not in *Liquor*.

4thly, That the allowance for shifting keels and lying tides be paid at the Fitters' Offices, with the keelmen's other wages.[2]

And it was resolved by the Coal Owners and Fitters concerned in the Works between Darwent and the Bridge, that the following Regulations will be proper to be adopted, with respect to the Keelmen employed in the Works above Bridge, and at or below Darwent.

1st. That the deduction of 1s. 4d. per tide from the Owners' Wages, which has been applied hitherto in stirring keels, as it is called, be abolished, and that, after Christmas next, 4d. only per tide instead of 1s. 4d. be allowed out of the Owners' Wages to the Skipper for furnishing the keels with proper geer.

2ndly, That the practice of deducting 1s. Can Money from the keelmen's dues each tide, and the payment of spout sixpences, be abolished at Christmas next, and that every keelman be at liberty to supply himself with liquor wherever he pleases, and not at any particular Can or Public House.

3dly, That each keel crew receive 1s. 4d. Beer Money instead of beer.

4thly, That the payment made at the staiths, called 'Making-in-Money', continue as before, but shall always be made in *Money*, and not in *Liquor*.

5thly, That the allowance for shifting keels and lying tides be paid at the Fitters' Offices, with the keelmen's other wages.[2]

And 6thly, That the further addition of 1s. 2d. per tide be added to their wages.

And it was resolved by the Coal Owners and Fitters concerned in the Works above Darwent, with respect to the keelmen employed in those Works,

That the same Regulations as those with respect to the keelmen employed between Darwent and the Bridge, except the last, will be proper to be adopted in these Works, and that instead of an addition of 1s. 2d. they shall receive an addition of 1s. 6d. per tide to their wages.

And it was also unanimously resolved by the Coal Owners that they would make such regulations at their respective staiths as would secure the accustomed use of the Spouts with the greatest impartiality.

And the Fitters resolved to take into early consideration the different proportions of the additional wages to be given to the Skipper and to the men.

And it was then unanimously resolved that immediate measures be taken to have the above Regulations carried into effect by having them engrossed on parchment and sanctioned by the same authority which passed the Regulations in the years 1710 and 1744.

J. E. Blackett, Chairman.

[1] A list of those present at the meeting 'in consequence of a summons issued by the direction of the Mayor' is in TWA 394/33.

[2] The further provision 'that 1s. be paid when the coals are taken in at a port hole which shall be five feet or upwards above the keel's gunwale' was crossed out.

194. The Keelmen's Response, 26 September 1791 [TWA 394/33]

All the people above Darwent are agreeable to the Bill [*i.e.* the proposed Regulations] with 1/8[1] more advance.

All from Darwent to the Bridge are agreeable to the Bill except Mr Blackett's and Mr Hood's employ who want 1/8 advance.

All under the Bridge are agreeable to the Bill.

[Those employed by Messrs] Bell, Scott, Lisle & Row, and Liddell &c., have sometimes to go to the staiths above Darwent, [and] when they are so employed they expect the same wages as others who are employed [there].

It is expected that every skipper have the 4d. for finding the geer.

It is expected that the determination of this day be printed with the Town Clerk's signature, and that a limited time be fixed upon when a parchment shall be signed, sealed and delivered as in 1710 and 1744.

[1] This is written as a fraction and it is not clear whether this means 1s. 8d. or one eighth.

195. Nathaniel Clayton, Town Clerk, to John Erasmus Blackett [TWA 394/29]

Westgate Street, Friday morning [late December 1791?].

Dear Sir,

I have enclosed a draught of the proposed regulation for the keelmen which you will be so good as revise. Perhaps it ought to be laid before the Fitters previous to its being ingrossed on parchment.

It is a curious fact that there is nothing either in the regulations of the years 1710 or 1744 which can be fairly applied to the wages of keelmen employed in any Work below Scotswood.

I remain, Dear Sir, yours very faithfully,
Nathaniel Clayton

196. Anthony Hood to Nathaniel Clayton [TWA 394/30]

Hanover Square, Sunday 1 January [1792]

Dear Sir,

Several fitters and others that vend their own coals from above Bridge have promised to stand with me in the distribution of the wages according to the mode which was unanimously agreed to, viz. 'That the Skipper should have 1s. per tide more than a common man, exclusive of 4d. for finding geer'.

I submit therefore to your better judgement whether the present situation of things does not require that this division of the wages should be engrossed upon the parchment as the most proper way to prevent any further trouble and confusion; indeed I believe it will be but partially signed if this is not inserted. Some of the Works above [Bridge] have bound on these conditions, more than a third of ours have done the same, and I have great reason to think the rest will follow their example, if they only see that we are firmly resolved not to do otherwise.

I am, Dear Sir, your most obliged Servant,
Anthony Hood

197. Further Regulations as to the Dues of the River and Owners' Wages[1] [TWA 394/36]

Newcastle upon Tyne, 3 January 1792

Each keel that shall be cast on board any ship shall be paid the sum of 1s. 4d. for beer, instead of being furnished with beer by the ship.

That the deduction of one shilling Can Money, and the payment of Spout Sixpences be abolished; and that no keelman be obliged to supply himself with liquor at any particular Can or Public House.

That the payments made at the staiths, called 'Making-in-Money' continue the same as before, but shall be always made in money, and not in liquor. And that the usual allowance for shifting keels and lying tides be paid at the Fitters' Offices with the other dues.

And in case any keel crew shall demand and receive such allowance when not justly due, such keel crew shall forfeit five shillings for each offence, out of which the Fitter shall be reimbursed what he has paid wrongfully and the remainder shall go to the keelmen's Fund, established by Act of Parliament.

And that instead of the deduction of one shilling and four-pence per tide, called 'Steerage Money', hitherto made in the Works above Bridge, four-pence only per tide shall in future be deducted, which shall be allowed to the Skipper of each keel for furnishing the keel with proper geer.

And it is recommended to the Fitters, that the Skippers be paid One Shilling per Tide (over and above the four-pence Geer Money) more than each Man.

	DUES		OWNERS' WAGES		TOTALS	
	s	d	s	d	s	d
From Stella to the New Quay	6	4	5	2	11	6
From Blaydon to the New Key	6	4	4	10	11	2
From Lemington to the New Key	6	4	4	6	10	10
From Denton to the New Key	6	4	4	2	10	6
From Scotswood to the New Quay	6	4	3	10	10	2
From all Places below Scotswood and West of the Bridge to the New Key	6	4	3	6	9	10
From Stella to below the Bourne or Ewes Burn	6	8	5	2	11	10
From Blaydon to below the Burn	6	8	4	10	11	6
From Lemington to below the Burn	6	8	4	6	11	2
From Denton to below the Burn	6	8	4	2	10	10
From Scotswood to below the Burn	6	8	3	10	10	6
From all Places below Scotswood, and West of the Bridge to below the Burn	6	8	3	6	10	2
From Stella to Snowdens Hole or Dents Hole	7	6	5	2	12	8
From Blaydon to Snowdens Hole or Dents Hole	7	6	4	10	12	4
From Lemington to Snowdens Hole or Dents Hole	7	6	4	6	12	0
From Denton to Snowdens Hole or Dents Hole	7	6	4	2	11	8

From Scotswood to Snowdens Hole or Dents Hole	7	6	3	10	11	4
From all Places below Scotswood, and West of the Bridge to Snowdens Hole or Dents Hole	7	6	3	6	11	0
From Stella to St Anthony's	7	8	5	2	12	10
From Blaydon to St Anthony's	7	8	4	10	12	6
Lemington to St Anthony's	7	8	4	6	12	2
Denton to St Anthony's	7	8	4	2	11	10
Scotswood to St Anthony's	7	8	3	10	11	6
From all Places below Scotswood, and West of the Bridge to St Anthony's	7	8	3	6	11	2
From Stella to Billlratch	9	0	5	2	14	2
From Blaydon to Billratch	9	0	4	10	13	10
From Lemington to Billratch	9	0	4	6	13	6
From Denton to Billratch	9	0	4	2	13	2
From Scotswood to Billratch	9	0	3	10	12	10
From all Places below Scotswood, and West of the Bridge to Billratch	9	0	3	6	12	6
From Stella to below the Pace	11	8	5	2	16	10
From Blaydon to below the Pace	11	8	4	10	16	6
From Lemington to below the Pace	11	8	4	6	16	2
From Denton to below the Pace	11	8	4	2	15	10
From Scotswood to below the Pace	11	8	3	10	15	6
From all Places below Scotswood, and West of the Bridge to below the Pace	11	8	3	6	15	2
From Stella to Shields	13	4	5	2	18	6
From Blaydon to Shields	13	4	4	10	18	2
From Lemington to Shields	13	4	4	6	17	10
From Denton to Shields	13	4	4	2	17	6
From Scotswood to Shields	13	4	3	10	17	2
From all Places below Scotswood, and West of the Bridge to Shields	13	4	3	6	16	10

Signed by the Magistrates and Fitters

[1] The keel dues remained as they were in 1710 (see above **Document 22**) and

repeated in 1744, but the owners' wages were increased. The amounts stated would have to be shared among each keel's crew. Provision was made for those working below Scotswood, to address the anomaly that Nathaniel Clayton pointed out in his letter to J.E. Blackett (see above), but, despite what Anthony Hood wrote to Clayton about the skippers' wages, it was merely 'recommended' that they should be paid one shilling more than the other men. The above Regulation was engrossed on parchment, sealed with the Corporation seal, and signed by seven magistrates and thirteen fitters (TWA 394/34).

198. Andrew Mitchell, Schoolmaster, *An Address to the Society of Keelmen on the River Tyne, with a correct Table of the Dues of the River* (Newcastle, 1792), printed for the author and sold at his School in Peter's Entry, Sandgate [NCL, John Bell, *Collections relative to the River Tyne: its Trade and the Conservancy thereof*, vol. I, No. 30]

I have been led to this when I consider the few friends you seem to have. I some time ago signified in a company my surprize, that, during the time your masters and you did not understand one another about the grievances you complained of, none appeared to give the public a view of them, as they had done to some others in like circumstances. But I was told you were such a set of men as few cared to trouble themselves with; however, I am happy to see matters turned out as well, both with respect to your fund and to your wages. I shall therefore give you a little advice about each. I was led also to those considerations from some discourses I heard in public companies, who would lay wagers, that in a few years, you would loss again what you had now obtained, that cans would be filled, and liquor taken at staiths, and sixpences given for spouts as formerly. What, said they, do not some fill cans already, and give spout sixpences too? But, as I know little of those affairs, I could say nothing to the contrary, but I thought if it were truth, that certainly you were the most simple men in the world, who, after so much trouble and expence, had obtained such good answers from the gentlemen to your petitions, should lose them again by your own simplicity. I thought who would pity such fools. But I hope better things of you, and if you please to follow the advice here given you, it will both tend to your own benefit, and keep the gentlemen from a deal of trouble with you.

My friends, were I persuaded you were such a set of men as you are represented by some to be, I should think my time ill-spent to give you my advice; but from my acquaintance of many of you I am inclined to think otherwise, and therefore make free to give you the following advice.

I have in the table of the dues, placed them as they were settled by the gentlemen on the 26th of September, 1791, which is undoubtedly the present dues of the river. They then established them, as had been done in the years 1710 and 1744, which statement stood fast from those years, until the beginning of the year 1792, when the statement made on the 26th of September took place, and how long it may continue no man knows, so that no keelman has any occasion to make any new bargains, no, not in the least, to hurt the said statement; and whoever attempts to do so, not only hurts the keelmen, but casts great dishonour upon the gentlemen; as you may be sure, they do not want to throw the river into a continual confusion, nor to have the keelmen's wages to settle every day.

Now, dear friends, it must give very much pleasure to all your well wishers, that after much expence and trouble, you have at length obtained a permanent fund for answering those good purposes mentioned in the Act of Parliament, which if you were all as sensible of as some are, you would endeavour to guard it with much prudence. I have considered your Act with great attention, and own, that though some things in it might have been better modelled, yet it is to a wonder; but if you take not special care of admitting members, it will not answer its original intention. And although your Guardians be gentlemen of benevolent, humane dispositions, yet it lies in your own power to guard against admitting of members who should not be admitted; and if you would take a pattern by other united societies, such as the Free Masons, and others, you will soon find its good effects. I think you are more proper to guard on this point than even your Guardians can be expected to be. So passing by what has been done formerly, I would advise you to be on your guard.

And 1st, Your Act that says, None shall receive any benefit from the said fund who has not contributed thereto one whole year without intermission:- Pray what is the sense of this? Does it mean any man, or does it mean a keelman? A keelman to be sure. The Act was got for the benefit of keelmen only: it was not for tradesmen. Should a tradesman serving under one fitter four months; three under another &c, until it be one year, is he then a keelman, or has he any title to the fund? No, absurd nonsense to imagine such a thing; undoubtedly then you are the best judges when a man may be said to be a keelman. If a man comes to the keels at 20, 30, or 40 years, and work one year, is he then a keelman? If so, I acknowledge I do not understand the word.

2d, But granting when men are scarce that men may come to the keels, yet I think you should have a fixed age agreed upon, that if any come above that age agreed upon that they should serve such a term of years as your guardians and stewards may fix upon in their by-laws, which, without doubt, will cast great light upon the Act.

3d. What relates to the regulation of the measure, both you and all concerned may think themselves happy, that that affair is so well settled already; and certainly no man of conscience will trifle with the oath of God; but if any such monsters may be, you have it in your power to try them by law; but always be sure you do justice, as you would desire justice done to you.

4th. I come now to consider your duty in your present circumstances. We ought all to be thankful to God that, in our days, freedom and liberty has spread so much among all ranks of men, but yet we are to beware that we use it not to bad purposes. You ought always to consider yourselves in the line God has been pleased to place you, viz. that of servants; the master's duty is to order and command, and that of the servant to submit and obey; and if this be duly attended to, your lives would be more comfortable than many times they are; yet I understand the master to command nothing but what is just and equitable, and, if so, then certainly it is your duty to obey, giving honour to whom honour is due.

5th. I think it your duty to remember with thankfulness and gratitude, the attention payed by the gentlemen to your petitions, 26th of last September, and the generous redress granted you to your several complaints, which I think you ought to guard with greatest caution and respect, and take care that no mean-spirited men among you use any means, either directly or indirectly, to ensnare the river and bring them back to their former bondage, such as filling cans, or giving six pences for spouts, or taking liquor at staiths for your work; these are the 3 articles you are in the greatest danger of being brought back to by mean ignorant men. Do not imagine that I would advise you against drinking; by no means, but only I would advise you to regulate it in such a manner as you might be respected and thought of as well as other tradesmen are for your money, and not to be used ill, as formerly you have been, but to have the pleasure that others have to lay it out, when you please, where you please, and what you please, according as you get good liquor and good usage. But in case there should be any such thoughtless men among you that through any intention, or by ill advice, should endeavour to ensnare the river again, I would advise each gentleman's servants, to enter into an agreement, that if any ignorant men shall, directly or indirectly, endeavour to break or infringe the present privilege of the keelmen, granted them on 26 September 1791, that the same be fined in the sum of ……. and the same payd into the secretary of the keelmen's fund to go into the same.

Now, my friends, if you should neglect to advert to the advice I lay before you and be led again into your former bondage, who will pity you? I should be sorry to hear of it. Now, if in case, in aftertime, I should happen to meet any of your sensible men coming in a body to town, and if I should ask them, My friends, where are you going to? and they should answer (going), We are going to throw in a petition to the mayor and the gentlemen. A petition (say I) what want you now? (Want man) we are worse than ever we were; we get nothing at staiths for our work but drink, and that very bad, and our can houses are as bad as ever, giving both bad usage, and bad drink, and if we go in to get a glass to ourselves, we must sit behind backs, or probably go to a room where there is no fire, and if we want a can or beer money, we must take it out of the house to drink it, or want it, and be snuft and sneard at, as if we were dogs, and is that right, think you? Right (says I), do you deserve any better, were you not at your freedom?, and was there not liberty granted you by the mayor and gentlemen already to drink where you pleased? Pray, do you imagine the gentlemen has nothing to do but mind you every day? You mind me of children who throw away their play things on purpose that you may give them again. How lost you your rights when you had them? Lost them, you may say so, why those poor simple silly men that were the occasion of losing them will not now shew their faces, but make plenty of noise about them. Fy, get us this and that, throw in a petition, make a stop &c., but if they had considered before, they would not have betrayed the men by their mean conduct.

Now follows the dues of the River: You must know that the gentlemen of the Corporation, foreseeing the confusion that would attend an unsettled state of the keelmen's wages in this river did in 1710 agree that the following dues should be settled as the dues of this river, which settlement was confirmed on the 4th day of August 1744 on parchment as the other was by the signatures of 8 magistrates and 24 fitters, now in the possession of the keelmen. You must understand further that the [1744] table is now altered, as the keelmen found themselves under the disagreeable necessity of giving in some petitions to the gentlemen, on the 26th of September, 1791, as the aforesaid wages was found not adequate to support them, on account of the high advance of the necessaries of life, which petitions were generously considered, and answered by one of the most respectable meetings that ever was held in Newcastle. [The further regulations] were signed by 7 magistrates and 17 fitters. If any fitters have not yet subscribed they are engaged by the agreement of 26 September 1791 in which all agreed to give the same security as in 1710 and 1744.[1]

So the keelmen must put them in mind of their promise before they engage for the year 1793, as they forgot last year.

That the foregoing table is the stated dues of this river is without doubt, and will remain as such, until they be altered by the same authority who settled them, which I wish never to see. And any individual who shall attempt in any manner of way to break, alter, or infringe upon the said statement, throws contempt and a daring affront upon a deed of the most respectable and judicious meeting of gentlemen that possibly ever met in Newcastle, and an insult upon the understandings of men, and calls their candid, wise, prudent determinations for good, both of masters and servants, folly and nonsense. Wonderful ignorance that men should be so blind and stupid as to study to hurt their own interest! Should any ignorant stupid person or persons demand more than was granted them, they would soon be deemed unreasonable. Are they not the same who would abridge them any manner of way of their just property? No skipper or any man has any right to want any of those privileges granted them. And if any such mean, unworthy, ignorant, cowardly men should be found as would any way endeavour to loss their properties, and endanger their brethren, how ought they to be corrected for their folly, I shall leave you to judge.

Now my friends, from what I have said, you will both see your duty and your interest. 1st, Your duty to the gentlemen who have been so kind to you in granting you an ample redress of your complaints; and you ought on the other hand to express your thankfulness to them, and your employers, by being good, honest, obedient servants; and I am in no doubt to think but what will engage them to do what is right to you. 2ndly, It is your interest to stand fast in that liberty with which you are made free, that you loss none of those privileges granted to you; for the man who will not mind his own interest and right will never mind his master's good. And if you pay attention to the advice I have given and laid down to you, I possibly may appear again in your favour, but if they be disregarded, as I am the first I know of, so I dare say I will be the last, that ever will appear in your favour any more.

[1] The tables of dues are set out above, **Document 197**.

RIOTS BY KEELMEN AT SUNDERLAND

199. The *Newcastle Courant*, 23 February 1793

Sunday evening a party of the Innesgilling Regiment of Dragoons marched into Sunderland, and on Monday morning 7 of the riotous keelmen were committed to Durham Gaol and there safely lodged under the escort of Mr Milbanke and Mr Errick, 2 Justices of the Peace, attended by a troop of horse. On the road through Bishopwearmouth they were assaulted with a shower of brickbats, filth, &c by a mob assembled in a riotous manner in the Panfield. The dragoons were then ordered to clear the streets through which they paraded, but luckily none of the inhabitants were hurt.

On Thursday a number of the well-disposed keelmen promised to restore the wonted lustre of business to that disturbed Town by again opening the flourishing trade of that Port which has been for several weeks suspended. A strong military guard was ordered to protect them from the insults of the refactory, and attended on the shore near to where the greatest number of keels are moored, but the dread of future treatment they might experience from their incensed brethren so far deterred them that not one of their party appeared to fulfil a promise so pregnant with benefit to all ranks of people concerned.

Early yesterday morning the dragoons marched from Newcastle, headed by some of the Magistrates for County Durham, to suppress the tumults now existing amongst the colliers upon the West, which they happily effected without any disturbance, and the colliers have quietly returned to their avocations.

Some insidious villains have certainly subverted the minds of the many, and might be happy, artificers, mariners, watermen &c in this neighbourhood, some of whom will long repent their illegal combinations which at present prey on the public and private peace of the community at large, but will, it is hoped, end in confusion of the villainous projectors of such vile machinations.

DISPUTE OVER THE LOADING OF SHIPS BY SPOUTS, 1794

200. *Newcastle Courant*, 19 July 1794

For some days past the keelmen have stopped work under a pretence of the spouts on the staiths below bridge where ships of small burthen are loaded without the aid of keels. Thinking themselves aggrieved, a part of the men more turbulent than the rest destroyed several spouts and did other damage. By the spirited exertions of the magistrates of this Town, and neighbouring magistrates of Northumberland and Durham, the business is in a fair way of accommodation and it is hoped the keelmen will in a few days go to work. At the instance of the magistrates a party of the Earl of Darlington's Durham Rangers marched into Town to aid the North York and West York Militia quartered here and at Tynemouth Barracks to suppress the commotion, if occasion requires.[1]

[1] On 6 June 1794, the High Sheriff of Northumberland, C.J. Clavering, had informed the government that from the 'peculiar situation of the County of Northumberland any attempt to raise volunteer cavalry consisting of gentlemen and yeomen would not be likely to be successful', and that a committee held on 5 June thought that 'under all existing circumstances' it would be most advisable to apply a subscription that had been made to raising a corps of 360 men on the terms mentioned. Henry Dundas, Secretary of War, replied that the King observed with great satisfaction the liberal subscription that had been made but disapproved of the corps being kept in constant pay. Dundas thought that if the committee should judge it expedient from any local circumstances that a force should immediately be called out and embodied in the county, the expense should be defrayed out of the funds subscribed (TNA, HO 43/5, Entry Books, pp. 213–14).

201. Charles Brandling to the Duke of Portland [TNA, HO 42/32/325]

Gosforth House, 19 July 1794

My Lord Duke,

Being considered by the keelmen on the River Tyne as the person who prevented their demands being complyed with, which was a violation of private property, I take the liberty of inclosing your Grace two handbills published by the Coal Owners which I trust will remove from your Grace's mind and the Government of this country every impression unfavourable to my conduct on this occasion. The mob remain (but with some hopes of their going to work on Monday next [21 July] in a state of sulkey discontent, and it is the opinion of the well disposed that a little success in their demands would induce them to come forward and avow principles of the worst kind, but I am convinced this will be prevented by the civil power aided by the steady conduct of the military.

I am, your Grace's most obedient humble Servant,

Charles Brandling

201a. Enclosure in above [TNA, HO 42/32/327]

11 July 1794

Whereas a report has prevailed among the keelmen that at a meeting of the Coal Owners and Fitters held at the Mayor's Chamber on Thursday last, Mr Brandling was the only person present who refused to remove the spouts at his staith at Felling, we whose names are hereunto subscribed publicly assert in justice to Mr Brandling that we perfectly agreed with him in opinion that it would be unjust to remove the spouts erected *at any staiths* on the River Tyne.

Signed by T.C. Bigge, Matthew Montagu, William Peareth, Richard Bell, William Row, William Cramlington, John Marley, Thomas Ismay, Anthony Hood, Robert Rayne, Robert Taylor for Wallsend and Usworth Main Collieries, William Surtees for Benwell, William Surtees for Sheriff Hill. H.U. Reay was not present but entirely concurs.

201b. Further enclosure in above [TNA, HO 42/32/326]

Newcastle, 15 July 1794

We whose names are hereunto subscribed feel ourselves particularly called upon at this time to declare our intention to persevere in loading coals at our respective staiths and spouts, both into the keels and ships, in the usual manner.

Signed by Thomas Charles Bigge (one of the Trustees of the late William Ord), William Peareth for Walker Colliery, Matthew Montagu for Mrs Montagu, William Cramlington, Aubone Surtees (for Adair's Main and Gateshead Park), Mr Brandling for Felling Colliery, Robert Lisle, George Johnson, William Row, Thomas Ismay for Greenwich Moor Colliery, Robert Taylor for William Russell Esq. & Co., David Crawford for Bowes's Main, James Row for Matthew Bell and Richard Bell, William Leaviss, Anthony Hood for Pontop-Pike and Bladon, John Buddle for John Silvertop.

202. *Newcastle Courant*, **26 July 1794**

The commotions of the keelmen still continue, but by the prudent and at the same time spirited measures pursued by the magistrates there is great reason to hope that the matter in dispute will in a few days be amicably terminated. Some of the most refactory keelmen have been apprehended and sent to Durham Gaol, under a strong escort of Light Dragoons.

On Tuesday morning two troops of Colonel Leigh's Lancashire Dragoons marched in here from Derby. Their march was uncommonly rapid, and their conduct since their arrival highly approvable.

Riots and Riotous Proceedings

For preservation of peace and good order a great number of the inhabitants of this Town have voluntarily offered themselves to the Magistrates and been sworn in constables, it is sincerely wished the inhabitants at large will stand forward and offer themselves for this truly and effectual assistance to the Magistrates now at this peculiar crisis. Magistrates will attend the Mayor's Chamber to swear in.

Upwards of 100 gentleman of the first respectability of town and neighbourhood have voluntarily been sworn in as extra constables, and should these riotous proceedings be persevered in, many more have offered their assistance to restore that order which can alone give happiness to every truly loyal British subject.

203. *Newcastle Courant*, 2 August 1794

On Tuesday [29 July] the keelmen quietly returned to their work by which the extensive commerce of the Tyne is restored to its usual vigour. It is sincerely to be hoped that the happy unanimity so very conducive to the welfare of a trade that gives sustenance to thousands will not be again interrupted.

204. *Newcastle Courant*, 2 August 1794

Charles Brandling: Address to the Public

Gosforth House, 30 July 1794

Whenever a dispute of any kind tends to the disturbance of the public peace, it becomes a subject of general concern, but it does not always happen that the popular decision on the conduct of the parties is free from error, because the information on which they form that decision is too often partial, and misrepresentations, industriously spread, frequently gain credit, while the plain truth is disregarded. It is for this reason that I conceive it a duty I owe to myself to lay before the public a concise statement of what happened during the late commotion.

It must be well known to the trade, though not to the public, that the dispute in which the parties were involved originated with the keelmen demanding that the spouts hitherto used for the loading of vessels at the staiths below the Bridge should be laid aside, and to enforce that demand, on Monday the 7th instant, they abandoned their work.

On the Thursday following, at a respectable meeting of the Coal-owners and Fitters, it was unanimously resolved that the demand of the keelmen, being a direct infringement of property, and of the right they legally possessed to ship their coals in the most eligible way that the situation of their work admitted, could not be acceded to without exposing all other property to claims equally incompatible with justice; and was therefore rejected. This resolution was communicated and explained to the persons acting as stewards to the keelmen by me, but a very unfounded report having gained general circulation among the keelmen, that I was the cause of their demand not being complied with, it was deemed necessary to remove so unfair an imputation by the circulation of the following hand bill:

Newcastle, 11 July 1794. Whereas a report has prevailed among the keelmen that at a meeting of the Coal Owners and Fitters held at the Mayor's Chamber on Thursday last, Mr Brandling was the only person present who refused to remove the spouts at his staith at Felling, we whose names are hereunto subscribed publicly assert in justice to Mr Brandling that we perfectly agreed with him in opinion that it would be unjust to remove the spouts erected *at any staiths* on the River Tyne.

Signed by T.C. Bigge, Matthew Montagu, William Peareth, Richard Bell, William Row, William Cramlington, John Marley, Thomas Ismay, Anthony Hood, Robert Rayne, Robert Taylor for Wallsend and Usworth Main Collieries, William Surtees for Benwell, William Surtees for Sheriff Hill. H.U. Reay was not present but entirely concurs.

Previous to the printing of this declaration, but on the same day, a conference was held with the Stewards of the keelmen at the Walker Office, who not giving up their demand, received the same answer as before; and matters remained in this situation until Monday the 14th instant when a numerous party of keelmen assembled and proceeded to demolish the ship spouts at Brandling's Main, Walker, Wallsend, and Usworth Main, which they not only in part effected, but actually stopt the pitts at the three first mentioned collieries, as well as at Bigge's Main and Heaton, damaged the staiths and some colliery materials, and threatened the pitmen with violence if they returned to their employment.

These outrages called forth the Magistracy who have protected person and property by the aid of the military power; and it was agreed by the Coal-Owners and Fitters, at a third meeting, to declare their intentions by the following hand bill:

Newcastle, 15 July 1794. We whose names are hereunto subscribed feel ourselves particularly called upon at this time to declare our intention to persevere in loading coals at our respective staiths and spouts, both into the keels and ships, in the usual manner.

Signed by Thomas Charles Bigge (one of the Trustees of the

late William Ord), William Peareth for Walker Colliery, Matthew Montagu for Mrs Montagu, William Cramlington, Aubone Surtees (for Adair's Main and Gateshead Park), Mr Brandling for Felling Colliery, Robert Lisle, George Johnson, William Row, Thomas Ismay for Greenwich Moor Colliery, Robert Taylor for William Russell Esq. & Co., David Crawford for Bowes's Main, James Row for Matthew Bell and Richard Bell, William Leaviss, Anthony Hood for Pontop-Pike and Bladon, John Buddle for John Silvertop.

On the Thursday following, a paper was received from the keelmen desiring that, instead of the total abolition of the spouts, no ships should be loaded at the staiths for London, and that 2 shillings per tide should be added to their wages, and 6 pence per keel on all coals put on board vessels from the spouts paid into their fund.

The answer they received was that the demand respecting the spouts and the additional dues could not be complied with, but that if they returned to their employment, any reasonable complaint would be taken into consideration and redressed.

The subsequent conduct of the keelmen must be known to every person in Newcastle and its vicinity; and I have only to add and I am confident I speak the sense of the Coal-Owners at large, that while they are ready to listen to and redress any real grievance that useful body of men may fall under, they are determined to resist, with firmness, every illegal and compulsory attempt on their *Rights and Property*.

Charles Brandling

205. *Newcastle Courant*, 16 August 1794

Address to the Public from the Keelmen employed on the
River Tyne, 9 August 1794

As Mr Brandling has given the public one side of the dispute between the Keelmen and some Coal Owners, we think it also our duty to lay before the public the other side of the cause of the dispute and let the public judge. It must be well known to the Trade, though not to the public, that a similar dispute originated with the Coal Owners above 30 years ago but was taken little notice of until 1771 when the Keelmen took the alarm and stopped working four weeks, and ever since has lain dormant, though still considered a grievance; but as its amazing progress threatens not only the hurt of many besides us, but also the free navigation of the River, it is thought high time to put those concerned in mind thereof, as no less than nine staiths below Bridge, each having two spouts (except one) for loading ships from 5 to 13 keels burthen, and more in forwardness, by which a large quantity of coals are shipped to the great hurt both of us and the public; it was therefore at the yearly meeting of the stewards of our fund unanimously agreed that a petition should be made setting forth the many evils arising from this practice, which should be laid before the gentlemen concerned, they having no doubt of its success; this was on July 2nd. But to the surprize not only of the gentlemen, but also of the majority of the Keelmen, a stop was all at once made of the keels on the 7th; then it became the duty of all concerned to have matters settled as soon as possible. The stewards for the fund found themselves under no obligation to act in this affair more than any other man, so delegates were chosen to let the gentlemen know what they wanted. Accordingly a petition was given to the Mayor to call a meeting of the coal owners, fitters and ship owners to hear the complaints of the Keelmen, so the Mayor gave orders for that purpose; but none of the ship owners attended, notwithstanding their former promises to stand by the Keelmen, as their complaints tended to inforce those of the Keelmen's; the whole business was therefore thrown on the Keelmen.

Accordingly the gentlemen met on the 10th and the Keelmen's delegates waited on them, who after hearing their complaints, viz. that by this practice their work was shortened, so that at the advanced prices of the necessaries of life they cannot earn a sufficient support to their families, and by this means many of their families are kept in very indigent circumstances, who might otherwise, if fully employed, be enabled to keep their credit with such persons as intrust them; and many of them being in such great distress that their Fund, to which they contributed out of their wages, for the support of their own poor, was greatly diminished by it; and on the gentlemen's hearing of these complaints, one would have supposed that a hand bill would have appeared to convince them of their error of stopping working until their bonds were fulfilled, and that no reasonable man would take part with them as they now stood, but that they were sorry to hear of the distress of their families and that enquiry should be made for a temporary relief to be granted them, and that a further enquiry should be made into the state of their complaints, and, if possible, should be redressed as circumstances occurred. But instead of anything consolatory, a bill appeared without the least glance at anything like a redress ever to be expected. Now what the consequence of this was is too well known. And what does commonly appear when those in power neglect salutary methods to prevent them? What was next done! A set of armed men was sent for, which raised an alarm as if the Keelmen intended to turn the world upside down! when it was well known we wanted no more than work to support ourselves and families, and for the good of the public in general, and the causes of the want to be removed, our highest ambition being always to work freely and to spend as freely, for if money be scarce, they are mistaken who imagine it to be in our possession. And had what was expended on them been given as relief to such Keelmen's families as were found to be in real distress for want of employment, with a few friendly words, the commotion, perhaps, would soon have been at an end. And which of these two methods would have been most honourable to the gentlemen, let the public judge. But instead thereof, horse and foot were employed to chase and affright women and children, and no regard paid to guilty or innocent. It appeared as if the gentlemen had wanted to excite a mob, to the disgrace of the country, when it was well known that we wanted no such thing, as most part of us were as great enemies to every disorderly practice as they were. However on the 15th, another hand bill appeared to the same import as the first, to stand to their resolutions, having no respect to the cry of the poor, nor any thought of that awful but certain text 'whoso stoppeth his ears at the cry of the poor, he also shall cry himself but shall not be heard'. And on appearance of which another general meeting was held on the Windmill Hills to consider what method we could fall upon to restore peace and good order, as it appeared to us that the gentlemen had missed it. So the delegates chosen proposed another plan, rather to amuse and persuade our brethren to go to work than expecting the request to be granted, but, however, it failed on both sides. The gentlemen told us it could not be granted, and the Keelmen told us it was not the mind of the majority, for nothing would satisfy them but their first object. So the next Saturday the stewards of the Fund were ordered to wait on the gentlemen who accordingly attended, and great pains were taken to convince them of their error; this was the easier done, as they were to a man, with many more of the Keelmen, were sensible, however enormous their grievances might be, they were not in a proper way to obtain redress, neither were they able to bring many of their brethren to think with them, but, however, they were advised to serve their year out quietly, and make better terms for the next. So on the Monday we had another general meeting on the Quayside, and, after some pains to convince one another, we agreed to go quietly to work on Tuesday the 29th.

Our general meetings were never intended to hurt any man's person or property, but we could not be answerable for the conduct of individuals when such numbers of men meet, but to know one another's minds that a good understanding may be maintained among us, as we have often intermixed in our employment when others are asleep, and when that subsists, we stand in no need of protection from any quarter whatsoever. We should think ourselves happy could the gentlemen concerned concert a plan for the preventing of this growing evil, so as to avoid in future, any uneasiness to us or others concerned.

Thus have we given the outlines of our grievances which we wish to have redressed, not doubting but the gentlemen concerned, after mature deliberation, perhaps, will condescend to redress the grievances we complain of, to the mutual satisfaction of all concerned.

By order of the Committee of Delegates for the whole body of Keelmen, John Wilson, Peter Cook, William Doctor, John Gray, John Walker.

THE KEELMEN STRIKE FOR HIGHER PAY, AND THE AUTHORITIES ATTEMPT TO SUPPRESS THEM, 1809

206. Petition to the Mayor and Fitters, 29 August 1809 [TWA 394/37]

To the Worshipful Joseph Forster, Esqʳ Mayor, and the other Trading Brethren of the Company of Hoastmen, the Petition of the Keelmen on the River Tyne

Humbly sheweth that your petitioners trust they have no need to remind the Worshipful the Mayor and the other Trading Brethren of the Hoastmen's Company of the very high price of every article connected with housekeeping, in so much that should your petitioners have constant employment, or as much work as they could do throughout the year at the present wages, this would be barely sufficient for the maintenance of their respective families.

Your petitioners humbly solicit for an addition of one shilling and six pence per tide each man above Bridge, and one shilling per tide each man below Bridge, and house and firing.

Your petitioners humbly presume in this manner to lay their case before the worshipful the Mayor and the other Trading Brethren of the Hoastmen's Company, in full confidence that it will be received with all due attention.

And your petitioners as in duty bound will ever pray &c.

207. *Aides Mémoires* for the Keelmen's Delegates [TWA 394/37]

The advance of wages craved in the petition bears little proportion to the advance of provisions and necessaries since the year 1710, nor the advances in wages of the other labouring classes.

The wages are irregular, whereas the most of others are [constant?]. The wages of others are proportioned to the different natures and circumstances of their employs, such as those that are exposed to weather, to hardships, to dangers, being more laborious, being mistimed, being from home, having to provide for themselves, separate from the families, being slavish, or dirty, &c, all of which the keelmen can plead, whereas others only a part of them, or occasionally.

The usefulness of the keelmen in the coal trade, as part of the machinery, as a nursery for seamen, and of consequence bearing a large proportion (comparing with their number) in rearing boys for the sea, and in consequence for the navy.

Having [a] boy to vi[c]tual and pay from our own wages.

Having to support our own poor out of our wages.

House rents being exorbitantly high.

208. Minutes of a meeting of Fitters and Keelmen's delegates held at the Mayor's Chamber, 7 September 1809 [TWA 394/37]

The keelmen above bridge wish to have 4s. 6d. a tide or 1s. 6d a man add[itional].

Those below [bridge] 3s. 0d. or 1s. 0d. a man additional, with house and firing.

Their ground is the high price of provisions, and they pretend that even if they were in full work they cannnot make enough to supply their families.

Mr Henry Strachan – Mr Temple's Work – 120 tides since Christmas

John Wallis – Tanfield Moor – 120 tides since Christmas

Joseph Crooks – Hebburn Main – 38 tides since Christmas

William Haine – Walker Owners – 60 tides and 4 bye tides since Christmas

Mr Strachan says that except the 2s. 6d. Bread Money and 1s. 2d. a tide above bridge, their wages have not been raised since 1710.[1] That since that time the necessaries of life are much increased. Particularly pressed at this time for want of work below bridge. Thinks that those who have families should have 2 pound a week. He has a wife and 6 children, the eldest goes in the keel. Last year about 270 tides which was more than in former years. In former years 12 score was a tolerable year.

The Walker keelmen get a trimming every nine weeks – 3 this year.

Within this 24 years every artizan has had his wages doubled. Strachan says that the boys have 13d. a tide. Boys above bridge have about 18d. House rents have advanced to such a pitch that there is no getting them paid. Strachan says he now pays £5 for one room and a backroom – lives near Carfs Landing.

Temple allows one waggon of small coals; Tanfield Moor 2 waggons; Walker Colliery 4s.0d. in lieu of coals.

Has understood that before there was a disturbance and the rates were then fixed, but they agreed amongst themselves for the increase mentioned in the petition and had much difficulty in keeping their expectations so low.

Adjourned to this day week at 11 o'Clock at which the Coal Owners are desired to attend.

At a meeting of the Coal Owners and Fitters held at the Mayor's Chamber this 14th September 1809,

Present: The Mayor, Mr Lambert, Mr Dixon Brown, Mr Gibson, Mr Blackett, Mr Chapman, Mr Crozer, Mr Humble Lamb, Mr Buddle, Mr Grey, Mr Dalton, Mr Ismay, Mr Potts, Mr Watson, Mr Robson

The meeting having taken the matter into serious consideration are of opinion that a committee should be appointed…who shall investigate the grounds of the keelmen's petition and into all the circumstances connected with them, and report their opinion thereon to a general meeting of Coal Owners and Fitters to be held here on Saturday 30th instant at one o'Clock, and that such committee consist of Mr Hood, Mr Dunn, Mr Chapman, Mr Buddle, Mr Crozer, Mr Blackett and Mr Potts.

[1] A marginal note states 'last year the making in money was increased'.

209. William Chapman to Nathaniel Clayton, 3 October 1809
[TWA 394/37]

Dear Sir,

I enclose you the resolutions relative [to] the keelmen which the Committee approve of, and have only made a slight addition throwing the blame where it lies, as they had done in their report.[1] They imagine that many amongst the keelmen will be actuated by reason and therefore they think detail necessary, particularly as it refutes the assertion of their ring leaders that no change has taken place since the reign of Queen Ann. It is thought advisable the paper should go from the Corporation Office to Mr Dees, and they will thank you to send it to him to make a copy for each work.

I am, Dear Sir, Yours truly,
William Chapman

[1] The resolutions are not present.

210. Chapman to Clayton, n.d. [TWA 394/37]

Kenton Hall, Wednesday evening

Dear Sir,

I am a convert to your reasoning and glad you suppressed the obnoxious passage.[1]

I remain, Yours truly,
William Chapman

[1] The contents of 'the obnoxious passage' are not known.

211. Minutes of a meeting of the Magistrates at the Mayor's Chamber, 22 October 1809 [TWA 394/37]

Sunday, 22 October 1809

Present: Mr Mayor, Alderman Blackett, Alderman Clayton, Alderman Smith, Mr Dunn, Mr Blackett, Mr Ismay, Mr Knowsby, Mr Taylor, Mr Crozer, Mr Potts, Mr Pearson

It was stated to the meeting that several keelmen had forcibly interrupted other keelmen discharging their duty on the River. That a ship was stopped at Felling Staith from loading at the spout. That a ship has also been stopped at Walker.

Thomas Onthat, Master of *The Ambulator* of Scarboro, casting his ballast at Walker Quay, was interrupted by several persons appearing to be keelmen, about quarter past 8 this morning, who threatened personal violence to those who continued to cast the ballast and threw several ballast shovels found upon the quay into the River.

Mr Dunn suggested that the Fitter of each work below bridge shall this afternoon call all their keelmen together and require them to go to work pursuant to their bond. That in case of their refusal they should resort to the proper magistrate, and make information of their refusal, who will issue the proper warrants for apprehension of the offenders.

The disturbance has been occasioned by the keelmen employed in the works below Bridge. These are: Felling, Ellison Main, Heaton, Bewick Main, Walker, Kenton, Walls End, Willington, Benton and Killingworth, Hebburn, Percy Main, Temples.

The agent for Walker informed the meeting that the five several persons bound keelmen in the Walker employment being asked and required by Mr William Heaton to go to their work, and a positive answer being also required whether they would or not, refused to go to their work – [Thomas] Gibb particularly replied that they would not go till what they had petitioned for was granted. The others answered to the same effect. James Sword, John Purvis, Thomas Gibb, David Cuthbert and Walter Usher, the latter a skipper. Sword, Cuthbert and Purvis said to be young men.

Mr Taylor informed the meeting that he last night ordered the several persons after mentioned, keelmen employed in the Wallsend Work, to go to work this morning, to which they in general answered they would go to work if others did, but they have absented themselves from their work: Cuthbert Birtley, John Stewart, Ralph Faddy, Thomas Brown, Robert Harrison, John Henderson, John Black, Thomas Caverhill, Taylor Coats, Thomas Malfin – all skippers and married men.

Ralph Harrison, running fitter to the Hebburn Owners, went among the keelmen last night and required them to go to work this morning. They answered they would go to work if the rest did. They have not gone to work. The names were: John Nixon, James Baxter, Robert Scott, Joseph Manvel, Thomas Watson, William Gill, Edward Oliver, Jacob Thrift, John Cole, William Gilchrist, Joseph Crooks, Thomas Raith, John Surtees, B. Carr, Joseph Noble, James Carr. All married men save Noble who is about 20 years old.

William Cash, Staithman at Felling, states that some of the keelmen had taken out 3 of their own body, who were employed trimming, forcibly, and telling them that if they did not discontinue trimming they would force. Called the men together to give them orders to go to work. They generally answered they would not till their demands for an increase of wages were complied with. They added that it was 3 shillings a tide [additional] with house and firing. On witness expostulating with them on the illegality of their proceedings, they said they were unable to live on their present wages and it was indifferent to them whether they were committed to the County Gaol or not. Their names are: Cuthbert Atkinson, skipper, Alexander Young, Archibald Parkin; Michael Young, skipper, Edward Oliver, [John Douglas, *crossed out*]; Christopher Richardson, skipper, Edward Richardson, married, John Grey, married; John Wallace, skipper, Henry Elliott, married, Thomas Wraith, married; [William Chance, skipper, *crossed out*], George Chance, John Simpson; F. Black, skipper, Edward Moor, senior, Edward Moor, junior; John Forster, skipper, George Forster, married; [J. Fairfull, *crossed out*]. Live chiefly on the South side of the River near Felling or Snowdons Hole.

John Thornhill called the keelmen of Sheriff Hill Work together and required them to go to work. All save James Emmerson said would go if others would let [them]. James Emmerson – lives at Felling Shore – said would not go till wages raised.

William Chicken called the men of Heaton together last night and required them to go to work. The following persons refused to do saying that they would not go till the wages are raised: Isaac Henzell, James Commons, John Tomlinson, but Thomas Tempest will stand as long as the rest. Live at Dents Hole and St Anthonys.

212. Return of the dispositions of the Keelmen employed in Heaton Work[1] [TWA 394/37]

1. Robert Stephenson, willing to go [to work] if others go, but will not go first.
   John Stephenson, [as above] though rather worse.
   Isaac Hensell, will not go till wages are raised.
2. Henry Wetherburn, Robert Stott, John Stott [no information].
3. William Tempest, if others will go he will.
   Thomas Tempest, will stand as long as the rest.
   Robert Turnbull, [no information].
4. William Darling, willing when the other men will let him.
   Edward Johnson [no information].
   Charles Miller, has been absent from his keel several weeks.
5. Joseph Craigs, if others go he is willing.
   James Craigs [no information].
   James Nelson, has been absent several months.
6. Thomas Marshall [no information].
   James Commons, will not go till wages are raised.
   Thomas Norton [no information].
7. William Brown, his keel is on the carpenters and will be ready about Thursday.
   George West, sick.
   George Hogg, will not go till wages raised.
8. William Carter, willing; has promised to start in the morning.
   William Chicken, as above.
   Michael Gray, as above.
9. John Tomlinson, will not go till wages are raised.
   George Gray [no information].
   Allen West, will go if others do but not else.
10. Thomas Brownlee, will go if others do but not else.
    Richard Coates, says very little but will not go till the others do.
    John Ellison [no information].

11.   Mark Ross[?], Thomas Smith, William Bewick, keel on the carpenters.

12.   John Brown, John Johnson [no information].
Robert Linsey, willing to go, but says that their puoys, deals &c are stolen.

13.   David Blakey, willing to go and has promised to start as usual.
James Robertson [no information].
Robert Row, has been absent from his keel nearly all summer.

14.   Thomas Jamieson [no information].
William Cockburn, will go if the others will go.

¹ The return is undated but closely associated with the preceding document (**212**). The numbers refer to each keel crew.

213. William Cash to J.B. Pearson, 23 October 1809 [TWA 394/37]

Felling Staith, 23 October 1809

Sir,

I have succeeded in collecting nearly the whole of our men together for the purpose of ordering them to work and also to learn the extent of their demands which they state to be: an additional 3 shillings per tide and to have *houses* and *firing* found them *gratis* – and they are determined not to go to work till this request is granted, even at the risk of being to a man impressed into his Majesty's service or sent to the County Jail. This they have told me in a very pointed manner and almost individually. Hope you will excuse the hasty manner in which this is wrote as I am anxious to send you the above information.

I am, Sir, your most obedient,

William Cash

Our men have all denied having any hand in stopping the waggons today or taking the Trimmers out of the vessel under the spout. They say it is not their intention to interfere with any other class of workmen than keelmen. I expect we shall have *The Providence* finished tomorrow.

[On *verso* of the above]: Edward Pearson for Bell and Brown's Work ordered his men to work yesterday. Did not refuse but said [they] would do as others did. The names are: John Watson, Roger Hall, Robert Forster, William Forster, senior, James Lowthian, Ebenezer Sinclair [of] Byker Buildings, Northumberland, Michael Marr [of] Ballast Hills, Newcastle.

214. Matthew White Ridley, junior, to Mr Brown of the Town Clerk's Office, 24 October 1809 [TWA 394/37]

Heaton, 24 October [1809]

Sir,

I found your letter here on my return home late last night. I beg you will assure the Magistrates of Newcastle that I shall be ready on all occasions to afford them any assistance in my power, but trust from what I have heard this morning that the interference of the civil power at the present time will not be required.

I remain your obedient Servant
Matthew White Ridley, junior

215. 'Information of Thomas Aiston, one of the Constables of the Town and County of Newcastle upon Tyne, taken on oath before me, one of His Majesty's Justices of the Peace, 26 October 1809' [TWA 394/37]

Who saith that by virtue of the warrant now produced, granted by Isaac Cookson, junior, Esquire, Mayor, and one of His Majesty's Justices of the Peace in and for the said Town and County of Newcastle upon Tyne, and indorsed by me, the Justice taking this Information, for the apprehension of one George Heads, he this informant in the presence of three other constables of Newcastle, namely William Russell, William Clarke, and James Makenzie, came up with the said George Heads upon or near a place called St. Peter Quay and then and there took him into custody, and that when he was so in their custody, Thomas Heads, John Heads and George Russell, and several other persons whose names this informant does not know, by force rescued the said George Heads out of the custody of this informant and the said other constables.

Thomas Aiston

Before me, M. W. Ridley, junior

216. Copy, The Mayor to Lieutenant General Dundas [TWA 394/37]

Mayor's Chamber, 26 October 1809

The Mayor of Newcastle presents his respects to Lieutenant General Dundas. Information has been brought to the Mayor that a tumultuous body of persons has this morning by force rescued a keelman who was taken up under a warrant issued against him, and the Mayor therefore fears that the assistance of the military power will be immediately necessary.

218. *Newcastle Courant*, **28 October 1809.**[1]

Hue and Cry

FORTY GUINEAS REWARD. Whereas on Thursday the 26th instant, THOMAS HEADS, JOHN HEADS, and GEORGE RUSSELL, keelmen, residing near Newcastle, did forcibly rescue from the Constables of the said Town the person of GEORGE HEADS, then in their custody by virtue of a warrant, granted by the Right Worshipful the Mayor of Newcastle, for his apprehension. Whoever will apprehend or give such information to any of the said Constables, as may lead to the apprehension of the said Thomas Heads, John Heads, George Russell and George Heads, or any of them, shall receive a reward of TEN GUINEAS each, on applying at the Mayor's Chamber. Newcastle, 27 October 1809.

[1] Repeated in issues of 4, 18, 25 November and up to 30 December.

218. Plan of Operations, Thursday evening, 26 October 1809 [TWA 394/37]

One troop of horse shall meet at the new parade near the Barras Bridge at 6 o'Clock tomorrow morning. The other troop at Gateshead at the head of the Bottle Boate [?] at the same hour.

One half of the first troop shall be guided by one who shall conduct them to Heaton. The other half by one who shall conduct them to the Ouseburn Bridge by Sandyford. The division marched to Heaton shall proceed under the direction of Mr Ridley to the West House near St Anthony's and then turn to the westward, returning up the riverside towards Newcastle. This will bring both divisions of that troop together as they will meet the Ouseburn Bridge division which will be under the direction of the Mayor of Newcastle.

The troop assembled at Gateshead shall, under the direction of Mr Ellison and Mr Phillpotts, be conducted to Felling Shore and so down to Snowdons Hole and shall be attentive to what passes on the north side of the River and to any keelmen who may pass from the north to the south side.

The principal object of the party under the direction of Mr Ridley will be to prevent those keelmen who are in the district of Newcastle escaping down the riverside and by cutting off that means of retreat to increase their alarm. And upon joining the other division under the direction of the Mayor, will endeavour to apprehend the persons named in the several warrants which are intended to be acted upon and will prevent them escaping through Newcastle to the westward, and will wait the joining the division under the direction of Mr Ridley.

The object of the troop assembled at Gateshead and proceeding eastward under the direction of Mr Ellison and Mr Phillpotts will be to observe the movements of the military on the north side and prevent the keelmen assembled on the north side from escaping over the River, and to aid the execution of the warrants issued against the offenders belonging to Felling who mostly reside at Snowdons Hole.

A proper officer will be sent with these warrants to meet Mr Ellison and Mr Phillpotts on their way to Felling Shore. The Corporation boats will be on the River attending to the movements of the military on each side and be ready to afford them the means of communicating with each other.

219. Directions for Mr Ostte and his Assistants. Thursday evening, 26 October 1809 [TWA 394/37]

They will proceed down the River from the Newcastle Quay at half past 6 [o'Clock] tomorrow morning in two boats, attending carefully to the motions of the keelmen on both sides of the River. When they reach the Ouseburn they will observe the military parties on the north side of the River. One boat is to stay there, the other to proceed to Felling Shore where another party of military [is stationed] and probably a third party on the north side nearly opposite. It will be Mr Ostte's business in one boat, and Mr Peter Row in another, to attend to the motions of the military on both sides of the River and be ready to fulfill any directions they may respectively receive from the Magistrates who accompany them and keep open the communication between them, also conveying any messages that may be sent from one to the other. They will also endeavour to prevent any keelmen passing from one side of the River to the other, and give notice to the Magistrates on either side of anything that appears to them worthy of their attention.

It is to be understood that one of the boats is to attend to the motions of the military on the north side of the River near the Ouseburn and the other to the motions of those at Felling Shore and the opposite side. The boat at Felling Shore will probably be called on to ferry Mr Cocke of that place from the north side to the south side which they will take care to do. Mr Cocke will be at Dentshole Ferry about 7 [o'Clock] in the morning or soon after.

220. Note to the Magistrates of Newcastle as to the appointment of Guides by the Fitters [TWA 394/37]

Friday evening, 8 o'Clock

The Committee [of Fitters] will attend to the recommendation of the Magistrates as to Guides to accompany the military detachments tomorrow and will thank Mr Brown for a list of the names of the men against whom warrants are issued.[1] [Signed] J.B.

[1] The list was duly provided and gives the names of 73 keelmen, their place of abode and the names of the informants against them. A further list of 21 persons against whom warrants were granted gives only the men's names and those of their employers. There is some duplication with the previous list (TWA 394/37).

221. Minutes of Proposition to the Keelmen [TWA 394/37]

Mayor's Chamber, 27 October 1809

On the keelmen's going to work, the Magistrates of the 3 Counties now present will themselves take into consideration the petition presented some time ago by the keelmen to the stewards of the Hostmen's Company, the answer of the Coalowners and Fitters to that petition, and the paper now presented, sealed and addressed to the gentlemen Coalowners and Fitters of the River Tyne. And that they will, after maturely considering the same, hand over the papers with their opinion upon them to the Coalowners and Fitters for their ['further' *crossed out*] consideration.[1]

[1] The next day the magistrates of the three counties met with representatives of nineteen works, of which thirteen had stopped but six were still working, though in the case of Brandlings, the men who would not work were 'a less number'; 'several [did] not dare to work'. Six works were not represented. A deputation of keelmen also attended (TWA 394/37).

222. Oath taken by 10 Special Constables sworn before Isaac Cookson, junior, Mayor, 31 October 1809[1] [TWA 394/37]

You shall well and truly serve our Sovereign Lord the King in the office of Special Constable for the Town and County of Newcastle upon Tyne for the space of fourteen days from this day according to the best of your skill and knowledge. So help you God.

[1] Two more special constables were sworn on 1 November, and a further seven on 4 November.

223. George Mowsley to Captain Charleton, 31 October 1809

[NCL, J. Bell, *Collections relative to the River Tyne: its Trade and the Conservancy thereof*, II, f. 90]

George Inn, 31 October 1809

Sir,

Mr Dixon Brown, Mr Joseph Lamb and myself have just had the pleasure of calling on you and are sorry to have interrupted you at dinner. We are deputed, Sir, by a meeting of the Magistrates and Coal Trade of Newcastle, assembled at the Mayor's Chamber this morning, to wait on you to state to you a plan which has been devised by the meeting and in which your aid and concurrence will be essentially necessary, and, as we have been requested to return to Newcastle as speedily as possible, you will oblige us by granting us an early interview, and, as the matter we have to propose is so essentially necessary to the interest of the Coal Trade, we trust will plead our excuse for our troubling you.

I have the honor to remain, Sir, your most obedient Servant,
George Mowsley

224. Joseph Lamb to Charleton, 31 October 1809 [NCL, J. Bell, *Collections relative to the River Tyne: its Trade and the Conservancy thereof*, II, f. 93]

Sir,

I have just left the Mayor with a deputation of Coal Owners and he has kindly given us every assistance we could wish to carry [out] our plan of navigating the keels by strangers tomorrow. The fair being held prevents his being able to assist us by his presence on the River, but Messrs Aldermen Cramlington and Smith, or one of them, will be in the Mayor's Barge and will give the necessary directions to the boats you were so good as to promise us if it is necessary to call their crews into action. We hope they will meet us tomorrow morning at St Anthonys at 9 o'Clock.

Your most obedient Servant,
Joseph Lamb

225. Copy Requisition from the Fitters of Newcastle to the Mayor, 2 November 1809 [NCL, J. Bell, *Collections relative to the River Tyne: its Trade and the Conservancy thereof*, II, f. 94]

The undersigned fitters of Newcastle being satisfied that Captain Charleton's boats have by appearing on the River yesterday and this day contributed in a great degree to keep the keelmen in check, request that the Right Worshipful the Mayor will be so good as to apply to Captain Charleton for his assistance tomorrow, and that Mr Mayor will at the same time communicate to Captain Charleton their best thanks for the aid which has been already afforded to them.

Signed: for Thomas Wade, John Henderson; for Thomas Gibson, John Dodds; George Dunn; for H. Lamb & Company, R. Cooper; for Matthew Clayton Esq., John Dalton; for John C. Blackett, Gilbert Gray; for John Grey & Company, R. Wilson; Wm. Surtees & Company; for Heaton Main Colliery, Ellison Main Colliery, Park Main Colliery, Sheriff Hill, Joseph Lamb; for Hebburn Main Colliery, P Hesleton, W. Turner; for Thomas Shadforth, William Heaton; for George Burdon Esq., Joseph Metcalfe; Rowland Wilson

226. Isaac Cookson, junior, Mayor to Charleton, 2 November 1809

[NCL, J. Bell, *Collections relative to the River Tyne: its Trade and the Conservancy thereof*, II, f. 95]

Sir,

In consequence of a requisition from the body of Fitters (a copy of which I take the liberty of enclosing you), I have to request a further continuance of this aid and protection which the presence of your boats afford to those now navigating the keels upon the River.

I remain, Sir, your most obedient humble Servant,

Isaac Cookson, junior, Mayor

227. Cookson to Charleton, 3 November 1809 [NCL, J. Bell,

Collections relative to the River Tyne: its Trade and the Conservancy thereof, II, ff. 96–7]

Dear Sir.

I have to thank you for your letter of this morning.

The disturbances excited by the keelmen have risen to great disorder and some acts of violence have been committed by riotous bodies of them assembled on the water and by forcibly stopping keels which were under way navigated by others. For these acts, and for the desertion of their service, many warrants have been issued, and, as the civil power is quite inadequate to the execution of them, it is proposed to call for the assistance of the military, and the Magistrates of the three Counties, who are now assembled, direct me to request that you will lend all the assistance on the water that your boats properly manned can afford.

The different parties will move about 12 o'Clock tomorrow noon, and if you would direct your boats to be at the Newcastle Quay about Eleven, they would be in time to aid the Magistrates who will act upon the water.

The Magistrates direct me to add that they would be highly obliged by your attendance at 10 o'Clock at the Mayor's Chamber, which would give them an opportunity of availing themselves of your assistance and advice, and when their plan of operations will be laid before you.

I remain, Sir, your most obedient humble Servant,
Isaac Cookson, jnr., Mayor

228. Draft, Cookson to Sir Edmund Nagle on the Leith Station, 3 November 1809 [TWA 394/37]

Sir,

I regret to have occasion to address you on so unpleasant a subject, but the public service seems to require an immediate exertion to preserve the peace in this district.

The keelmen or lightermen employed on this River are now in a state of riot and have assembled in large bodies on the water and forcibly stopped the trade of the Port until their demand of increased wages are complied with by their employers, though they are under bonds which do not expire till Christmas. It has occurred to the Magistrates that if an armed ship was sent to the Port it might materially assist them in the discharge of their duties, and they beg the favor of you to direct any one under your command to sail forthwith to Shields. A copy of this letter will be sent immediately to the Admiralty.

I have the honour to be,
Your most obedient Servant,
Isaac Cookson, jnr., Mayor

229. Nagle to Cookson, 4 November 1809 [TWA 394/37]

Admiral's Office, Leith

Sir,

I am honored by the receipt of your letter of yesterday's date, and agreeable to your request have ordered 'The Strenuous', gun brig, to Shields without a moment's loss of time. Lieutenant O'Conor, a relation of mine, you will find an active intelligent officer. He has directions to carry into execution the suggestions of the Magistrates for the maintenance of the public peace.

I am extremely sorry the conduct of the keelmen should be of such a nature as to call for this assistance and trust that your exertions will soon restore them to tranquillity.

I have the honor to be, Sir,
Your most obedient humble Servant,
Edmund Nagle

230. Plan suggested by the Coalowners and Fitters for the operations of the 4th November 1809 [TWA 394/37]

The following plan is submitted to consideration of the Magistrates for reducing the keelmen of the River Tyne to a state of subordination:

That a certain number of men be apprehended immediately, for which purpose it appears necessary to issue a number of warrants, and that such number of those warrants as shall be thought necessary be executed by the civil power of the three Counties. As it is apprehended that considerable difficulties will be encountered by the constables in the execution of these warrants, should they alone attempt to carry them into effect, it is recommended that they should be supported in the discharge of their duty by a military force. The apprehensions which the Committee entertain that a serious resistance will be made by the keelmen to the civil power is grounded upon the experience of yesterday, as during that day the keelmen not only manifested a riotous disposition but some of them committed acts of violence. As unity of action is absolutely requisite in this instance, the following plan is submitted to your consideration:

1. That the Magistrates of the Town should proceed up the River tomorrow at 12 o'Clock with such military force as they may think necessary, and when they shall arrive at Dunston they should then divide into two parties, one of which to remain at Dunston and the other to proceed up to Derwenthaugh.

2. That the Magistrates of the Counties of Durham and Northumberland proceed up their respective sides of the River at same hour, viz. 12 o'Clock, accompanied by a military force also, and proceed to the following points to carry into effect the warrants, viz:

South side: Team Gut, Swalwell, Derwent Gut, Bladon
North side: Bells Close, Lemington

The Committee beg leave to observe that, as it may not be convenient to the cavalry to act with effect close to the shores of the River, a small detachment of infantry might assist to prevent [the] escape of those men against whom the warrants were directed.

As a necessary part of the plan the Fitters will [precede?] the Magistrates early in the tide to man some of their keels and endeavour to bring them down, which in all probability will have the effect of drawing the attention of the keelmen and assembling them in bodies at some of the above mentioned points, and that proper persons who can identify the persons of the keelmen informed against will be deputed by the Fitters to attend the Magistrates on both sides of the River.

231. Plan of Operations (fair copy), **3 November 1809** [TWA 394/37]

The force required will be the two Troops of Horse and four Companies of Infantry, one Troop of Horse and one Company of Infantry to be employed on the North side of the River, one Troop of Horse and two Companies of Infantry on the South side of the River, and one Company of Infantry in boats upon the River. A Magistrate will accompany each detachment.

The Troop of Horse intended for the North side to meet at Westgate Turnpike Bar at 12 o'Clock at noon tomorrow, whence they will be conducted to Bells Close adjoining the River and from thence to Lemington; the Company of Infantry to meet at the Forth at the same hour from whence they will be conducted by the Maidens Walk to the River and so to Bells Close and Lemington.

The Troop of Horse intended for the South side to meet at Gateshead at the same hour, from whence they will be conducted to the West side of Team Gut, where it is proposed that one half shall remain and other half proceed on to Swalwell, Derwent Gut and Bladon. The two Companies of Infantry to meet on the South end of Tyne Bridge at the same hour, whence they will be conducted by the river side to Team Gut and from thence to Swalwell, Derwent Gut and Bladon.

The Company of Infantry intended to act upon the River to meet at the same hour in the courtyard before the Mansion House where they will be embarked in boats and proceed up the River.

The objects to be attained are the execution of the several warrants issued by the Magistrates for the apprehension of the offenders, the Civil Power having been resisted in the execution of them, and the prevention of any opposition by the keelmen to the navigating of the keels down the River which will be manned by seamen and others employed for the purpose.

It is submitted to the consideration of Lieutenant General Dundas that the officer commanding the military force should accompany the river detachments by which means he will have an easy communication with the detachments on both sides of the River. The Magistrates accompanying each detachment will be able to give more detailed instructions as circumstances may require.

232. *Newcastle Courant,* **4 November 1809**

Very considerable agitation still exists among the working people on the Tyne. This week the few keels of coals that have been put on board of ships were navigated by waggonmen, pitmen, sailors &c, the regular keelmen refusing to work.

233. Major J. Handasyde to the Mayor, 5 November 1809 [TWA 394/37]

Sir,

I am directed by Lieutenant General Dundas to acknowledge the receipt of your letter of this day, and to acquaint you that the cavalry required will be in readiness to march to the points mentioned in your plan of operations at 10 of Clock in the morning. You will be pleased to order the Peace Officers to attend at the place of assembly of the different detachments in Newcastle and Gateshead.

I have the honour to be, Sir, your obedient Servant,

J. Handasyde, Major

234. Lieutenant General Dundas to Isaac Cookson, Sunday evening [5 November 1809] [TWA 394/37]

Sir,

I have this moment received your letter of this day, having been previously informed by Major Handasyde that you had done me the favour of calling here this morning, and am sorry being out of Town I had not the pleasure of seeing you.

The troops will be detached and in readiness to attend the Magistrates tomorrow as you desire, and I have the honour to be,

Dear Sir, your obedient and humble Servant,

David Dundas

235. Heads of a proposed handbill to be published 5 November 1809 ['Invite all well disposed keelmen to return to work', *crossed out*] [TWA 394/37]

The Newcastle Magistrates with those of Northumberland and Durham having shown their determination to compel the bound keelmen of the River Tyne to perform their contract by serving for the term of their respective bonds, the Fitters, having taken into consideration the dangerous and serious situation in which the keelmen have placed themselves and families by their late violent and illegal proceedings, recommend to them in the most earnest manner immediately to return to their respective employments in order to avoid the dreadful consequences of the law which must inevitably take place should they any longer persevere in their present line of conduct.

As it is the wish of the Fitters that the well disposed keelmen should have the opportunity of avoiding the consequences that must ensue as above stated, [they] request them to return to their employment immediately, and also give in their names to the running fitters who will attend at the respective staiths for that purpose during the tide on Monday morning and the remainder of that day. All keelmen returning to their employments shall be protected.

236. Handbill. The Mayor's Chamber, Sunday Morning, 5 November 1809 [TWA 394/37]

Public notice is hereby given that all bound keelmen of the River Tyne who shall not return to their respective employments on or before Tuesday first will be considered to have deserted their service, and [be] immediately proceeded against as the Law directs. And in order to remove all pretence of the well disposed being kept from their employment under fear of violence from the riotous and disorderly keelmen, a force fully adequate to their protection, and the apprehension of the offenders, will be stationed on the water and on both sides of the River during tide time until order is restored.[1]

[1] In a manuscript draft of the above, a reward of 50 guineas (altered to 20) was to be offered for the apprehension of each offender, to be paid on the conviction of anyone opposing any keelman in discharge of his duty, but the proposal to offer a reward was finally crossed out.

237. Draft Plan of Operations for 6 November [TWA 394/37]

In order to carry into effect the object of the enclosed handbill, it is proposed with Lieutenant General Dundas's approbation, to send out small detachments of horse tomorrow to several points to remain there a given time and to return. [It is] intended by this merely to shew the keelmen that the Magistrates continue to employ the military to assist their endeavours to restore order amongst them.

The Magistrates have despatched proper persons this afternoon to inquire and report what convenient quarters can be obtained for some infantry at particular points on both sides of the River, and when they are able to communicate to the Lieutenant General the result of this inquiry as to quarters, which they will be able to do tomorrow morning, it is their purpose to request that he will have the goodness to direct that 4 or 5 small detachments of the infantry shall on Tuesday be quartered at these particular points, and, that during the time of their remaining in such quarters, small detachments of horse shall continue to march each day to the respective points to remain there a proper time and then return to Newcastle.

The points for the march of the horse tomorrow will be:

Below Tyne Bridge on the South side of the River, Snowdons Hole. On the North side, Dents Hole, by the Ballast Hills.

The South side party to march from Gateshead, and the North side party from Newcastle at 10 o'Clock in the morning and return at four in the afternoon, and to consist of 15 men each.

Above Tyne Bridge on the South side, Swalwell, where one half are to remain whilst the other half march into Blaydon and who, after remaining there an hour, shall return back to Swalwell. This detachment to consist of 30 men and to march from Gateshead 12 at noon and return from Swalwell at 4 in the afternoon.

On the North side, Lemington. This detachment to consist of 15 men and to march from Newcastle and return at the same hour as the last. Inquiries [are] being made for quarters at Dents Hole and Willington Quay, Dunston, Whickham, Swalwell, Blaydon, Scotchwood, Bells Close and Lemington.[1]

A mounted Peace Officer will attend to conduct each detachment to the fixed points and back.

[1] The return of quarters for the infantry on both sides of the river gave the totals as follows: Number of houses, 70; number of men from publicans' account, 202; number of men who may be quartered, 263 (TWA 394 /37).

238. Minutes of a Meeting of the Magistrates with a Committee of the Coal Trade held in the evening of 6 November 1809 [TWA 394/37]

Resolved that the Water Bailiffs' boats be at the bridge at high water who shall wait the arrival of any keels from above bridge and shall conduct them to Shields.

That Lieutenant General Dundas be requested that 15 Dragoons march from Newcastle to Dents Hole by the Ballast Hills, and the *like* number from Gateshead to Snowdons Hole, at 6 o'Clock *tomorrow* morning – that they should remain at or about the places to which they are respectively marched till 10 o'Clock when they may return to Newcastle. Each party will be attended with a Peace Officer and a guide.

For [the] North side, who will muster at the Sandhill, Mr Chicken, Guide; Mr [John] Scott, Peace Officer.

For the South side, who will muster at Gateshead, Mr Gilbert Grey, who is a Special Constable, and will be also a Guide.

239. Draft letter to Lieutenant General Dundas, 6 November 1809 [TWA 394/37]

The magistrates having great hopes that the disturbances amongst the keelmen are more likely to be composed than they yesterday expected, they are anxious to avoid giving unnecessary trouble to the military who have so readily lent their assistance, and therefore have only to request that Lieutenant General Dundas would have the goodness to direct that 15 dragoons assemble on the Sandhill and march from thence at 6 o'Clock tomorrow morning by the Ballast Hills to Dents Hole, and that 15 dragoons assemble at Gateshead to march from thence at the same hour to Snowdons Hole. That these two detachments should patrol about these points till 10 o'Clock when they may march home.

The following Peace Officers and Guides will be ready at the places of assembly:

North side, Peace Officers, Mr John Scott and Mr Heppel; Guide, Mr Chicken.

South side, Peace Officer and Guide, Mr Gilbert Grey.

240. Further Proposals against the Keelmen [? made at the above meeting] [TWA 394/37]

Monday evening, 6 November 1809, 6 o'Clock

If the keelmen do not go to work in the morning, it is recommended that the troops should march to the places already appointed above Bridge, and also that a guard of soldiers should be sent to each of the under mentioned places below Bridge, viz. Ouse Burn, Dents Hole, Willington, Felling Shore.

Every endeavour should be made to execute the warrants issued against the men in *the below Bridge works*, the military having previously surrounded the places where they live to prevent their escape.

It is submitted that the troops, accompanied by proper guides, should move from Newcastle at 6 o'Clock in the morning, and that the Water Bailiffs' boats should be stationed on the River at the following places: Dents Hole, St Anthonys, Willington Quay.

As the constables appointed to take into custody certain keelmen against whom warrants are issued have been disappointed in meeting with the individuals described in these warrants, but have met with others absenting themselves from their lawful employment and being assembled with the intention of preventing others from going to their regular employment, it is strongly recommended that no exception should be made, but that every bound keelman absenting himself from his work should be instantly taken into custody.

241. Minutes of Order to the Water Bailiffs [TWA 394/37]

Mayor's Chamber, 6 November 1809

The Water Bailiffs' and Newcastle Quaymaster's boats, properly manned, to be at Newcastle Bridge tomorrow morning at High water where [they] will wait for loaded keels coming from above bridge and protecting down to Shields such colliery keels as may be inclined to avail themselves of it. After seeing the keels cast, the boats will afford them protection up the River to the same point where they took them in charge. Both boats will receive for self defence a sufficient number of pikes at the Mansion House. Mr Peter Rowe, under the Water Bailiffs' direction, will take charge of the Quaymaster's boat.

242. Minutes of examination of prisoners before the Mayor and Aldermen Hood, Forster and Cramlington, 6 November 1809 [TWA 394/37]

Thomas Gibb of Walker Work: William Heaton sworn [and] produces the bond marked by the prisoner. Left service without leave; bond expires on the 31st [December]. Comm^d [committed to prison] 1 month.

Aaron Tempest, Benwell Work. Witness Joseph Wigham proves binding to 31 December. Same charge. Says his skipper, John Richardson, refused to let him work. Discharged.

Timothy Tempest, same witness and charge, but says he will not go to work. Committed 1 month.

Edward Lindsay, Mr Hood'sWork. Thomas Blackett produces bond. Same charge. Committed 1 month.

John Tad, Knowsley and Chapman's Work, produces bond and proves absence. Keel was repairing the first week. Committed 1 month.

George Hutchison Mr Turner's Work. Master produced bond, proves absence without leave. Committed 1 month.

Cuthbert Dobinson, Scott & Forsters' Work. William Winn produces bond and proves desertion from service. Committed 3 months.

Elizabeth Richardson, sister of John and Jane Hutchinson, mother of George Hutchinson, said in Jane Hutchinson's Friday evening that if Richardson was not liberated by Monday night the house would either be burnt or come down by the keelmen. Informer was at the outside window shutters.

On Thursday George Orrick said if constables came to take him he would murder them.

243. [Further] Minutes of examination of prisoners, 8 November 1809 [TWA 394/37]

David Sword, Skipper, James Sword, John Purvis, keelmen in the Walker employ. The Steward of Walker Work lives in Petrees Entry, Sandgate, and is named David Haine.

James Sword brought before Magistrates, admitted he had deserted his service, but was prevented from going to work by over 100 keelmen who threatened him if he went to work he must stand the consequences, by which he understood they would throw him overboard. Didn't know their names but knew them to be keelmen. Made no application to his master or a magistrate regarding these threats preventing him going to work.

Henry Forest (Russell's Work), James Jameson, Skipper – lives in Sandgate, John Ions. Peter Gilroy of Sandgate is the Steward.

[Henry Forest] admits he deserted work on Monday morning last. Was in bed asleep when his skipper called him up about 3 o'Clock and told him the above bridge men had come down to prevent their going to work. Let skipper in and learnt his story – went to bed again. Skipper said that one of the men in their own employ had called him out of bed and told him what they were about to do, and some of the men had said if they attempted to work they would knock them down. Got up at 7 o'Clock, went to low end of New Quay. Several keelmen talked of the upper works men having come down to stop the work. Has heard the Felling keelmen sent 4 boys up to Dunston on Friday to desire them to stop. Did not apply to master or to any magistrate.

James Jameson, the Skipper, appeared. Denied all Forest had said. Called on Forest Monday morning; got him up, carried him with him about 100 yards from his house when [they] met several persons who took his sack from him and threatened if they went to work would knock him down. On going back they gave him his meat again. Knows they were not above bridge men. They could not be. Never told Forest they were. Neither he nor Forest knew anything of the disturbance. One Coverhill called him up but he knew as little of the disturbance as witness did.

Jameson and [John] Ions both said they were ready to go to work and would go under the direction of the Magistrates and their protection.

Joseph Burdis, Bell and Browns' Work: Edward Pearson proves the bond. Prisoner admits the offence. Committed 1 month.

John Heads, Scott and Forsters' Work: William Winn proves the bond and the absence from service. Prisoner admits the offence. Committed 1 month.

James Hutchinson, Kenton Work: George Meffin[?] proves the bond and the offence. Prisoner says he is willing to work when he can get redress; has no other defence. Committed 2 months.

Robert Mitchell, Kenton Work: Same witness proves the bond and absence. Committed 1 month.

Thomas Purvis admits sign[ature] to bond. Told by his skipper and fellow when he called him up. That he was then told that he had better go home for there was a disturbance and they would get mischief if they went to work. Went home and to bed. Never applied to master or magistrate or attempted to work. His account proved by his skipper.

William Johnson – scalded – discharged.

244. Draft letter, the Mayor to Lieutenant General Dundas, 8 November 1809, sending return of quarters which may be obtained at certain points on each side of the River, as requested by the Mayor on 5th instant, and requesting detachments of infantry as early as convenient [TWA 394/37]

South Side

Snowdons Hole and Bell Quay [below bridge]	30 men
Dunston, Whickham, Swalwell, Bladon and Stella [above bridge]	100 men

North Side

Lemington, Bells Close and Scottswood [above bridge]	50 men
	Total 180

This number deemed necessary, but numbers [are] subject to the Lieutenant General's approbation. The detachments [to be] stationed at these points with a view to enable the Magistrates the more readily to call in their aid should necessity require it, and that without such request they will not have to act. The Mayor will provide guides to the several stations and to assist in procuring billets.

245. Omissions of the Keelmen's Petition [TWA 394/37]

Lying tides to be paid at the same rate as keels slung, or, as the ballast keels are when detained, which is at the rate of the dues for one tide for each day, and double on the Sabbath.

Coming over land from Shields for orders to be paid 3s. 0d., and if ordered back with the coals, to have a full tide without any deductions.

Gentlemen, we expect you will give us a verbal hearing patiently and candidly upon these and the other articles of our petition, as, perhaps they may not be properly understood, not doubting that then our petition will not be found unreasonable, as also we expect you will give our paper already given in, addressed to the Gentlemen Coal Owners and Fitters of the River Tyne, an impartial reading.

246. [Draft] Proposition of the Coal Trade, 10 November 1809
[TWA 394/37]

The gentlemen of the Coal Trade are anxious to reconsider the requests of the keelmen, but they cannot enter on the subject without the men first going to work. As soon as they do so, the Trade will meet for that purpose and will lay the result before the Magistrates, and will propose nothing that shall not first have the approbation of the Magistrates consulted, who shall be those of the three Counties [who] pledged themselves to the keelmen to meet on the business the moment they went to work.

If the keelmen go to work on Monday, the Trade will meet on Tuesday.

247. The Fitters' Proposal [TWA 394/37]

The Fitters propose that 1s.6d. per tide [per keel[1]] be added to the earnings[2] below Bridge to *commence immediately*. [The keelmen below bridge have this year earned much less than usual.[3]]

That the addition of 1s.10d. be added to the earnings above bridge to *commence immediately*. [Those above bridge have had at least equal work.]

That the further[4] addition[5] as formerly proposed to the keelmen above bridge shall take place on 1 January next, and that this addition shall be as follows:

From Stella, 2s. 4d., in all 7s. 6d.

[From] Lemington, 1s. 8d., in all 6s. 2d.

[From] Denton, 1s. 4d., in all 5s. 6d.

[From] Derwenthaugh and the staiths between it and the bridge, 1s. 0d., in all 4s. 6d.

2s. 6d. [2s. 0d.] addition to lying tides.

1s. 0d. addition to the messenger coming for orders.

Six chaldrons of coal to each keel for a year.

The gear money as before.

The binding money: All below bridge, £1. 0s. 0d. per keel; Dunston, £1. 10s. 0d. per keel; Benwell, £2. 0s. 0d. per keel; Denton, Kenton and Lemington, £3.0s.0d. per keel; Whitefield, £12.0s. 0d. per keel.

[1] 'Per keel' added later.
[2] 'Keel Dues' crossed out and 'earnings' substituted.
[3] This sentence added in pencil.
[4] 'Proposed' crossed out and 'further' substituted.
[5] 'Owners' Wages' crossed out and 'as formerly proposed' substituted, but the addition was in fact to be made to the owners' wages, as comparison with the scale set out in 1792 shows; see above **Document 197**. These terms were agreed by the magistrates on 16 November 1809, see below, **Document 250**.

248. Isaac Cookson, junior, Mayor, to Richard Rider, Home Secretary, 11 November 1809 [TNA, HO 42/99/593–5, and TWA 394/37]

Sir,

I am honoured with a letter from Mr Beckett [Permanent Under-Secretary of State for Home Affairs] communicating your wish that I should lose no time in reporting to you the particulars of the disturbance amongst the lightermen (or keelmen as they are here called) employed on this River, and whether tranquillity has been restored.

For three weeks that class of persons have combined with a view to obtain an advance of wages; and in furtherance of their object have absented themselves from their services, and in one or two cases they have proceeded to acts of violence in preventing the well-disposed from returning to their work, and in rescuing persons apprehended under warrants issued by the Magistrates. Several of the offenders have been committed to the House of Correction, and I would persuade myself that the bulk of them are about to return to order and their duty.

The Magistrates of this Town and the two adjoining Counties met a deputation of the keelmen today, and the conference seems to have produced a determination in the latter to return peaceably to their employments, which I have much reason to think will take place on Monday. If it should not, I shall take the liberty of again addressing you on the subject.

I feel a duty on this occasion to express to you that the Magistrates think the country much indebted to Lieutenant General Dundas, commanding the military in this district, and to Captain Charleton, the Regulating Captain of the Port, for their zealous and active exertions in every way in which the Magistrates could suggest that those exertions could be of service.

I have the honour to be, Sir, your most obedient Servant,
Isaac Cookson, junior, Mayor

249. [Copy] Cookson to Lieutenant General Dundas, 13 November 1809 [TWA 394/37]

Sir,

I am happy in having it in my power to notify to you that in consequence of the keelmen having this morning gone to work it will be unnecessary that the detachments of infantry which you were so good as to station on each side of the River should any longer remain there.[1]

Permit me on behalf of myself and the other Magistrates to express to you how much we feel obliged by your ready acquiescence in assisting the Civil Power with the aid which we were under the necessity of calling upon you for.

I have the honor to be, Sir, your very obedient Servant

[1] Major Handasyde to Cookson, 13 November, acknowledging the above in the absence of Dundas, states that the detachments would be ordered to join Head Quarters 'tomorrow morning' (TWA 394/37).

250. Terms agreed to be offered to the Keelmen, 16 November 1809 [TWA 394/37]

That the earnings of the keelmen shall be increased in the following ratio:

To those below Bridge,1s.6d. per tide.

To those above Bridge, 1s. 10d. per tide, and the further addition of 2s. 4d., 1s. 8d., 1s. 4d., 1s. 0d. per tide according to the situation of the respective staiths.

And these additions the Magistrates assembled approve.

These additions of course could not take place till the expiration of their present contract, but the Fitters have proposed, in consequence of the *Below Bridge keelmen* being much abridged in their work, that their addition take place immediately, and that the addition of 1s.10d. to the above Bridge [keelmen] shall take place immediately, and the further advance according to the distances of the staiths shall commence the 1st January next.

DOCUMENTS CONCERNING THE IMPRESSMENT OF
KEELMEN, 1803–11

**251. Copy of Protection of Keelmen and others granted to the
Mayor, 1803** [NCL, John Bell, *Collections relative to the River Tyne: its
Trade and the Conservancy thereof*, vol. II, f. 6]

By the Commissioners for Executing the office of Lord High
Admiral of the United Kingdom of Great Britain and Ireland, &c., to
all Commanders and Officers of His Majesty's ships, Pressmasters
and all others whom it doth or may concern

Whereas there is now in the hands of the Mayor and Aldermen
of Newcastle upon Tyne, and several other gentlemen of that Town
whose names are mentioned on the other side, a list of such Keelmen,
Coblemen and Shipwrights as are employed in the River Tyne, you
are hereby required and directed not to impress into His Majesty's
Service any of the said Keelmen, Coblemen and Shipwrights,
provided it shall appear to you that an oath is made at the end of
the list aforesaid that none of them are seamen, and that the ages
and descriptions of the persons hereby intended to be protected be
inserted therein, the same to continue in force for 3 months (calendar
months) from the date hereof.

Given under our hands and seal of the Office of Admiralty, the 8th
day of April 1803.

Underneath Thomas Clennel, Esq., Mayor, and Aldermen: Sir Matthew
White Ridley, Bart., John E. Blackett, William Yielder, Francis Johnson,
William Cramlington, Anthony Hood, Robert Clayton, Robert
Shaftoe Hedley, Archibald Read, Joseph Forster; and Isaac Cookson,
Alexander Adams, Thomas Emerson Headlam, Esqrs.

**252. Thomas Brown to Captain Adam MacKenzie, Regulating
Officer, 17 April 1803** [NCL, John Bell, *Collections relative to the River
Tyne: its Trade and the Conservancy thereof*, vol. II, f. 11]

Sir,

I am directed by the Mayor to transmit you duplicates of the lists[1]
upon which Protections have been granted on Friday and Saturday,
and to inform you that every person to whom any such Protection
hath been granted hath made oath that he hath not been at sea,
except a few shipwrights,... and to these men Protections have been
granted upon condition only of your deeming them not seamen
when they have been at sea as carpenters.

The Mayor will thank you to inform him whether you will receive from the civil power any landmen who they may be inclined to turn over to you, and between what ages.

I am, Sir, Your most obedient Servant,

Thomas Brown

[1] The lists are not present.

253. Newcastle Advertiser, 23 April 1803

The scandalous outrages that have been recently committed by press gangs call for the immediate interference of the Board of Admiralty. Custom and state necessity authorise the practice of impressing *seamen*; but it never was intended that persons not accustomed to a seafaring life, and pursuing useful industry should be deprived of their liberty, dragged like felons through the streets, beat and cut with hangers [short swords], and put on board a tender, merely because it pleased a set of ruffians called a Press Gang to do so.[1]

[1] The *Tyne Mercury*, 29 March 1803, reported that soldiers had been stationed at the outlets of North Shields to prevent escape while the press gang paraded the streets and seized an immense number of all descriptions without distinction. The principal inns and public houses were examined and gentlemen, shipowners and tradesmen indiscriminately arrested. An ex-naval officer who remonstrated was beaten.

254. *Tyne Mercury*, 10 May 1803

A remarkably hot press commenced yesterday on the Tyne, no protections were respected; all seamen were indiscriminately seized.

255. Captain Mackenzie to Sir Evan Nepean, Secretary of the Admiralty, 10 May 1803 [TNA, ADM 1/2141]

Sir,

…[There is] a vast body of fine men in the keels who are protected by their Lordships. Captain Skene and I determined to take as many of the younger ones as we could this morning, leaving all skippers. It is the general opinion here that nothing will be done in the River until the keelmen are again protected; in the meantime we will get all we can.

I am, Sir, your most obedient Servant,

Adam Mackenzie

Endorsement to the above: 'Approve and direct him not to impress any more of the keelmen and to apprize the Mayor that he has received these instructions'.

256. *Tyne Mercury,* **17 May 1803**

Scarcely was our last publication issued when the press service was practically extended much beyond the expectation of every person and greatly to the distress of some. On Tyne and Wear the keelmen, unapprized of their danger, were suddenly *put in requisition.* In fact the orders received by those who are at the head of the Impress Service were so *express* that they could neither be misunderstood nor safely disobeyed. *No protections were to be regarded.*

257. Handbill: The Mayor to the Keelmen [NCL, John Bell, *Collections relative to the River Tyne: its Trade and the Conservancy thereof,* vol. II, f. 13]

Mansion House 26 May 1803

The Mayor was last night favored with a letter from Captain MacKenzie, the Regulating Officer of this Port, inclosing the following copy of a letter received by him yesterday from the Admiralty:

Admiralty Office, 23 May 1803

Sir,

In further answer to your letter of the 10th instant, respecting the Keelmen whom you have impressed belonging to Newcastle, I am commanded by my Lords Commissioners of the Admiralty to signify their direction to you to discharge them, notwithstanding my letter to you of the 20 instant.

I am, Sir, your very humble Servant,

Evan Nepean

Captain MacKenzie

As there now can be no doubt of the impressed Keelmen being discharged immediately on their arrival at the Nore, and as a gentleman will be there *this Day* for the express purpose of providing them a passage home,[1] it is expected by the Mayor that the Keelmen will immediately return to their employment.

---

[1] Before instructions to discharge the impressed keelmen arrived, the men had been shipped to the Nore. As stated above, arrangements had been made to return them to Newcastle immediately they disembarked, but the Admiralty suddenly countermanded the order to discharge them. After much difficulty it was agreed that substitutes for one tenth of the whole body of keelmen should be provided. See account by George Dunn senior of what took place (Minutes of a Meeting of the Fitters, 30 March 1811, **Document 271**, below).

258. Resolution of a Meeting of Coal Owners and others, 10 June 1803 [TWA 394/38]

At a meeting of Coal Owners and others interested to consider of the best means of procuring the liberation of the impressed keelmen,
    Resolved

That the gentlemen whose names are undersigned, forming a majority of the Coal Owners and persons interested in the Trade in London, will undertake, upon the liberation of those impressed, and Protections being granted to the keelmen on the Tyne during the war, to use their utmost endeavours to procure 80 serviceable men* to serve in his Majesty's Navy within two months, or sooner if possible.

*'out of the body of keelmen' *interlined but crossed out.*

Matthew White Ridley, R. Burdon, William Pitt, W. Russell, George Silvertop, Matthew Bell, Robert William Brandling for Charles John Brandling

259. Thomas Clennell, Mayor, to Captain Charleton,[1] 23 June 1803

[NCL, John Bell, *Collections relative to the River Tyne: its Trade and the Conservancy thereof*, vol. II, f. 18]

Sir,

I was favored with your polite letter of the 21st instant the contents of which I have communicated to the Committee of Fitters, and am requested by them to say how much they feel themselves obliged by your attention, and to state that as they procure men very fast, and there being no receiving ship at Shields, they will be much obliged to you to allow Mr Horn to examine the men at Newcastle for the present, as they are under the necessity of paying a part of their bounty[2] here, in which they will not be safe unless the men are previously approved of by a proper surgeon. Under the authority of your letter, Mr Horn has this morning entered upon the examination, but leaves any man who he conceives doubtful for your subsequent regulation.

I have the honor to be, Sir, Your most obedient Servant,
Thomas Clennell, Mayor

---

[1] Captain Charleton, who succeeded Mackenzie as Regulating Officer of the Impress, served for seven years in that capacity and was later promoted to Rear Admiral of the Blue (note by J. Bell, *Collections*, II, f. 74).

[2] The bounty offered to volunteers (upon approval) was eleven guineas to an able seaman, ten guineas to an ordinary seaman and eight guineas to a landsman. The

keelmen had entered into a subscription for that purpose (*Newcastle Advertiser*, 25 June 1803).

260. Sir Evan Nepean, secretary of the Admiralty, to Charleton, 24 June 1803 [NCL, John Bell, *Collections relative to the River Tyne: its Trade and the Conservancy thereof*, vol. II, f. 19]

Sir,

I am commanded by my Lords Commissioners of the Admiralty to acquaint you that the gentlemen of Newcastle have agreed to provide Eighty men for the Service in consideration of the protection of the keelmen and that you are to receive any able men that may be delivered to you in consequence of that agreement.

I am, Sir, your very humble Servant,

Evan Nepean

261. Clennell to Charleton, 28 June 1803 [NCL, John Bell, *Collections relative to the River Tyne: its Trade and the Conservancy thereof*, vol. II, f. 22]

Sir,

I communicated your favor of this date to the gentlemen who compose the Keelmen's Committee, and agreeable to your directions fifty of the volunteers will be sent down to you tomorrow at noon. I have to inform you that the whole number is now raised and must now take the liberty of requesting that you will have the goodness to send off by the Tender as many as you think prudent, as the keeping of them at Newcastle entails an enormous expence upon the Coal Trade. The bearers of this will explain more fully the situation of the Coal Trade.

I have the honor to be, Sir, your obedient Servant,

Thomas Clennell, Mayor

262. [Copy] Samuel Walker Parker, Chairman of the meeting of Merchants, to Sir Evan Nepean, Bart. [NCL, John Bell, *Collections relative to the River Tyne: its Trade and the Conservancy thereof*, vol. II, f. 29]

Newcastle upon Tyne, 20 August 1803

Sir,

I have the honor to acquaint you that, at a general meeting of the merchants of this place employing keelmen and watermen upon the River Tyne, it was resolved that an application should be made to Government for protections for such keelmen and watermen during the war upon condition of their providing a quota of men for the navy in the same manner as the keelmen employed in the Coal Trade upon the River Tyne, and in such proportion according to the number to be protected as should by Government be thought reasonable.

This application was handed to the Mayor of Newcastle with a request to transmit it to Government, but no answer having been received and it being apprehended that the application may not have been communicated to the proper department, I am directed by the merchants and others concerned to renew the application to you with a request that you will have the goodness to lay the same before their Lordships for their consideration.[1]

I beg leave further to acquaint you for their Lordships' information that the merchants have agreed to include in this application all such ballast keelmen, wherrymen and watermen upon the River Tyne, not being in the employment of any particular merchant, who may contribute their quota towards the expence of raising the men, and that such men should likewise be considered upon this condition as protected during the war.

Should their Lordships be pleased to accede to this proposal, nearly all the keelmen and watermen upon the River Tyne will have contributed towards providing men for the navy. Such as do not may be easily distinguished as their names cannot appear upon the list of men intended to be protected.

Samuel Walker Parker, Chairman.

[1] The Mayor sent the letter concerning the merchants' proposal to Captain Charleton, who enclosed it in a letter to Nepean of 6 July, but the Lords Commissioners could give no directions on the subject until they had further details (Bell, Collections, II, f. 25, Nepean to Charleton, 11 July 1803).

263. Sir Evan Nepean to Charleton, 14 November 1803 [NCL, John Bell, *Collections relative to the River Tyne: its Trade and the Conservancy thereof*, vol. II, f. 37]

Sir,

The Mayor of Newcastle having requested that the watermen, ballast and other keelmen employed upon the River Tyne may be exempted from the Impress upon their procuring for His Majesty's service such number of men as may be deemed reasonable, I am commanded by the Lords Commissioners of the Admiralty to signify their direction to you to accede to the Mayor's proposition on the express condition that the men so furnished be raised out of their own body; but you are not, on any account, to discharge those already impressed.

I am, Sir, your very humble Servant,
Evan Nepean

264. Charleton to Nepean, 18 November 1803 [TNA, ADM 1/1634]

Sir,

In pursuance of the Lords Commissioners' directions of 14th instant to accede to the propositions of the Mayor of Newcastle for the watermen, ballast and other keelmen raising such a quota from their own body as their Lordships should deem reasonable in consideration of their being protected, I yesterday met the Mayor and settled with him, in conjunction with the principal manufacturers, owners of ballast keels &c on the River Tyne, that they shall raise one in ten upon the gross number they employ, and in consideration of which their keels &c shall not again be interrupted by the officers on the Impress till the mode of their being protected shall be finally arranged by their Lordships. Everyone is anxious that the number be raised as soon as possible.

I beg to request instructions as to how the Lords Commissioners would in future have the business of protections arranged upon the River Tyne, as without regularity I have no doubt that we shall be subject to much imposition. I understand that in former wars the mode adopted was for the Lords Commissioners to grant a warrant to the Mayor of Newcastle authorizing him to give protections, renewable every three months on proof that the keelmen &c had never been to sea, and thus the business was arranged in the Town Clerk's office, very much to his emolument, and without anybody from the naval service [being] present. I beg leave to suggest that in future this should be done in the presence of officers of the Impress, and for twelve months, as the [keelmen's] bond is for a year and they are held for that term. There is no need for the Town Clerk's fee every three months. No protections [to be granted] but to workmen of those fitters &c who have subscribed towards raising their proportion, and in case of their extending their number of workmen beyond their present establishment, to raise for the navy one in ten for every such addition.

I am, Sir, your very humble Servant,
William Charleton

265. Nepean to Charleton, 21 November 1803 [NCL, John Bell, *Collections relative to the River Tyne: its Trade and the Conservancy thereof*, vol. II, f. 42]

Sir,

Having laid before my Lord Commissioners of the Admiralty your letter of the 18th instant acquainting me of the proportion of men proposed to be raised out of the body of watermen, ballast and other keelmen at Newcastle in order to exempt the remainder from the Impress, I am commanded by their Lordships to acquaint you that they are pleased to approve of the arrangement proposed, and to signify their direction to you to take care that the stipulated number of men are duly furnished, and that no imposition be practised.

I am, Sir, Your very humble Servant,
Evan Nepean

266. Joseph Lamb, and others to Charleton, 21 November 1803 [NCL, John Bell, *Collections relative to the River Tyne: its Trade and the Conservancy thereof*, vol. II, f. 44]

Dear Sir,

The committee acting for the body of ballast keelmen, trimmers, wherrymen and others employed on the river have the pleasure to inform you they have enrolled the names of upwards of two hundred men who are willing to contribute the necessary sum for providing men for the navy. They have offered bounties for volunteers as per the inclosed bill, and also given certificates of which they inclose one.[1] They hope very soon to get the number wanted, and shall use every exertion to forward the business.[2]

We remain your most obedient Servants,
Joseph Lamb, Isaac Cookson jnr, Samuel Walker Parker

---

[1] The enclosures are not present.
[2] By 23 November there were nearly 300 men on the list (NCL, Bell, *Collections*, II, f. 46).

267. William Marsden, Secretary to the Admiralty, to Charleton, 27 February 1805 [NCL, John Bell, *Collections relative to the River Tyne: its Trade and the Conservancy thereof*, vol. II, f. 58]

Sir,

I am commanded by my Lords Commissioners of the Admiralty to send you the enclosed extract of a letter I have received from Rear Admiral Phillip relative to the mode by which the keelmen of

Newcastle and Sunderland procured their quota of men to serve in the navy, and to signify their Lordships' direction to you to explain the circumstances therein mentioned

I am, Sir, your very humble Servant,
William Marsden

268. Extract Phillip to Marsden, 26 February 1805 [NCL, John Bell, *Collections relative to the River Tyne: its Trade and the Conservancy thereof*, vol. II, f. 57 *verso*]

The keelmen in the North and the fishermen in some parts of Scotland to avoid the Impress agreed to give one man in ten to the Service, but they did not give that number of men from among themselves but raised a sum of money and procured men by a bounty from among the seafaring men by which the Government lost the chance of procuring these men for the Service, none taking the bounty but men who were subject to the Impress, and the quota [of] men thus raised has not been general but procured from particular places only.

269. Resolution of a Meeting of Fitters at the Mayor's Chamber, 21 September 1807, concerning a Proclamation of 18 September seeking volunteers of seamen employed in Greenland and British fisheries, or who are otherwise protected, to assist, fit out and navigate to British ports Danish ships and vessels of war at Copenhagen which lately surrendered to his Majesty's arms[1] [NCL, John Bell, *Collections relative to the River Tyne: its Trade and the Conservancy thereof*, vol. II, f. 77]

An application having been made by Mr Mayor to know whether any and what portion of the keelmen employed in the River Tyne can be spared to enter as volunteers for the service pointed out by the proclamation issued by the Lords of Admiralty bearing date the 18th instant, resolved that it is deemed expedient to permit one out of twelve men in each work so to volunteer their services, upon the express condition that the men so volunteering shall not by that means be rendered more liable to the Impress Service for the future than they now are.

[1] See NCL, Bell, *Collections* II, f. 75.

270. Joseph Lamb to Charleton, 16 October 1809 [NCL, John Bell, *Collections relative to the River Tyne: its Trade and the Conservancy thereof,* vol. II, f. 89]

Sir,

I take the liberty to address you in consequence of one of the keelmen in my employment [John Smith], and who has been 2 years with me, being impressed. I find he has been at sea, therefore you may probably not be willing to grant his release, but, as he has a family whom he leaves in distress, you may probably be induced from humanity to oblige me so far as to give him a place in the Gang if there is a vacancy.

I am, Sir, your obedient Servant,
Joseph Lamb

271. Minutes of a Meeting of the Fitters, 30 March 1811 [TWA 394/38]

At a meeting of the Fitters held at the Mayor's Chamber on Saturday 30 March 1811, Present: Mr Alderman Cookson, Mr Lambert, Mr Humble, Mr Ismay, Mr Dunn senior, Mr Pitt, George Ellison, Mr Wilson, Mr Chapman, Mr Croser, Mr Dunn junior.

It was stated to the meeting that two keelmen employed in Pontop Work, one in Mr Dunn's and the other in Sheriff hill, had been impressed. The 3 first are liberated and the other yet detained, he having on a former impressment claimed exemption as being under age, and the three that have been liberated have been so on Mr Dunn junior undertaking to produce them hereafter if the Admiralty do not order their release.

Mr Dunn senior stated that in May or June 1803 he applyed to the Admiralty, [and] had an interview with Sir Thomas Troubridge and Admiral Markham. At this time 51 keelmen had been impressed and were on their passage to the Nore. [He] received an order sealed directed to Lord Keith for their liberation, contradicted by a telegraphic message, after a part [of them had] landed. Mr Dunn returned to Town to the Admiralty, [and] again saw the same Lord commissioners in the presence of Sir Matthew White Ridley, Mr Burdon &c. The cause [of the countermand] avowed was the Sunderland keelmen being content with the protection of one man and a boy to a keel. Mr Dunn stated the difference between the two rivers. Then stated that the above 800 effective keelmen were [then] employed on the Tyne. Proposal to find one in ten within 2 months. [The 51] men to be kept as hostages. [The one in ten] men to be found out of the keelmen. Objected to this.

Sir Evan Nepean, Secretary, declined to see several Members [of Parliament] got together. Then went to the [Prime] Minister. He gave an order that if men to the amount of 80, either landmen or seamen, were found, the men should be released. The protection thus purchased was to be for protection during the war.

Captain Charleton had no written instructions. The [present] Captain contends that the men impressed have come into the Trade since and [are] therefore liable. Answer to this that the body is fluctuating and the whole number [has] not increased.

To write [to] Admiralty as from the Mayor. Refer the Admiralty to Sir Matthew White Ridley. Send him the copy of the letter. To request the Mayor will be so good as [to] sign the letter. Change of officers. One [of those now impressed] kept because he used a former excuse, namely under age.

[*Endorsed*] Committee appointed: Mr Alderman Cookson, Mr Lamb, Mr Dunn or his son, Mr Lambert, Mr Dixon Brown, Mr Taylor.

272. Captain Wilson Rathborne[1] to John Wilson Croker,[2] Secretary to the Admiralty, 30 March 1811 [TNA, ADM 1/2416 Capt. R 398]

North Shields, 30 March 1811

Sir,

Three young men belonging to the keels on this River were yesterday impressed on the ground of their not being any of the men who found substitutes in 1803, and knowing the fishermen of the coast of Scotland and the keelmen of Sunderland find men as substitutes every year for the young men who arrive at the age of 18.

The people here inform me that at the commencement of the war there were 800 keelmen on the Tyne and found 80 substitutes, and that the Admiralty had informed them they were not to provide any more substitutes during the war.

From the great increase of trade I think that there must be many more keelmen at present, as well as the number that were only boys at that period. Therefore I beg leave to know whether their Lordships consider any protected except the original 800, and if the rising men are to find substitutes in the same proportion that the others have.

I have the honor to be, Sir, your most obedient humble Servant,

Wilson Rathborne

---

[1] J.K. Laughton, revised by A.W.H. Pearsall, 'Rathborne, Wilson (1748–1831)', *Oxford Dictionary of National Biography*.
[2] William Thomas, 'Croker, John Wilson (1780–1857)', *Oxford Dictionary of National Biography*.

273. Draft, Thomas Burdon, Mayor, to John Wilson Croker, 30 March 1811 [TWA 394/38]

Mayor's Chamber, Newcastle, 30 March 1811

Sir,

I have the honor to address you at the instance and on behalf of the gentlemen of the Coal Trade, who are under great apprehension that a measure which has been lately taken by the Regulating Officer of the Impress in this Port will be productive of much mischief to their trade.

I should explain that in former wars it had been the invariable usage to protect from Impress the lightermen who navigate the vessels which are employed to convey the coals from the repositories on the River to the ships lying at the mouth of the sea shore, and who are here called keelmen, on satisfactory proof being made of their not having used the sea. In the Spring of the year 1803, however, several of them were impressed, and all the rest in conseqence left their employment and great interruption of the coal trade of the Port took place. After much discussion with the Lords of the Admiralty it was agreed, with the approbation of his Majesty's Minister, that if these lightermen or keelmen would unite and find eighty men for the service of the Navy (being about the proportion of one tenth of the whole body), the whole body of keelmen should be exempted from the Impress during the war. The men were found at a very great expence and supplyed to the Navy, and the protection stipulated has ever since been enjoyed by them.

It now has, however, unfortunately occurred to the Regulating Captain, who has lately been appointed to that duty, that such men as have come into the employment since that period are not entitled to the exemption, though the whole number of keelmen are not increased but rather diminished, in opposition to the understanding of the parties at the time and to the practice ever since the agreement took place, and he has directed four of them coming under that description to be impressed.

This has created much dissatisfaction amongst the keelmen, who view the act as a breach of faith, and we have reason to dread great public inconvenience will result from it unless the Lords Commissioners of the Admiralty shall be pleased to order their discharge and to give such directions as will prevent the recurrence of a similar measure, and the Trade direct me therefore to lay the matter before their Lordships and to crave their early attention to it. It is hoped that the minutes of the Board in the latter end of May 1803 will confirm this statement, and, if further testimony should be required of the nature of the compact, Sir Matthew White Ridley, one of the Members for this Town, can bear witness to it for their Lordships.

I have the honor to be, Sir,

your most obedient humble Servant,

Thomas Burdon, Mayor

274. Sir Matthew White Ridley to Nathaniel Clayton, Town Clerk, 1 April 1811 [TWA 394/38]

Portland Place, 2 April 1811

Sir,

I had the honor of receiving your letter of 30 March this morning. I have had an opportunity of conversation with Mr Croker on the subject. I learnt from him that the subject had engaged the attention of the Board *in some degree* this day. He assured me that he would now officially submit it to their consideration and inform me of the result. Mr Croker intimated that the conduct of the officer of the Impress had been produced by some attempts (as he conceived) to misapply the terms of the agreement for the protection of *young men*, who were not keelmen truly, but were adopted as servants and apprentices by that body for the purpose of the privilege of exemption. I flatter myself that the Admiralty feel no intention to break the terms of the original agreement.

I am, Sir, your most obedient Servant,

Matthew White Ridley

275. John Barrow, 2nd Secretary of the Admiralty, to Thomas Burdon, Mayor, 2 April 1811 [TWA 394/38]

Admiralty Office, 2 April 1811

Sir,

Having laid before Lords Commissioners of the Admiralty your letter of 30 ultimo relative to the protection of the keelmen on the River Tyne from the Impress, I am commanded by their Lordships to acquaint you that it never could be intended to extend protection beyond the eight hundred individuals who were keelmen at the commencement of the war, and who are of course to continue protected during the war; but that on no consideration can any others be protected from the Impress as they become liable thereto, unless they submit to the same conditions on which the eight hundred persons before mentioned obtained their exemption.

I am, Sir, your very humble Servant,

John Barrow

276. Copy Nathaniel Clayton to Captain Charleton, 6 April 1811
[TWA 394/38]

Dear Sir,

A question of some importance has arisen between the Admiralty and the Coal Trade as to the construction of the agreement which took place in 1803 for the protection of the keelmen on the River Tyne from the Impress in consideration of the Trade having furnished 80 men for the service of the Navy, the Admiralty alledging that the men then employed in the keels were alone exempted, [while] the Trade [contend] that the whole body of keelmen were exempted during the war. It is stated to us that the keelmen of Sunderland have ever since their agreement (for some agreement was about the same time made with them), acted in conformity to the opinion of the Admiralty by furnishing a man for every ten new men that have since come into the employment. We are not aware of the nature of their agreement, but we argue that it cannot be of the same nature as that for the keelmen of the River Tyne, the conduct of the latter since the agreement having been directly the reverse of the conduct of the Sunderland keelmen. We believe that during the whole time you conducted the Impress Service you never required the fitters to supply a further contribution for the men coming into their service subsequently to the agreement, and in truth the aggregate body of keelmen has not been increased, the supplies being only in lieu of those worn out by age or infirmity.

This leads us to beg the favor of you to inform us what the agreement of the Sunderland keelmen was and what circumstances induced the Impress Service to act so differently towards the keelmen on the Wear and those of the Tyne during the eight years which have elapsed since the agreements were made.

An answer by return of post will very much oblige the Trade who fear that if the question be not soon set at rest the Trade of the Port will be interrupted.

I am, Dear Sir, yours &c
Nathaniel Clayton

277. Captain Wilson Rathborne to Thomas Burdon, Mayor, 5 April 1811 [TWA 394/38]

North Shields, 5 April 1811

Sir,

I have this day received a letter from the Secretary of the Admiralty acquainting me the Lords Commissioners do not consider any keelman exempt from the Impress except the eight hundred who found substitutes at the commencement of the war, and that you are made acquainted therewith by the same post.

I have therefore to request you will make it known to those concerned for the purpose of lists being made out of the number of men that have come into the keel service, and that have grown up in it, since the year 1803, in order that they may find substitutes in the proportion of one for every ten men.

I will not allow the Trade to be interrupted for a reasonable time, to give the parties concerned an opportunity of making such arrangements as they may deem necessary.

I have the honor to be, Sir, your most obedient and very humble Servant,

Wilson Rathborne, Captain RN

278. Nathaniel Clayton to Rathborne, 6 April 1811 [TWA 394/38]

Sir,

The Mayor of Newcastle was favoured with your letter of yesterday and immediately laid it before the gentlemen of the Coal Trade interested in the question that has arisen as to the exemption of the keelmen from the Impress, by whom I am directed to express to you their best thanks for the communication and for your assurance that the Trade will not be interrupted for a reasonable time to give an opportunity of making the necessary arrangements.

Though the Trade do not concur with the Lords of the Admiralty in the construction given to the agreement which took place in the year 1803, they have thought it right to direct that the lists which you recommend should be immediately made out that they may be at liberty to act as soon as the final determination of the Admiralty is known.

I have the honor to be your most obedient Servant,

Nathaniel Clayton, Town Clerk

279. Captain Charleton to Clayton, 7 April 1811 [TWA 394/38]

North Shields, 7 April 1811

Dear Sir,

I am favored with your letter of yesterday requesting to be informed of the circumstances causing such difference of the Impress Service, whilst under my direction, in its conduct towards the keelmen employed upon the Rivers Tyne and Wear, and feel truly sorry at not thinking myself authorised to explain such circumstances to the Coal Trade upon the Tyne.

My conduct upon this point, whilst regulating the Impress Service at this Port and neighbourhood, was never hid in secrecy; of course I can have no possible objection to that being appealed to by the Trade in any way which they may chuse and where they think it can apply. It continued seven years, and was never either directly or indirectly construed to be different from the intentions of the Admiralty.

I remain, Dear Sir, your obedient Servant,
William Charleton

280. Copy [Thomas Burdon] to John Barrow, Secretary to the Admiralty, 13 April 1811 [TWA 394/38]

Sir,

I took an early opportunity of assembling the gentlemen interested in the Coal Trade of this Port and of communicating to them the answer which I had the honor of receiving from you to my letter on the subject of some keelmen having been impressed.

It is to be regretted that the sense they entertain of the Agreement of the year 1803 should differ so much from the construction put upon it by the Lords of the Admiralty. The Coalowners have employed the interval since the meeting in an inquiry into all the circumstances attending that transaction, which has produced no alteration in their sentiments. They lay much stress on the conduct of all parties under the Agreement as best proving its intention, and appeal particularly to the conduct of the Impress Service as being in strict conformity to their construction of it. Under these circumstances, they earnestly request the Lords of the Admiralty will be pleased to review the transaction and the minutes of the Agreement, and call for information as to the conduct of the Impress Service here under the directions of the Board who made the Agreement, before they finally decide the question, and that, if their Lordships should ultimately think it right to support the new construction put on the Agreement, they will be pleased to allow a sufficient time to supply the quota of men which shall be required.

I have the honor to be, Sir, your most obedient Servant,
[Thomas Burdon]

281. John Barrow to Burdon, 17 April 1811 [TWA 394/38]

Admiralty Office, 17 April 1811

Sir,

I have received and laid before my Lords Commissioners of the Admiralty your letter of the 13th instant conveying to me the sentiments of the persons concerned in the Coal Trade of Newcastle with regard to the impress of certain keelmen employed upon the River Tyne, and referring to an arrangement formerly made with respect to the men in question.

In return I have received it in command to acquaint you, for the information of the parties interested in the Trade, that, considering the pressing exigency of the Service, their Lordships conceive their demands upon the keelmen to be exceedingly moderate – that they are not disposed to alter the determination which they have formed upon the subject, and that they have caused directions to be given to the officer regulating the Impress Service at North Shields to allow one month for receiving the substitutes, after which he is to impress such as may be found liable to serve and for whom substitutes shall not have been provided.

I am, Sir, your very humble Servant,
John Barrow

282. Wilson Rathborne to Burdon, 20 April 1811 [TWA 394/38]

Sir,

I beg leave to inform you that I have received an order from the Lords Commissioners of the Admiralty to receive one seaman or 2 landsmen for every ten keelmen serving on the River Tyne who have not already found substitutes at the commencement of the present war. That their Lordships had allowed one month for the raising of such substitutes, at the expiration of which time I am to cause to be impressed such keelmen as have not certificates from me of having found such substitutes.

Herewith I send you the form of the certificate which I beg, when you may have shown it to any concerned, you will give to Mr G. Dunn.

I have the honor to be, Sir, your most humble Servant,
Wilson Rathborne

Form of Certificate

A list of ten men belonging to the keels on the River Tyne who have found a substitute, or substitutes, to exempt them from the Impress during the war.

Names, Age, Height, Complexion, Colour of Eyes, Colour of Hair, Marks if any

I do hereby certify that I have received one seaman or two landsmen (as the case may be) as substitutes to exempt the above men from the Impress during the present war.

Given under my hand this day of…1811. W.R. Captain

283. John Barrow to Nathaniel Clayton, 14 May 1811 [TWA 394/38]

Admiralty Office, 14 May 1811

Sir,

Having laid before my Lords Commissioners of the Admiralty your letter of yesterday's date, requesting on behalf of the persons interested in the Coal Trade of Newcastle upon Tyne that the time appointed for raising the substitutes for the keelmen employed upon the Tyne may be extended. I am commanded by their Lordships to acquaint you that directions are given to the Regulating Officer at North Shields to extend the time for another month.

I am, Sir, your very humble and obedient Servant,

John Barrow

284. George Dunn to Nathaniel Clayton [in London], 24 May 1811 [TWA 394/38]

Newcastle, 24 May 1811

Sir,

I wrote you the 18th instant in reply to yours of the 13th and 15th instant, since which I am without any of your favours.

I have now to advise you that some keelmen having volunteered for the Navy, the Regulating Officer has refused to accept them as substitutes for the body of keelmen, saying his orders from the Admiralty are to receive none but able seamen. This appears rather unreasonable on the part of the Admiralty, and I have no doubt when the case is properly represented to their Lordships but they will accede to the measure of taking *one sufficient able keelman* as a substitute for *ten* of their body, and, as it is more than probable that more of the young men will offer their services, it is very material to the interest of the Trade that this should if possible be understood with the Board.

At the request of the Committee I have therefore to request your immediate particular attention to this subject, and hope to receive your reply in course of post, or as early as the nature of the business will admit.

I remain, Sir, your most obedient Servant,

George Dunn

285. Draft, Clayton to Barrow, 28 May 1811 [TWA 394/38]

3 Lincolns Inn, New Square, 28 May 1811

Mr Clayton, after offering to Mr Barrow the thanks of the gentlemen of the Coal Trade of the River Tyne for his early attention to their request for further time to raise the substitutes for the keelmen on that River, is instructed to state to the Lords Commissioners of the Admiralty through Mr Barrow that the gentlemen of the Trade, finding great difficulty in raising the required number, have been obliged to call upon the keelmen who are not protected under the former arrangement with the Lords of the Admiralty to select some of their own body to serve as substitutes for the rest, and that after having obtained the consent of the keelmen to the measure, they have been prevented proceeding in it by the Regulating Officer declining to receive such persons as substitutes, and to entreat that their Lordships will be pleased to direct that such persons may be received as substitutes if they shall be found able and fit for the Service.

286. George Dunn to Clayton, 10 June 1811 [TWA 394/38]

Newcastle, 10 June 1811

Sir,

I received in course your favours of the 27th and 30th ultimo and communicated their contents to the Committee, and in consequence a general meeting was called for the 8th instant at which it was resolved to address the Lords of the Admiralty in a body, and the memorial enclosed being read, was agreed to unanimously and ordered to be transmitted to you for *your signature*, with an earnest request that you would be pleased *personally* to present the same to their Lordships.[1] The time allowed for finding substitutes expiring the 14th instant, it is of the utmost consequence that the Trade should have as early an answer to their memorial as possible; and I beg further to remind you that next week being our *Race Week*, a number of substitutes will most probably be obtained, provided their Lordships accede to the prayer of the memorial; and, if they refuse, it seems to be the general feeling of the fitters &c that it would be better to let things take their course rather than submit to so serious a demand as that one fifth of their people being required for the naval service.

Your early reply to the present will be anxiously looked for, and I hope their Lordships will be satisfied that nothing unreasonable or unfair is requested by their memorialists.

I am, Sir, your most obedient Servant,
George Dunn

P.S. None of the keelmen who have entered *have been passed before the Regulating Officer*, it having been thought prudent not to do so, unless they are received in the proportion of *one* for *ten* of their body, as it would afford a precedent which in future wars might be of the most serious and irremediable injury to the Coal Trade.

[1] The memorial is not present.

287. Extract, Barrow to Clayton, 17 June 1811 [TWA 394/38]

Admiralty Office, 17 June 1811

I have received [your letter] and in return I am commanded to acquaint you, for information of the parties who signed the letter, that their Lordships consider the request to be exceedingly unreasonable, and, in the present scarcity of men for his Majesty's service, are rather disposed to withdraw the indulgence altogether than to continue it to men who, though strictly liable to the Impress, are not satisfyed to commute their services by finding one able seaman or two landmen for every ten.

I am &c, John Barrow

288. Captain Wilson Rathborne to the Right Honourable Charles Philip Yorke, first Lord of Admiralty, 24 June 1811 [TNA, ADM 1/2416 Capt. R 510]

North Shields, 24 June 1811,

My Lord,

The Coal Owners and Fitters of this Port, not satisfied with the decision of the Board relative to the finding one seaman or two men out of their body as substitutes for every ten keelmen, held a meeting last Saturday [22 June] and agreed to send a deputation of 3 to remonstrate with either the Naval Lords or the Board, and these gentlemen are to leave Newcastle for Town tomorrow. It appears by the number of substitutes raised in 1803 that the number of keelmen, watermen and trimmers must have been 1070. Since then the trade has increased. Each man at that period paid £5 towards raising the substitutes, 107 in number, to Joseph Lamb, one of the deputies going up. Mr Lamb has also granted protections at £2 for each to every man that has come to work on the River from that year, till I put a stop to it by impressing some of them.

Those men I have granted protections to in consequence of my late orders have procured their substitutes at the rate of £60 for an able seaman, which for 10 men is only £6 per man, of course no hardship to keep clear of the Impress during the war, when an able seaman is glad to pay £80. Those gentlemen talk of the Trade stopping work and London being distressed for coals if their demands should not be acceded to, but I should hope they would not try the experiment, as on the last striking a Coal Owner informed me it was a loss to him of £150 per diem. Therefore I should hope self interest would induce them to make their men conform to the regulation of 1 seaman or 2 landsmen for every man working on the River. I have no doubt the men would be governed by the Coal Owners and Fitters.

I have the honor to be your Lordship's most humble obedient Servant,

Wilson Rathborn

289. Letter from 'A Keelman' to the *Newcastle Courant*, 23 May 1815[1] [NEIMME 3410/ZD/70, pp 25–9]

Sir,

While the subject is again afloat respecting a permanent fund for the relief of distressed colliers, their widows, &c on the plan of the Keelmen's fund, I am desirous to give my mite (as I have been long) before it gets aground again, although it should be in that clumsy bundling manner which may be expected from one bred from his childhood, and is professionally what he signs himself.

Then, Sir, in narrating some facts, and suggesting a few hints respecting the Keelmen's fund, I hope the concerned will very easily make the application to the subject in hand: then it must be known there were several attempts made for raising a permanent fund amongst the keelmen (with one of which they built their hospital), but they all failed, from various causes, except the last; and some of the principal reasons were that the managers had no authority adequate to enforce obedience, nor punish transgressors; therefore the people entrusted with their money abused the confidence put in them, which caused the others to withhold their respective contributions; which failures suggested the idea of having an act of parliament for its establishment; accordingly that was attempted by them about the year 1769, but not being supported by the gentlemen of the corporation, nor any individual gentleman of weight enough, it also failed; but still, the subject being considered of importance, it was again revived by some keelmen (the principal of whom were the late Henry Strachan and John Day, senior) who with indefatigable zeal, the assistance of the late Mr William Tinwell, and the present Town Clerk (to whom great praise is due from the keelmen for his unremitted exertions hitherto in their behalf), together with the compliance of the gentlemen of the corporation, at the last an act for that purpose was obtained: yet, Sir, notwithstanding its acknowledged utility in easing parishes and townships near the navigable part of the River Tyne, not one individual, company, nor society whatever has given the least pecuniary assistance to it, except a donation lately of five guineas from the Perseverance Steam Packet Company, for which they deserve peculiar respect and thanks from the keelmen on the river Tyne, as they lead the van, and I hope, as they have broke the ice, many will be induced to follow the good example; for the keelmen are not altogether insensible that although many very liberal subscriptions have of late been made for seamen, fishermen, colliers and others (which they do not envy them of) yet not one of any kind has been made for them individually, which makes them think that they must be considered as of very little importance in the community, or greatly disregarded; which, I am sorry to say, they have too much reason to blame themselves for, but like others who are bred to great exertions and hardships, they are not so courteous nor polished as those are whose business lies behind the counter and obliging customers (but there are some exceptions). I only name these things, Sir, to stimulate some in favour of the keelmen, for although such great disasters do not happen to the keelmen as happen to others at certain times, yet their necessities and wants may be considered more permanent, as such a number of sick, old men superannuated, widows, children and orphans are constantly receiving relief from the fund, which takes an average of above 36£ per week to pay them.

There is one way which they have been long looking at, a way which was promised them in the year 1794, a way which has been attempted by them without effect as yet, and a way which they think they are with some justness entitled to; it is that ships loading, or taking a part of their loading in at spouts should be charged the small sum of one penny per chalder for all coals taken in by them at the spouts, for the use of the keelmen's fund, which could easily be done by the gentlemen coal owners and fitters. Thus, when a ship takes on for the spout at any office, the person taking her on may be told that one penny per chalder will be charged more than usual for all coals taken in at the spout, which sum or sums can be given separately with the other collections made at the fitting offices, and I think no objection whatever will be made to it.

But, Sir, what I consider a hardship is that when any person entitled to relief from the keelmen's fund applies for parochial relief, they do not receive the same quantum of relief as others in the same situation of life with themselves; but what they receive from the fund is added to what they get from the overseers, to make them on a par with the others; this is considered a great hardship by the keelmen, because they pay their share either directly or indirectly to the poor-rates, as the others do, besides this which they save off their earnings; therefore they think that they are entitled to the same parochial relief as the others receive – and that independent of the fund, because, as they rightly argue, the fund never was established for its support to be blended with parochial relief, neither has it a right to be so, because the others may save their earnings in some such manner as the keelmen do; but no doubt these wise oeconomists think they save by it, and may ask, without doing thus, what would the parishes and townships be the better for the establishment of the keelmen's fund? I answer it has indeed the appearance of saving, but there are some who save at the tap and run out at the bung, and so it fares with this, inasmuch as it discourages and prevents others from forming similar societies; for according to the best information I can get, this is the principal reason why the colliers did not agree to form into a society of this kind when it was attempted before, because, said they, neither us nor our relatives will be any better when we or they are necessitated to apply for parochial relief, and we may as well take the good of all our earnings now as give them for the good of the parishes, for we see plainly the keelmen are no better in that case than we are, notwithstanding their fund; and this is the principal reason why so many when they leave the keels leave the fund likewise: but they are greatly better, because few do apply to them until they are necessitated to do so, and the relief got from the fund prevents them in so far as it goes for their subsistence, which upon the whole is considerable; and in my opinion if they were allowing them one half of what they get from the fund over and above the common parish allowances it would have a better effect, because, when the keelmen with their relatives were made more comfortable with their own money, it would prompt others to form into similar societies; and I am persuaded if the colliers were satisfied on this point, there would be very few obstacles in the way; and I do not know of a better way to satisfy them, than to do it with the keelmen and their relatives.

Thus, Sir, the colliers have beacons set up for them to steer by, as it appears plain from the above narration that nothing short of an act of parliament will answer the purpose, and they have now a better prospect than ever the keelmen had, for the keelmen, as was before observed, had no pecuniary assistance whatever, and the act cost them, I believe, upwards of £200, and in order that a fund might be raised, the contributions for two years were taken and no relief given whatever, whereas the colliers are receiving great assistance at this time, such as may pay for the act and give them immediate relief: and there is a beacon for the overseers and others concerned in granting parochial relief, as they may hereby see what made the failure last time it was in agitation for the colliers, and steer clear in future; and

I hope they will be more wise than heretofore; and I heartly wish that many similar societies to the keelmen's may be formed, and succeed better than theirs, for it is very poor, and I am afraid that the benefits will have to be lessened, unless they get assistance from some quarter, which I hope will soon be as before hinted; and I as a member, and of consequence a well wisher thereto, sign myself

23 May 1815   A Keelman

---

[1] The letter does not appear in the *Newcastle Courant* about the above date or in several subsequent editions of the paper. It must have been published eventually as it appears in the Bell Collection as a press cutting.

THE KEELMEN'S STRIKE OF 1819, THE GREAT RADICAL REFORM MEETING THAT COINCIDED WITH IT, AND THE ALARM OF THE AUTHORITIES

290. (rough draft) Joseph Forster, Mayor, to Lord Sidmouth, Home Secretary, 28 September 1819 [TNA, HO 42/195, and TWA 394/42]

Newcastle, 28 September 1819

My Lord,

It gives me much concern to have occasion to apprise your Lordship that in the course of yesterday a strong body of the lightermen employed on this river assembled and proceeded to prevent by force the navigation of the keels or barges carrying coals from the staiths to the ships.

They have, however, since sent a respectful petition to their employers stating the cause of their disssatisfaction, and as the gentlemen interested in the coal trade have appointed a general meeting to be held on Friday first [1 October], for the purpose of taking that petition into consideration, I entertain the hope that they will soon return to their duty. I have not, my Lord, any reason at present to suspect the influence of any kind of political notions amongst them, but I cannot help feeling apprehensive that much industry may be used by ill-disposed persons to inflame them to mischief.[1]

I beg leave to represent to your Lordship that the military and naval force now here is small, consisting I believe of only two weak troops of cavalry and two revenue cutters.

I have the honor to be your Lordship's most obedient humble Servant,

Joseph Forster, Mayor

Endorsed by Henry Hobhouse, Under Secretary of State for the

Home Department, 'Directions have been given by the Admiralty for a sloop of war to proceed to the Tyne from the Firth of Forth'.[2]

[1] A week earlier Forster wrote to Sidmouth: 'Though I have strong reason to think that the inhabitants of this part of the country are generally well disposed, and that there is not any disposition on their part to aid and encourage those at a distance who are engaged in measures tending to disturb the public peace, I think it my duty to inform your Lordship that a handbill has been lately distributed about the Town soliciting the attention of the public to a very mischievous publication under the title of an appeal to the people of England on the necessity of parliamentary reform. I have the honor of transmitting to your Lordship the handbill and also the publication to which it refers.' (TWA 394/42). The two enclosures are not present.

[2] This and extracts of many other Home Office papers relating to the strikes of 1819 and 1822 are printed in A. Aspinall, *The Early English Trade Unions* (London, 1949).

291. Copy Joseph Forster, Mayor, to the Duke of Northumberland, Lord Lieutenant of Newcastle, 28 September 1819 [TWA 394/42]

Mayor's Chamber, 28 September 1819

My Lord Duke,

I consider it my duty to apprise your Grace that yesterday a strong body of the keelmen on this River, under the pretence of some real or supposed greivances, proceeded to prevent and actually did prevent the navigation of the keels upon the River.

I crave leave farther to represent to your Grace that the military and naval force at present here is small, consisting I believe of not more than two weak troops of cavalry and two revenue cutters under the command of Lieutenants of the Navy.

I have the honor to be your Grace's most obedient humble Servant,

Joseph Forster

292. Joseph Bulmer, an acting Magistrate, to Sidmouth, 28 September 1819 [TNA, HO 42/195]

South Shields, 28 September 1819

My Lord,

As the spirit of discontent is beginning to show itself in this district, I deem it my duty to give your Lordship early information. The keelmen, from real or pretended grievances, yesterday struck off work, and this morning I have seen many of them in boats on the river preventing keels going with coals to the ships.

I understand the men allege that their employers load the keels with more than the usual quantity of eight chaldons (which over-quantity the coalminers give to the shipowners instead of reducing the price) and only pay the same wages. This is not a time, my Lord, for masters to do anything that looks like oppressing their labourers, and therefore I think the Mayor and Magistrates of Newcastle should lose no time in getting those differences adjusted, for I fear if the keelmen remain long in this state, the sailors will begin to feel uneasiness, and those two great bodies of men may join.[1] 'Tis certain the reformists will endeavour to promote discord as much as they can. We have some of them here, but 'tis only among the labouring class. I have learnt they intend to hold a meeting to-night.

I have the honor to be your Lordship's most obedient humble Servant,

Joseph Bulmer

[1] The authorities were always fearful that when one body stopped work the others who were consequently affected would join the strikers. During the seamen's strike of 1815 the Mayor wrote to Sidmouth: 'The great bodies of keelmen…of pitmen and of waggonmen whose bread depends on the coal trade (now entirely stopped) must in a very few days be without employment and it is greatly to be feared that their strength will be added to that of the seamen' (TWA 394/42, 7 October 1815). In 1740 the magistrates' worst fear was that the keelmen who would be put out of work by the pitmen's strike would join them, as they soon did. See above **Document 93**.

293. Petition of the Keelmen, 28 September 1819 [Enclosed in a note from Nicholas Fairles to Sidmouth, 3 October 1819] [TNA, HO 42/196/427]

To the Gentlemen Coalowners and Fitters on the River Tyne, the Petition of the Keelmen employed on the River Tyne humbly sheweth

That your petitioners have suffered very great privations from want of employment chiefly owing to the vend by spout having increased *so much of late*.

Your petitioners humbly beg that no ship be allowed to take in more of her cargo or loading at any spout than *six keels* [48 Newcastle chaldrons].

Your petitioners humbly beg that no keel be permitted to carry more than *eight chaldrons*, the danger being very great in stormy weather or strong tides if the keels carry more than that quantity.

Your petitioners humbly hope that the Keelmen's Fund will not be forgot at this time, an institution, they believe, all the gentlemen in the trade are friendly to, and without whose assistance it cannot continue. Your petitioners humbly beg that *one penny* per chaldron, for every chaldron vended by spout, be allowed to relieve the funds of that Institution.

And your petitioners shall ever pray, &c

294. Abstract Account of the state of the Funds of the Keelmen's Society [TNA, HO 42/196/427 and TWA 394/42]

Collected from Fitters' Offices			
1815	1816	1817	1818
£1777 15s. 9d.	£1772 15s. 4d.	£1613 19s. 11d.	£1812 2s. 10d.
Collected at 6d. per week			
£286 16s. 6d	£276 5s. 10d.	£268 2s. 5d.	£244 15s. 8d.
Collected bye–tides			
£123 13s. 9d.	£87 12s. 5d.	£83 1s. 10d.	£83 6s. 7d.
Totals			
£2188 6s. 0d.	£2136 13s. 7d.	£1965 4s. 2d.	£2140 5s. 1d.
Paid sick keelmen, superannuated members, widows and orphans			
£2235 19s. 0d.	£2234 15s. 0d.	£2127 4s 0d.	£2241 7s. 6d.
Balance against the Fund			
£47 13s. 0d.	£98 1s. 5d.	£161 19s. 10d.	£101 2s. 5d

Upon the Fund at present, 138 superannuated members; 182 widows; 6 orphans and 22 sick, making a total of 348.

295. Nicholas Fairles, J.P. to Lord Sidmouth, 30 September 1819 [TNA, HO 42/195]

South Shields, 30 September 1819

My Lord,

…The whole of the keelmen upon the River Tyne have stopped work. They complain of short employment and of being obliged to convey a larger quantity of coals in their craft than usual, without additional pay. They also require that no vessel above the burthen of 96 chaldrons of coals shall be allowed to load at the spouts. Your Lordship will observe that at these spouts vessels of [small] burthen are laden without the employment of craft, and it is doubtful, in case this stop continues, the pitmen, who are a numerous and ignorant race, may join them. Some Radicals have appeared amongst them. Added to this, we have a very large fleet in port, and consequently the seamen unemployed, and unfortunately no ship of war with us. The *Alert* left about ten days ago for Sheerness, and report says she is not to return. As I have stated before to your Lordship, Shields harbour never should be without a ship of war. Had we had one with us I think it likely this matter might have been prevented. My advice this morning is that a meeting of the coalowners and a deputation from the keelmen will be held at

Newcastle on Saturday, and that some of their demands are likely to be acceded to, but that of the spouts will not. I am of opinion we should be provided against the worst.[1]

I have the honor to be your Lordship's most obedient humble Servant,

Nicholas Fairles

[1] Fairles later reported that on the day he wrote the above 'I experienced much insult and contempt from about 200 ballast keelmen who attempted to prevent any ballast being landed from ships at the wharves' (to Sidmouth, 3 October 1819, TNA, HO 42/196).

296. William Richardson to the Mayor of Newcastle, 30 September 1819 [TWA 394/42]

North Shields, 30 September 1819

Sir,

I am one of those who cannot sit still and see the laws and institutions of Great Britain trampled upon.

This morning a body of riotous people, under the name of keelmen, forcibly obstructed peaceable labourers (trimmers) and waggoners at Bardon Main Staith on the Tyne and compelled them to cease their daily employment.

This, I need not tell you, is only the forerunner of that awful rebellion, plunder and rapine, now in embryo, and which will in a few days shew its daring head if the arm of the law and force, civil and military, put not a stop thereto.[1]

I trust that others may have informed you of these proceedings, but I cannot reconcile myself to sit at ease without adding my notice thereof likewise.

Very respectfully, Worshipful Sir, your oedient Servant,
William Richardson

[1] Richardson, a special constable, later wrote to Sidmouth, 21 October 1819: 'The small wicked pamphlets must be suppressed, and some restraint put upon the newspaper editors, or the liberties of England will be trampled under foot and that under guise of preserving them' (TNA, HO 42/197/32–3).

297. Robert Wheldon to Lord Sidmouth, 2 October 1819 [TNA, HO 42/196/440–1]

North Shields, 2 October 1819

My Lord,

There are now in the harbour of Shields about 300 sail of ships, and in consequence of the keelmen having for the present refused to do their duty and preventing any coals being sent down to the ships, the pitmen and the seamen who are both numerous bodies, are laid idle. For the present they are quiet, but should they become tumultuous, we are without any military or ships of war to assist the civil power in case of need.[1]

I have the honor to be your Lordship's most obedient humble Servant,
Robert Wheldon

[1] As the keelmen's strike continued, Archibald Reed, now Mayor, greatly feared that 'towards the latter end of the week we shall have the pitmen and sailors in a state of insubordination' (to Sidmouth, 5 October 1819, HO 42/196). By 12 October two sloops of war had arrived in the Tyne (Fairles to Sidmouth, HO 42/196).

298. *Newcastle Chronicle*, 2 October 1819

The keelmen last week struck work and have not suffered any keel, and a few wherries, to be worked. We understand that their object is to make the coals shipped from the staiths by spouts contribute to the maintenance of the hospital for the support of their sick and decayed brethren. This hospital is supported by a rate of 8d. a tide imposed on every keel navigating the river. When the Act authorising this rate passed, nearly all coal shipped in the Tyne was carried by keels, but since that period, at the staiths of nearly all the collieries below bridge, spouts have been erected by which the coals are now put on board the ships immediately from the waggons without the intervention of keels. This has superceded the use of so great a number of keels that the remainder are not equal to the support of the hospital. Under these circumstances, the keelmen are desirous that the coals shipped by the spouts should pay a rate of a penny a chaldron to the hospital. They have made a represention of their grievances to the gentlemen of the coal trade and that body will (we understand) take it into consideration this day.

299. Resolutions of the Coalowners, 2 October 1819 [TWA 394/42 and HO 42/196/430]

At a general meeting of the coalowners of this Port held at Newcastle on Saturday, 2 October 1819, the following resolutions were passed unanimously:

It appearing to the meeting that the Keelmen's Fund has fallen into arrears to the amount of £161, owing to the number of claimants upon it, and to the difficulties of the Coal Trade, and this meeting, wishing to encourage the same, and to assist it with subscriptions, *it is ordered* that the sum of Three Hundred Pounds be raised by a voluntary subscription of the Coalowners, and paid into the bank of Messrs Ridley and Company to be placed to the credit of the Guardians of the Keelmen's Fund.

That no keel be allowed to carry more than 8 chaldrons, and that in order to prevent the violation of this order, the Secretary of the Coal Owners be directed to call upon the off-putter at each staith to take the oath prescribed by the Act for establishing the Keelmen's Fund; and that any off-putter neglecting or refusing to take such oath within one week shall be discharged from his employment.

That the request of the keelmen to put any limitation or restraint on ships loading at the spouts, or to impose any duty or charge upon coals vended by spout, is illegal and therefore impracticable; and that an attempt to do so would be a violation of private property and of the principles on which all trade is carried on.

That the contribution of £300 be paid as above directed as soon as the keelmen shall return to their respective employments.

And lastly, that these resolutions be printed, and a copy sent to the Stewards of each Work, and to each Fitting Office.

Matthew Bell, Chairman

300. Petition of the keelmen, 5 October 1819 [TWA 597/79]

To the Right Worshipful the Mayor and Aldermen of Newcastle upon Tyne, the Petition of the Keelmen employed on the River Tyne Humbly Sheweth

That your petitioners have suffered very great privations from want of employment, chiefly owing to the vend by spouts having increased so much of late. Your petitioners therefore humbly beg that no ship be allowed to take in more than six keels of her loading at any spout, and that no keel be allowed to carry more than eight chaldrons, as we have for a considerable time been suffering the loss of one tide in every eight by extra measure. And as the Fund by the same means has suffered greatly, we humbly hope that you will so advocate the cause of the Fund of which you are the Guardians as to induce the Gentlemen Coal Owners and Fitters on the River Tyne to grant the small sum of one farthing per chaldron for the coals vended from every staith to be paid for the support of that useful institution; and that the waggons both above and below the Bridge be made to contain no more than one stricker Measure.

Added below: There are about 200 men out of employment at present and like to be more at the binding time, A. Strachan (one of the leaders of the strike).

301. *Tyne Mercury*, **5 October 1819**

We regret to state that the keelmen upon the Tyne have held meetings and generally struck working on two grounds of dissatisfaction. The first is that the coal owners load more coals on board the keels than formerly, i.e. they keep up the nominal price by giving larger measure to the shipper and thus increase the labour of the keelman without any additional pay. The other complaint is against the extension of the colliery spouts (the termination of railways on the river) below Newcastle bridge, by which vessels of almost any burthen can now receive their coals without the intervention of keels, thus throwing many keelmen out of employment.

It is the desire of the keelmen to restrict the loading at the spouts to vessels of small burthen, such as formerly could alone go under them. It is said that the keelmen also wish the spouts to pay a small tax to their hospital fund, which owing to the decrease of their employment is greatly exhausted. We have understood that a proposal was made to allow the keelmen £300, but that has been rejected and they still continue off work.

302. Archibald Reed, Mayor, to Lord Sidmouth, 5 October 1819
[TNA, HO 42/196]

Newcastle 5 October 1819

My Lord,

In consequence of the keelmen having yesterday evinced a disposition to mischief, I deemed it my duty as Chief Magistrate (having been elected yesterday) to proceed at an early hour this morning upon the River, the principal assemblage being about four miles from hence. Upon my appearance the men dispersed, but, as I was anxious to have an interview, I quitted the steam packet, attended by three gentlemen, and obtained a full meeting about half a mile from the River. It proved more satisfactory than I expected, and having convinced the men of the illegality of their proceedings and the impossibility of my receiving their petition or attending to their complaints until they returned to work, they expressed their conviction that the whole of them would comply with my advice.

I am with the highest respect, my Lord, your Lordship's most obedient humble Servant,

Archibald Reed

303. Reed to Sidmouth, 6 October 1819 [TWA 394/42 and HO 42/196/417–8]

My Lord,

I am extremely sorry to inform your Lordship that at a meeting held this morning by the keelmen they have come to the resolution of continuing off work. I shall immediately communicate with the Magistrates for Northumberland and Durham and request their co-operation without which we can effect little. I shall also write to General Byng who commands the District and request some infantry. I beg leave also to state to your Lordship that I greatly fear we shall towards the latter end of the week have the pitmen and sailors in a state of insubordination, and I trust your Lordship will give such instructions as are deemed prudent for the preservation of the Port and shipping, which it is utterly out of our power to protect without a strong naval force.

Your Lordship is aware that a requisition was presented to me to call a meeting to take into consideration the *Manchester Magistrates*, which is a mere pretext for a reform meeting. They have appointed it upon their own responsibility to be held on Monday next.

I am, &c.

Wrote by the same post to Major General Byng commanding the Northern District, Pontefract, requesting at least four companies of infantry to be sent here immediately, to co-operate with the Magistracy on the water if necessary.

304. Reed to Sidmouth, 12 October 1819 [TNA, HO 42/196/209–10 and TWA 394/42]

My Lord,

It affords me pleasure to inform your Lordship that the [reform] meeting which was held yesterday terminated peaceably. The number of Reformers that marched in regular order to the meeting are estimated by military gentlemen to be about 12,000,[1] the total amount assembled about 40,000, but the observers did not in any way identify themselves with the Reformers, who were men of the lowest order. The Magistrates will collect in the course of 2 or 3 days all the informations that they deem worthy of your Lordship's notice.

I am sorry to report the keelmen [to be] in the same state as when I last had the honor of writing to your Lordship.[2] I feel myself particularly obliged to Lieutenant Colonel French of the 6th Dragoons for his readiness to act in co-operation with the Magistrates in case of necessity.

I am, &c,

Archibald Reed

[1] The number of marchers was later revised to be from 18 to 20,000 (see below, **Document 312**).

[2] According to Joseph Bulmer, the keelmen were 'living by plunder, taking turnips and potatoes from the farmers in open day' (to Sidmouth, 8 October 1819, TNA, HO 42/196).

305. Nicholas Fairles to Lord Sidmouth, 12 October 1819 [TNA, HO 42/196]

South Shields, 12 October 1819

My Lord,

From the peaceable termination of a public meeting of Reformers held yesterday in the neighbourhood of Newcastle, and the little interest which both keelmen and pitmen took in the business, I augur that they will return to their employment about Monday first. Their poverty, and the advice given them by their employers, I trust will have the desired effect. Should this fail, I see no other line but to apprehend some of them by warrant. Two sloops of war are arrived in the Tyne.

I have the honor to be your Lordship's most obedient humble Servant,

Nicholas Fairles

306. (draft) Archibald Reed, Mayor, to Lord Sidmouth, 14 October 1819, 10pm [TNA, HO 42/196/404–5, TWA 394/42]

My Lord,

I am sorry to inform your Lordship that an attempt to open the navigation of the River Tyne (which, as your Lordship is already informed, has been interrupted for some time by a riotous combination of the keelmen) has been attended with the most alarming consequences. A furious attack was this afternoon made by the mob at the mouth of the harbour on myself and the civil power, and on the boats of his Majesty's ships stationed here.[1] Some shots were fired by the boats' crews in their own defence, but as far as I have yet been able to ascertain, only with blank cartridges.[2]

I take the liberty of urging most earnestly upon your Lordship the necessity of sending to this Port without loss of time an adequate force of ships of war and marines, and also of increasing the military force in this neighbourhood.

I am, &c, Archibald Reed

[1] The Mayor issued a handbill offering 100 guineas reward for information leading to the apprehension of the offenders, 15 October (TNA, HO 42/196/415).

[2] This was incorrect; one man was killed. See Joseph Bulmer's letter to Sidmouth of 15 October (**Document 310**) and other items below.

307. Copy Reed to the Commanding Officer at Sunderland, 14 October 1819 [TWA 394/42]

Sir,

I am sorry that the violent proceedings of the mob makes it necessary that I should request you to send here without an hour's delay as large a body of the infantry under your command as you can possibly spare.[1]

I have the honor to be, Sir, your most obedient,

Archibald Reed

[1] A party of 230 men of the 40th Regiment was accordingly supplied and arrived in Newcastle during that night (*Newcastle Chronicle*, 16 October 1819).

308. Copy Reed to Major General Sir John Byng, 14 October 1819 [TWA 394/42]

Sir,

The disturbed state of this part of the country renders it absolutely necessary that the military force stationed here should be forthwith increased.

The mob proceeded to acts of violence this afternoon, and I have sent to the Commanding Officer at Sunderland requesting as many infantry as he can possibly spare. Until the arrival of the force he may send, our whole strength consists of 4 troops of the 6th Dragoon Guards. I must therefore entreat that you will make such arrangements as will add to the force here.

I have the honor to be, Sir, your most obedient,

Archibald Reed, Mayor

309. Copy Reed and John Collinson, J.P., to the Earl of Darlington, 14 October 1819 [TWA 394/42]

My Lord,

The disturbed state of this part of the country renders it necessary that the military should be called upon to aid the Civil Power. The military stationed here are not of an adequate strength to afford security, and the Magistrates therefore request that the South Tyne Yeomanry Cavalry may be called out with as little delay as possible.[1]

This request we have the honor of referring to your Lordship, and are &c

Archibald Reed, Mayor, John Collinson, J.P., County Durham

[1] Darlington ordered the Yeomanry to assemble and placed them under the authority of the Newcastle magistrates, 'who must be responsible if they order the military to act, and I have strongly urged them not to do so, unless the civil power

is overcome or incompetent' (to Sidmouth, 15 October 1819, TNA, HO 42/196/413–14). See also Darlington to Sidmouth, 21 October, below **Document 319**.

310. Joseph Bulmer to Lord Sidmouth, 15 October 1819 [TNA, HO 42/196/411–12]

South Shields 15 October 1819

My Lord,

….About six o'clock yesterday evening a few keels (four or five) came down the river, loaded with coals, protected by eight of his Majesty's boats; the keelmen came to North Shields in great numbers, and from the warf annoyed the men so much, who were casting the coals into the ships, that they were obliged to desist. The Harbour Master accompanied the men-of-war boats, and when he and his officers attempted to land on the Duke of Northumberland's quay (which is a very spacious place), they were assailed with brickbats, &c, &c, and obliged to retire. I am informed that the Mayor of Newcastle (who had also come down) at last effected a landing; the marines being stoned most dreadfully by the mob (and I understand several of them wounded) at length *fired* over their heads, but this only had the effect of causing greater violence. At length the marines fired amongst them and *killed* one man and wounded others. The mob became very furious and demolished all the windows of the principal inn (kept by one Mrs Carr, a widow) because several special constables had gone there for safety. The mob at length dispersed but threatened to assemble again this morning….

The keelmen were joined by a great number of the Radicals of North Shields, and the circumstances seemed greatly to interest those of South Shields, but we remain quiet. I believe my Lord that the lower orders here are ripe for anything.[1]

I have the honor to be your Lordship's most obedient humble Servant,

Joseph Bulmer

---

[1] There were various opinions as to whether there was any connection between the keelmen and the radicals. The Duke of Northumberland believed that the keelmen's strike was 'totally unconnected with politics'; Bulmer reported that the keelmen were determined to remain off work until the reform meeting had been held, but, according to Fairles, the keelmen and pitmen had taken 'little interest' in it; the Earl of Darlington believed that the refractory keelmen and the radicals were perfectly separate, though 'very inflamatory language and seditious writings are defused amongst the former'. Archibald Reed declared that almost the entire body of pitmen entertained the 'mischevious and abominable principles' of the radicals, but did not attribute them to the keelmen (Northumberland to Sidmouth, 1 October 1819, TNA, HO 42/196/443–4; Bulmer to Sidmouth, 8 October, HO 42/196/423; Fairles to Sidmouth, 12 October, HO 42/196; Darlington to Sidmouth, 15 October, HO 42/196/413–14; Reed to Sidmouth, 27 October, HO

42/197/692–4). Sir Matthew White Ridley described the radicals as 'the very lowest class of blackguards' (to 2nd Earl Grey, 8 October 1819, The Earl Grey Papers, GRE B49/12/1).

311. Minutes made in the Mayor's Chamber, 15 October 1819
[TWA 394/42]

Present Mr Mayor, Mr Cramlington, Mr Clayton, Mr Smith, Mr George Forster, Mr Isaac Cookson, Mr Sorsbie

Mr John Brown told Mr Scott that he came from Mr Mayor and requested his prohibition as a Magistrate from a number of people riotously assembled near Mr Carr's 'Northumberland Arms' in North Shields. Mr Scott stated his state of health. Went to Mr Wright with Mr Donkin the High Constable. Mr Stephen Wright said that it was of no use his going without a force. Mr Brown replyed that his appearance and the reading of the Riot Act might intimidate the mob. The High Constable with several constables accompanyed Mr Brown on his return to Mr Carr. Mr Brown was himself sworn by Mr Scott a special constable. On his return to the quay [he] saw several persons and women and boys assembled about the Tavern and saw that the windows and door of the Tavern had been broken.

Mr William Brandling attended at the Chamber and required the interposition of the Magistracy of Newcastle in order to protect the property of himself and his partners vizt. a keel of coals lying at Shields. The keel was made fast to *The Piggy* of Newcastle by witness who is staithman of Coxlodge, George Mangham, the running fitter, Stephen Wilkinson, the off-putter and John Knox, a messenger at the staith. These persons navigated the keel and made her fast. All quitted the keel…and know not what has become of [her]. They durst not return to [her] for fear of the mob.

Mr Donkin went amongst the crowd and after avowing himself High Constable he demanded peace in the King's name and that he was determined that the peace should be kept at the hazard of his life. They seemed very violent and said that a man had been murdered and that they would have blood for blood. They stated that there was a man in custody in the Tavern and they were determined to have him out. Donkin went into the Tavern to inquire after him – found him there and took him out and liberated him amongst the mob, saying that he was known and he would be afterwards answerable.

Mr Brown was went on the message to Mr Scott about 10 minutes after 5. On his return it was near dark.

The Mayor expressed a desire that Mr Reed and Mr William Brandling as Magistrates of the County of Northumberland would remain near Newcastle, as from the narrowness of their limits it might be found necessary to have recourse to them if any riotous body should pass those limits into Northumberland.

Mr Robson of Collingwood Main Staith [was] wounded with a large stone. Whilst Mr Brown was upon the message a shot had been fired and a man killed. The Mayor was on shore at the Tavern when the shots were fired by the Marines. Upon the firing Mr Mayor ran out and seeing a man on the edge of the quay throwing a stone laid hold of him and conducted him into the Inn. This was the man that was afterwards liberated. Mr Donkin advised Mr Mayor to leave the house privately, the mob without demanding the Mayor and persons within to be turned out. The women about threatened that the inn and Dockeray Square would be fired that night. It appeared that they had the impression that the Mayor had been the cause of the man being shot. The Mayor, Mr Brown and Mr Donkin then left the house by the back door and went to the George Tavern. The Mayor then got a horse which he mounted, but afterwards Mr Mayor got a gig by Mr Donkin's means and he and Mr Brown arrived in it at Newcastle a little after 9 o'Clock.

It is suggested that a formation of corps of yeomanry might be very advisable in this Town.

A letter from Mr Buddle was brought in expressing apprehension about the safety of 8 or 9 Hoastmen who conveyed some keels down the River yesterday of whom he had not heard and expressing a wish that they should be looked after. The letter stated that they were on board the *Sea Nymph* by the last account.

The Mayor laid before the meeting the sketch or form of an instrument partaking of an axe, a scythe and a spear, and an intimation that it is believed that some thousand of instruments like the above are manufacturing in this neighbourhood. This was sent to him through the Newcastle post and was anonymous.

Forsyth, the Sergeant, stated that after making fast the keel to a vessel he called a skuller to go on shore – informed that if he went to the steam boat they would be killed. When he came alongside the steam boat a stone from the same quay struck Forsyth in the hand. Saw on the shore about a hundred hands [raised?] up with stones as in the act of throwing. He was again struck down by a stone hitting him upon the neck – was drawn into the cabin by Christopher Jackson, one of the constables. Stones continued to be thrown. Heard the mob on shore: 'There are six of the buggers, we know. We will murder them and scuttle the steam boat and send them all to hell'. Stones were again thrown into the steam boat from the shore from which there were not above five yards from the shore. The steam boat was at anchor and the steam let off. …In a short time two boats from the armed vessel came to our assistance…when the boats came up to the steam boat the officer asked for the Mayor or a Magistrate. Forsyth told him the Mayor was on shore and no Magistrate on board, but he was their officer and would attend him. At this moment more showers of stones came both against the steam boat and the officers' boats. He then heard one of the two officers present say, or someone, 'Fire in the air'. Witness said, 'For God's sake don't fire'. Two seamen then fired in the air. Great confusion took place. The Man of War's boats then endeavoured to get behind the steam boat and witness went into the steam boat's cabin for protection from the stones. Witness then heard the report of 2 or 3 more guns. One of the steam boat's men came into the cabin with a musquet and expressed a wish to have some ammunition. The armed boats then left the Packet and witness saw no more of them. Witness made the best of his way to the south shore in order to make his escape. Several of the constables on the deck of the steam boat received several hurts from being struck with the stones. All the stones were thrown from the people on the north shore save one which must have been thrown from a ship or boat afloat. John Braithwait, a constable, will speak to some of the above facts.

Mr Collinson and Mr Askew attended and requested the opinion of the Magistrates whether they considered it lawful for the Magistrates to stop persons in large bodies coming from a distance and apparently making their way to a place where a riotous assemblage of persons had taken place last night, and may probably yet continue, and, more generally, if any meeting should now take place in numbers evidently as large as to overawe the civil power, whether Magistrates might by law, with the civil power aided by the military force, proceed to disperse such meeting and endeavour to prevent different bodies of them congregating in one place before any outrage is committed or actual tumult has taken place.

A question is suggested whether in case of emergency the Tyne Legion could be called upon to serve out of the County of Durham.

The Mayor having received a letter from Mr Wright of Dockeray Square stating that the Coroner was sent for and a wish for a further force of Dragoons, a further force was sent, and under their protection the following witnesses were dispatched to be examined before the Coroner, viz. Thomas Forsyth, John Braithwaite, George Rutherford and Thomas Aiston.

The Mayor stated that as he went down to Shields yesterday he met one of the steam packets returning to Newcastle on board of which was a man with a white hat and black cloaths who made some gestures and uttered something which could not be heard but impressed the Mayor with the notion that he meant to presage that the civil power would be worsted in the attempt they were making to restore the peace of the Port. It was since said that this man was Hodgson of Winlaton who is believed to have been most active in corrupting the minds of the people, and to have spoken most violently at the meeting held on Monday.

Mr Peter Row came in and said that the riot at Shields was occasioned by fetching down the keels. He thinks that those who navigate the ballast keels were very forward in the mischief. One Blackelock appeared to be most active. They have little to do at present and Blackelock plys a skuller. He was standing upon the stairs of the New Quay and seemed disposed to obstruct the landing of the boat on board of which the Mayor was.

312. Minutes for further letter to Lord Sidmouth [TWA 394/42]

The Mayor's Chamber, 16 October 1819

Present: The Mayor, Mr Alderman Forster, Mr Alderman Cookson, Mr Alderman George Forster

The numbers who marched in procession under leaders [at the Reform Meeting on 11 October] appeared to be more than estimated before. They are now calculated at from 18 to 20,000 and the whole number was full as large as before stated. The sentiments therefore of these reformers are more widely diffused than expected. They are classed under leaders and appear to be in great discipline.

A rumour prevails that arms are manufacturing at Winlaton and that several of the men attending the procession had them concealed upon their persons. The form of a pike has been anonymously sent to the Mayor.

[It is] the opinion of the Magistrates that a very large force should be at all events collected without loss of time, or this part of the country cannot be in safety. That [it] seems necessary that the well disposed in all parts of the country should be put upon their guard and should be stimulated or required to form themselves into bodies under the direction of the leading men of the country and should be taught a portion of discipline and the use of arms. That means should be used to possess their minds with the conviction that they should enable themselves to act in conjunction with and in aid of the military force.

Mr Brown returned from Shields with an account that the Inquest at Shields was proceeding with regularity, and that the Coroner had determined that no lawyer or attorney should attend and that no notes should be taken.

The person was upon the quay when he received the shot and he fell on the quay. He was a sailor but had a sculler on the water which he plied for his livelyhood. He was taking an active part in the riot.

313. *Tyne Mercury*, 19 October 1819, Letter from a Correspondent

North Shields, 17 October

On Thursday afternoon a rumour prevailing that a steam-boat was towing loaded keels down the river, a number of the inhabitants assembled on the Duke of Northumberland's quay. Several gentlemen and others said to be special constables from Newcastle were on board of the boat, the former of whom as soon as she was moored at the quay repaired to the Northumberland Arms, and were hooted, hissed &c. Those who remained on board were assailed with stones thrown by idle boys, said to have been urged thereto by women, so that the Peace Officers were forced to take shelter in the cabins. It appears that a message had been sent to the brig cutter for assistance, and about 6 o'clock two boats arrived in each of which were marines, when without the least warning for the crowd to disperse, a musket was fired and soon after a second, but those who used these murderous engines pointed them in such a manner as not to injure the unsuspecting, and most of them innocent spectators, who did not fly, from the supposition that the guns were fired to disperse the boys, but the third person that fired convinced them that their security was wrong placed: he levelled his piece at the multitude and, melancholy to relate, the bullet entered the heart of a seaman, Joseph Clackson, an unoffending man who had not been on the quay five minutes, and he almost instantly expired. The act was so unexpected that the multitude could not credit the report of those near the dying man, but when assured of the fact, the scene became truly terrific. Personal safety was forgot and shouts for vengeance issued from every tongue. The person who fired the musket took advantage of the moment and escaped. The gentlemen in the mean time issued from the inn and seized a youth who, being lame, had been upset by the crowd, whilst it was imagined that he was picking up stones. They succeeded in dragging him to the Northumberland Arms whilst others laid hold of a man dressed in a light coat, caught in the act of bombarding the boat; the last, on the alarm being given, was instantly rescued, when the populace repaired to the inn to liberate the other. The doors were found shut, but by the application of some gas pipes which were lying near, the hinges were soon broken and the mob with stones totally demolished the panes and sashes of the lower windows and a number of squares in the second story. A window where the gentlemen were assembled, which faced the back of the house, shared the same fate; so that those within were assailed on both sides. The door was no sooner opened, than a party rushed in and demanded the liberation of the young man which was instantly complied with. The gentlemen then escaped by the back door, and retreated up the bank.[1]

[1] The *Newcastle Chronicle*, 23 October 1819, adds some details: 'the mob searched almost every part of the house and sought to wreak vengeance on the officers of the steam boat, but they escaped to the other side of the river. The mob continued on the streets till a late hour. A party of dragoons arrived and somewhat quietened the fears of the inhabitants. Crowds of disorderly persons have since nightly assembled and alarmed the inhabitants by their threats and frightful shouts, and on almost every door and wall has been written "blood for blood" and other terrible and threatening expressions.'

314. *Tyne Mercury*, 19 October 1819

Yesterday morning a Court of Inquest was held at the County Court, in this town, before Thomas Clennell, Esq., and a full bench of magistrates, under an Act of Parliament passed in the reign of Henry IV, when the jurors found that there was a riot at North Shields on Thursday last, and that Thomas Custard of North Shields, shoemaker, was then and there present, which decision amounted to his conviction as a rioter. Mr Clennell, in passing sentence, said that this was almost the first instance of such a court having been held in this County – the court was vested with very great powers, and their object was rather to show that they had that power than to punish the prisoner, as he had been found to be a person of excellent character. The sentence was that he should be fined 20s. and become bound to keep the peace, himself in £40, and two sureties in £50 each.

The court also decided that there had been a riot at Wallsend staith on Wednesday, and that three keelmen who were named, but who were not in custody, had been present thereat. They were fined £15 each.[1] The Court was adjourned till yesterday week.

[1] The *Tyne Mercury*, 2 November 1819, printed an extract from *The Star* of 22 October which strongly criticised the proceedings against the three keelmen, fined £15 – a heavy penalty for a keelman – in their absence without opportunity of making a defence. The right of being heard before being condemned is 'a right on which everything like justice must eternally hinge…if such are the "great powers" which the magistrates of Newcastle wished to show they possessed by reviving the Court of Inquest…we do say at once they are powers wholly unknown to the existing laws of England and a positive infringement on some of the oldest and best recognized rights of Englishmen'.

315. Archibald Reed to Lord Sidmouth, 19 October 1819 [TNA, HO 42/197]

My Lord,

The keelmen refused to accept of the terms offered yesterday by the Coal Owners. I am in hopes of giving these men satisfaction today, as their only wish is now that for 100 to 140 of them who have not employment may be found work, and I have summoned the Common Council to attend within an hour for the purpose of proposing that the Corporation employ the men who have not work in dredging the River. I am, &c,

Archibald Reed

316. A meeting of the Common Council held on 19 October 1819 [TWA, MD/NC/2/10, Minutes of the Common Council, 1817–24, p. 135]

The Mayor having communicated to this body that he had called it together to suggest that it might be an encouragement to the keelmen, now absenting themselves from their service, to return to their duties if employment could be furnished by this Corporation to such of the keelmen as cannot get employment as keelmen, and it appearing to this body that a considerable quantity of ballast and soil has accumulated at or near several of the ballast and other quays and at the staiths and spouts and other places in the River, and this body being of opinion that such of the keelmen as are in want of work might be usefully employed in cleansing the several places, it is ordered that a committee be, and the same is hereby appointed, viz. Mr Alderman Smith and Mr Alderman Cookson, Mr John Anderson, Mr David Cram and Mr Thomas Smith of Saville Row, to direct such employment to be given, and that such committee to be desired to call upon the coal owners, and others whose acts have contributed to the accumulation of such ballast and soil, to assist in the measures proposed and to contribute to the expense, and that any three of the said committee be a quorum, and that the Water Bailiff and Harbour Masters be directed to attend such committee when required, and it is further ordered that the said committee be and they are hereby empowered to apply the revenues of this Corporation in paying such keelmen their wages.

317. Terms offered by the Coal Owners to the Keelmen, 20 October 1819[1] [TWA 394/42]

1. That an application shall be made to Parliament at the next sessions to empower the Guardians of the Keelmen's Fund to collect from the owners of Collieries upon the River Tyne a

farthing per chaldron upon all coals shipped in the Port after this day and to apply the same in aid of that Fund, and that the £300 already subscribed by the Coal Owners shall be paid into the Bank for the like purpose within a week after [the keelmen's] return to work.[2]

2. That the over-measure, which has been carried in the keels beyond the eight chaldrons in each keel, shall be accounted for to the keelmen at their respective Fitters' offices, as far back as the first of January last, and be paid within a fortnight from the date of this instrument. A small proportion of the above will be paid on application at the Fitting Office.

3. That the bonds of each Fitter's office in future be printed and that a duplicate of the bond be given to each keelman on his binding; but it is understood that local situations may possibly make a difference in the covenants.

4. That the Makings-in shall be two shillings and sixpence per keel, and always paid in money, and the keelmen [shall] not be compelled to drink at the staiths.

5. That one shilling per keel for casting be paid by the Master of ship when the port is above five feet from the gunwale, and one shilling per foot more for every foot exceeding six feet; and in case of any dispute the Harbour Master to decide.

6. That if any complaint arise amongst the keelmen in future, two keelmen shall immediately be deputed to apply to a Magistrate, who is requested to receive their complaint and transmit the same in writing to Mr Buddle, or the acting secretary of the Coal Owners, and that the names of the two persons shall not be mentioned.

7. That the keels in future are only to carry eight chaldrons. Off-putters at the respective staiths shall be immediately sworn to that effect.

8. That one pound be paid to each man at the binding in aid of house rent.

It is understood that the Corporation of Newcastle by a vote of Common Council this day will employ all the keelmen out of employment in cleansing the New Quay of the gravel and other sand and mud at so much a ton, and a committee is appointed to treat with the keelmen.

None of the keelmen will be discharged from any of the Works for any thing that has passed, and they shall all be bound again.

Signed this 20th day of October 1819,

Thomas Clennell, Joshua Donkin

Mr Clennell begs to add that he this day advocated their cause about the spouts in the Common Council, and was satisfied that a petition from the keelmen to that body will meet with every attention.

[1] These terms were brokered by Thomas Clennell, 'one of the most active magistrates in this County [Northumberland], to whose decision the keelmen had referred the arrangement of their grievances. After much difficulty his efforts have been attended with success, almost to the entire satisfaction of the keelmen' (Duke of Northumberland to Sidmouth, TNA, HO 42/197).

[2] The *Newcastle Chronicle*, 23 October 1819, estimated that this would raise the hospital funds from £1,800 to about £2,700 per year. The above terms were also printed in this newspaper, 30 October 1819.

318. Archibald Reed to Lord Sidmouth, 20 October 1819 [TNA, HO 42/197/669–70]

My Lord,

The keelmen have not returned to work; they are now holding a meeting in a body about a mile from this Town, and a deputation is to meet me this morning, but I much fear the result.[1] The coal owners have acted most liberally, and the Corporation of this Town offered to employ every keelman who has not work.

I received a letter from Sir John Byng urging the return of the 40th to Sunderland barracks. I have only to assure your Lordship that a diminution of force at this place will probably be attended with the most fatal results, and I most earnestly entreat your Lordship's attention to the inadequate force which we have, both military and marine.

We have the most formidable set of men to contend with, consisting of sailors, lightermen, pitmen, and, I am truly sorry to add, of Radical Reformers. I stated to your Lordship the immense value of the shipping now lying in the River, the inadequacy of the naval force and military to protect Shields, Newcastle and populous surrounding country…

I am, my Lord, &c,
Archibald Reed

[1] The men, however, agreed to return to work and would have done so the next day but 'they had not money to furnish their baskets'. Their employers agreed to advance some money on account, and most of the keelmen resumed work on 22 October; but the owners of two collieries refused to accept the terms to which the others had agreed, and Reed feared that the whole body would strike again the next day, an event he could not contemplate 'without the utmost dread of the consequences' (to Sidmouth, 21 and 22 October, TNA, HO 42/197).

319. Lord Darlington to Sidmouth, 21 October 1819 [TNA, HO 42/197/577–8]

My Lord,

...The keelmen then [at the time of the Reform Meeting on 11 October], in a state of insubordination, proceeded to do some unjustifiable acts and appeared so riotously inclined that the Magistrates in the northern district of this County as well as the Mayor of Newcastle applied to me by express for the assistance of the Yeomanry Cavalry, with which request I thought it right to comply, and immediately ordered the South Tyne Yeomanry to assemble and place themselves under the orders of the Magistrates on whom all responsibility must rest. I also ordered the whole yeomanry force of the County to be in readiness if I issued the order, not yet found to be necessary. I understand that no compromise has been reached with the keelmen yet. Some of the collieries are guarded by constables and the military lest the coal trade should be stopped. This state of things cannot remain long, but I am satisfied that *compulsion* is not the way to ameliorate the state of the country. The Magistrates have applied for an addition of military force near Newcastle which I believe is desirable. The South Tyne Yeomanry are yet on duty.

I am your Lordship's obedient Servant,

Darlington

320. Archibald Reed to Lord Sidmouth, 23 October 1819 [TNA, HO 42/197]

My Lord,

As it was of the utmost importance to the country to keep the keelmen at work, I agreed to advance the men 20 shillings each, upon condition that if the owners of Bewicke and Craisters did not repay me, the [rest of the] coal owners would do so. I named to your Lordship that the owners of the above colliery refused to complete the conditions which the others had agreed to, and I am to meet them this morning and hope to convince them of the policy, if not the absolute necessity, of their complying. The advance made had the effect of setting all the keelmen upon the river to work.[1]

I am, my Lord, &c,

Archibald Reed

---

[1] William Richardson reported that the keelmen had resumed working on 22 October 'and so wishful are the well disposed people to keep the *mania* from the sailors, that many loaded vessels sailed this morning though a high and perilous sea raged on Tynemouth bar' (to Sidmouth, 23 October 1819, TNA, HO 42/197/69).

321. Minutes taken at a meeting of the Mayor, Mr Clayton, Mr Askew and Mr Collinson, 23 October 1819 [TWA 394/42]

The summons [to the great reform meeting on 11 October] was to the inhabitants of Newcastle and its vicinities. The Mayor stated that the pitmen were enrolled and trained. That [another] meeting of the Radicals [is] intended on or about the 1st of November. That about 700 of those who met before were probably armed. That arms continue to be manufactured somewhere for the use of the disaffected. Suggested that a general rising is in contemplation and that it will take place at once.

A house to be provided for the accommodation of the Infantry to guard against the troops being contaminated. No necessity for removing the troops before 1st November as it would probably be desirable to bring them here then if they were removed before.

Mr Thorp stated that a search had been made at Winlaton but no pikes found, though a model of one was. Colonel Shelton suggested that the pikes might be easily concealed and put out of the reach of a search, and cited instances of such concealment having been practiced in Ireland previous to the Rebellion there.

The sailing of ships loaded at Shields to be communicated immediately as it takes place to Colonel French. The Bywell troop wish to go home. The gunpowder had better be removed to the Fort at Tynemouth and might be sent down by water. See Harbour Master thereon. Letter to the Commanding Officer of Artillery in the Fort. On further consideration it is thought better to place the gunpowder at the Barracks. There are no artillery waggons [at Newcastle?]. Query if any at Tynemouth Fort.

Colonel French has in some degree been thought to have acted hastily in suffering his men to have been split into small divisions in order to protect the staiths. It is deemed right to take proper opportunity to express public thanks to Colonel French and Colonel Shelton.

322. Petition of the Keelmen, 23 October 1819 [TWA, 597/79]

The Right Worshipful the Mayor, the Aldermen and the Common Council in Common Council Assembled,

The Humble Petition of the Keelmen on the River Tyne Sheweth

That there are only three ways in which the keels can be navigated on the River Tyne, the first is by setting,[1] the second by rowing, and the third by sailing. Your petitioners consider the River as the King's Highway, and consequently any impediment or obstruction to the craft employed on the River they conceive to be an infringement of their privileges, and therefore contrary to Law; and as it is well known to your honourable body that there are several staiths, gears or spouts placed in, or projecting into the River on both sides, from the high end of Shields to a little higher up the River than Dents Hole, which spouts prevent your petitioners of availing themselves of the means of *setting*, in taking the keels past the said spouts. There is also great danger when the keels are navigated by *rowing* or *sailing* by reason of the keels getting foul of the ships laying at the spouts, especially when it is dark and the tide low, and owing to this, one man did lose his life and others have been in great danger.

Your petitioners pray that such staiths, gears or spouts may be removed, that they may not obstruct the navigation of the keels in the said River Tyne, and put your petitioners in danger of their lives or getting hurt or lame, and the keels sunk or damaged.[2]

And your petitioners as in duty bound will ever pray.

[1] In shallow water it was usual to propel the keel by 'setting', whereby each man in the keel manipulated a 'puoy', a long slender pole shod with an iron fork. To 'set' the keel, the crew stood at the bow and faced the stern, each man quickly thrusting his puoy forward and downward to the river bed and then leaning with his whole weight against its upper part as he moved forward, thus driving the keel along. The crew then returned to the bow and repeated the process, 'all done with the smartness of a drill exercise, the movements timed and in unison' (R. Oliver Heslop, 'Keels and Keelmen', NEIMME, ZD/71).

[2] At a meeting of the Common Council, 23 December 1819, it was ordered that consideration of the above petition be referred to the River Jury and to a Committee of the Common Council and to report their respective opinions as to the effects which 'the projecting point, called Whitehill Point, and the staith, geers and spouts there have upon the navigation of the said River' (Minutes of the Common Council, 1817–24, TWA, MDNC/2/10).

323. The petition is rejected by the River Jury and Common Council, 24 August, 14 September 1820 [TWA 597/79 *Verso*]

We the undersigned of the River Jury, having this day considered the prayer of this petition, are of opinion that the same is unreasonable and therefore ought to be rejected. With respect to the matter referred to us by the Common Council as to the effects which the projection point called Whitehill Point and the staith there have upon the navigation of the River, we are of opinion that the quay built at the said point and the geers erected there have not materially injured the navigation of the said River. All which, &c

Signed: Robert Cram, foreman, George Fothergill, James Archbold, Robert Rayne, Cuthbert Liddell, William Wright, William Whitaker

Spence, Lancelot Atkinson, Robert Hall, R. Farrington, Alexander Dale, John Carr, Ralph Naters, Brough Pace[?].

Attached 14 September 1820

We the undersigned Committee of the Common Council, having this day considered the prayer of this petition and the foregoing report of the River Jury thereon, do entirely concur with the River Jury in opinion as expressed in their report.[1] All which &c.

Signed: Robert Clayton, Thomas Smith, H. Cramlington, Nicholas Naters, Sheriff, James Bulman, James Archbold.

[1] The keelmen complained that the River Jury was composed principally of trades people and persons unacquainted with navigation (Correspondent in the *Durham Chronicle*, 2 November 1822).

324. Colonel French to the Mayor of Newcastle, 24 October 1819
[TWA 394/42]

My Dear Sir,

Since I had the pleasure of seeing you this morning I considered with every possible attention our conversation, and beg leave to submit to you my ideas on the matter, viz:

It appears that the disputes of the keelmen are now fortunately on the point of being settled, and as this was the cause, in a certain degree, of the drawing in troops here, and subsequently dispersing them, perhaps you might approve of the following arrangement, if the situation of the Counties of Northumberland and Durham would with reference [?] to the dissaffected, admit of its being acted upon.

I now beg leave to submit as follows, viz:

1st That the Companys of the 40th Regiment stationed here might return to Sunderland from which place, in the event of riots at this place, they might very soon be brought in.

2nd That the Troop of the 6th Dragoons might be called from Shields, leaving a detachment of (say) six to keep up a communication between that place and here.

3rd That the Corps of Yeomanry might return, under, however, a previous arrangement for their being held in readiness to return here at the shortest notice.

4th That the small parties of the 6th Dragoons stationed along the River might be called in.

By this arrangement there would be the following distribution, viz: 4 troops of the 6th Dragoons at Newcastle, which would give a force of about 120 mounted Dragoons at the shortest notice. One Company at Shields and one at Tynemouth.

In submitting this arrangement for your consideration and that of the Magistrates of Northumberland and Durham, I beg leave to be understood that I can not be so well acquainted with the general state of the country as what you and they are, but I am quite certain of being able with my Regiment to protect this place against any attack which may be made upon it. I am likewise equally certain that Shields and Tynemouth would be equally safe with the force I propose to leave at these places.

I have the honor to be, Dear Sir, yours most sincerely,

G. French

325. *Tyne Mercury*, 26 October 1819

The inquest on the body of Joseph Claxton, after a patient and laborious investigation of 5 days, returned a verdict of justifiable homicide. This unhappy affair, though in its origin apparently unconnected with politics, created a strong sensation in the minds of the populace at Shields; before and during the investigation threats were made to intimidate the jury and influence them to bring in a verdict of wilful murder. It was necessary to protect the coroner, the jury, and the witnesses by a military guard, and on the evening of Wednesday, after the verdict had been recorded, bullets were fired through the windows of the foreman of the jury, and the windows of other of the jurors were broken, but happily without injury to any of their families. The inhabitants of the parish met yesterday (Thursday), and offered a reward of 300 guineas for a discovery of the offenders.

326. Archibald Reed to Nathaniel Clayton, 26 October 1819 [TWA 394/42]

My dear Sir,

I will be obliged by your forwarding a case by first post to the Attorney General, as it is of great importance that I should determine upon the line of conduct which I shall pursue in case of another Radical meeting. I am informed that the intended meeting upon the 1st of November is postponed.

I am, my Dear Sir, yours most sincerely,

Archibald Reed

327. Draft Case as to the Power of the Magistrates in cases of Numerous Meetings [TWA 394/42]

The Magistrates of Newcastle, surrounded by a very dense population, and having reason to believe that much pains have been taken by the ill-disposed to excite discontent in the minds of His Majesty's subjects and to urge them to tumult and disorder, are very anxious to be possessed of the Attorney General's opinion as to the powers they possess to interpose their authority in guarding against the dreadful mischiefs which may ensue from an uncontrolled mob.

A short time ago, a meeting was held at Newcastle of those persons who are designated Radical Reformers. A week or ten days before the meeting, a requisition was delivered to the Mayor by four or five unknown to him who stated it to come from the persons resident in Newcastle whose signatures were subscribed to it. They were between 2 or 300 in number, and, with the exception of about ten or twelve, not known to the Mayor, and generally so obscure as to make it impossible to find out who they were. Several of the names subscribed were also evidently written by the same hand.

The requisition requested the Mayor to call a meeting of the inhabitants to consider of the recent transactions at Manchester. The Mayor civilly refused the request, but added that he did not mean to repress, by the exercise of the authority he possessed, any peaceable meeting of the King's subjects held for constitutional purposes. With this answer the bearers of the requisition seemed gratified, and, a day or two after, there issued from an obscure press in the Town a printed handbill calling a meeting of the inhabitants of *Newcastle and its vicinities* for the purpose expressed in the Requisition, and, a day or two before the meeting, the Mayor received a letter from a printer in the Town apprising him that he was desired to act as chairman of the meeting, and that it would be necessary, in discussing the avowed subjects of the meeting, to treat on the business of reform. To this letter, of course, no answer was given, and the meeting was held.

About an hour before the time appointed for the meeting, two numerous trains of persons approached the Town from different directions, in number about 8,000, and made their way through to a large open ground adjoining it called the Moor, where a waggon was drawn and formed into a sort of hustings. Here upwards of 30,000 people were collected and …inflamatory and violent resolutions were made and come to. The persons who came into the Town did not belong to it but to other places. They marched in columns with banners with inscriptions on them, with drums, pipes and music, and did not appear to be armed or to carry any offensive weapons, and in the most regular order. After the meeting, those who had come into the Town in columns marched through it on their return in the same order, and the whole meeting dispersed without tumult or disorder.

It is now said that these persons proposed to have another meeting at an early period and, however peaceable the former one has passed over, the Magistrates cannot but be apprehensive that any such assemblage of persons must at last endanger the public peace, and that slight unforeseen circumstances may produce very mischievous consequences. They therefore beg the opinion of the Attorney General on the following questions, being perfectly aware, however, that whatever legal powers they may possess, the exercise of them must depend on circumstances and on the urgency of the occasion which may call for them.

First, whether great bodies of persons proceeding in array and in columns attended with banners, drums, pipes and music to a general place of meeting, called for purposes avowed and not illegal, but in such number as to occasion considerable alarm and dismay on the minds of the peaceable and well disposed, and to overawe the civil power, may be prevented by the civil power, aided if necessary by a military force, from making their way to the place of meeting, and

Second, whether such persons being congregated at the place appointed, the Magistrates can legally interpose and disperse the meeting by the powers of the Riot Act or otherwise, though no outrage or actual tumult may have taken place.

328. R.W. Brandling [a Northumberland Magistrate] to Nathaniel Clayton, 25 October 1819 [TWA 394/42]

My Dear Sir,

The question appears to me to be whether or not a body of people summoned to meet with drums beating and marching under banners in regular array, though their professed object was legal, can be prohibited by the Magistrates from proceeding in that manner, and whether, if they actually so meet, they can be dispersed under the Riot Act, or not. And to both I answer that I think they may.

I take it to be the Common Law of the land that no persons are justified upon any pretence in assembling in such a *manner* as shews a *manifest intent* to strike terror into the people, and to obtain their object by dint of their numbers.

In Lord George Gordon's case, Mr Erskine very properly contended that there must be a criminal *intent* (the traitorous *purpose* being in fact the treasons) accompanied by an overt act proving that *intent*, but he did not deny that an unarmed multitude may be guilty of acts shewing such intent, so as to bring them within the highly penal statute upon which this prosecution was founded. In the same trial Lord Mansfield observes 'Though the form of an indictment for this species of treason mentions drums, trumpets, arms, swords, fifes and guns, yet none of these circumstances are essential – the question always is whether the intent is by force and violence to attain an object of a public nature, or by dint of their numbers'. If therefore the manner of proceeding (notwithstanding the declaration of the parties) may be taken as an overt [act?] to explain the *intent* so as to bring it within this statute, surely the Magistrates are justified in looking at similar arrangements as a proof of the *intent* of an assemblage of persons to strike terror into the people, and to attain their object by such means and by dint of numbers, so as to justify them in prohibiting such an assembly as illegal, or in dispersing it if assembled under such circumstances.

I conceive it to be highly important in the present day, that it should be clearly understood what power is vested in the Magistrates for the protection of the innocent and well disposed and for the coercion and punishment of the disturbers of the public peace. When it is proper to exercise them must depend upon circumstances; in the present case, I think the prudence of so doing may well be doubted. The extravagant pretensions of the radical reformers, raised and kept alive by abandoned profligates and men of desperate fortunes, must I think work their own destruction; all that I conceive necessary for the well disposed is to be *actively* upon their guard. Unfortunately in the present day it is necessary that both truth and justice should be so armed, but they must not hope to effect any permanent conquest over erroneous opinions, except by the force of Reason.

I remain, Dear Sir, very sincerely yours,
Robert William Brandling

329. Duke of Northumberland to 2nd Earl Grey, 30 October 1819

[Grey Papers, Durham University Library, GRE/B42/11/1]

Alnwick Castle, 30 October 1819

My Lord,

I regret that your health is not yet re-established, but I trust that my servant will bring back an account of your convalescence.

I am sure your Lordship will be pleased to learn that our meeting went off yesterday with that entire unanimity which is so essential at the present moment, and which it will always be my object to preserve in this County.

We came to a general resolution declaratory of our determination to support the civil power in defence of our property and persons. With a view to render that support as purely constitutional as possible, it was proposed that a very large number of special constables should be sworn in. Where the nature of the population required it, armed associations were recommended to be enrolled to act under the Magistrates of the districts, which might supersede the necessity of raising any force of more military character – a measure to which, with my view of the Constitution, I should unwillingly resort, unless the agitation and danger of the country should increase rather than diminish.

I have the pleasure to be, my Lord, your obedient Servant,

Northumberland

329a. Copy Grey's reply to Northumberland, 31 October 1819
[Grey Papers, Durham University Library, GRE/B42/11/2]

Howick, 31 October 1819

My Lord,

A very bad night had left me at the moment of the arrival of your Grace's servant utterly unable to attend to, or to answer your very obliging letter.

I now hasten to beg that your Grace will, in the first place, accept my thanks for your kind enquiry after my health, of which I cannot give a very good account. I hope, however, that what I now suffer may rather be ascribed to extreme weakness than to any remaining disease.

I must next offer you my best acknowledgement for the manner in which you have communicated to me the result of the meeting held at Alnwick Castle on Friday last. I have read with sincerest pleasure the expressions of your Grace's disinclination to the extension of the military force of the country and the constitutional views which you entertain on the subject. But I am sorry to add that the resolutions taken at the meeting, however unobjectionable they may appear to be, could not in their present form have had my concurrence, at least without some very important additions. At the same time that we repress the violence of the people, we have a corresponding duty to perform in evincing an equal disposition to redress their grievances, under circumstances of great distress, and to protect them against any undue exertion of power. The circumstances of the time seem to me to call with as powerful a claim for the performance of the last as of the first of these duties, and the resolutions of the meeting of Friday last, taken, as far as I am informed, under circumstances of no immediate urgency, and unaccompanied with any proceeding on the part of the leading proprietors of the County to manifest their feeling for the rights and interest of their fellow subjects, appears to me to proceed on a partial view of our situation, and to have a direct tendency to countenance a system of policy, which has, I am persuaded, principally contributed to produce our present danger, and must, if persevered in, I fear at no distant period involve us in consequences which I dare not contemplate.

I cannot pursue this subject further at present, and for any indistinctness which may appear on this letter I must plead the state in which it is written. I regret sincerely any difference that may appear to exist between your Grace and me on this as on every other occasion; possibly had there been the means of a freer personal communication it would have been less; at all events, I beg your Grace to be assured that the desire which you express to preserve the unanimity in the County will always find in me a corresponding disposition as far as honor, conscience and duty will admit.

I have the honor to be &c

[Grey]

330. Archibald Reed to Lord Sidmouth, 4 November 1819 [TNA, HO 42/198]

My Lord,

I most deeply lament to inform your Lordship that Messrs Lamb, &c, owners of the Bewicke and Craisters, Wallsend, having refused to comply with the conditions agreed upon between the coalowners and keelmen, the others have this day refused to work, and the whole body of keelmen will be off work tomorrow.[1]

I am, my Lord, &c, Archibald Reed

[1] Some of the other coal owners had tried to evade the terms of the agreement. Reed reported on 6 November that all the keelmen were off work, that a deputation was to meet him, and that the coal owners also were to meet. The next day he reported that a large majority of the coal owners had settled with the keelmen. By 8 November all but those employed by six collieries had returned to work. The next day the men of only one colliery remained off work and Reed intended to meet the men, the colliery agent, and Thomas Clennell, and was confident of settling their differences (TNA, HO 42/198).

331. James Losh to 2nd Earl Grey, 11 November 1819 [University of Durham Library, Grey Papers, GRE B40/7/6]

Jesmond, 11 November 1819

My dear Lord Grey,

As I am called from home and shall be about for some days…. I have, however, set on foot enquiries both as to [the Radicals] and as to the keelmen; and I trust I shall be very soon able to collect information on which you may depend. What you have heard, however, with respect to the keelmen is sufficiently correct as to the outline. Their first demands were certainly just, and had been long refused or evaded, but when they made their stick they got heated, felt their strength, and demanded more.

The arrangement made by the Magistrates was I think upon the whole fair, and had the keelmen well content. But it is quite true that some of the coal owners attempted to evade the new regulations, and this immediately produced great irritation. All however is quiet again, and Mr Clennell told me yesterday that he thought it would continue so.[1]

I was truly sorry to hear of your indisposition when I was at Alnwick last week, and sincerely hope that your long journey may do you no harm.

Believe me, my dear Lord Grey, always very faithfully yours,

James Losh

[1] Losh, a barrister who had interests in coal mines and was often consulted in industrial disputes, had had 'a good deal of conversation with Clennell as to the keelmen' and was satisfied that 'their masters were more to blame than the poor men themselves' (Edward Hughes, ed., *The Diaries and Correspondence of James Losh, 1811-23* (Surtees Society CLXXII, 1962), p. 103.

332. Losh to Grey, 19 November 1819 [University of Durham Library, Grey Papers, GRE B40/7/7]

My dear Lord Grey,

Enclosed with this I send you a statement with respect to the keelmen upon the accuracy of which I can rely, it having been given to me by one of the best informed Fitters in Newcastle.[1] I can also myself confirm this statement, as far as it relates to the demands of the keelmen, a deputation of five from their committee having been sent to take my opinion, or rather advice. In my conversation with them I succeeded in shewing them the folly of their attempting to interfere with the spouts and other machinery, and in preparing them to accede to the first fair and moderate proposals made to them by the coalowners. The 2nd dispute originated entirely, as Mr Clennell told me, in an attempt made by some coalowners to evade the terms to which they had agreed.

By tomorrow's post I hope to send you some account of the Radicals of this district which has been promised to me by a sensible clergyman of the Established Church, who has better means of obtaining information than any person I know. From what I have yet learned, their numbers are not so great as has been supposed and are lessening. Their organisation is constructed upon the plan of the Methodists, to whom however they are hostile, and indeed stand in the most deadly opposition.

I was much pleased to see Mr Lambton's letter in today's Newcastle paper. I think it will do much good, but it certainly appears to me wrong to confound all the Radicals with their leaders.

Believe me always with great respect, sincerely yours,

James Losh

[1] This has not been found.

333. Archibald Reed to Sidmouth, 6 April 1820 [TNA, HO 40/12/72]

My Lord,

I am extremely sorry to inform your Lordship that I am much afraid of the renewal of the [disputes?] of last October with the keelmen. They dare not send a deputation to me, as several of the keelmen who acted as deputies were discharged by their employers notwithstanding the indemnity which was promised. They sent a confidential person to communicate with me, and I immediately wrote Mr Buddle [secretary to the coal trade] and enclose a copy of my letter.

The offputters were sworn not to put more than 8 chaldrons of coals into each keel. The keelmen dare not complain as they would lose their employ, and will rise in a body unless relieved.

I am my Lord, &c

333a. Enclosure, Copy Reed to John Buddle, 5 April 1820 [TNA, HO 40/12/74]

Sir,

I am extremely sorry to inform you that great discontent prevails among the keelmen in consequence of the overmeasure which they are now carrying, and which, notwithstanding the oath administered to the offputters, is as great now as it was previous to the month of last October. They have other complaints, but it appears to me that a rupture may be prevented if their employers either lessen the measure, or pay for the overmeasure which they carry. You will oblige me by laying this statement before the coal owners.

THE 'LONG STOP', 1 OCTOBER–6 DECEMBER 1822

334. Nathaniel Clayton (colliery owner) to Michael Green, Staithman at Dunston, 2 October 1822 [TWA 394/45]

Dear Sir,

I learn from Mr Reynoldson's letter of yesterday that nine keels loaded and ready to sail were yesterday stopped by a great number of men who, he says, came down from the staiths above, and I find that none [of the keels] have come down this morning. I must therefore beg you will immediately inform yourself by enquiry of our skippers what has caused this, and what persons interrupt them in the discharge of their duty. If there be any cause of complaint I presume you will learn what it is, and be able to inform me. If it arises in our work and is well founded, I shall readily inquire into and redress it. If it arises elsewhere, I trust our men will not obstruct Mr Pitt's work for matters with which he has nothing to do.

I shall expect you at half past 10 tomorrow morning with two or three of the skippers that I may better judge what is proper to be done.

I am, Dear Sir, yours truly,

N. Clayton

335. Petition of the Keelmen on the River Tyne to the Gentlemen Coal Owners and Fitters, 3 October 1822 [TWA 394/46 (copy in 394/45)]

Humbly sheweth that your petitioners feel greatly hurt that so many of the keelmen are at present out of employment, by which they and their families have not the necessaries of life, and your petitioners have no prospect of being better, but the contrary. They therefore humbly pray that the gentlemen would please to grant the favour that no more than six keels of coals be put into any ship or vessel by the spout, until the employment get better for the keelmen.

Also your petitioners pray that the allowances and binding money be given to the keelmen as before the agreement of 20 October 1819, besides the one pound granted in the said agreement in aid of house rent.

And likewise your petitioners pray that they may receive Earnest Money (as usual prior to the above agreement), at least 3 months previous to the binding in each year, and that they may be bound in every other respect upon the same terms as this year.

And our petitioners shall, as in duty bound, for ever pray.

[*Endorsed*: copy of the petition…presented to the Mayor, 3 October 1822.]

336. Minutes of a Meeting of the Magistrates in the Mayor's Chamber, attended by a Deputation from the Coal Owners and the Keelmen's Stewards, 4 October 1822 [TWA 394/46]

Present: The Mayor, Mr Alderman Clayton, Mr Alderman Smith, Mr Alderman Cookson; ten Stewards; and Mr Dunn, Mr Potts, Mr Buddle, Mr Thompson, Mr Armstrong – the Committee of the Coal Owners and Fitters

The Mayor stated the Keelmen's breach of their Agreement of 20 October 1819 in stopping the Trade before they presented their petition to the Magistrates.

300 keels were formerly employed, 280 now.

The Stewards stated they had done their [best] endeavour to prevent the men stopping, but they could not help it. They stated that they had to support themselves from their families and also their home establishment. They stated that there were near 900 keelmen on the River; 280 keels would require 840 men. It follows then that there are only 60 men unemployed, though one of the Stewards asserted that there are 300 men [un]employed.

The Stewards said that a suspicion prevailed of a new arrangement about the keels being meditated by the Coal Owners,[1] and that alone occasioned the stop. They impute the intention to the Pontop Owners. They complain that obstructions to the navigation of the keels arise from the mooring of the ships at the spouts and by ships lying more than two abreast.

[1] Imposition of a rent-charge for use of the keels.

337. Statement of the Number of Keels and Keelmen above Bridge, n.d. [TWA 394/46]

Colliery	Number of Keels	Keelmen
Townley	22	66
Wylam	12	36
Newmarsh	28	84
Benwell	11	33
Elswick	17	51
Eighton	20	60
Tanfield	13	39
South Moor	16	48
Lem[ington]	4	12 unbound

Pontop	16	48
Total	175	525

338. Earnings of the Keelmen of Tanfield Moor (one of the above bridge collieries), exclusive of by-tides, 1 January–5 October 1822
[TWA 394/42]

Date	Number of Tides	Keelmen's Pay
19 January	38	£44 13s. 0d.
26 January	26	£30 11s. 0d.
2 February	63	£72 19s. 6d.
9 February	58	£67 11s. 8d.
16 February	51	£59 18s. 6d.
23 February	59	£68 5s. 6d.
2 March	59	£68 5s. 6d.
9 March	42	£47 12s. 0d.
16 March	13	£14 11s. 6d.
23 March	53	£58 4s. 2d.
30 March	32	£34 16s. 0d.
6 April	1	£1 3s. 6d.
20 April	25	£27 5s. 2d.
27 April	12	£14 2s. 0d.
4 May	4	£4 14s. 0d.
18 May	29	£31 13s. 10d.
25 May	53	£61 11s. 6d.
1 June	30	£35 0s. 6d.
8 June	44	£49 19s. 0d.
15 June	16	£18 16s. 0d.
22 June	34	£39 5s. 0d.
29 June	25	£29 7s. 6d.
6 July	44	£46 16s. 0d.
13 July	40	£44 14s. 8d.
20 July	44	£48 3s. 4d.
27 July	36	£35 18s. 4d.
3 August	29	£33 14s. 6d.
10 August	39	£43 0s. 6d.

17 August	42	£45 13s. 8d.
24 August	38	£41 5s. 0d.
31 August	28	£28 9s. 8d.
7 September	43	£46 6s. 6d.
14 September	35	£37 12s. 6d.
21 September	28	£30 9s. 0d.
28 September	34	£37 17s. 0d.
5 October	1	£1 3s. 6d.
Totals 40 weeks[1]	1248	£1401 10s. 6d.

1248 tides @ £1401 10s. 6d. Deduct 1s. per tide to boys = £1339 2s. 6d. for 13 keels employed at Tanfield Moor = £103 0s. 2d. per keel [with 3 men] = £34 6s. 8d. per man for 40 weeks = 17s. 2d. per man per week.

[1] The strike began at the beginning of October, hence the cut-off point at 40 weeks. A report in *The Times* of 15 October 1822, quoting the *Durham Chronicle* of 12 October, stated that in Mr Newmarch's colliery [above bridge] where 100 keelmen were employed more constantly than most on the river, their wages had not averaged more than between 14s. and 15s. per week during the existing year, while many below bridge had not averaged more than 7s. or 8s. a week, 'a sum very inadequate to the support of themselves and families'. A correspondent in the *Tyne Mercury* of 10 December 1822 disputed these figures and claimed that some keelmen earned four or five times as much, and that the yearly average wage of those employed by the Grand Allies was not less than 30s. per week, but Matthias Dunn, author of *A Treatise on the Winning and Working of Collieries* (London and Newcastle, 1852), stated that on account of the spouts, the below bridge keelmen had been earning 'very bad wages' of between 10 and 12s. per week (Diary, 1 October 1822, quoted by R. Oliver Heslop in 'Keels and Keelmen' (NEIMME, NRO 3410/ZD/71).

339. Robert Bell, Mayor, to the Commander of the 66th Regiment of Foot at Sunderland Barracks, 5 October 1822 [TWA 394/46]

Sir,

The keelmen on the River Tyne having assembled in great numbers and proceeded to acts of riot and violence, it has been deemed prudent to have a proper military force at hand to aid the civil power, and I have therefore to beg the favor of you to direct two companies of the Regiment under your command to march forthwith to Newcastle.

I have the honor to be, Sir, your most obedient Servant,

Robert Bell, Mayor

340. Robert Bell to Robert Peel, Home Secretary, 5 October 1822
[TNA, HO 40/17/6, and TWA 394/46]

Sir,

I feel it my duty to inform you that since Monday last the public peace has been disturbed, and the navigation of the river interrupted by a riotous body of keelmen, who navigate the lighters or keels, which convey the coals from the repositories or staiths upon the river to the ships at the mouth of the harbour, and that I have been obliged to call on a part of the military force stationed here and in the neighbourhood, in aid of the civil power.

The prompt measures which have been taken by the Magistrates of this Town and the adjoining Counties to restore order will, I trust, be effectual, and I hope soon to be able to convey the intelligence that the disturbance is at an end.[1]

I have the honor to be, Sir, your most obedient Servant,

Robert Bell, Mayor

---

[1] According to an endorsement on the draft of the above it was also to be sent to the Duke of Northumberland, but the draft of a longer letter to him appears below.

341. Draft, Robert Bell to the Duke of Northumberland, 5 October 1822 [TWA 394/46]

My Lord Duke,

I regret that I have to inform your Grace that the trade of the Port and the navigation of the River have since Monday last been interrupted by a riotous body of keelmen who have forcibly prevented the well disposed part of them from following their employments and discharging this duty to their employers.

They have had the audacity to send a deputation to the different spouts on the river, at which ships are laden with coals, to require them to cease their work, accompanied with a threat of violence if they did not comply. This has led the Magistrates to station small detachments of cavalry at the different spouts for their protection, and to require their assistance to the civil power in resisting the attempt of the ill-disposed to prevent those who are willing to do their duty from navigating their vessels.

I should mention to your Grace that in the year 1819 similar outrages were committed by the keelmen, but as it was at the time thought that some hardships were imposed upon them, a magistrate and a ship owner acted as referees between them and their employers and published a sort of award which ultimately restored order. By this award it was provided that, if any complaint arose among them in future, two keelmen should be immediately deputed to apply to a magistrate who was to receive their complaint and transmit it to the coal owners.

On the present occasion, the keelmen proceeded to acts of violence in the first instance, and after an interval of three days sent me their petition. Notwithstanding this conduct, it was taken into consideration and their allegations fully examined into, and their complaints were found to be frivolous and without foundation.

I have now only to express my hope that the prompt measures that have been taken by the magistrates will soon put an end to the disorder.

I have the honor to be, &c.

342. Duke of Northumberland to Robert Bell, 7 October 1822
[TWA 394/46]

Alnwick Castle, 7 October 1822

Sir,

I beg that you will accept my best thanks for the information you have given me with respect to the confusion which exists among the Keelmen on the River Tyne.

It is earnestly to be advised that this meritorious but misguided set of men speedily return to their accustomed industry and good order. I feel the firmest conviction, Sir, that within the limit of your jurisdiction you will take every step towards conciliation which may be compatible with magisterial firmness and with the just interests of individuals.

You will I trust, Sir, as long as possible confide in the ordinary operation of the civil power and dispense with military interference till the last extremity.

I am, Sir, your obedient Servant,

Northumberland

343. Handbill [NEIMME, The Bell Collection, Vol. 13, 605]

The Mayor's Chamber, 7 October 1822

Whereas several Informations have been made before the Magistrates of Newcastle upon Tyne, Northumberland and County Durham, that divers bound Keelmen on the River Tyne have deserted the service of their employers and left their respective dwellings, and are now wandering abroad and committing acts of vagrancy; Notice is hereby given to all watchmen, constables and other peace officers that it is their bounden duty to apprehend the persons so offending and bring them before the nearest Magistrate in order that they may be dealt with and punished according to law; and as an encouragement to such officers, they are hereby informed that they will be rewarded as is prescribed by law.

344. *Tyne Mercury*, 8 October 1822

The Keelmen of the Tyne

We regret to state that the keelmen employed on the river Tyne have within the last few days refused to work as usual until certain alleged grievances are removed. We regret it for their own sakes, for the sake of all the parties concerned, and for the injury our trade must inevitably sustain....

Apprehensions, it seems, have been entertained that the keelmen would endeavour to destroy the staiths by which coals are conveyed into the vessels, and in consequence small parties of the military have been stationed at the different parts of the river where such attempts were likely to be made. We are happy to state, however, that these precautions appear hitherto to have been unnecessary. We think it proper to mention that several keelmen are averse from these dissensions and would willingly have gone to work as usual but for the intimidation to which they have been subjected by others. In conclusion we may add that the keelmen, up to this moment, appear to have conducted themselves peaceably, and we have heard of no instance of an act of violence having been committed except what is related in the following letter.

North Shields, 7 October

On Friday a number of keelmen visited this place, apparently with no object but mischief and plunder, each having a stick with a flat end, which they freely bestowed on the shoulders of those who passed them. They repaired on board several vessels where ballast was casting and made the men desist from their labour. Amongst other ships, they boarded 'the George', and wounded a trimmer named Rochester on the face with a stone, and aimed a deadly blow at another with a ballast shovel, who had a very narrow escape. On shore, plunder was the watchword: they met a baker's cart carrying bread to the country, which they took possession of, and threatened the boy for complaining. As to apples, turnips &c on the stalls, they made not the least hesitation in seizing them as they passed.[1]

---

[1] A similar report in the *Durham County Advertiser*, 12 October, adds that they ploughed up potatoes and turnips and carried off large quantities from the fields.

345. Handbill: Resolutions at a meeting of the Coal Trade at Newcastle, 8 October 1822 [TWA 394/45]

At a general meeting of the Coal Owners and Fitters held here this day, Richard Bell, Esq in the chair, the Coal Owners and Fitters on the River Tyne finding it impracticable to carry on the trade of the Port whilst the conveyance of their coals to the ships is under the control of a body of men who, in violation of their engagements and the laws of their country, have deserted their own duty, and riotously obstructed the performance of it by others, it is unanimously resolved that a committee be appointed to take into their serious considera-tion the best means of rescuing the trade from these difficulties and guarding against a recurrence of them in future.

Resolved also that it is the unanimous opinion of this meeting that the frequent interruptions which have thus been produced in the coal trade of this Port, must, if their recurrence be not prevented, end in the destruction of the trade of the Tyne, and in forcing the consumers of coals to resort to inland and other places for their supply; and that such a result will be fatal to the prosperity of this part of the Kingdom and destructive of its best interests. And that, under this conviction it is the duty of this meeting, promptly to adopt firm but temperate measures to aid the Civil Power in preserving peace and restoring order.

It appearing to this meeting that several Coal Owners and Fitters had made informations before the Magistrates against their respective keelmen and had obtained warrants for their apprehension, resolved that the other Coal Owners and Fitters whose keelmen have deserted their service be requested to take the same steps in order that all the offenders, who do not immediately return to their work, may be brought to a proper sense of their duty, and of the illegality of their proceedings.

Resolved that each Coal Owner and Fitter do forthwith apply to the Magistrates to appoint and swear in as Special Constables such persons at their respective collieries and staiths as they think proper to recommend, and that lists of them be sent to the Magistrates with as little delay as possible.

Resolved that each Coal Owner and Fitter be requested forthwith to transmit to the Secretary a list of their respective bound keelmen, specifying their places of abode and whether married or singlemen; and Resolved that as the bound keelmen have generally deserted their dwellings and their service, it is highly expedient that public notice be given that prosecutions will be instituted against those who shall harbour or employ them during the continuance of their present engagement, and exhorting all persons to assist the Civil Power in apprehending and bringing them to justice.

Resolved that a copy of these resolutions be handed to the Mayor of Newcastle with the request of the meeting that he will have the goodness to communicate them to the other Magistrates of this Town, and to the Magistrates of the Counties of Northumberland and Durham acting with him upon the present occasion.[1]

---

[1] The above resolutions were also published in the *Tyne Mercury*, 15 October 1822.

346. James Atkin to Thomas Forsyth, the Mayor's Sergeant, 8 October 1822 [TWA 394/46]

Swallwell, 8 October 1822

Sir,

I write to inform you that after we came here, Mr Collinson sent for the constable and granted a warrant against one of the keelmen and ordered him, in company with us, to apprehend him, and as many more as could be found near this place. We have kept watch all yesterday, last night, and this morning, and have not seen one keelman that is a bound man. It is reported they are at Whickham, Winlayton Mill, Winlayton Town, Blaydon and other parts of the West.

Yesterday after noon, some of our men got drunk and quarrelled amongst themselfes and the people of the place, and caused great disturbance untill the Horse came and peace was restored by eight O'clock at night. The men who got drunk were sent to Town this morning by a guard.[1] We wait farther orders and hope to hear as soon as possible.

Yours,
James Atkin

---

[1] A separate note states that three soldiers were arrested and that a peace officer 'behaved ill and was drunk'.

347. Rough Draft [Nathaniel Clayton] to Robert Bell, [c. 8] October 1822 [TWA 394/46]

I beg you to pardon me if I cannot after serious consideration bring myself to think that the step General Byng is about to take is right. It seems not to have occurred to him that you were on the spot and that the responsibility of the acts done rested with you and the concurring Magistrates. If a General Officer commanding a District and having his Head Quarters at the distance of 100 miles must be consulted ere the aid of the military can be obtained, that aid may often come too late. With this feeling I have to beg you will have the goodness to allow me the referensal of the dr[aft] of your letter to the General.

348. Robert Bell to Nathaniel Clayton, [c. 8] October 1822 [TWA 394/46]

Dear Sir,

Thinking no time ought to be lost, I sent the letter to the Post, and I regret to say I have not kept a copy. I am quite of your opinion of the absurdity of waiting in case of riot for permission from the General commanding the District, perhaps a hundred miles off, to have his leave to apply for troops, as much mischief might take place before they were, by this tedious method, procured.

I think had we written immediately to the General, his ire might have looked over this omission. If you can get the letter out of the office, I should wish you to make any alterations you might think proper.

I regret I cannot attend at court today. I was seized with a shivering fit yesterday, and today I have some fever which obliges me to keep my bed. If you procure the letter, and write another, I will with pleasure sign it.

Believe me, Sir, very truly yours,
Robert Bell

349. Aubone Surtees to Robert Peel, 9 October 1822 [TWA 394/46]

Sir,

Referring to a late letter to you from Robert Bell, Esq., the Mayor, who, I am sorry to say, is confined by indisposition, I have the honor to acquaint you that the disturbances amongst the keelmen stated in that letter still prevail, though the measures taken have prevented the destruction of private property, which had been threatened by them, and have opened the navigation of the Port, which had been forcibly interrupted.

The promptness with which the Commanding Officer of the 3rd Dragoon Guards, stationed at the Barracks here, and of the 66th Infantry stationed at Sunderland, complyed with the requisition of the Magistrates has mainly contributed to that improved state of things which I describe and for which the Magistrates of the Country are truly grateful. I must here, however, lament that two Companies of the 66th, which had been marched to this Town and Gateshead at the request of the Mayor, have been this day withdrawn and ordered back to Sunderland by the Commander in Chief of the District, without any previous communication with the Mayor or the other Magistrates, and it is to be feared that this measure may be prejudicial to the public service. I owe it, however, to the General of the District to state that amongst the various objects and duties which pressed on the Chief Magistrate's attention, it escaped [him] to inform the Commander of the District of the steps he had thought it prudent to take with respect to the military, and it may be owing to that irregularity that we are deprived of the benefit of the presence of the infantry.

> I have the honor to be, Sir, your most obedient Servant.
> Aubone Surtees, late Mayor

350. Major General Byng to the Mayor, 10 October 1822 [TWA 394/46]

> Pontefract, 10 October 1822

Sir,

I am favored with your letter of the 8th instant, just received, and for which I feel obliged.

With the very small force at present under my command, I am necessitated to restrict Commanding Officers from moving detachments without a previous reference to me, which, to save time, they are permitted to do by express (except in a case where actual riot exists), as it may happen they may be sent from where their presence is actually necessary to another place where there is only a probability of their services being required. I hope you will see with me the necessity for such directions, and do me the justice to believe they are not given from any unwillingness to cooperate most cordially with the Civil Authorities.

> I have the honor to be, Sir, your very obedient humble Servant,
> John Byng, M.G.

351. Handbill: Address of the Keelmen of the River Tyne, 9 October 1822 [NEIMME, The Bell Collection, Vol. 22, ff. 38–40]

'The Poor is hated even of his own Neighbour: but the Rich hath many Friends'. Solomon.

We, the Keelmen of the River Tyne, having been much misrepresented by the unfeeling and uncharitable relative to the differences which have unhappily taken place between us and our employers, and our conduct, object, and views having also been greatly misstated, we beg leave to lay the facts of the case before the public at large, and appeal to their candour and generosity in extenuation of the charges against us.

The peculiar grievances under which we labour are numerous: some of them, perhaps, under present circumstances do not admit of a remedy; but there are others, which would admit of modifications, by which the body of keelmen on the River might be materially benefitted. The Spouts for instance. This has become a great evil to us, and of late has been considerably increased by the use of steam-boats in towing ships from the Spouts, by which means vessels of 16 and 18 keels can now come up and take in their loading at these erections. The Magistrates, we apprehend, have it in their power, as Conservators of the River, to restrict the Spouts, several of which are evidently encroachments on the boundaries of their jurisdiction; and in some instances, from the great extent of the projections, they are clearly nuisances, and, as such, ought to be abated. But in our petition to the Mayor, on this head (presented on Thursday last), we have not presumed thus far; we requested only that the Coal Owners would take into consideration the propriety of limiting the quantity of coals taken in at the Spouts to six keels for each vessel. The reason for which is obvious – a greater number of keelmen would by that means be employed.

Previous to the last stop, in 1819, our Binding Money, two pounds a keel, and one guinea for a binding supper, was paid regularly every year. Since that period these allowances have gradually been diminished, till the last Binding, when they were wholly taken from us.

One principal reason for the present stoppage is the demand which has been made by some of the Coal Fitters on the Tyne of one shilling and sixpence a tide for the use of the craft or keel, as a kind of rent charge, which is neither more nor less than reducing in that proportion every man's wages. This we consider a peculiar hardship, especially to those who have little employment.

It was customary every year to enter into conditions for the next, and to arle the men three months before the expiration of the term of their agreement. This gave us time and opportunity to make engagements more agreeable to our interests. That good old custom being now laid aside, we are compelled either to comply with the terms dictated to us, or be turned adrift without employment.

Though bound to our employers by articles of agreement, we conceive we are with them under mutual obligations, and hope we are not bound to starve. It is well known that many of us, especially the keelmen below Bridge, are very imperfectly employed. Some of us have had only 56, others only 53 tides this year, and others again still fewer. It is easy to conceive the privations and distress which such of us and their families have suffered under these circumstances.

By a vote of Common Council, in 1819, the Corporation of Newcastle engaged to employ all keelmen out of employment in cleansing the New Quay of the gravel, &c. at so much a ton. This continued only about three months, and the keelmen out of employ have not since been employed by that body.

The disbursements from our Fund for the support of our sick and aged brethren and their widows and orphans last year amounted to £2,583. 7s. 9d. This Fund which we have long laboured to support, for purposes to ourselves the most invaluable, is also, we conceive, of general advantage to the Town and neighbourhood in which we live, as it greatly relieves the parishes from burdens which they would otherwise have to sustain. But if our employment be abridged, and our wages and privileges be diminished, poverty and wretchedness must overtake us, and we shall finally be unable to support this noble Institution, which has so long been our hope and our pride.

We ask for nothing unreasonable, and only wish to be dealt with as beings capable of the discourse of reason. All violent measures we deprecate. We wished to meet quietly and peaceably to confer with each other on our own affairs; but by the military arrangements which have been made, with a view to threaten us, the evil time has been protracted, and that amicable adjustment of all our differences, which we so anxiously wish, has been hitherto prevented.

We greatly lament and condemn the irregularities and misconduct of some of our body, and hope the candid and discriminating will exonerate us from any charge of countenancing such conduct; as our object is neither rapine nor riot, but to labour honestly with our hands and 'to do our duty in that state of life unto which it has pleased God to call us'.

The Keelmen of the River Tyne

352. Handbill: Coal Trade, Newcastle, 12 October 1822 [TWA 394/45]

The owners of the undermentioned collieries, proprietors of staiths on the River Tyne, in order to remove the vain hope which some of the keelmen seem to entertain respecting the spouts, think it proper, publicly and solemnly to declare that no consideration whatever shall induce them to abandon the right to the free and lawful enjoyment of their property. They erected their staiths in strict conformity to the regulations established by the law of the land, and to that law only will they consent to be amenable. For the work required of the keelmen they have been paid liberally; their employers have scrupulously performed their part of the contract, and they are aware that under such circumstances they might be excused from entering into any explanation with their workmen till they had as honestly performed theirs; but, in order that those who are made the dupes of the idle and designing may have no pretence for not returning to their duty, they think it proper to state that they never entertained any idea of making any reduction in their wages, though the price of provisions may seem to justify it. And, moreover, that they have no object[ion] to establish a general time of hiring, previous to the expiration of the former contract, as is the case with some other labourers. Beyond this they will not go, and if this offer is not accepted, it is the firm resolution of the proprietors of the undermentioned collieries to petition the legislature to be relieved from the tax, which they voluntarily imposed upon themselves in 1819, for the relief of a body of men, who, by such refusal, will then shew that they are insensible of the benefits conferred upon them, careless of their solemn engagements, willing to exert the most unlawful means of securing to themselves a temporary advantage at the expense of others, and vain and presumptuous enough to imagine that they can with impunity array themselves against the well known laws of the land.

Walls End, Willington, Cox-Lodge, Killingworth, Percy Main, Manor Wall's End, Heworth, Burdon Main, Backworth, Whitley, Hebburn, Jarrow, Penlaw Main, Heaton, Walker, Sheriff Hill, Tyne Main

353. Resolutions of the Magistrates, 12 October 1822 [TWA 394/46]

At a meeting of the Magistrates of the three Counties of Northumberland, Durham and Newcastle [in the Mayor's Chamber], adjourned from the Moot Hall in Northumberland, present: Sir Thomas Burdon, George Anderson, Esq., Thomas H. Bigge, Esq., and Robert W. Brandling (all for Northumberland); Adam Askew, Esq., Revd John Collinson (both for County Durham), and Revd C. Thorpe (for County Durham and Northumberland); Mr Alderman Surtees (for Newcastle). Adam Askew, Esq., in the chair.

A committee of the Coal Trade attended the meeting, consisting of: 1, Mr James Potts; 2. Mr Benjamin Thompson; 3, Mr Cuthbert Liddell; 4, Mr George Thomas Dunn; 5, Mr Joseph Croser; 6, Mr John Buddell; 7, Mr William Armstrong, who produced a set of resolutions entered into by the gentlemen interested in the Coal Trade below

Bridge, and the same were read to the meeting. The petition of the Keelmen to the Coal Owners and coal Fitters was read.

It was represented to the meeting that a military force would be necessary to be continued for the protection of the staiths below Bridge, and the apprehension of the Coal Trade that if the present military force should be withdrawn, that the staiths will be in danger of being destroyed by the Keelmen.

Mr Buddle stated that he highly approved of the arrangements made in October 1819, that the military force then placed at the staiths be considered amply sufficient; there were 24 Dragoons stationed at the staiths on the North side of the River below Bridge, and that on the South side below Bridge about 18 Dragoons were stationed, and he suggested the propriety of having a similar force at present. It was also intimated that a military force above Bridge may be wanted, and that a Reserve will be necessary in case of any riot or tumult in any other part.

Mr Benjamin Thompson stated that a party of 10 men will be necessary at Scotswood. Mr Croser thinks they should have occasion for 6 men at Benwell Staith, and it was suggested that 6 men would be necessary at Lemington. Mr Armstrong suggested the propriety of about 10 men being stationed at Dunston, and that about 10 men should be stationed at Swalwell.

Mr Dunn stated as a reason for having the military stationed above Bridge, that prior to the detachments being stationed above Bridge, the keelmen prevented transportation upon the River, and that after the military were stationed the keelmen were awed and have not since attempted to prevent such craft from proceeding except coal keels navigated by keelmen.

The Magistrates resolve that application be immediately made to Colonel Holmes to be informed if he can supply the requisite number of troops to compose the above parties, and that if Colonel Holmes cannot, then that application be then made to the Lords Lieutenants for Northumberland and Durham to continue the Northumberland and Newcastle Yeomanry Cavalry on duty, and the Ravensworth Yeomanry Cavalry on duty also; and they direct also an enquiry of Colonel Holmes whether the two troops which have lately joined from Carlisle can be detained for duty here.[1]

---

[1] According to a separate summary of the above, the term of permanent duty of the three bodies of Yeomanry Cavalry was due to expire on 14 October.

354. George Dawson, Under-Secretary of State at the Home Office, to [Aubone Surtees], 12 October 1822

Whitehall, 12 October 1822

Sir,

In Mr Peel's absence I have opened your letter of the 9th instant. It will be a matter of considerable regret to him to learn from your communication that the hopes held out by Mr Bell's letter have not been realized by the return of the refactory keelmen to their usual employments.

I find upon enquiry at the Horse Guards that from the *very limited Force* which can be appropriated to the Northern District, the Detachment of the 66th Foot could not be allowed to remain at Newcastle without material injury to the public service in other quarters. As, however, there are still *four* Troops of the *3rd Dragoon Guards* stationed at Newcastle, the Magistrates will have at their disposal a *strong military force*, should their services be unfortunately required in assisting the Civil Power to restore tranquillity.

I have the honor to be, Sir, your most obedient humble Servant,

G. Dawson

P.S. In the event of the Magistrates requiring the assistance of Infantry Soldiers, it would be desirable that they *should put themselves in communication with the General Officer commanding the District*

355. *Durham Chronicle*, 12 October 1822

With respect to the spouts, do these deluded men imagine that they have any right to say to their employers, or to any body of men, 'You shall not increase the value of your property; you shall not adopt inventions or introduce improvements by which your interests may be served and the public benefited because *we* may suffer some inconvenience from such means?' Are they so ignorant or misled as to suppose that if this principle were admitted society could exist and flourish?…No concession will or ought to be made to them while they continue refactory.

356. Handbill: Collieries above Bridge, 14 October 1822 [TWA 394/45]

The Owners of colleries and Fitters situated above Bridge having seen a resolution put forth by the proprietors of spouts below Bridge, think it proper also publicly and decidedly to declare their feelings and determination with regard to their keelmen.

Resolved that those Fitters who have not already *arled* their men do so on the first Saturday after their returning to work, but that they hold themselves at liberty, and they are also determined to engage only such men, and such number of men, as they shall deem proper.

That the terms for the ensuing year shall be the same as present.

That the one pound per man towards house-rent be continued, and no binding money paid, except at Stella, where it has already been agreed for.

That the intention of the proprietors of spouts to petition the Legislature for relief from the tax which the Coal Owners generally and voluntarily imposed upon themselves in 1819, in the event of the keelmen not immediately returning to their duty, is deemed highly proper, and the undersigned will cordially unite with them in such petition, feeling as they do, an unqualified abhorrence at the ungrateful conduct of men who have manifested, not merely an indifference to the benefits conferred upon them, but also a total disregard of their duty, and the interests of their employers.

Elswick, Benwell, Fawdon, Wallbottle, Wylam, Townley, Pontop, Garesfield, Tanfield Moor, Team, Liddle's Main, South Moor

357. James Potts, J. Croser, and G. T. Dunn of the Coal Trade Committee to the Mayor, 15 October 1822 [TWA 394/45]

Newcastle, 15 October 1822

Sir,

We beg to inform you that the keelmen employed at several of the staiths above bridge have expressed their determination to return to their employment tomorrow morning, but we have strong apprehensions that an attempt will be made by the men from Newcastle and below bridge to deter them in the same manner as was done last week. We therefore beg to suggest to you the propriety of stationing the civil and military force under your direction in such situations as you may deem proper effectually to prevent the assembling of any body of keelmen during this night and early tomorrow morning. As the keels will be coming from Lemington about four o'Clock, it is probable, if the attempt is made, that the men will proceed there soon after midnight, to prevent which it is most desirable they should be stopped from going through Newcastle to the westward, for which purpose patrols of cavalry and civil officers from the bridge eastward to the Ouse Burn and westward to the Skinner Burn and Westgate would be highly useful. We further beg to recommend that the police boats should be on the alert upon the River from midnight, proceed to Derwenthaugh about three O'Clock, remain there untill the keels get under weigh, then come to Dunston staiths and remain till the keels go past; also that two of the boats should proceed with the first keels as far as Bill Point. If the keels come away [it] is probable they may be annoyed from the Bridge and the north shore to which points we also beg to direct your attention.[1]

We are, Sir, your most obedient James Potts, J. Croser, G. T. Dunn

[1] *The Durham Chronicle*, 19 October 1822, reported that the keels under strong guard had little impediment until they reached Bill Point, where about 700 keelmen on the banks nearby assailed them with large stones. The crews were obliged to lower the sails and shelter in the hurrocks of the keels. Eventually the crews abandoned the keels and went home over land, not daring to return by water or to renew the attempt. One man was severely wounded by a stone and the coal owners offered a reward of 100 guineas for the apprehension of the person who threw it, and five guineas in respect of everyone who participated in the disturbance, to be paid by the Secretary of the Coal Trade on conviction of the offenders (Handbill, 16 October, NEIMME, Bell Collection, XXII; *Tyne Mercury*, 22 October).

358. *Tyne Mercury*, 15 October 1822

The Keelmen of the Tyne

…The dispute appears no nearer a termination than when we first drew the public attention to the subject. We believe we do not exaggerate when we state that the number of keelmen thus thrown out of employment considerably exceeds 900. These men for the most part continue to wander about the country without any apparent means of subsistence, except the precarious pittance extorted from the hand of charity. On Friday last they assembled on the Windmill Hills to the number of about 600, and we understand they parted with the same views with which they met, a determination to abstain from all work until their masters shall have acquiesced in the terms they proposed. Their chief ground of complaint appears to be that large ships are laden at the spouts, thereby rendering their labour less necessary. The question between the coal owners and their servants appears to be no other than a breach of contract between the parties. …It is complained that the coal owners do not restrict the use of the spouts to loading a certain quantity of coals. Have the coal owners then swerved from any agreement in loading vessels at the staiths beyond the quantity of six keels to every ship? The answer is decidedly in the negative, because it is known the practice has been uniformly exercised since the last stoppage in 1819 and there has been no stitpulation that it should cease.[1]

The keelmen allege that one principal reason of their stoppage is the demand made upon them of 1s.6d. a tide for keel rent. The public will naturally infer that this reduction of their wages, which they rightly state it in effect to be, is now attempted to be enforced by their employers. The fact is entirely [the] contrary. Some one or two collieries, imprudently we think, made this proposition to the keelmen they employed; the *arles* were paid, and an engagement was entered into with [this] condition for the next year. Observe, this bargain was only made by one or two collieries, and of course with a small proportion of the body of the keelmen. The workmen repented of it, and their masters consented to their release.

It is not to be disguised that the keelmen have suffered from want of sufficient employment, but they err in supposing their masters are under any obligation to sacrifice their own property to afford them relief; they cannot demand that as a right which may be granted as a boon. They hold an attitude of intimidation, and they think that necessity will obtain for them what they do not expect from justice. In leaving their employments they have committed a breach of their contract. We do not discuss the policy which has rendered the greater employment of the keelmen unnecessary – that policy which has induced the proprietors of our collieries to keep up the price of coals, while provisions are low, by combining to restrict the supply. The coal owners have expressed their determination not to abandon the advantage they derive in certain cases from spouts rather than keels in loading the ships.

In 1819 they voluntarily contributed a farthing a chaldron on all coals conveyed in keels in support of the keelmen's fund, and they now declare that if they continue to hold out they will 'petition the legislature to be relieved from the tax'. We mention this in connexion with the policy of the present differences. That those who suffer, and have repeatedly suffered, from these combinations should endeavour to contrive means to prevent their recurrence is nothing more than might be expected. Application, we are credibly informed, was made within the last few days for steam boats to tow the keels down the river, but for reasons we need not mention, the request was not complied with. Should any such measure be adopted as a temporary substitute, the keelmen's future employment would be held by a weak tenure. In conclusion we may observe that the coal owners above bridge, for a considerable time, have had it in contemplation to convey their coals on the South side of the Tyne, with the assistance of steam, by land carriage down to Shields, and we need not hazard any observations on the tendency of such a measure.

[1] There was no such agreement in 1819. The keelmen did call for spout loadings

to be restricted to six keels but the coal owners absolutely rejected any limitation to be placed on their use of the spouts. See above, **Document 300**.

359. Handbill: The Second Address of the Keelmen of the River Tyne, 15 October 1822 [NEIMME, The Bell Collection, vol. 22, ff. 41–4]

'Hear this, O ye that swallow up the Needy, even to make the Poor of the land to fail'. Amos viii.4

We the Keelmen of the River Tyne, beg leave most respectfully to return our sincere and humble thanks to those of the Coal Owners, Fitters, &c. who have renewed their agreements with their keelmen on the same terms as last year; and we, at the same time deeply lament the inconvenience these gentlemen have suffered, or may continue to suffer from the stoppage of their Works on account of the unwillingness of the other Coal Owners to accede to the prayer of the great body of the keelmen – to limit, in some degree, the number of keels taken in by the different vessels laden at the spouts of the collieries below Bridge. This may appear to some an unjustifiable interference with the rights of private property. But when it is considered how much the interests of a large body of men are injured by these encroachments, and also the obstructions they present in the River, some of them projecting into it to the extent of 50 feet, to the great annoyance of ships, keels, and smaller craft, we may be permitted to presume that no man or body of men ought to be allowed to use their property in a way productive of injury to the community. However 'vain our hopes' may be, an Appeal in this case, we apprehend, must lie, either with the government of the Town, as Conservators of the River, or with the Legislature of the Country.

The objections of our body to the unlimited use of spouts may appear, to the casual and superficial observer, absurd and untenable; and also destructive of the principle by which it is supposed everyone has a right to make the best or most advantageous use of his own property. However, if we look at Trade generally, we will find it subjected to various legislative regulations and restrictions. This is, in a special manner, the case with the Coal Trade; for, added to the legislative enactments, the Coal Owners have themselves, from time to time, adopted other regulations and restrictions for the purpose of supporting their own interests. The legislature in granting a *Monopoly* to the Coal Owners of Newcastle, by which the inhabitants of the Metropolis and other parts of the country are deprived of the advantage of working the mines in their own immediate neighbourhood, did not surely intend the exclusive benefit of those whom we serve. No, the policy of the government appears clearly to have been to support the shipping and commercial interests of the country, and especially to encourage a nursery for seamen, for the important purpose of national defence, in the Newcastle Coal Trade. And it is well known that during the last war, besides furnishing our quota as required for the service of the state, the navy was supplied with a number of its best seamen from our body. It may not therefore be ultimately advantageous to the Coal Owners themselves to seek, by oppressing and annihilating us, to deprive themselves of their chief claim to the Monopoly they enjoy, and by which their property has been rendered so valuable.

The Coal Owners very well know we have not sought any advance of wages, though the very great advance in the price of coals at market (which has been more than doubled within late years) may seem to justify it. And though we have not participated in the advantages of the high prices, we have not complained of those well-concerted plans by which they have been effected; though suffering at the same time, as we must have done, together with the public at large, by the Vend being restricted. Neither have we armed ourselves or called in the aid of the Military to support our interests; though, in the case of these restrictions, the interests of the public were more intimately involved than our own.

The owners of the collieries say they never entertained any idea of making any reduction in our wages. But how does this agree with the demand which has been made of a rent charge for the use of the craft, in some instances to the amount of one shilling per man for every tide; and also taking away our binding money and other allowances formerly paid? These are things of which we complain justly. But most of all do we complain of the deficiency of employment, and this we believe to be occasioned principally by the now extended employment of spouts, and also by the restrictions imposed on the vend by the Coal Owners, which by keeping up the price of coals must necessarily diminish the consumption.

The owners of some of the collieries have published a threat, in case we should not accede to their views, to apply to Parliament to be relieved from the obligation, which they say they 'voluntarily imposed upon themselves' by the Act of Parliament passed in 1820, of contributing to the Fund for the support of our sick and aged brethren, our widows and orphans, &c. Under such circumstances, and considering the inadequacy of our means to the support of this noble institution, so extensive in its objects, it may be deemed prudent on our part at the same time to pray to be relieved from the heavy payments imposed on us by the same Act. In this case the maintenance of our sick and aged brethren, their widows and orphans (which last year cost our Fund £2,583 7s. 9d.) will eventually fall upon the parishes and townships in which we reside; towards which the Coal Owners will most probably be obliged to contribute much more than they do at present. In fact, in the preamble to the Act for establishing our Fund it is expressly declared that it is not our interests alone which are provided for by the Institution, but that also 'great benefits have resulted therefrom to the parishes and townships where we are legally settled'. The importance therefore of our Fund to the public at large being recognized by the Legislature, it is highly probable in the present depressed circumstances of the country that the public would deeply interest themselves in the question by which, if the Coal Owners succeeded, very heavy additional burdens would be imposed upon them.

We are more than once reminded by the Coal Owners of the 'established' and 'well known laws of the land', against which we are advised not to array ourselves. So far as this advice is dictated by a spirit of benevolence and good will, we are thankful for it, and hope that these laws will not be left to the administration of interested persons who might be tempted to 'pervert justice and judgment' for their own sinister purposes. Such we would remind that there are also laws of God and Nature, which have likewise been declared to be 'part and parcel of the law of the land', the precepts of which are of still higher obligation, and cannot be contravened with impunity. These laws provide in a special manner for the interests of the poor, and are inimical to every species of oppression.

To deprive us of the 'public sympathy', to which they tell us 'we are not entitled', various erroneous statements have been made by the hireling journals in our neighbourhood; and through the same corrupt channels have been propagated the most malicious falsehoods relative to our designs and intentions, evidently with a view to excite alarm, and give a colourable pretence for the employment of the Military. It has also been erroneously stated that 'we have a kind of Committee appointed for representing our grievances'. The truth is, we are associated together on the same principle on which the Coal Owners themselves are united, namely for the protection and advancement of our own interests, though we have not, like them, entered into any 'solemn engagements', neither have we 'bound our souls with an oath'. In fine, we have not, like our masters, any regular organization for the management of our interests. Neither have we, like them, any Committee, Chairman, nor 'Secretary for collecting Lists'.

The Keelmen of the River Tyne

360. Copy the Mayor to General Byng, 17 October 1822 [TWA 394/46]

Sir,

The disturbances amongst the keelmen of this Port still continuing, and some aggravated cases of riot having taken place, and, as by a letter received from the Secretary of State's Office,[1] the Magistrates are advised in the event of their requiring the assistance of Infantry soldiers to put themselves in communication with the General Officer commanding the District, I beg to state to you that it is highly probable that such assistance, if necessary at all, will be required in the instant, and it may therefore be important to the public service that the officer commanding at Sunderland Barracks should have your directions, on the Magistrates requiring aid, to detach to Newcastle and Gateshead such part of the 66th as he can prudently spare, without waiting to make a communication to you. If you shall concur with me in that opinion, I rely that you will have the goodness to give directions accordingly.

I have the honor to be, Sir, your most obedient Servant.

[1] G. Dawson to A. Surtees, 12 October 1822, See **Document 354**, above.

361. Minute of a meeting held in the Mayor's Chamber, 17 October 1822 [TWA 394/46]

Present: The Mayor of Newcastle, Mr Alderman Cookson, Mr Alderman Smith; Mr William Brandling (Northumberland); Mr Askew, Revd. Mr Liddell, Revd. Mr Collinson (County Durham).

Mr Collinson and Mr Liddell propose to be at and about Felling Shore this day at two O'clock, accompanied with forty Dragoons and three of the Serjeants at Mace of Newcastle, mounted as special constables for the County of Durham, and afterwards to assist in the execution of the warrants already issued against the bound keelmen.

The Mayor proposes to embark forthwith in a steam boat, accompanied with 20 of Colonel Brandling's dismounted troop, with Peace Officers, and to proceed to Friar's Goose and Felling Shore and the neighbourhood and thus assist in the preservation of the peace upon the water.

362. [Nathaniel Clayton] to Revd John Collinson, 18 October 1822 [TWA 394/46]

Mayor's Chamber, 18 October 1822

Dear Sir,

The Mayor desires me to state to you that he has been applyed to by the Agents for Team, Pontop and Tanfield Moor (whose staiths are at or near Dunston) for protection on the water whilst they bring down several keels with coals now lying loaden there with sailors and others ready to navigate them, with which application he proposes to comply, and the force upon the water destined for that purpose will set out from the Newcastle Quay at 6 o'Clock tomorrow morning, the keels proposing to move from the staiths at 7 o'Clock.

It seems agreed on all heads that protection must be also given at the shore at Dunston by a Magistrate, aided by a proper military force there, and the Mayor hopes therefore that you will have the goodness so to arrange matters so as to give that aid. If the party under your direction set out at 6 or soon after 6 o'Clock, they will arrive in good time at Dunston.

I am, Dear Sir, yours faithfully
N.C.

363. The Keelmen to Adam Askew, one of the Magistrates for County Durham, 18 October 1822 [TWA 394/46]

Dunston, 18 October 1822

Sir,

We the Keelmen of the River Tyne, having been much misrepresented by the unfeeling and uncharitable relative to the differences which have unhappily taken place between us and our employers, and our conduct, object, and views having also been greatly misstated, we beg leave to lay the facts of the case before you at large and appeal to your candour and generosity in extenuation of the charges against us.

We the Keelmen of the River Tyne, beg leave most respectfully to return our sincere and humble thanks to those of the Coal Owners, Fitters, &c. who have renewed their agreements with their keelmen on the same terms as last year; and we, at the same time deeply lament the inconvenience these gentlemen have suffered, or may continue to suffer from the stoppage of their Works on account of the unwillingness of the other Coal Owners to accede to the prayer of the great body of the keelmen – to limit, in some degree, the number of keels taken in by the different vessels laden at the spouts of the collieries below Bridge. This may appear to some an unjustifiable interference with the rights of private property. But when it is considered how much the interests of a large body of men are injured by these encroachments, and also the obstructions they present in the River, some of them projecting into it to the extent of 50 feet, to the great annoyance of ships, keels, and smaller craft, we may be permitted to presume that no man or body of men ought to be allowed to use their property in a way productive of injury to the community. However 'vain our hopes' may be, an Appeal in this case, we apprehend, must lie, either with the government of the Town, as Conservators of the River, or with the Legislature of the Country.

The objections of our body to the unlimited use of spouts may appear, to the casual and superficial observer, absurd and untenable; and also destructive of the principle by which it is supposed everyone has a right to make the best or most advantageous use of his own property. However, if we look at Trade generally, we will find it subjected to various legislative regulations and restrictions. This is, in a special manner, the case with the Coal Trade; for, added to the legislative enactments, the Coal Owners have themselves, from time to time, adopted other regulations and restrictions for the purpose of supporting their own interests. The legislature in granting a *Monopoly* to the Coal Owners of Newcastle, by which the inhabitants of the Metropolis and other parts of the country are deprived of the advantage of working the mines in their own immediate neighbourhood, did not surely intend the exclusive benefit of those whom we serve. No, the policy of the government appears clearly to have been to support the shipping and commercial interests of the country, and especially to encourage a nursery for seamen, for the important purpose of national defence, in the Newcastle Coal Trade. And it is well known that during the last war, besides furnishing our quota as required for the service of the state, the navy was supplied with a number of its best seamen from our body. It may not therefore be ultimately advantageous to the Coal Owners themselves to seek, by oppressing and annihilating us, to deprive themselves of their chief claim to the Monopoly they enjoy, and by which their property has been rendered so valuable.

The Coal Owners very well know we have not sought any advance of wages, though the very great advance in the price of coals at market (which has been more than doubled within late years) may seem to justify it. And though we have not participated in the advantages of the high prices, we have not complained of those well-concerted plans by which they have been effected, though suffering at the same time, as we must have done, together with the public at large, by the Vend being restricted. Neither have we armed ourselves or called in the aid of the Military to support our interests, though, in the case of these restrictions, the interests of the public were more intimately involved than our own.

The owners of the collieries say they never entertained any idea of making any reduction in our wages. But how does this agree with the demand which has been made of a rent charge for the use of the craft, in some instances to the amount of one shilling per man for every tide; and also taking away our binding money and other allowances formerly paid? These are things of which we complain justly. But most of all do we complain of the deficiency of employment, and this we believe to be occasioned principally by the now extended employment of spouts, and also by the restrictions imposed on the vend by the Coal Owners, which by keeping up the price of coals must necessarily diminish the consumption.

The owners of some of the collieries have published a threat, in case we should not accede to their views, to apply to Parliament to be relieved from the obligation, which they say they 'voluntarily imposed upon themselves' by the Act of Parliament passed in 1820, of contributing to the Fund for the support of our sick and aged brethren, our widows and orphans, &c. Under such circumstances, and considering the inadequacy of our means to the support of this noble institution, so extensive in its objects, it may be deemed prudent on our part at the same time to pray to be relieved from the heavy payments imposed on us by the same Act. In this case the maintenance of our sick and aged brethren, their widows and orphans (which last year cost our Fund £2,583 7s. 9d.) will eventually fall upon the parishes and townships in which we reside; towards which the Coal Owners will most probably be obliged to contribute much more than they do at present. In fact, in the preamble to the Act for establishing our Fund it is expressly declared that it is not our interests alone which are provided for by the Institution, but that also 'great benefits have resulted therefrom to the parishes and townships where we are legally settled'. The importance therefore of our Fund to the public at large being recognized by the Legislature, it is highly probable in the present depressed circumstances of the country that the public would deeply interest themselves in the question by which, if the Coal Owners succeeded, very heavy additional burdens would be imposed upon them.

We shall now proceed to state our grievances.

1st It was customary every year to enter into conditions for the next and arle the men three months before the expiration of the term of their agreement. This gave us time and opportunity to make engagements more agreeable to our interests. That good old custom being now laid aside, we are compelled either to comply with the terms dictated to us, or be turned adrift without employment.

2nd That one shilling per keel for casting be paid by the Master of the ship when the port is five feet from the gunwale, and one shilling more per foot for all that is above the stated height.

3rd With respect to Measure, we have generally to carry one chaldron more than was agreed to in 1819, which is reducing our wages 2s. 6d. per tide.

4th That the Corporation of Newcastle engaged to employ all keelmen out of employment in cleansing the New Quay of the gravel &c at so much per ton. This continued only about 3 months, and the keelmen out of employ have not since been employed by that body.

5th It is our fixed determination that not one man will return to work untill every man is liberated who is or may be arrested during the continuance of the stop.

6th That we consider the placing of Buoys in the channel of the River to be a dangerous nuisance which ought to be removed.

We ask nothing unreasonable, and as soon as these grievances are satisfactorily redressed, we will instantly return to our employment.

On behalf of the Keelmen of the River Tyne

364. Minutes of a meeting of the Magistrates of the three Counties of Northumberland, Durham and Newcastle, together with Gentlemen of the Coal Trade, 19 October 1822 [TWA 394/46]

The Mayor's Chamber, 19 October 1822 Present: Robert William Brandling, Esq. and William Clark, Esq. (Northumberland); Adam Askew, Esq. (County Durham); The Mayor, Mr Alderman Clayton, Mr Alderman Smith, Mr Alderman Cookson (Newcastle).

The Gentlemen of the Coal Trade attended the meeting, consisting of: Cuthbert Ellison, John Buddle, James Potts, Robert Johnson, Benjamin Thompson, John Grace, John Walters, Richard Lambert, Joseph Bainbridge, George Dunn, George Thomas Dunn, Joseph Croser, William Armstrong, Nathaniel Grace

Mr Askew stated that he had received a petition from the Keelmen which he had promised to lay before the meeting, and he read such petition to the meeting.

1st One of the claims made by the Keelmen is that they should be re-engaged 3 months before the year expires, and they stated that that has been the custom. Mr George Thomas Dunn stated that what is asserted by the Keelmen that it had been the custom to earl [i.e. re-engage] them 3 months before their year expires is not founded in fact, for that many of the Fitters did not earl them at all. That the Fitters above Bridge are pledged this year to earl them for the ensuing year on the first Saturday after they go to work, but that that pledge does not extend to any future earling.

The Gentlemen below Bridge do not consider themselves pledged to earl.

Mr R.W. Brandling moved that it be left to the Magistrates of the three Counties in their respective sessions to fix the time of hiring each year. Seconded by Mr George Dunn.

Mr Lambert moved that they should be earled on the …..and that the year should commence on the ….of March.

Mr Ellison recommends that an agreement should be come to this day, and he hoped that the Coal Trade would agree to hire their men 3 months before their year shall expire. He does not think that that can be considered as a concession.

Mr Brandling abandoned his former motion and instead of it he moved that they should be hired 3 months before the year expires – carried by 9 to 4. Condition that they immediately go to work. It was moved that for this year the men should be hired on the first Saturday after they shall go to work.

2nd The Keelmen next ask that one shilling per chaldron per keel for casting should be paid by the master of the ship when the port is above 5 feet from the gunwale. The Coal Trade say they cannot interfere with this matter as it must rest with the ship owner and refer to the agreement of 1819.

3rd The Keelmen complain that they have generally to carry one chaldron [more] than was agreed in 1819 which reduces their wages 2s. 6d. per tide. The Coal Trade refer to the Agreement of 1819, and say that then this point was provided for in 1819.

4th The Keelmen complain that the Corporation employed the Keelmen only about 3 months on cleansing the Quay. The Mayor will reply to this.

5th The Keelmen's demand for release of prisoners. Inadmissible.

6th The buoys are under the direction of the Conservators and the Trinity House and who must attend to the whole navigation, not to that of the keels alone.

365. Report of the above meeting for publication [TWA 394/46]

Mayor's Chamber, 19 October 1822

At a meeting of the Magistrates of the three Counties of Northumberland, Durham and Newcastle, attended by deputations from the Owners and Fitters concerned in the Coal Trade and from th+e Keelmen of the River Tyne, a paper which had been presented to Adam Askew, Esq. on behalf of the Keelmen was read and fully considered; and the Magistrates think it right to communicate to the parties concerned the result of the discussion that took place. [*The report was to be printed, and for this purpose each of the keelmen's griev-ances listed in the manuscript as 'first', 'second', &c., bears the note 'here insert the grievance from the Keelmen's paper'. As the grievances have been set out in full in the preceding letter to Adam Askew, they are merely summarized here.*]

First, [*The 'good old custom' of arling being laid aside.*] To this it was answered by the Coal Owners and Fitters, that, though no such old custom had generally existed in the Trade, and though in practice it had been usual to give the keelmen not intended to be employed in the following year six, and sometimes twelve, months notice of that intention, yet the Coal Owners and Fitters are ready to agree allways to arle three months before the end of the subsisting year the keelmen intended to be employed in the following year, and that the keelmen intended to be employed for 1823 shall be arled on the Saturday after they return to work, provided they return to their duty not later than Wednesday next.

Second, [*payment to be made by the ship Master when the keelmen have to cast above certain heights.*] To this it was answered that, as what is required to be paid is to be paid by the Master of the ship over whom the Coal Owners and Fitters have no controul, they cannot interfere further than to remind the ship Master that it was agreed in 1819 that this payment should be made, and, it was added, that in many cases the payment continues to be made.

Third, [*concerning overmeasure.*] To this it was answered that under the direction of the Board of Customs the waggons and keels used in the Coal Trade had been, since the year 1819, strictly weighed and measured, and that since that time there has been no just cause of complaint of overmeasure.

Fourth, [*discontinuance of employment of unemployed keelmen by Newcastle Corporation.*] To this it was answered that the Coal Owners and Fitters cannot interfere with the discretion of the Corporation in the application of their funds, but they are aware that a considerable sum was expended by that body in supplying work to the Keelmen, after the agreement of 1819.

Fifth, [*that arrested strikers be liberated.*] Here the Magistrates inter-posed, declaring that the administration of the laws of the Country could not be interfered with, and to this declaration all present at the meeting submitted.

Sixth, [*the danger from buoys in the River.*] To this it was answered that the power of placing buoys in the River belongs to the Conservators, and to the Master and Brethren of the Trinity House, and are placed as those bodies think will best promote the trade of the Port and the general navigation of the River.

The limitation of the use of Spouts being mentioned by the deputation from the Keelmen, they were referred to the resolution of the 12th Instant published by the Owners of collieries below Bridge, and the Magistrates present unanimously concurred in the propriety of those resolutions.

366. The Keelmen's Response, 21 October 1822 [TWA 394/46]

We the keelmen of the River Tyne assembled this day on the Windmill Hills for the purpose of taking into consideration the communication from the meeting of the Magistrates, Coal Owners, &c held at the Mayor's Chamber on Saturday last, the 19th of October instant, having taken the same into our serious consideration, we beg to call the attention of the Gentlemen concerned to two things not adverted to in the printed communication above referred to, and also to a third which the petitioners deem of much importance to themselves.

In the first place we beg to express our thanks to the Coal Owners and Fitters for all the declarations they have made in our favour relative to the non-reduction of our wages, and for their agreeing to enter into conditions with and arle us, as formerly, before the expiration of the present year ensuing.

All therefore that we would now petition for is that our binding money, namely, two Pounds per keel, and one Guinea in lieu of a binding supper, which was formerly allowed, may still be continued to us.

And we also pray that the Coal Owners and Fitters will be pleased to take into their consideration the propriety of restricting every vessel laden at the Spouts to take in from thence not more than eight keels of coals; a regulation by which we presume little loss or inconvenience would be sustained by the proprietors of coals; while, we are persuaded, it would give more employment to our body, and long stifle the voice of complaint among us.

We also pray that the Coal Owners and Fitters will be pleased to use their influence to obtain as speedily as possible the liberation of such of our body as may have been put into confinement since the commencement of the present stop and on account thereof.

And finally, we beg leave to state that it is our earnest wish and desire, and we do hereby declare that we will, each and every of us, return to our employment so soon as it shall appear that our employers are impressed with a desire to attend to the prayer of our petition, and evince towards us a spirit of reconciliation.

The Keelmen of the River Tyne

367. Michael Green, staithman, to Mr Watson, Tanfield Owners' Office, 21 October 1822 [TWA 394/46]

Dunston, 21 October 1822

Dear Sir,

I had some hopes this morning that the Keelmen's meeting would come to a resolution to go to work, but it is quite the contrary. They do not mean to work till some arrangement take place +++++ respecting the Spouts.

I am sorry to observe that our staith will be full tomorrow, and our [waggons?] will cease to go, without you can come up and take away a few keels as you did on Saturday last, or at least get the light keels into the spouts which may give us another day.

Mr Pile's Box, in which many of the Keelmen is in, gave out ten shillings a man to enable them to live during the stop, also Piscard's Box on Saturday, 5s. 0d per man, so that they may stand this week very well.

I am not aware whether Mr Clayton is in Town or not; if he is, show him this letter.

I am yours truly,
Michael Green

I've wrote to Mr Archless respecting this unpleasant business.

368. Copy [Nathaniel Clayton] to the Magistrates John Collinson and Adam Askew, 21 October 1822 [TWA 394/46]

Dear Sir,

Application has been made to the Mayor for protection on the water for some keels to be brought from Dunston and elsewhere tomorrow morning, and, as protection will also be required on the Durham side of the River, we have to beg the favor of you to make arrangements for that purpose. If you approve of this being done, the bearer of this will convey your commands to Colonel Holmes as to the force which may be deemed necessary for the purpose, and it will be expedient that it should be at Dunston tomorrow morning at quarter before eight o'Clock.

I remain, Dear Sir, Yours faithfully,
[Nathaniel Clayton]

369. John Collinson to Nathaniel Clayton, 21 October 1822 [TWA 394/46]

Gateshead, 21 October 1822, Half past ten o'Clock,p.m.

Dear Sir,

I received your letter about an hour ago, and sent it on immediately to Mr Askew. In answer to the application conveyed by your letter, I may state as our joint opinion that we do not think ourselves authorized in the present case to call for the assistance of the military.

I remain, Dear Sir, faithfully yours,

John Collinson

370. Resolutions of the Coal Trade Committee, 22 October 1822 [printed but marked 'Private' and addressed to Nathaniel Clayton, Tanfield Moor Office.] [TWA 394/45]

At a meeting of the special committee appointed to attend to the interests of the Coal Trade during the present stop of the keelmen, Resolved:

1. That in the opinion of this meeting, formed upon the best information they have been able to collect, the bound men above bridge, for the most part, are earnestly desirous of returning to work, but are prevented so doing by the keelmen below bridge, together with the unbound men generally.

2. That the attempt of the above-bridge men to return to their duty on 16th instant was frustrated by the opposition presented at Felling Shore and other places by the men from Dunston, below bridge, and other unbound men.

3. That the proprietors of spouts be requested to order their respective bound keelmen to return to their employment, and also to use their best endeavours to keep them from riotously assembling to obstruct the passage of keels down the river; and it is recommended to the proprietors of collieries above bridge to make another united and simultaneous effort to get down their keels, soliciting the Magistrates of the two Counties and the Town of Newcastle to afford them a competent protection upon and along both shores of the river.

4. That if, and consequent upon, the Magistrates agreeing to support the proposed attempt to take down the keels, it is thought the intended protection would be most effectually afforded by the following arrangement: by placing Special Constables, supported by such military force as the Magistrates may deem proper at the following points: Derwenthaugh, Dunston, Fryar's Goose Quay, Felling Shore, Bill Quay, Hebburn Quay, South Shields, Tyne Bridge

to Ouseburn, Dents Hole, St Anthon's, Bill Point, Willington Quay, Howdon. And also by embarking such force on board steam or other boats as the Magistrates may deem proper.

5. That the staithman, offputter and running fitter of each colliery be ordered to attend at the Mayor's Chamber tomorrow morning at 10 O'Clock to be sworn in as Special Constables.

371. Printed Order to the Keelmen to Return to Work, 22 October 1822 [TWA 394/45]

In consequence of a general resolution of the Coal Owners and Fitters of the River Tyne, you the bound keelmen of[1]...... are hereby ordered to go to your work on Thursday first [24 October], when ample protection (see accompanying declaration) will be given you in the lawful discharge of your duty. But in case of your refusing, or neglecting to comply with this Order, your bond will be immediately cancelled and the owners of the said Colliery will feel themselves at liberty to engage other keelmen, or to avail themselves of any other means they may think proper for navigating their keels.

[1] In this example, 'Tanfield Moor Colliery' is inserted by hand.

371a. Declaration of the Magistrates (under the above) [TWA 394/45]

Information having been given to the Magistrates of Northumberland, Durham and Newcastle that several of the keelmen are willing to return to their employments but are intimidated by the threats of the ill-disposed, and are fearful of being molested in navigating the river. Notice is hereby given that ample arrangements have been made for the preservation of the public peace and for the personal safety of individuals employed in their lawful occupations. The said Magistrates think it right to add that they are resolved to put the laws in force, as well against those who may be actively employed in riots or breaches of the peace, as against all who, by their presence, are aiding and abetting in such illegal acts.

Robert Bell, Mayor, R.W. Brandling, William Clark, Adam Askew

372. *Tyne Mercury*, 22 October 1822

The Keelmen of the Tyne

...What confidence can be placed in men who have no regard to their engagements? What interest can they expect their employers to take in their welfare, when they have evinced such a total disregard for the interest of their employers? On Wednesday morning last, some of the keelmen above bridge shewed a disposition to return to work, and actually proceeded with their keels down to Shields. They were, however, interrupted in their progress by stones thrown from the sides of the river by those of their body less peaceably inclined. One keelman was severely wounded, and has since been conveyed to the Infirmary. A reward of 100 guineas was offered by the owners of Team Colliery for the person who threw the stone, and a further reward of 5 guineas each for the apprehension of such as were engaged in the disturbance. A few below bridge also went to work on Thursday under the protection of the civil authorities, but the spirit of intimidation held by the majority has prevented their continuance in their employment....

The effect of such a great body of men out of employment has been severely felt in this district by the trading part of the community. Ships belonging to the Tyne have been under the necessity of going to Sunderland for lading, and shopkeepers from the highest to the lowest are sensible of a material defalcation in their business.

373. Printed Notice [TWA 394/45]

Whereas information having been given to the Justices of the Peace of the West Division of Castle Ward in the County of Northumberland that several keelmen, who are at present in a state of unlawful resistance to the commands of their employers, have threatened to damage the staiths and other property of the Coal Owners, and that divers of them are at present wandering about the County of Northumberland committing Acts of Vagrancy and Trespass, they, the said Justices, think it right, as a caution to the persons so offending, to state that by an Act of Parliament passed in the 56th year of his late Majesty's reign, persons unlawfully assembled who shall with force demolish, pull down, destroy, or damage any fire engine or other engine, erected, or to be erected, for making, sinking, or working collieries, coal mines, or other mines, or any bridge, waggonway, or trunk, erected or made to be erected, or made for conveying coals or other materials from any colliery, coal mine or other mine, to any place, or for shipping the same, or any staith, or any other erections or buildings for depositing coals or other minerals, or used in the management or conduting of the business of any such colliery, coal mine or other mine, whether the same engines, bridges, waggonways, trunks, staiths, erections, and other buildings or works shall be respectively completed, finished, or only begun to be set up, made or erected, shall be adjudged Felons, and shall suffer Death, as in the case of Felony, without Benefit of Clergy; and by an Act passed in the 3rd year of his present Majesty's reign, all persons wandering abroad, and lodging in Ale houses, barns, outhouses, or in the open air, or under tents, or in carts or waggons, and not giving a good account of themselves, as also all persons gathering alms under any false pretence, shall be deemed Rogues and Vagabonds within the meaning of the last mentioned Act, and such person when brought before a Justice is made liable to be committed to the then next General Quarter Sessions of the Peace, or for any period not exceeding 3 months or less than one month, and during such confinement to be kept to hard labour. And by the 1st George IVth cap 56 it is enacted that if any person shall wilfully or maliciously do or commit any damage, injury, or spoil to or upon any building…or to or upon real or personal property of any nature or kind soever, and being thereof convicted, shall forfeit and pay to the person aggrieved such sum of money as shall appear to be a reasonable satisfaction and compensation for the damage…together with all the costs, charges, and expenses attending the prosecuting and convicting the party offending, and if the same be not forthwith paid, then the Justice before whom the matter shall be heard is empowered to order the offender to be confined in the Common Gaol or House of Correction for any period not exceeding three calendar months, and during such imprisonment to be kept at hard labour. By the same Act power is given to any Constable or other Peace Officer, and the owner of the property so damaged,…*without any warrant* to seize and detain any person or persons so committing such damage and carry such person or persons forthwith before a Justice.[1]

[1] This was also published in the *Tyne Mercury*, 22 October 1822.

374. Minutes of a meeting of the Magistrates of the three Counties, 23 October 1822 [TWA 394/46]

The Mayor's Chamber, 23 October 1822
At a meeting of the Magistrates of the three Counties of Northumberland, Durham and Newcastle, Present: Robert Bell, Esq., Mayor, Aldermen Thomas Smith, Robert Clayton and Isaac Cookson, junior (Newcastle); Robert Brandling and William Clark, Esqrs. (Northumberland); the Revd. Liddell (County Durham).

Mr Potts attended the meeting and stated that he has had a letter from Mr Taylor of Backworth Colliery intimating that the keelmen at Whitehill Point Staith had gone to work and that the keelmen at Wallsend and Walker had promised to go to work tomorrow morning. Mr Potts read a letter (circular) which had been sent by the Committee of the Coal Trade to the owners of collieries below Bridge.

The Magistrates approve the suggestion of the Coal Trade Committee, viz., that Special Constables supported by a military force [should be stationed] at the following points: Derwent Haugh, Dunston, Fryer's Goose Quay, Felling Shore, Bill Quay, Hebburn Quay, South Shields; Tyne Bridge to Ouseburn, Dents Hole, Saint Anthony's, Bill Point, Willington Quay and Howdon. This is approved by the Magistrates of the three Counties.

The Mayor proposes to embark…tomorrow morning at half past 9 o'Clock in his barge, accompanied by the military and civil power, and to proceed up the River and to be at Lemington at half past 10 o'Clock, there to afford protection to the keels.

Mr Alderman Smith will accompany a patrol of 4 Constables and 10 Dragoons mounted from Tyne Bridge to St Peter's Gate near St Peter's Quay, Sandhill.

375. Copy Nathaniel Clayton to J. Wilson Croker, Secretary to the Admiralty, 24 October 1822, 1 O'Clock P.M. [TWA 394/45]

Sir,

In the absence of the Mayor who is now upon the River with some troops in order to resist the riotous attempts of the keelmen of this Port to put a stop to the trade of the Port, it is my duty to communicate to the Lords of the Admiralty that intelligence is this moment brought to the Town that a riotous body of sailors are proceeding up the River from Shields in boats with intent to prevent the ships which have been loaded with coals at the spouts from proceeding to sea.

Under these circumstances it seems highly necessary that the force in this neighbourhood should be strengthened by a ship or ships of war, and I have therefore, under the direction of the Magistrates, to entreat their Lordships will immediately order such a force to be sent here as soon as shall seem to them proper, with a strong body of marines on board.

It is presumed that the Mayor will by tomorrow morning's mail write to the officer commanding the ships of war on the Leith station to forward to this Port any ship of war that can be spared for that service, and it is hoped their Lordships will approve the measure as it will of course save much time.

I have the honor to be, Sir, your most obedient Servant,
Nathaniel Clayton, Town Clerk

376. Copy the Mayor to Sir J.P. Beresford, Bart., or Officer Commanding at Leith, 24 October 1822 [TWA 394/46]

Mansion House, Newcastle, 24 October 1822

Sir,

I beg to enclose you a copy of a letter which has been forwarded by this day's post to the Secretary of Admiralty and which will sufficiently explain the circumstances under which I request you to dispatch to this Port a sloop or brig of war with a strong body of Marines.

I have the honor to be, Sir, your most obedient humble Servant,

[Robert Bell, Mayor]

377. Copy Robert Bell to The Duke of Northumberland, 24 October 1822 [TWA 394/46]

My Lord Duke,

I am sorry to have to report to your Grace that in addition to the continuance of the illegal proceedings of the keelmen, the seamen have today attempted to obstruct the navigation of the Port. Immediately on hearing what was taking place, I proceeded down the River, with the River Police, supported by a military force, and succeeded in apprehending and securing a considerable number of the offenders in the act of riotously obstructing the navigation. I trust that the measures which have been taken will be productive of a salutary effect and that I shall soon be able to apprise your Grace that the aspect of affairs is improved.

I have the honor to be, my Lord Duke,

Your most obedient humble Servant,

Robert Bell, Mayor

378. Robert Bell to Robert Peel, Home Secretary, 25 October 1822 [TNA, HO 40/17/47 and TWA 394/46]

Sir,

Since Mr Alderman Surtees' letter of the 8th instant, the Magistrates of this Town in conjunction with those of the adjoining Counties of Durham and Northumberland have been sedulously employed in endeavours to bring back the keelmen to a sense of their duty and in protecting such part of the navigation of the River as could be carried on without the assistance of the refactory keelmen, but I am sorry to say that the great body of them still continue obstinate and have withdrawn themselves entirely from the service of their masters, so that no coals can be shipped except from the spouts below the Bridge which deliver their coals immediately into ships of small burthen without the intervention of keels or lighters.

Having strong hopes that some of the keelmen were willing to return to their duty and navigate their keels, if they were protected from the violence of the ill-disposed, strong measures were yesterday adopted to afford that protection by means of the River Police, a detachment of the Company of Infantry attached to the Northumberland and Newcastle Yeomanry Cavalry, in barges, and several detachments of Cavalry stationed on both sides of the River, but so far from any part of the keelmen availing themselves of the arrangement and performing their duty, a large and riotous body of sailors belonging to the ships at Shields, in concert probably with the keelmen, assembled in boats on the River, and by violence compelled several of the sailors employed on board the ships loaded at the spouts, to quit their ships. The Civil Magistrate, however, under the protection and with the assistance of the military force stationed as above mentioned, was enabled to arrest twenty-eight of the rioters who were secured on board the Swan Sloop, Lieutenant Stewart, lying at Shields for safe custody for the night, and will be brought up to this Town today, under a strong escort of the third Dragoons and the Northumberland and Newcastle Yeomanry Cavalry, for examination.

Under these circumstances, the Magistrates directed an immediate application to the Lords of the Admiralty for a Ship or Ships of War with marines to be sent to this Port, and, as it would save time, made a similar application to the commanding officer on the Leith station.

I trust you will approve of what has been done here, and, as the bodies thus opposed to the Civil Power and arrayed against the due administration of the law are very numerous, you will also approve of the force now employed in resisting them being considerably strengthened.

I have the honor to be, Sir, your most obedient Servant,

Robert Bell, Mayor

379. The Duke of Northumberland to Robert Peel [TNA, HO 40/17/54]

Alnwick Castle, 29 October 1822

Sir,

...The keelmen have as yet abstained from any acts of general violence or aggression, although they obstruct the passage of any craft down the River which their late employers have endeavoured to navigate by persons unconnected with themselves. The Magistrates and Lieutenant Colonel Brandling have both endeavoured to secure the transit of coals, so conveyed, but hitherto, I grieve to say, with only partial success. The windings of the River, the difficulty of access, and a variety of other causes, present many impediments to their exertions….

I think, Sir, I may venture to assure you that there is no bad disposition amongst the seamen, but they who are serving on board vessels of large tonnage are totally dependent upon the craft [i.e. keels] for freight, and they see with some degree of jealousy the smaller ships loaded by the spouts from the staiths to which their small draught of water allows them to approach. They are now, however, peaceable and have acknowledged their error to some of the Magistrates who have been amongst them, although I must fear that a continued withholding of their loadings by the obstructed navigation of the Tyne may be a severe trial of their temper.

It is right also to add that the keelmen, however improperly they may have acted upon this occasion, are, generally speaking, a decent body of men; that, misguided as they are, it is by no political delusion, and that their present ill behaviour is mainly to be accounted for by the constant hostility of unenlightened manual labourers to the improvement and facilities of machinery.

I am, Sir, your obedient Servant,
Northumberland

380. *Tyne Mercury*, 29 October 1822

The Keelmen of the Tyne

The keelmen have now been a month entirely without employment, and, as yet, we can see no likelihood of the existing differences between them and the coal owners being soon settled. The servants are still loud in their complaints of their hardships they have long laboured under, and their masters are equally resolute in resisting the invasion of their private property. Considering the relative situation of the parties, we cannot conceive how the conduct of the keelmen is capable of justification. We do not pretend that the agreement between the employers and the employed is of the most eligible description for the latter, but it is a contract for a year and as such it ought undoubtedly by both to be held sacred. It was not less disadvantageous in January when it was entered on than it is in October. But it is urged in defence of their proceedings that this, if ever, is the time for the keelmen to resist, because now their services are in the greatest

requisition. Instead of a defence, we consider this rather an aggrava-
tion of their conduct. For their own individual interests it is taking an
undue, and ungenerous advantage of the situation of their employers.

The coal owners above bridge, we are informed, are very anxious
to come to some adjustment as they have been the greatest sufferers
by the stoppage; for, as they load no ships by spouts, they have no
means of vending their coals without the assistance of the keels. With
the collieries below bridge the case is considerably different: their
chief dependence is upon the spouts; they are benefitted to a certain
extent by the distress of the coal owners above bridge, and though
they suffer temporary inconvenience from the keelmen continuing
refractory, it is not of so serious a nature. It has justly excited surprise
how so numerous a body of men obtain subsistence for so great a
period without employment. They have not depended, it seems, on
the precarious pittance they could extort from the hand of charity
but have drawn liberally on certain boxes or private funds belonging
to their society. They cannot long be maintained from these sources,
and they would act wisely for themselves to come to some reasonable
arrangement while they may with decency. The coal owners, they
must be well aware, will never restrict the use of the spouts to 8 keels
in opposition to their most important interests, and when they are
authorized by law to use them without such limitation. It is not to be
concealed that the trade of this port has suffered from the combination
of the coal owners to restrict the vend, and it is with sincere regret we
observe that these proceedings of the keelmen have a tendency to do
it greater and more lasting injury by diverting it into other channels.

381. Copy, Robert Bell to Robert Peel, 30 October 1822 [TWA 394/46]

Sir,

I have the honor to inform you that the riotous proceedings of the
sailors were suppressed on the 24th ultimo and reported to you by
my letter of the 25th instant, and I trust the arrival of His Majesty's
Sloop Nimrod, which Sir John Beresford promptly dispatched to this
Port at my request, together with a further force promised by the
Admiralty, will have the effect of securing tranquillity amongst that
body of men and materially assist me in restraining the keelmen,
who, I am sorry to inform you, still continue refactory from inter-
rupting the navigation of the River.

I have the honor to be, Sir, your most obedient humble Servant,

Robert Bell, Mayor

382. *Newcastle Chronicle*, 2 November 1822

Letter to the Editor

It is now upwards of a month since the keelmen struck to their own loss as well as that of their employers and every person in this district, who are all more or less connected with the coal trade.

It seems to me that the origin of this unfortunate measure was the apprehension on the part of the keelmen that the fitters and coal owners by whom they were employed would attempt to take off the charge of 2s. 6d. per keel under the name of bread-money, laid on several years ago, and which by mutual agreement was to continue until the price of wheat should fall below 12s. per boll or 48s. per quarter.[1] Some of the coal owners and fitters above bridge, anxious to prevent their work being laid in at a time so important to their interests as the month of October, thought it prudent to earnest (arle) the keelmen in their employment for the ensuing year, on the same terms as they have for the present, and it was expected by them that this measure would be the means of quieting their apprehension. The keelmen above bridge could therefore have no reason of complaint, and it could only be to assist their brethren employed below bridge in their demand to limit the quantity of coals shipped by the spouts which prevented their going cheerfully to work, for as to the attempt made on the 16th ultimo by the above bridge keelmen to resume their employment, it was very clear that this attempt was any thing but in earnest.[2]

They have since avowed their resolution of sticking till Christmas rather than submit without gaining *something* from their employers, and their argument is a pithy one, that they never yet made a stick but they obtained *some concession* from their masters, therefore they have only to starve them out as before to gain their object.

This time they appear to have outshot their mark and have taken the most effectual steps in their power to ruin themselves and their families by making it the interest of their employers to dispense with them. One obvious mode, the use of steam boats by the owners above bridge to tow the keels. As a result, these blind and misguided men may be reduced to cast coals aboard ship for 2 or 3 shillings a day, instead of 5 or 6 shillings, which I am informed, from good authority, the majority above bridge have averaged for 18 months past. As this calamity has been brought on themselves by their own short-sighted folly, few will pity or relieve their necessities, and they will have accelerated, by their mistaken conduct, the march of the steam engine, which has already obliged so many workmen to turn their hands to other employments than they were brought up to.

...The bond for a year on various occasions has proved the most signal service to them, besides giving at all times the grateful assurance of constant and well requited employment. They have for a month past considered this as waste paper. If I am correctly informed, this instrument will very soon have an equal value in the eyes of their employers, and then the keelmen may consider the first act of their tragedy to be completed.

[Yours faithfully], Z

[1] This allowance had been granted in February 1800 as a temporary measure, but in course of time it became regarded as permanent. The coal owners denied that they had ever thought of reducing the keelmen's wages 'though the price of provisions may seem to justify it' (Statement issued by the Coal Trade, 12 October 1822, see above **Document 352**, p. 300).

[2] The attempt was made in earnest but abandoned on account of the strong opposition it incurred. One man was seriously wounded (see above p. 304, **Document 357**, footnote 1).

383. Minutes of a meeting of the Coal Owners, 4 November 1822 [TWA 394/46]

Newcastle, 4 November 1822

At a meeting of the Coal Owners (above Bridge) held here this morning, it was determined to make an effort to take keels down from the under-mentioned collieries, and they request the Magistrates of Newcastle and of the Counties of Durham and Northumberland to afford them such assistance and protection as they may deem sufficient for preserving the peace, &c.

Stella 6 [keels]; Walbottle, 5; Wylam, 8; Fawdon, 5; Elswick, 5; Benwell, 6; Team, 3; Pontop, 6; South Moor, 4; Tanfield Moor, 6. 54 in all.

384. Plan of Operations submitted by the Coal Trade, 4 November 1822 [TWA 394/46]

Protection for getting the Keels to work Tomorrow

A chain of Guard Boats to be stationed on the River, from Askew's Quay to Lemington. As soon as the last laden keels pass Lemington, the chain of boats to move by signal and proceed to Shields with the keels, taking care to preserve the distances, and to return in the same order.

Land protection to be established at Dunston, Tyne Bridge, Felling Shore, Jarrow Quay, Bill Point, and Willington Quay.

385. Minutes of Meeting of the Magistrates, 4 November 1822
[TWA 394/46]

At a meeting of the Magistrates of Newcastle, Northumberland and Durham held in the Guildhall, Present: the Mayor and Alderman Smith of Newcastle, Robert William Brandling, Thomas Clennell and William Clark, Esqrs., Northumberland; Coal Fitters Present: Messrs George Thomas Dunn, John Buddle, Joseph Croser, Nathaniel Hindhaugh, Matthew Atkinson, William Armstrong, Charles Robson, John Brandling, George Newmarsh, Richard Lambert, Benjamin Thompson.

Mr Buddle stated that an effort will be made tomorrow morning by the Coal Fitters both above and below Bridge to get keels down the River, and that on behalf of the Coal Owners he begs that protection may be afforded them upon the River and upon the shores on the North and South sides of the River. Mr Buddle further stated that the Coal Fitters had agreed upon a plan of opertions [*see above*] which he submitted to the consideration of the Magistrates.

386. George Dawson, Under-Secretary of State at the Home Office, to Robert Bell, 4 November 1822 [TWA 394/46]

Whitehall, 4 November 1822

Sir,

I am directed by Mr Secretary Peel to acknowledge the receipt of your letter of 2nd Instant, and to express his regret that the keelmen still continue in their insubordination. Mr Peel hopes that the spirited and meritorious exertions of the Magistracy and yeomanry united with the strong force of marines, which have been stationed at Shields by his directions, will have the effect of convincing these deluded people that their tumultuous conduct can have no other result than that of aggravating their own distress.

I have the honor to be, Sir, your most obedient Servant,
George Dawson

387. *Tyne Mercury*, 5 November 1822

The Keelmen of the Tyne

The keelmen, we regret to state, still hold their employers at defiance. They have not recently evinced the slightest disposition to return to their duty, and the prospect of their submission is not greater now than it was a month ago. In their first Address they declared their only wish was to be dealt with as beings capable of the discourse of reason. Their whole conduct has falsified this declaration. They have persisted and still persist in their demand that the use of the spouts should be limited to 8 keels per ship: no argument is sufficient to convince them of the folly of this demand. They have attempted no show of reason that it should be complied with from inherent justice of the measure, nor have they sought to support their claim from any precedent. They have proved that they mean by 'the discourse of reason' nothing less than the entire acquiescence with their demands, however preposterous.

The policy by which the coal owners have been actuated may reflect credit on their humanity, but as a means of inducing their servants to return to their employment it has been eminently unsuccessful. They held out a threat that if the keelmen did not proceed to their work by a particular day, they would cancel their bonds. This menace produced no immediate effect, and the proprietors of the collieries shewed it was an empty parade. They did not destroy the bonds, and the keelmen were encouraged to continue to hold the attitude of intimidation.[1] The manner in which the police and military have been employed has only had the tendency of confirming them in their refractory conduct. The have committed acts of violence, they have interrupted the navigation of th river, and yet the police and the military have availed nothing.

On Thursday last, Alderman Forster, it seems, went up the water to escort some keels down. He proceeded nearly as far as Lemington, and sent forward the police boats to Wylam staith. The dismounted cavalry were in this barge with the magistrate, but they returned down the river without waiting to see if the police boats succeeded in bringing away the keels. Four keels at Wylam, it appears, were got under weigh and proceeded with little molestation till they reached Scotswood where they were assailed by showers of stones from a great body of keelmen, who put off in an empty keel from the shore, and soon gained possession of the 4 keels, obliging the police to fly to the boats to save their lives. The magistrate and his troops were out of danger. They had come down the river as far as the King's Meadows, before they were overtaken by the police boats. They did not return to the scene of action. We should do an injustice to the military if we did not state that they, one and all, desired to go in pursuit of the aggressors. It was, however, decreed otherwise. What, then, we would ask, has the employment of the military effected? They are on duty, or ought to have been, to prevent violence, and to protect the navigation of the river. They have done neither. The rioters have acquired strength and courage, because they have been suffered to act with impunity. The soldiers have been parading on the Town

Moor and in the streets, when they should have been supporting the craft on the river by their attendance on the shore. They are not to blame, and the discredit of these unpunished outrages must rest on those under whose controul they are placed.

… The time for compromise is past. The coal owners have in a few instances cancelled the bonds between them and their servants. They have erred in not cancelling the whole, even at the commencement of the differences….[The keelmen] are bound servants and are as much amenable to the law as indentured apprentices. This [the coal owners] should have had recourse to in the beginning as a right, they should now do it as a measure of policy.[2] The permanent interests of the keelmen have shown that submission ought to have been their course. The remissness of the proprietors of the collieries has been attributed not to a spirit of lenity but timidity, and if these men continue refactory we should conceive the interference of the civil authorities not warrantable only, but advisable and necessary.

[1] The *Durham County Advertiser* of 2 November reported that the magistrates charged the coal owners with 'great laxity' for failing to put in force the warrants taken out against 'so many refactory individuals'. The keelmen's stubbornness was 'a monstrous evil', and 'the sooner the hydra were crushed the better'.
[2] The *Durham Chronicle* of 2 November stated that tradesmen on both sides of the river were beginning to be affected by the stoppage, with numbers of industrious men thrown out of work and their families in great distress.

388. Copy of Mr Williamson's Opinion on the arming of Special Constables [NEIMME, The Bell Collection, vol. 22]

Agents and servants of the owners of collieries, as well as other persons, in consequence of the unlawful proceedings of the Keelmen, having been sworn in as Special Constables for the execution of warrants and the preservation of the public peace,

Are the Magistrates justified, and can they legally put into the hands of such Special Constables, as well as the regular Constables annually appointed, fire-arms, swords, or other weapons?

I think the Magistrates cannot, in the first instance, put into the hands of the Constables, either special or regular, fire-arms, swords, or other weapons; but they may do so upon calling them into service upon any occasion, which, in their judgement, may require such extraordinary means of action in the Civil Power; or the Constables may, on their own authority, arm themselves in such manner as the existing circumstances may make necessary.

Newcastle, 6 November 1822   Robert Hopper Williamson

389. 'A Friend to the Coal Trade' to the Keelmen of the River Tyne
[NEIMME, The Bell Collection, Vol. 22, p. 15]

Newcastle, 12 November 1822

Situated as you are at present, under circumstances which, at least, must be distressing to some, and inconvenient to all of you, I have no doubt but a few words, by way of admonition, will be thankfully received; although, perhaps, some designing persons may attempt to make you believe that all those who profess opinions and sentiments different to yourselves are influenced by some corrupt or interested motive, yet I can assure you that the few words I shall say are purely by way of advice, and unconnected with any party, either for or against. I am neither a keelman nor a Coal Owner: I have nothing to gain from the one, or to lose by the other.

I have read the Addresses issued under your name, and there are really some things which might be very easily remedied, and which I am happy to learn the Coal Owners have consented to ameliorate; while, on the other hand, there are requests and demands so inconsistent, and so absurd, that I cannot help attributing them to the wicked designs of some who tamper with your grievances, than to your own actual thoughts upon the subject. Nay, I am confident that had you been left to yourselves, had no individual, possessing a greater wish to stir you up to acts of mischief, than to better your condition, meddled with your affairs, the Trade of the Tyne would not have been thus interrupted, but harmony and good-will between your employers and yourselves would have existed at this very hour! If you are not already aware of the absurdity of the demands already alluded to, I will refer to them, and I think the most important one, at least that to which you have been advised to adhere to most strictly, is the case of the Spouts. You, at first, were so far opposed to every reasonable feeling, as to insist upon a total abolition of their use; but you afterwards, as appears from the Addresses I have already mentioned, reduced your demands to a limitation of quantity. Now, my Friends, where is there a precedent for such a demand as this? Where is there a manufacturing district and a body of labouring individuals that have not been more or less injured by things of this nature, and to which, of course, they have submitted without resistance? The Coal Owners are the same as proprietors of any other species of property; they have a right to do and act as they like (legally and lawfully); they have a right to employ who they like, and as few as they like; and if the use of manual labour has diminished, it can only be attributed to this age of inventions and improvements, and by which every part of the labouring classes throughout the United Kingdom, as well as yourselves, have been in a larger or smaller degree affected; but which, from the stagnation of trade, and other causes too well known to require repetition, is perfectly without remedy. And even were we to suppose you had the least shadow of a claim for such a demand, let me for a moment dwell upon the singular course you have been advised to adopt, in order to enforce compliance with it. You illegally break your engagements with your employers, who, of course, are chiefly those owners whose collieries are above the Bridge: you, after refusing to navigate the keels yourselves, forcibly prevent any other persons from doing so; you direct all your animosity – all your plans, against the collieries above Bridge, while you permit those loading coals by spout to reap all the benefits therefrom; while you are seeking a limitation of quantity, you give *them* the opportunity of having the whole trade of the Port to themselves; and thus preventing and depriving those, whom you ought to cherish as your only remaining friends, from having any opportunity of affording employment to you. You must be well aware that the greater the demand for 'below Bridge' coals, the less must be your chances of employment, and such a course of proceeding, you will find upon the least reflection, can only end in total ruin to yourselves and families. You ought to reflect too, that the farthing per chaldron granted to your Hospital Fund was a boon you could not have enforced; and that were the donors to recall their gift, and you in consequence to throw your families upon the parish, you would not be injuring those you are at variance with, but simply the inhabitants who are unconnected and unconcerned in the business. The only line of conduct you can pursue with advantage to your-selves is the reverse of this; you ought to assist your employers above Bridge to ship their coals without molestation; thus giving them every opportunity of extending their connexions and increasing the consumption of the coal: this is the only possible means by which you can limit the spouts, and by which your interests and your welfare can be increased.

Little more, I think, need be said to convince you of the error you have been led into; return then to your lawful work, fulfil your agree-ments with your employers, and enjoy the only source of prosperity which is left to you, and which you have long enjoyed happily and satisfactorily. Few words need be said to those who advise you to follow a different track; their motives may be easily seen through, and their sinister designs may be as easily controverted; and better it would be were they to bestow their time upon some more laudable pursuit than in attempting to render a body of men unworthy the confidence of their employers, and causing them to swerve from that honest line of conduct which they have long pursued, and which, I firmly believe, you are anxious to maintain.

A Friend to the Coal Trade

390. *Tyne Mercury*, 12 November 1822

The Keelmen of the Tyne

Six weeks have now elapsed since the keelmen deserted their employment and there is yet no prospect of their returning to their engagements. Of their voluntary submission there appears not the most distant probability and we can perceive no chance of regaining their services except by their being reduced to actual necessity or by the adoption of prompt and vigorous measures on the part of the civil authorities.[1] The unaminity they have evinced, and the secrecy and cunning which have distinguished all their proceedings, are truly remarkable. In the different meetings they have held, especial care has been observed to have as few individuals present belonging to the neighbourhood as possible, thus preventing their recognition by presenting only strangers to the notice of the inhabitants. For some time past considerable numbers of the keelmen have been dispersed in different parts of the Counties of Northumberland and Durham, with no other object apparently than to extort by intimidation the charity they cannot always obtain from the pity of those to whom they apply. Their success in these excursions has enabled them in a great measure to live without work, and it is not easy perhaps to determine how long this may endure, if the magistrates in the several districts do not exert themselves to check the progress of this vagrancy, so oppressive to the country, and so injurious to the most important interests of this town. Many of the keelmen have betaken themselves to other employments at some distance rather than remain here to fulfil their engagements with the coal owners. A considerable number have been, and are still, working at Sunderland as casters, and from the increased trade of the Wear, owing to the inability of many of our collieries to send coal to market in consequence of the stoppage, it is conceived they will meet with liberal encouragement.

On Wednesday last [6 November], the Mayor proceeded up the river in his barge, accompanied by a party of marines from the ships of war, and succeeded in conducting from 30 to 40 keels in safety down to Shields.[2] Proper precautions had been taken to have the shores lined with military, so that though numbers of keelmen appeared in sight, no violence was attempted. This management, however, appears to have been of short duration. No sooner do the coals arrive in safety at their destination, than the *men* are left to return as they may without guard or protection. On the following morning one of these keels on coming up the river was obliged from the state of the tide to stop at St Anthony's where the 3 men left it and went on shore. They were proceeding it seems towards Dent's Hole when they were overtaken by about 100 keelmen who beat them with great cruelty. One of them, indeed, from the severe wounds he received remains in a dangerous condition.[3] They all agree that they must certainly have perished but for the interposition of some women. Other keels were also subjected to insult on their return. On Wednesday also one of the King's boats was assailed by stones in proceeding down the river, and the men were obliged to fire in their own defence.

Last Saturday [9 November] a general meeting of the coal owners of the Tyne was held to take into consideration a proposition from the proprietors above bridge. It appears that in consequence of the immense quantity of coals they had wrought, and the great advance they were called upon to make for wages &c without any prospect of effecting sales, it was deemed advisable to suspend their workings. But as their pitmen are by their contract entitled to receive a certain sum per week, even though unemployed, it was proposed that those men should be employed by the collieries below bridge. This proposition has, we understand, been acceded to upon certain terms arranged between the parties subject to the management of a committee. In consequence, several pitmen have already gone from the pits of Adair's Main, Elswick, Beaumont's Main, &c, which will afford relief of the highest importance to their late employers.

Yesterday 5 of the armed boats from the ships of war proceeded upriver to give protection to some keels coming down from Dunston, but from the late guarded conduct of the keelmen, little interruption is apprehended. ...The magistrates, we hear, have expressed the most decided disapprobation of the irresolute conduct of the coal owners. They have neither cancelled all their bonds nor attempted to have their servants apprehended; and, though warrants have been granted some time ago, comparatively few men are in custody. It is idle to pretend this is impracticable, while it is obvious to all that their unwillingness, or their fear to proceed to extremities, have given courage and confidence to their refactory servants which render their submission uncertain, and impose a duty on the civil authorities at once painful and difficult.

[1] The *Durham County Advertiser*, 9 November, declared that lenity and forbearance with these 'turbulent and dissatisfied men' was evidently misapplied, and the general opinion was that nothing would avail but 'strong and coercive measures'.
[2] The *Durham Chronicle*, 9 November, stated that keels manned by inexperienced men required double the number of hands, who required more than the usual wages. Accidents occurred and the keels sustained great injury.
[3] The *Newcastle Chronicle*, 9 November, reported that besides the three men attacked at Dents Hole, a crew at Scotswood was ducked and brutally beaten, and three keelmen belonging to Stella who had returned to work were waylaid and 'most inhumanly beaten'.

391. Minutes of a Meeting of the above Bridge Coal Owners and Fitters, 12 November 1822 [TWA 394/46]

At a general meeting of the Coal Owners and Fitters interested in the collieries above Bridge held in the Merchants' Court, it was resolved that it is the opinion of the meeting that the trade may be partially carried on by the Works above Bridge if a sufficient protection can be afforded to those who navigate the keels as well on their return with the light keels as in going down loaded to the ships to which they engaged to carry their coals.

That this protection must, in the opinion of the meeting, be afforded as well on land as by water, and they respectfully submit to the Magistrates for their consideration the following plan of affording it:

That all the Works should use their utmost endeavours to have their keels ready loaded and prepared for being navigated by sailors either from the coal ships or the ships of war or others. That the boats of the ships of war should set out from Shields at the early flow of the tide and proceeding up the River carry up to the staiths under their convoy all the light keels ready to proceed. That two armed boats only need proceed to the higher Works (leaving the rest near Derwenthaugh and Dunston) and, having brought their keels away, convoy them down the River, the keels at the lower staiths, and the armed boats left there, putting off when the first boats and their convoy reach them, and joining them as they proceed down the River.

That the keels on arriving at Shields should be put alongside the ships they are destined for, and wait there till the tide makes *the next day*, when the Men of War's boats will again take them under their protection as before and proceed up the River, and thus continue to navigate up and down the River for several successive days.

That the land stations for the troops above Bridge appear to be Derwenhaugh and Dunston on the South side of the River, and Scotswood on the North. Below Bridge, St Anthony's on the North and Felling on the South. It is deemed essential that these stations should not be left without troops at any time during the whole time of making this attempt to restore the navigation, and the number of troops required are as follows, which it is hoped will not deprive the Commanding Officer of the power of giving them the usual relief:

Above Bridge, South side, at Dunston, 8, at Swalwell, 8; North side, at Scotswood, 6.

Below Bridge, South side, [at] Felling Shore, 10; North side, [at] St Anthony's, 8; in all, 40, or any greater number which the Magistrates and the Commanding Officer should think necessary. At all these stations Special Constables should be kept in constant attendance to act as may be required.

It has been suggested that some of the Works may be able to employ steam boats in towing the keels, and there is great hope that this will be effected if 12 Marines can be permitted to be stationed on board the steam boat and remain on board till the service is over, the proprietors maintaining the Marines whilst with them.

If some such plan as the above be approved and executed, the meeting entertain the hope that the keelmen, when they see that the trade is in part carried on without their assistance, and other persons receiving wages which they ought to earn, may be induced to break up their combination; or, if it should not have that effect, the collieries above Bridge will be enabled, by the partial trade thus obtained, to keep their collieries in work and to prevent great numbers of their pitmen, carriagemen and other workmen being thrown out of employment and deprived of the means of earning their bread.

392. The Mayor to the Magistrates of Northumberland and Durham, 13 November 1822 [TWA 394/46]

The Mayor of Newcastle, in consequence of the application from the Coal Owners, requests the Magistrates of Northumberland and Durham will do him the favor of meeting him in the Mayor's Chamber on Thursday morning at 12 o'Clock in order to consider a plan for the protection of the navigation submitted by the Coal Owners above Bridge to the consideration of the Magistrates.

393. Minutes of a Meeting of the Magistrates of the three Counties, 14 Nov. 1822 [TWA 394/46]

Present: the Mayor, Aldermen Cookson, Sorsbie, Forster and Cramlington (Newcastle); The Revd Mr Liddell, the Revd. Mr Collinson, the Revd Mr Thorp and Adam Askew Esq. (County Durham); Sir Thomas Burdon, Northumberland.

Coal Owners Present: Mr Robson for Wylam, Mr Hindhaugh for Walbottle, Mr Atkinson for Team, Messrs Dunn for Elswick, Mr Lambert for South Moor, Mr Croser for Benwell, Mr Newmarsh for Fawdon.

The plan sent to the Mayor for giving protection to the Coal Trade above Bridge was read and considered.

Mr Mayor suggested that the seamen of the Man of War should have some remuneration for their exertions and also for the extra wear of their clothes.

Mr Thorp put these questions to the Coal owners: First, whether in case the military are stationed as wished, the Magistrates may rely on the exertions of the Special Constables, and that persons will attend at the staiths who can identify the rioters. Second, whether it is the serious intention of the Coal Owners to execute the warrants that have been issued against the keelmen. Mr Thorp suggested it was his opinion that each Coal Owner was desirous of protecting his own men from their capture under the warrants.

Mr Mayor suggested the giving notices to the persons who employ the bound keelmen at Sunderland of their being bound. Mr Mayor suggested that some notice should be given by handbills that the well disposed be cautioned to refrain from any interference.

Mr Thorp suggested that each Work should determine to execute a certain portion of their warrants and abide by it. Mr Mayor suggests that the keelmen say they combine because their masters combine.

Mr Liddell stated that before he would consent to the employment of the military, he must be satisfied that the Coal Owners are determined to execute their warrants to a proper extent, and that the persons at Sunderland and elsewhere employing bound keelmen are prosecuted for doing so, and that immediate steps be taken by the Coal Owners to ascertain who the employers and employed are.

Sir Thomas Burdon will apply to the Commanding Officer for the requisite number of troops for Scotswood and St Anthony's. The Durham Magistrates will apply for troops to be stationed at Dunston, Swalwell and Felling Shore. The Newcastle Magistrates will apply for the naval force and the marines.

Mr Askew had a conference with George Farquerson, Charles Swallow and George Lesleigh [keelmen?] of whom he speaks well.

393a. Letter to the Commanding Officer enclosed in the above
[TWA 394/46]

Sir,

At a general meeting of the Magistrates of the three Counties held this day at the Mayor's Chamber, a plan for restoring the navigation of the River was proposed by the Coal Owners and Fitters for their consideration, which was approved, and in order to execute it, it will be highly expedient that detachments of cavalry should be stationed at different places on the North and South shores of the River to remain there for a few days.

The numbers that are deemed sufficient for each station are:

Above Bridge on the South side: at Swalwell, 8; at Dunston, 8.

On the North side: at Scotswood, 6.

Below Bridge on the South side: Felling Shore, 10.

On the North side: St Anthony's, 8.

In all, 40.

We have therefore to beg the favor of you (as the stations at Swalwell, Dunston and Felling Shore are within the County of Durham) to direct that the above mentioned number of troops be sent to those stations at about 2 o'Clock in the afternoon.

This letter will be conveyed to you by a deputation of Coal Owners who will confer more fully on the nature of the plan proposed, and we trust that proper accommodation will be provided for the troops at the respective stations.

We are your most obedient Servants

394. The Third Address of the Keelmen of the River Tyne, in Reply to the Snake in the Grass, who calls himself 'A Friend to the Coal Trade', 14 November 1822 [NEIMME, The Bell Collection, vol. 22, 45–50]

Unwilling as we are to obtrude on the notice of the Public, we feel our duty to ourselves obliges us to offer at least some apology for our conduct, and to prevent our neighbours and fellow townsmen from being imposed on and misled by interested and designing men, who by means of the press have attempted to prejudice the Public against us, traducing, vilifying, and degrading our character, with the view to deprive us of the respect and sympathy of the generous and good.

The motives of this writer, who has taken upon himself to admonish us, are clearly to justify the Coal Owners, and shew the extreme folly and ignorance of the Keelmen. He appears, however, wholly uninformed on the subject of the present disputes, and of the nature of the complaints of the Keelmen; contenting himself with idle declamation on the case, plentifully interlarded with sophistry and falsehood.

This declaimer, like other mercenary scribblers for the Press, supposes himself intimately acquainted with the subject, and particularly with the objects and views of the Keelmen, whom he describes as men utterly devoid of all discourse of reason, wholly inadequate to the management of their own affairs, but who have been guided and directed, in all their misconduct, by some wickedly mischievous persons, by whom they were also instigated and persuaded to leave their employments during a '*prosperity* which they had *long enjoyed happily and satisfactorily*'. The persons to whom this language is addressed must be considered by the writer as the most imbecile of men. Indeed, were there any truth in his assertion, it would not only justify his own opinion of them, but also point them out as fit subjects for a Lunatic Asylum. But why proceed to admonish men so entirely 'void of understanding'? Why talk about the inconsistencies and absurdities of men so completely idiotic, 'whose conduct has been opposed to every reasonable feeling'. Here we discover a Snake in the Grass. The warmth of his prejudices against us shews a strong sinister feeling which we have no doubt would immediately have appeared had the writer had the honest boldness to put his name to the paper. He must be a bad logician who would attempt in this way to prepare the persons whom he addressed to 'receive thankfully his admonition'.

The admonisher says 'he has read the Addresses of the Keelmen, and admits there are really some things which might be very easily remedied, and which the Coal Owners have assented to ameliorate'. How generous are the Coal Owners! and how wicked and stupid are the Keelmen! But what, pray, have the Coal Owners given up? Any thing of a pecuniary nature? No, not even the prayer for the paltry binding-money, or for the small allowance for a binding-supper, has been granted. No, they have not met us in a spirit the least conciliatory, or shewn any disposition to attend to the voice of our petitions and complaints. Instead of this, many of the Keelmen, after being hunted like wild beasts, by the Military and Police, have been dragged out of bed at midnight, driven away naked from their homes and families, and thrown into dark and unwholesome dungeons, condemned, against all law, to solitary confinement, and deprived of all intercourse with and assistance from their friends. The force of the arguments which have been urged on our behalf, and all our petitions and remonstrances have been met only with the *argument of force* – 'the last reason of kings': and to us the laws have been attempted to be promulgated, as they were to the Israelites of old from Mount Sinai, 'amidst thunders and lightnings'. The Coal Owners indeed have availed themselves of every advantage against us which their opulence and rank in the community has given them, whether as Magistrates or as Commanders of local armed corps. Through their influence and for the support of their interest, exclusively, the local authorities have been arrayed against us, and all the military force in the district has been put in requisition for the same purpose. And not satisfied with this tremendous power at their disposal, against a body of peaceable, unarmed men, they have not scrupled to bribe the mercenary Editors of the public papers in their favour, who are continually breathing out threatenings and slaughters against those whom they esteem poor and defenceless, and instigating their employers to still more coercive measures.

Disputes relative to the Spouts have existed between the Keelmen and the Coal Owners on the Tyne for a number of years, and petitions and remonstrances on the subject have frequently been made by our body. So late as the year 1819, the Keelmen presented a petition to the Common Council of Newcastle, stating that such 'erections were impediments or obstructions in the navigation of the River, and that, by reason of them great damage had accrued to the keels and other craft, as well as great danger to themselves, and that one man's life had actually been lost by them'. And it must now we think be admitted, by every impartial person who is at all acquainted with the subject, that these Spouts, several of which now project into the River greatly beyond low water mark, and by having the vessels lying moored at them by buoys laid in the stream, and some of them beyond it, are clearly obstructions to the navigation of the River. Not only our keels, but also the steam vessels and other craft on the River are not only impeded, but frequently receive serious injury from these obstructions. Indeed, one of the first law authorities in this part of the country has admitted that 'the spouts ought to be indicted as nuisances, and the case tried at common law'. The knave lies when he says 'we at first insisted on the total obolition of spouts'; our object was, as set forth in our petition, only to limit their use. But, says the knave, 'the Coal Owners have a right to do and act as they like with their own property', forgetting that, on the principles of English law and civilized society, no person is allowed to make use of his property in a way which shall be injurious to any portion of the community. Forgetting also that the labourer is the creator of wealth, and that to him the proprietor is indebted for giving a value to his property. The river is considered as a highway, on which it is not allowable to individuals, however wealthy, to make erections for their own benefit, by which a free passage to all persons may be prevented, or impeded. On this principle it is, we presume, that, by a late Act of Parliament, Windmills are not allowed to be erected within 100 yards of a public road.

There is something specious in the argument, if such it may be called, against our proceedings, that the Coal Owners above Bridge, who are presumed to be our friends, are made to suffer more than those below Bridge, who are more directly opposed to our interests. This, like other sophisms, is partly true and partly false. The Owners above Bridge are clearly and confessedly combined against us with those below, and have associated their interests together for the purpose of opposing our claims. How, then, can we discriminate, or detach the one from the other, seeing that they act in concert with each other. We lament that the Coal Owners above Bridge should be so blind to their own interests as well as ours, as to join a *Combination* alike injurious to the real interests of the Coal Trade and to the public at large – a Combination which, by restricting the Vend, enables the parties considerably to reduce consumption, and to double the price of coals to the consumer! – And hence the interests of the Pitmen, the Keelmen, the Ship-owners, and Seamen employed in the trade, are sacrificed to that of the Coal-owner. When mercenary writers talk of the interests of the Coal Trade, they generally mean only that of the Coal-owners, a body of men in number not more perhaps than fifty or sixty, whilst they leave out of the calculation the interests of the great body of Keelmen on the Tyne, which, with their families, would amount to not less perhaps than four thousand; also a much greater body of pitmen, waggon-men, Ship-owners and seamen employed in the trade. These are treated as the small dust in the balance, of no account. The interests of all this large body of people are made subservient to the interests of a Combination of a small body of Coal-owners!

The apologist for the Coal-Owners and the Spouts seems to attribute the distresses of the Keelmen to the great progress of inventions and improvements, and the introduction of machinery, by which, he says, all classes of labourers throughout the kingdom have suffered more or less; but to this, he says, 'they have submitted *without resistance!'* This is notoriously false. What he here refers to has been the fruitful source of riots and disturbances in various parts of the country for several years past; and the papers have been filled with accounts of riotous assemblages for the breaking of machinery, both in the manufacturing and agricultural districts of the Kingdom, down to a very late date. Indeed riots and disorders are at all times to be dreaded, and indeed seriously apprehended, when a number of useful mechanics or labourers are by any unfortunate circumstance thrown out of employment and deprived of the means of obtaining a livelihood by honest industry. Then, prompted by famine, 'a rebellion of the belly' may be expected, which, of all others, says Lord Bacon, are the most dangerous and difficult to subdue.

Lastly, we are reminded that 'we have *illegally* broken our engagements with our employers'. Now this is 'the head and front of our offending'. The legality of these engagements is, we believe, questionable. By the bond, the servant appears to be bound to the master, but not the master to the servant; and as no mutual obligation is included, the instrument cannot be good in law. Indeed the masters have shewn us that they can, when they please, discharge themselves of the obligation. For, in answer to our last Petition to the Mayor, the Coal-owners issued an order to a number of the bound Keelmen in their employment, that if they did not come to work the following day, their bonds should be cancelled; and again, on the 1st of this month, several bound Keelmen were summoned to appear at Newcastle town court to 'shew cause why they should not be discharged from their service, and the masters from keeping them', when a number were actually discharged. Previous to our leaving work, the engagements on the part of several of the masters were at least virtually broken, by their not entering into conditions with us at the usual period, before the termination of our term of binding. This, added to a practice which appeared to bid fair for becoming general, of making us pay a rent-charge for the keels, and thereby reducing our wages, gave us reason to believe that farther encroachments were meditated. And whilst many of us had little employment, and our masters were not compelled by their engagements to provide us with either sufficient work or sustenance for ourselves or families, we could not consider ourselves bound by the laws of either God or man to starve for their benefit.

The Keelmen of the River Tyne

395. A Second Letter to the Keelmen of the River Tyne from 'A Friend to the Coal Trade', 19 November 1822 [NEIMME, The Bell Collection, vol. 22]

I should have thought any further admonition unnecessary, had not these men by whom you are deluded, stung with the justice of my remarks, again appeared in print; had not the viper, writhing under the acuteness of suffering too justly felt, again appeared forth, and under your name issued a third address to the public at large. The principles by which such a reply has been actuated may be easily discovered by any person possessing the most moderate share of intellect, and with all the candour with which its authors are possessed, they proceed to style me a Snake, a Knave, and a Liar, because I differ with them, and wish to remove you from that delusion under which you have now too long laboured, and which is to be attributed more to your inexperience of the views of such men, than to any mischievous design on your own parts. When I published my Address to you I did not expect it to have any effect upon those by whom Reason is termed absurdity, Truth, sophistry, and Candour, corruption and partiality, I despaired of ever bringing those to a sense of shame who have long, too long, walked in the paths of mischief and iniquity; but I addressed myself to you, the Keelmen of the River Tyne, a body of men who, as supporters of our local wealth and our local prosperity, are entitled to consideration and advice. And I now repeat the assertion; I am neither a Keelman nor a Coal Owner; I have nothing to gain from the one or to lose by the other; I am unconnected with any party, unallied to any *combination* of interests; and am only influenced by the desire of leading you out of the labyrinth in which you are involved, and out of which, without a struggle of your own, you will find it difficult to extricate yourselves. I treat you with no contempt; on the contrary, I consider you as men who, had you not been deluded and misled, would have long since regretted your error, and have returned to that work which is the only source of your prosperity and happiness. You would have soon discovered that instead of opposing those Coal Owners who are your supporters and employers, and yielding up the Trade of the Tyne for the benefit of those very spouts you are condemning; instead of deserting the collieries above Bridge, and *'starving for the benefit'* of those below; instead of arraying yourselves against your friends, and leaving those you term your *enemies* in possession of the spoil, as those sapient counsellors have advised you to do; you should even now have been navigating those very keels which are lying idle, and affording to all beholders a most undeniable proof of the imbecility, the absurdity and folly of the measures you have been induced to adopt.

These argumentative and candid *Gentlemen*, however, cannot deny that the decrease of manual labour is to be attributed to the use of machinery of different kinds, inventions and improvements in which this age abounds, and where is the proprietor of any of these inventions that has been obliged to relinquish the legal and lawful use of his property? Let us look to your neighbours on the Wear; there are inventions and spouts on that river as well as on this, yet the keelmen go on peaceably, and with far greater cause of complaint than yourselves. The trade of the Wear is now more flourishing than ever, and the coal prices in London will clearly shew that the collieries even now at work are more than sufficient to supply that great mart for coal. Even admitting that there may have been attempts to destroy machinery in some parts of the kingdom by persons aiming more at plunder than redress, yet such attempts have been invariably discomfited, the plunderers punished, and if by chance any poor mechanic had been led into the snare, such conduct always proved ruinous to himself and his offspring. However seriously such riots are to be dreaded, their consequences always must entail ruin upon the aggressors; and however greatly such arguments as proceed from your advisers may tend to advocate such a breach of your country's laws, yet I hope you will have more sense and more foresight than to lend an ear to them, or to proceed to acts of violence which can only be resorted to by ruffians and plunderers, and which while they disgrace the man, ruin the cause.

Your deceivers, lastly, after a series of prevarications, wish even to justify your breach of engagements, although they call it *the head and front of your offending*; they attempt this justification, however, in a manner equally futile with their other assertions; and I think, my friends, it is time for you to scorn the assistance of such men, when they dare to set at defiance every honourable and legal tie, when they have presumption enough to advocate an act which can only have proceeded from a blind delusion, and which would long ago have been repented of by unprejudiced and uninfluenced minds.

To men like these, admonition is of no avail, although I might advise them to drop their pens in silence, and abuse not that Liberty of the Press, which is our country's glory; to be content to vent their calumnies in that den out of which they avail not, and to forbear from leading the Keelmen of the Tyne to ruin and to misery. To you, I would again, with all the earnestness and entreaty which I possess, call upon you as men and as friends to the community, to return to your lawful work, to enjoy in peace the produce of your honest industry, to restore again to your lamenting families the blessings of prosperity; and, above all, never more to put yourselves in the power of those, who, from the first, have proved themselves the advocates of discontent, and the enemies of the people.

A Friend to the Coal Trade

396. *Tyne Mercury*, 19 November 1822

The Keelmen of the River Tyne

The return of the keelmen to their employment now appears an event of so much uncertainty that it has ceased to be a matter of calculation. As long, indeed, as they remain at large and are at liberty to pursue other avocations more lucrative, nothing seems more improbable than that they should voluntarily come to fulfil their engagements with the coal owners. By their refractory conduct they have succeeded in putting a stop to the entire trade of the collieries above bridge, but if they intended to annihilate for a time the whole coal trade of the port, they could not have adopted a plan less efficacious. It may appear somewhat anomalous to affirm that the very contrary effect has been produced; that the sale of coals, instead of being limited, has been greatly increased; but this fact is capable of demonstration. The coals shipped coastwise from this port by *all the collieries* in September, the month before the stoppage of the keelmen, exceeds 55,000 chaldrons, and in October, the very month after they had deserted their employment, the quantity of coals shipped *by the collieries below bridge alone* is upwards of 59,000 chaldrons. This is a singular fact, and at once evinces the futility of the keelmen's attempt to injure the collieries below bridge, who are the parties that have given them so much umbrage by the use of spouts. The spouts were never since their erection of so much importance to these coal owners as they are at the present moment. Ships of 20 keels have been brought up to the staiths and loaded with the greatest facility by the assistance of steam boats, which would never have been attempted under different circumstances. The interests of the coal owners above and below bridge are hence manifestly at variance. Indeed they appear so entirely opposite that some change in the mode of carrying on the coal trade seems indispensible. The coal owners above bridge can do nothing without the keelmen, those below are the greatest gainers by their absence. Some collieries that we could mention reap still more evident advantage from the stoppage for they have even raised the price of their coals *two shillings a chaldron* to the shipowners in consequence. The proprietors of the coal mines below bridge have lately discovered a means of conveying their coals down river with little or no interruption, which to us is quite inexplicable. A considerable number of keelmen, it seems, have been employed as trimmers, while the trimmers have taken upon them the office of keelmen… and the probability is that there is an understanding between these trimming keelmen and their brethren, *if it does not extend further*, for it can hardly be supposed that the main body would suffer them to be employed if they did not partake of some advantage. In this manner for the last week many keels have gone down the river with no more interruptions than if these differences had never existed. A few keels have also been brought down under guard as far as Newcastle Quay where some vessels of from 12 to 18 keels had been brought by extraordinary assistance to load.

On Friday last, upwards of twenty of the keelmen who have been working at Sunderland as casters were taken into custody and have been since committed to Durham gaol, but there is a circumstance attending their apprehension which we cannot allow to pass without notice. We have heard, and from the respectability of the channel from which we derive the information we cannot doubt its accuracy, that many of the men were absolutely apprehended without warrants. It is true they were afterwards discharged by the magistrates, but we cannot too strongly express our reprobation at such conduct. If these men have acted wrong, there is a constitutional mode of proceeding to effect their punishment, and there is no excuse for their tampering with the freedom of the subject. We are told they were special constables who did this, but they have shown how unfit they are to exercise the duties of the police.

On Sunday three boats sent up to Lemington to conduct some keels down the river yesterday were entirely destroyed by the keelmen. Two of them are in custody. Many of the keelmen are working at the Stockton and Darlington railway, while others continue begging up and down the country, but no effectual attempts have been made to prevent their entering into illegal engagements, or to check this disgraceful but *formidable and oppressive vagrancy*.

397. Handbill, 22 November 1822 [NEIMME, The Bell Collection, vol. 22 and TNA, HO 40/17/52b]

The Civil Authorities regret to find the deluded Keelmen still continue to insult His Majesty's boats by throwing stones when protecting those that are willing to work; and finding that forbearance any longer will endanger the lives of those so employed, – This is to caution the peaceable inhabitants, and women and children, to keep within their houses during the time the keels are passing from the staiths to Shields, as the Marines have orders *to fire on the first man that shall dare to throw a stone at them.*

398. *Newcastle Chronicle*, 23 November 1822

It was stated in last week's paper that a number of keelmen from the Tyne had found employment at Sunderland casting coals out of the keels into the ships. On Friday [15 November] a number of these men were apprehended for having left the employment of their masters to whom they were bound, and brought to this town escorted by a detachment of the 66th Regiment. Next morning they were brought before the magistrates at Gateshead, and 15 of them were committed by them to the tread-mill in Durham Gaol, to which they were conveyed the same afternoon in carts escorted by a detachment of 3rd Dragoon Guards, who were much hooted and pelted as they proceeded up Gateshead. Since then some more have been committed to the same Gaol under the vagrant act, having been found sleeping about glasshouses &c in Sunderland; as also five men who were apprehended by the revd C. Thorp in the village of Blaydon on Monday morning. In all, about 30 men have since our last been committed to Durham Gaol.[1]

Four men have also been apprehended on this side of the water and committed to Morpeth Gaol. To the apprehension of two of these men at Scotswood on Sunday morning last, the greatest opposition was made by their friends and neighbours. The police officers and guard of a corporal and 6 men of the Dragoons were set upon by near 200 persons of both sexes and most severely handled. The officers and soldiers, however, so resolutely did their duty that the attempt at rescue failed, and they succeeded in taking shelter, with their prisoners, in a house near [at] hand. Here they maintained themselves, notwithstanding the violent threats of these riotous assailants to pull down the house if the prisoners were not released, until word was sent to the barracks of their situation, and a reinforcement under the command of an officer arrived to their assistance. Upon the appearance of this party, the rioters immediately dispersed and offered no further opposition to the removal of their comrades who were taken away in a cart tied together.

The conduct of the people engaged in this riot, we have heard represented as most violent and daring; the forbearance of the military in the difficult circumstances in which they were placed, from making use of the arms in their hands, is deserving of the highest commendation; indeed it is only justice to them to say that they have on all occasions merited the thanks of the community by the patient and forbearing temper displayed by them, even though frequently exposed to assault and insult. The resistance shewn to the execution of the warrant, so different from the conduct of the keelmen in general, we have heard ascribed to the mistaken idea that it was not legal to execute a warrant on a Sunday.

The same evening two boats' crews of seamen, who had arrived at Lemington to assist in the removal of some keels the next morning, were set upon immediately on their landing by a large body of keelmen and obliged to disperse. The boats were instantly broken to pieces by the keelmen. During the night 2 keels were scuttled at the lower end of the quay here and some others set adrift.

The keelmen still refuse to return to their usual employment, but the efforts of the coal owners to conduct their business without their assistance have this week attained an efficiency which must convince these misguided men of the utter hopelessness of the struggle in which they are engaged. By the aid of steam boats, and through the increasing skilfulness of the men who have been engaged to navigate the keels, considerable numbers have each day this week been brought down from the staiths above bridge to the ships at Shields and again conveyed back under the escort of the boats from ships of war at Shields. On their passage they have occasionally been assailed with showers of stones from the shore, and some of the keels which straggled behind the rest have been boarded by parties from the shore and brought to anchor. On Wednesday and Thursday these showers of stones were answered by discharge of firearms from the men of wars' boats without injuring any person, so the shots were fired more by way of intimidation than with intent to injure. The number of keels which were brought down on Thursday amounted to near 50 which is very near the average number from the collieries above bridge. As to the collieries below bridge they are fully able to meet their demand for their coals by means of their spouts and have in fact shipped more than is usually done by them in ordinary times. The trade of the Tyne may thus be said to be in full activity, without the intervention of the ordinary keelmen. The present appearance of things has, it is said, made a deep impression upon these men, and it would not be surprising if we should shortly have to announce their return to work.

[1] The *Durham Chronicle*, 15 November 1822, stated that for absenting themselves from work bound keelmen were imprisoned for one month and in some cases for two months. Those arrested for vagrancy were sentenced to 14 days imprisonment.

399. Henry Hobhouse, Under Secretary of State, Home Department, to the Mayor of Newcastle [TWA 394/46]

Whitehall, 23 November 1822

Sir,

Mr Secretary Peel having received a representation which gives him reason to suspect that the keelmen are receiving support from the funds of the Friendly Societies, I am directed to request that you will acquaint him whether you consider there is any ground for supposing that this representation is founded in truth.

I am, Sir, your most obedient humble Servant,

Henry Hobhouse

400. Robert Bell to Henry Hobhouse, 25 November 1822 [TNA, HO 40/17/19 and TWA 394/46]

Sir,

The Magistrates have had no information nor have I ground to suppose that the Keelmen have received pecuniary assistance from the funds of the Friendly Societies. They are much dispersed through the country and chiefly support themselves by begging and perhaps enforcing their requests by the terror of their numbers, and I have been told that they have been assisted by small subscriptions from other bodies of men employed in the Coal Trade.

I regret to add that they still continue in a state of disorder and insubordination, though a further continuance of measures, carried on by the indefatigable exertions of Captain Nicolas and the naval force under his command, assisted by the military, promises to make a strong impression upon them.

I have the honor to be, Sir, your obedient Servant,

Robert Bell, Mayor

401. The Fourth Address of the Keelmen of the River Tyne in reply to a 2nd Letter of the Snake in the Grass who calls himself 'A Friend to the Coal Trade' [25 November 1822] [NEIMME, The Bell Collection, vol. 22, pp. 50–6]

'A Bridle for the Ass, and a Rod for the Fool's back'. Solomon

Being plain uneducated men, and not possessed of the advantages of a learned education, it may be some apology for our not having learnt the art of disguising our feelings, and for using great plainness of speech when called on to defend ourselves at the bar of the public. Our adversary, fearful that his own name would at once betray his real motives, has chosen to assume the fictitious one of 'A Friend to the Coal

Trade'. It would scarcely perhaps be worth the trouble of stripping the Knave of his visor, were it not to shew still farther his ignorance and incapacity for the task he has undertaken, and the want of discrimination on the part of those who have employed him. We are not, however, wholly ignorant of the real name and character of this clerical gentleman who has kindly taken upon himself the thankless office of admonishing a body of men on subjects with which he has shewn himself almost wholly unacquainted. If we mistake not he has been employed in the field of controversy in defence of some of the Coal Owners when he was obliged abruptly and ingloriously to retreat.

The most conspicuous feature of this Second Letter is the arrogance and consummate vanity of the writer, which is, indeed, truly ridiculous. He may rest assured there is not a Pee Dee on the River that has read his Letters, who has not laughed outright at the conceited folly of the witless soul who could hope to palm such stuff upon the understanding of the most stupid with any hope of success. No: all the solemn gravity of the owl, which he assumes to cloak his purpose, though it might perhaps suit that class of persons who usually attend to the admonitions of this *hireling*, certainly is not adapted to impose on the more masculine understanding of the Keelmen.

It is truly amusing, after having convicted him of falsehood and ignorance, in our last Address, he should still continue to talk of 'the justice of his remarks', and like the village pedagogue, 'though thrice confuted, he must argue still'. His candour and Christian charity urges him to assume, as a truth, our utter incapacity for managing our own affairs, and our total want of discrimination of character, exemplified by our employing, for that purpose, 'vipers' and persons 'instigated only by mischievous designs'. No, Sir, we can confidently assure you, that if the Keelmen have at any time got advice, it was always contrary to the steps they have spontaneously and unadvisedly taken; and we are certain none of our body can say that he has been advised by any person (not a Keelman) to strike work. Your insinuations, therefore, are unfounded, base, and unmanly. We know not what may be the views of that class of men against whom the writer wishes to caution us; but we have of late had sufficient 'experience of the views' of that class to which he belongs to deter us from again putting any trust or confidence in them. Living in great part on the plunder of the poor, we find them constantly arrayed against their interests, and their bitterest enemies – attached only to the wealthy and insolent oppressors of the land – of many of them it may truly be said, 'their gospel is their maw' and 'their god is their belly'.

On all subjects connected with Trade, Commerce and

Manufactures, the writer seems quite confused in his ideas, and wholly unacquainted with even the rudiments of that species of knowledge. Of the nature of wealth, either public or private, he appears entirely ignorant. Information on these subjects may not be expected from men of his cloth, but we may certainly expect that a man shall not begin to teach before he is himself instructed. He has evidently assumed that the progress of inventions and machinery, by reducing the quantity of manual labour must necessarily occasion distress from want of employment among 'labouring individuals'. A position absurd and untenable. The Nations of the South Seas might then be accounted the most wealthy, as their population would be little subject to such distress. Without stopping farther to instruct his Reverence in the real causes of the great and important evils which at present afflict our Country, we might be permitted to ask him, Is this the cause of distresses in Ireland? and of the general distress among the farmers and other classes of the community? 'Where', he exultingly asks, 'is the proprietor of any of these inventions that has been obliged to relinquish the *legal* and *lawful* use of his property?' We will tell him, as he seems much in need of instruction on all points. We are informed from the public prints that a great number of gentlemen and farmers in the counties of Norfolk and Suffolk have agreed to lay aside the use of their Thrashing Machines this winter in order to employ the poor agricultural labourers in their district. And in some parishes the more opulent inhabitants are compelled to employ a certain number of people, or pay a certain additional poor cess. What we have demanded, therefore, is not altogether without precedent.

Intending, no doubt, a compliment to the Keelmen, he says, 'they are supporters of our local wealth and local prosperity', but, to prevent us laying 'the flattering unction to our souls', in another place he reverses the compliment, and calls 'the Coal Owners our supporters'. It would be difficult, we presume, to attach any precise meaning to this language. Had he understood the subject he would have known that all *Wealth* is the produce of *Industry*. It would therefore have been more correct to have said, 'they are a body of men by whom a large portion of our local wealth is *generated*'. When we speak of wealth, we are necessarily led to divide the community into two classes, the productive and the unproductive – the bees and the drones; and we believe it will be found that the distresses of the former arise rather from the great increase of the latter, than from any cause referable to the increase of machinery – and also to the increased ingenuity of those unproductive classes in possessing themselves of the fruits of productive industry. This great evil will be corrected when the different members of the community are better instructed in their interests: they will then cease to listen to those *hired 'deceivers'* and tools of tyrants, who, in order to enslave both soul and body first require of their devotees, 'an entire prostration of the understanding'.

This sorry advocate of the Coal Owners, in his Second Letter, again attempts to plead for his friends above Bridge, whose collieries, he says, 'we have deserted for the benefit of those below', who, he reminds us, are more directly opposed to us. We have hitherto pursued and intend to pursue only peaceable means for the attainment of our object, which we think just and reasonable. What other methods would he recommend to prevent those he stiles our enemies from 'possessing themselves of the spoil', as he terms it? Would he advise we should 'look to our neighbours on the Wear, who', he says, 'go on *peaceably*, with far greater causes of complaint'. He forgets, or perhaps is not informed of the conflagrations and destruction which took place there not many years ago, for which some of these *peaceable* people, whom he desires us to 'look to' (for example, no doubt) were imprisoned two years.

We would advise the reverend admonisher to 'drop his pen in silence', till he has better acquainted himself with the subject, and particularly the question relative to the Spouts. He will then find that our complaints are not entirely without foundation. Some years ago, when the Corporation of Newcastle ordered a survey of the river to be made, the celebrated engineer, Mr. Rennie, who was employed on the occasion, gave it as his opinion, that the greater part of the staiths (and particularly that of Whitehill Point) had been the productive causes of the great accumulation of sands which have of late years taken place, by which the navigation of the river has been so much injured. The question is not, as the Parson conceives, 'whether the Coal Owners below Bridge have a right to use their private property to the best advantage?' but, Have the Conservators of the River Tyne a right in law to legalize the projection of Spouts, the laying of Buoys, &c. so as to impede or obstruct the free navigation of the River? We presume they have no more right to do this, than the Magistrates would have to give leave for a projection from a house into any street of Newcastle, so as to impede or obstruct passengers or carriages.

We have not yet met with any person who has recommended us 'to set at defiance every honourable and legal tie'. The manner in which the Parson's patrons have treated these ties is already noticed in our third Address. They have since given us additional proofs of the little regard they pay to such ties, and of the justice of our former remarks on this subject. Several of our sons who were *bound* to the collieries as pitmen have of late been discharged by their masters from their service, solely because their fathers were keelmen who had left the employ; thus shewing the inutility of the bond for the purpose of binding the master, and at the same time (through the instigation of the Parson, perhaps, who generally interprets both law and the gospel to his own advantage) 'visiting the sins of the fathers upon the children'. Another instance of the *fidelity* with which engagements are kept with us, was afforded in the affair of the stop in the year 1819 when we were induced to return to work under an express promise that if we would give in a petition to the Common Council respecting the various matters then in dispute, it should be attended to. A petition was accordingly drawn up and presented; but though a deputation of six of our body waited at the same time to explain and enforce the arguments, they could procure neither an audience nor an answer. In short, the petition was never attended to, and the evils complained of have increased ever since.

While we are advocating our own interest we cannot but be surprized at the apathy and indifference of the great and respectable body of Ship-owners connected with the trade, who are even more concerned than ourselves in the better regulation of these affairs, deeply suffering as they evidently are from the operation of the Combination by which the Vend of Coals is restricted.[1] On this account the Ship-owners are obliged to give for their coals whatever price is asked, and have it not in their power to purchase at the best markets, like other merchants in a free trade. Thus they have become merely carriers for the Coal Owners, and are thereby robbed of the ordinary profits of trade, without any advantage accruing to the Public at large, who are also injured by the Combination. Were this Advocate of the Coal Owners really 'a Friend to the Coal Trade', he would now labour to convince the Proprietors above Bridge that their interests are insepa-rably linked with ours and those of the Ship- owners. Thus might they be persuaded to break off a connexion which has been productive only of injury to the trade in general and to the public at large – then might the Keelmen be very easily induced to resume their labours, under a persuasion that the principal grievance of which they complain would be easily and speedily remedied, and legal redress obtained, under the auspices of both Ship-owners and Coal Owners, whose interests are equally concerned in the question.

The manner in which the Keelmen have been treated while quietly endeavouring to obtain redress of their grievances is perhaps without precedent in the annals of the country. From Coal-owner and Clerical Magistrates they have suffered much cruelty and injustice. In their case the ordinary laws of the land have been dispensed with, and many of them have been arrested, even without warrant, dragged from their homes and their families, and illegally imprisoned, where they have been treated contrary to all law, and worse than felons under sentence of death. The effect of this Irish mode of administering justice has been to foster only the feelings of hostility, prolong a season of suffering to all parties concerned, and prevent the operation of conciliatory measures, so necessary for putting an end to these unhappy differences.

The Keelmen of the River Tyne

25 November 1822

[1] The North-East coal owners limited production through the 'Regulation of the Vend' by allocating a fixed quantity allowed to be mined from each colliery, in an attempt to maintain steady prices.

402. *Tyne Mercury*, 26 November 1822

The great body of keelmen is still refractory. In the memory of the oldest person connected with the Coal Trade there has been no stoppage that can form any parallel with the present, in point of duration, or for the obstinacy, cunning and determination by which the servants have distinguished themselves in resisting the fulfilment of their engagements. They do not perceive that this perseverance affords another argument against their deserting their employment. That such a number of men for so long a period could contrive to subsist without working at all will surely be adduced as a proof that their wages were not insufficient to prevent them from starving. We are not contending that their earnings were as great as they ought to be, but this is not the question. They have been encouraged to hold out thus long not because their situation is more pitiable than it was, not because this is a time of greater pressure than any other – for there is no foundation for either supposition. They deserted their employment at a time when they knew their services were in the greatest requisition, and they hoped to profit by the necessities of the coal owners. They have been induced to delay their return to their duty from the hope that they will at least gain something, and this expectation has been strengthened by the knowledge that in former stoppages some advantage has always been obtained. The resources of the coal owners are now, however, greater than at any former period, and such indeed that with the protection of the civil authorities and the marines, the inconveniences to which they are subject are comparatively trifling. The exertions of the magistrates and police have enabled the proprietors of the majority of the collieries to get so many keels up and down the river that the keelmen have ceased to appear of the first importance. They no longer hold with any success the attitude of intimidation. They have for a considerable time past persisted in insulting and annoying the keels in their passing through, navigated by seamen and others and protected by armed boats from the ship of war. The marines have fired repeatedly upon them on these occasions but without doing any execution. This emboldend the refactory to take even greater liberties, and the civil authorities found themselves called on to publish a declaration that 'the marines had orders to fire on the first man that shall dare to throw a stone at them'. This threat was carried into effect on Friday last, when a person of the name of Aaron Marr, a glassman, who had mingled with the keelmen, received a wound on the thigh and has since been committed to prison.

The keelmen have not confined themselves to interference with the craft passing in the river, but have sunk several keels moored on the shore side and thus prevented their employment when they were required and the tide answered. The increased vigilance of the police and marines, it is hoped, will at least prevent any successful attempts at violence or any further interruption of the navigation of the river. There appears at present greater probability of these deluded men returning to their engagements than has hitherto been observable. Their own necessities, the additional resources of the coal owners, and the increased vigour of the civil authorities cannot fail to effect at no distant period a return to work, an object now become so desirable. The most unequivocal symptom of this conclusion occurred yesterday, when part of the keelmen belonging to Northumberland Wall's End Colliery returned voluntarily to their employment. They are part of the men mentioned in our last as having been acting as *trimmers* while the *trimmers* officiated as keelmen. It is singular perhaps (and certainly highly creditable to the individual himself) that one of the skippers who have returned to their employment is from Dunston where the chief meetings have been held and where the strongest opposition seemed to prevail. His name is Sadler. It is a remarkable fact, and strongly evinces the folly of these men, that, during the last week, the *trimmers* who officiated as keelmen actually earned £4 per man. This is a circumstance that can be necessarily of rare occurrence and is attributable entirely to the absence of the keelmen. The most sensible part of this numerous body, and especially the elderly men, are now so decidedly tired of the present state of proscription that it is conceived they are only withheld from making submission by the threatened violence of the hotheaded, unruly young men amongst them. They have now stood out so long they seem to want only some little colourable pretext to surrender. The least acknowledgement from their masters, we doubt not, would be thankfully received, and they would return triumphantly to their engagements. The keels have certainly received material injury by being dragged up and down the river by steam boats or navigated by inexperienced men, but this is an inconvenience the coal owners submit to from necessity. The keelmen now perceive that they are doing themselves the greatest injury – that their employment is now in a great measure superseded, and may soon become not only not desirable but nugatory.

403. Proposal of the Keelmen to the Coal Owners, 28 November 1822 [TWA 394/46]

We the Keelmen of the River Tyne assembled this day on the South Banks of the River for the purpose of taking into consideration the best mode of terminating the unhappy differences at present existing between us and the Coal Owners, and being wishful as far as possible to discharge ourselves of all blame for prolonging a season of suffering to all parties concerned in or connected with the Coal Trade, beg leave therefore to propose, and do unanimously agree to propose, to the Coal Owners with a view to prevent further evils which must necessarily arise from a longer continuance of the stop, and to effect an amicable reconciliation between the contending parties:

That we shall agree to relinquish, for the present, the question of the Spouts, hoping that the Coal Owners will, in the same spirit of conciliation, also agree to restore to us those privileges we formerly enjoyed, namely our binding money and an allowance for a binding supper. And that such of us as may at any time be out of employ be employed, as far as needed, in trimming at the staiths, in preference to any other class of persons.

We beg leave also to renew our prayer that the Coal Owners and Fitters will be pleased to use their influence to obtain, as speedily as possible, the liberation of such of our body as may have been put in confinement since the commencement of the present stop, and on account thereof.

Finally, hoping that the Gentlemen Coal Owners will be pleased to meet our concessions with a similar spirit and disposition, we beg leave to state that it is our earnest wish and desire, and we hereby declare that we will, and each and every of us, return to our employments so soon as our employers shall express their willingness to comply with our very humble requests.

The Keelmen of the River Tyne

404. Minutes of a Meeting of Coal Owners and Fitters, 29 November 1822 [TWA 394/46]

At a meeting of the Coal Owners and Fitters held at the request of the Mayor,

Present: William Clark, Joseph Lamb, William M. Lamb, Nathaniel Clayton, Esqrs; Mr James Potts, Mr Matthew Atkinson, Mr Newmarsh, Mr Buddle, Mr George Thomas Dunn, Coal Owners and Fitters; Mr Hindhaugh, Mr Charles Robson, Mr Edward Robson, Mr Richard Lambert, Mr Robert Taylor, Agents.

The Mayor stated that he had called the Trade together for the purpose of reading to them a petition or resolution from the keelmen, and requested that it might be read, and the same being read, to these requests the Owners and Fitters gave the following answers which were delivered in writing to the Mayor who undertook to give them to a deputation from the keelmen:

To the first [request], the binding money and binding supper were included in their first petition and then refused by the Coal Owners and Fitters, and surely they cannot be expected to comply with them after the keelmen have for many weeks deserted their employments, interrupted the trade of the Port and occasioned most serious loss to many of the Coal Owners and Fitters, but this meeting does not mean to interfere with the discretion of each master to deal with his men at the binding as liberally as he may think proper.

To the second request that such of the keelmen as may at any time be out of employ be employed, as far as needed, in trimming at the staiths, in preference to any other class of persons, the Owners and Fitters replied that the men employed as Trimmers have generally conducted themselves well and, must not be deprived of their bread.

To the last request that the Coal Owners and Fitters will use their influence to obtain as speedily as possible, the liberation of such of the keelmen as may have been put in confinement since the commencement of the present stop, and on account thereof, they replied that those men who are suffering the penalty of the law for their offences are not in the power of the Coal Owners and Fitters, nor can it be expected that those who have by illegal means injured their interests will be deemed fit objects for the exercise of that power, if they possessed it. Where, however, the Magistrates think a discrimination may be made, the Coal Owners and Fitters will readily give their assent, but they are unanimously of opinion that those who have been guilty of personal violence ought to feel the severity of the law.

405. *Tyne Mercury*, 3 December 1822

The keelmen have not yet returned to their employment, and as their engagements with the coal owners will expire on 31st of the present month, there appears little probability of their doing any more work this year. The proprietors indeed have discovered so many efficient resources that their employment hereafter will be held by a very precarious tenure. The inconveniences to which their masters have been subjected appear at length to have given rise to a determination on their part to prevent the possibility of their recurrence. Some of the coal owners have already come to a resolution not to enter into any more bonds with their servants, or to enter into any future engagements with them for twelve months. Whatever may be the nature of their next contract, if there be one, there is little doubt that the number of keelmen required will be seriously diminished. The proprietors of the collieries, as might be expected, are anxious to have recourse to expedients which shall be equally efficient as the present measures and less expensive. In consequence of this disposition prevailing, a model of a steam vessel calculated to carry eight keels of coals has been submitted to the owners of Fawdon Colliery. It is calculated that the same number of men now employed in one keel will be adequate to its navigation. Other plans are in contemplation which it is conceived will be of the greatest advantage to the coal owners though permanently injurious to the keelmen. Much as we regret the adoption of any scheme which will have the effect of curtailing the employment of a great body of men and dispensing with the labour of many entirely, it is not surprising the proprietors of the collieries should have recourse to such expedients. The refactory conduct of the keelmen has rendered such a course indispensible to their interests.

We mentioned in our last that part of the keelmen belonging to the Northumberland Wallsend Colliery had gone to work. What will the public think when they are told that they were actually, soon after they had commenced, dismissed by their employers? Yet so it is. We have never defended the conduct of the coal owners when it was culpable, and this proceeding we do think was highly reprehensible. If their own interests were to be regarded only, perhaps this measure was justifiable. But they should have had some consideration for the general good, some care for the interests of the port, for it cannot be supposed that this would not form a colourable pretext for the great body of the keelmen to hold out if they were so disposed. It is said that they had other men employed and therefore had no need of the keelmen, but granting this, they should have had regard to their own engagements, which, if one mistake not, are imperative on their employing the keelmen when they are willing to work. These men have so often promised to return to their engagements that we have now no faith in them. It was generally understood they were to pursue their avocations yesterday morning, but this expectation was disappointed. On Friday last a proposition was made on their behalf that they would return to work if the coal owners would give them £2 for binding money and a guinea for a supper, but this, of course, they refused to accede to. The differences, therefore, between these men and their employers have no prospect of immediate adjustment; indeed the season is now so far advanced that many of the ships have been laid up for winter, and with some of the collieries, on this account, a settlement of the dissensions is no longer desirable, while with others, for reasons we need not mention, it would be a subject of regret.

406. Minutes of a Meeting of Coal Owners and Fitters above Bridge, 5 December 1822 [TWA 394/46]

Present: Mr Dunn, junior, Townley Main; Mr Croser, Benwell; Mr Newmarsh, Fawdon; Mr Hindhaugh, Hallowell and Elswick; Mr Armstrong, Pontop; Mr J. Clayton, Tanfield Moor; Mr Atkinson, Team; Mr Robson, Wylam.

Resolved:

1st That the keelmen be engaged for next year on the same terms as last year, and on no other – but the Fitters are understood to be at liberty to bind or not as they please.

2nd That no more than three men and one boy be engaged for each keel or recognized as servants by the Fitters.

3rd That such keelmen as have been legally discharged from their obligation shall not be employed during the present year.

4th That the consideration of the question whether or not any inter-cession shall be made with the Magistrates for the discharge of any of the men imprisoned be adjourned until Saturday [7 December] at 12 o'Clock.

407. Minutes of a Meeting of the Coal Owners above Bridge, 7 December 1822 [TWA 394/46]

Resolved:

That all such keelmen as are now imprisoned, against whom the Trade have alone to complain for having deserted their work, and who have suffered an imprisonment of a month or upwards, be liberated if the committing Magistrate approve thereof.

That all against whom any charge is made of assault or personal violence be indicted at the respective sessions where the offence was committed.

That all men against whom proof of their having riotously obstructed others in the navigation of their keels, or of being guilty of riot on those, be also prosecuted.

That it be recommended to the Coal Trade to appoint a committee of three to conduct these prosecutions and to examine and select the different cases.

Resolved unanimously that the warmest thanks of this meeting, which consists of the Gentlemen interested in the Coal Trade above Bridge, be given to Captain Nicolas and the officers, seamen and marines under his command, for the important services rendered by them to the trade of the Port, and for their zealous and unremitting exertions distinguished equally by their firmness and moderation in protecting and assisting those who were employed in navigating the keels in opposition to the interruptions given by the keelmen, and that this resolution be laid before the general meeting of the Trade to be held on Tuesday next. That Mr Clayton and Mr Lamb be requested to wait upon Captain Nicolas[1] with a copy of this resolution.

[1] J.T. Nicolas, Captain of HMS *Egeria*, at this time senior officer of HM's ships in the Tyne; see J.K. Laughton, revised by Andrew Lambert, 'Nicolas, John Toup (1788–1851)', *Oxford Dictionary of National Biography*.

408. Captain J.T. Nicolas to Messrs Clayton and Lamb, 7 December 1822 [TWA 394/46]

Gentlemen,

When you did me the honor to call upon me this morning, I fear I did not sufficiently express to you my sense of the thanks which you so handsomely conveyed to myself and the officers and men under my command from the Gentlemen interested in the Coal Trade above Bridge. I therefore hasten to assure you that we all duly appreciate the favor that has been done us, as it shews us that in executing the unpleasant duties on which we have of late been employed, we have given satisfaction to those whose interest we were called upon to support against the interruptions of a misguided set of men.

I have the honor to be, Gentlemen, your obedient and humble Servant,

J.T. Nicolas, Captain of H.M's Ship Egeria, and senior Officer of H.M's ships in the Tyne

409. *Tyne Mercury,* **10 December 1822**

The Keelmen of the River Tyne

This numerous and useful body of men, we are happy to state, have at length returned to their employment. We have no desire unjustly to detract from any merit they might possibly have in now regarding their engagements after an absence of 10 weeks, but we believe their submission at this moment arises less from a sense of duty than their own necessities. It appears to have been the intention of Mr Dunn's men to have returned to work on Tuesday morning last [5 December], but they were prevented by a great assemblage of keelmen amounting to from 300 to 400 who were collected together at Stella staith for that especial purpose. The Revd Charles Thorpe, the magistrate was sent for about 7 o'Clock and on his arrival read the Riot Act, but before the expiration of the hour allowed by the Statute the mob had dispersed. A number of marines and armed seamen were in attendance, and from the insult and provocation to which they were subjected from the refactory keelmen, there is little doubt that some lives must have been lost but for the laudable interference and exertions of the magistrate. Yet, notwithstanding these disturbances on Tuesday, there was manifested a most evident desire on behalf of the well-disposed to return to their employment. Three of the regular keelmen, indeed, belonging to Wylam Colliery that day applied for permission to return to their usual occupation, and that having been granted, they united with the inexperienced men at that time employed to do the duty of the absentees. On Wednesday these 3 men were joined by 10 others, and on Thursday their number amounted to 36, which is the full complement engaged by that colliery. On the same day their example was followed by the Townley and Walker men, and on Friday the whole keelmen of the Tyne had returned to their ordinary avocations.

No concessions having been made by the coal owners, the men themselves took an additional hand into each keel, as if this were at least something gained. But this is mere deception. Before the existence of these differences, the practice was for the coal owners to employ three men to each keel, and they of their own accord and at their own expense employed a lad, commonly called a *pee dee* or P.D. Instead of this lad, who received only a trifling allowance, the keelmen have taken another man, previously unemployed, and actually admit him as an equal partner in their earnings. To their employers it matters little whether they have 4 men or 40, for they only pay a certain settled price per tide for each keel, and they enter into articles of agreement with 3 men merely because they are considered adequate for its management. It has been stated that one great motive with the keelmen in this stoppage was the desire to relieve such of their body as were out of employment by inducing their masters at *their* cost to take into each keel a man additional. We observed some weeks ago that these men only waited for a colourable pretext to resume their labours. The event has shown the correctness of that remark. In confirmation of this, the fact of their having themselves taken a fourth man at their own charge may be adduced. Whatever their motive was, there is no doubt their conduct was highly reprehensible, and if they before had reason to complain of not receiving wages enough, it is obvious they cannot afford to reduce them by maintaining a fourth man at their individual expense who earns nothing towards his own subsistence.

On Sunday and yesterday over 20 keelmen in custody were discharged by the magistrates on the application of their employers.

410. Robert Bell to Robert Peel, 10 December 1822 [TNA, HO 40/17/52 and TWA 394/46]

Sir,

I have the satisfaction to inform you that the Keelmen of the River Tyne, after persisting for nearly ten weeks in a system of combination amongst themselves and intimidation towards others, have at length yielded to the power of the laws and returned to their duty. For this happy result we are greatly indebted to the exertions of Captain Nicolas and the officers, seamen and marines of His Majesty's ships Egeria, Nimrod and Swan stationed in the Tyne. By their aid, protection has been afforded by night and by day, and on all points, to the navigation of the River, and through their coolness and discretion this long struggle with a numerous and daring body of men has been unattended with bloodshed.

As far as the Civil Power has required support by land, it has been promptly afforded by Lieutenant Colonel Holmes of the 3rd Dragoon Guards and the Regiment under his command, and I have the pleasure to bear testimony to their exemplary conduct on all occasions.

It will be the care of myself and the Magistrates of this and the neighbouring districts to select for prosecution any flagrant instances of outrage or violence which may have occurred during the late disturbances.

I have the honor to be, Sir, your most obedient humble Servant,
Robert Bell, Mayor

411. Bell to John Wilson Croker, secretary to the Lords of the Admiralty, 10 December 1822 [TWA 394/46]

My Lords,

The disturbances amongst the Keelmen of the Tyne being happily terminated by the restoration of order and the return of the refactory to their duty, I should feel myself very deficient in gratitude did I not express to your Lordships my conviction that this result is mainly to be ascribed to the promptness with which you were pleased to comply with my application for a naval force, and to the zeal and ability with which Captain Nicolas and the officers, seamen and marines of His Majesty's ships Egeria, Nimrod and Swan under his command have performed the arduous duties to which they have been called. It is to their laborious and unceasing exertions that the trade of the Port has been indebted for effectual and continual protection, and it is by their means that the Civil Power has been enabled to controul the rioters and preserve order upon the River.

The tranquillity of the Port being now, I trust, permanently restored, Captain Nicolas proposes to sail today with the Egeria, and the Swan will leave us in the course of the week.

I have the honor to be, my Lords, your most obedient humble Servant,
Robert Bell, Mayor

412. Bell to the Duke of Northumberland, 10 December 1822 [TWA 394/46]

My Lord Duke,

I have much satisfaction in confirming to your Grace the intelligence which my late letter conveyed of the keelmen of this River having at length returned to their duty.

Order appearing to be completely restored, Captain Nicolas with His Majesty's ship the Egeria has left the Port and sailed this morning for his station off Yarmouth, and the Swan cutter will sail in the course of the week.

I cannot close my correspondence with your Grace on this subject without expressing to your Grace the high sense which the Magistrates entertain of the exemplary conduct of the naval and military force which has been employed on this occasion in support of the Civil Power, and to whose indefatigable exertions we are much indebted for the happy result.

I have the honor to be, my Lord Duke,
Your most obedient humble Servant,
Robert Bell, Mayor

413. Copy letter from the Coal Trade to Robert Bell, 10 December 1822 [TWA 394/46]

Sir,

I have the honor to convey to you and the other Magistrates of Newcastle, the unanimous thanks of a general meeting of the Coal Trade of the River Tyne, for your and their active services during the late disturbances amongst the keelmen.

Adverting to the heavy portion of duty which your situation of Chief Magistrate has imposed, they would be culpably wanting in a due sense of gratitude were they not to mark their sense of the very able and indefatigable exertions which the discharge of that duty called forth by avowing the deepest sense of obligation to you and their conviction that those exertions mainly contributed to the support of the trade of the Port and the preservation of the public peace during this protracted struggle.

I have the honor to be, Sir, &c. [No signature.]

414. The Duke of Northumberland to Home Secretary Robert Peel, 13 December 1822 [TNA, HO 40/17/23]

Alnwick Castle, 13 December 1822

Sir,

…The Magistrates as well as the military and naval forces have performed their harassing duty with a degree of temper and firmness which merits the highest commendation. It is but justice, Sir, to the keelmen to say that they have conducted themselves with more moderation than could have been expected, and have abstained from committing acts of violence except in preventing others from performing that labour which they were unwilling to do themselves.

They have at length voluntarily returned to their duty without any concessions on the part of the Coal Owners, and seem aware that they have been the dupes of mischievous and designing individuals.

I am, Sir, your obedient Servant,
Northumberland

415. *Tyne Mercury*, 17 December 1822

The keelmen of the Tyne continue to follow their occupations as usual, and there appears now little danger of a relapse.

There is a large steam boat of 34 horse power at present building at Howden Pans for the express purpose of giving greater facility to the loading of ships of great burthen without the assistance of keels by towing the vessels up and down the river. We understand the keelmen have been taking the opinion of counsel as to the spouts being a nuisance to the navigation of the river and Mr Brougham, it is stated, has given them so much encouragement that they are determined to set apart weekly a small portion of their ernings in order to raise a fund that they may try the question at the next assizes.[1]

[1] A meeting of the keelmen's deputies, 21 December 1822, resolved that a subscription should be raised to try the question of the spouts, and earnestly called on gentlemen, tradesmen and other public-spirited individuals in the area to aid them 'in this important purpose, in which the public at large are also so materially concerned' (NEIMME, ZD 70, p. 81).

416. The Humble Petition of the superannuated Keelmen, Widows and Orphans of the Township of Swalwell belonging to the Keelmen's Fund at Newcastle [to the Mayor], 21 December 1822 [TWA 394/46]

Sheweth that your petitioners have for many years past been supported by the fund established by the Keelmen on the River Tyne, but, in consequence of the late difference which existed between the Keelmen and their employers, your petitioners found the benefitt of the said fund closed against them, which has brought your petitioners almost to starvation. From the cravings of nature, your petitioners made application to the officers of Whickham Parish for relief, but found no redress; the said officers refused to comply with their request. Four weeks have gone their round since your petitioners received any support from the aforesaid fund.

Extreme necessity compels your petitioners to lay their case before your Honour, as a Governor of the Keelmen's Fund, most humbly imploring your interference on our behalf in order that your petitioners' weekly income may again be restored to them, that our existence may be continued a little longer in the vale of life. Surely by so doing the blessings of the humble poor will rest upon your Honour's head, and your petitioners shall as ever bound in duty pray for your prosperity in this life and in the world to come life for ever more.

417. Nathaniel Clayton, Town Clerk, to Richard Nicholson and James Potts, 28 December 1822 [TWA 394/46]

I have stated your case to the Magistrates assembled today at Gateshead who are of opinion that the Keelmen's Fund, not being now sufficient to r+elieve all the claims upon it, each Parish or Township in which the Keelmen... deprived of relief [are] legally settled, must provide for the Keelmen applying for relief in the same manner as for other persons relieved by such Parish or Township, if they are proper objects; and that such relief must continue so long as the relief from the Fund is necessarily withheld. It will be your duty, therefore, to apply to the Vestry for the same relief which is given to the other persons obtaining it as legally settled in Whickham Parish, and it will be your duty also to give notice to the Vestry as soon as the allowance from the Fund is restored to you.

This instruction will suit the case of any other Keelmen legally settled in the same Parish.

Nathaniel Clayton

418. *Tyne Mercury*, 31 December 1822

On Friday last, being St John's day, the members of the Keelmen's Benefit Society made their annual procession through the streets of this town and dined together at the Three Tens, Old Flesh Market. Notwithstanding the late long 'stick' amongst this body of men, they never made a more respectable appearance. Instead of the *pea* (a short jacket that used to be pretty generally sported on these occasions), they were mostly dressed in new long coats, and some had on silk stockings and silver buckles. They were also accompanied by a regular band of music instead of the numerous old and infirm *catgut* scrapers in the town and neighbourhood, who used to be employed rather from a feeling of charity than ostentation. This procession cannot be justly said to be simply a procession of keelmen, for they were accompanied by their wives, daughters &c &c, some of whom paid due attention to their friends by plying them well with *spirits* to 'keep out the cold'. Two circumstances of note are that the keelmen did not give three cheers according to invariable practice on reaching the Town's Court, and some opposition was made to the band playing 'God save the King'. We suppose this may have arisen on account of the active interference necessarily imposed on the Magistrates during the late stoppage. Now that the employers and the employed are agreed, we should wish all bad feelings to be buried in oblivion.

419. *Tyne Mercury*, 21 January 1823

Letter from a correspondent: The Keelmen of the Tyne
Mr Editor,

Through the medium of your excellent Journal, I beg to make a few observations on the situation of the keelmen of the river Tyne.

The historians of Newcastle, on noticing the building called the

Keelmen's Hospital, I perceive, take occasion to compliment that body of men on their prudence, independence and foresight by providing, without assistance, by small contributions from their own hard earnings, a fund to support their fraternity in the hour of sickness and infirmity. I fear their recent conduct will not tend to raise their character in the public estimation. Their defeat in their struggle with the coalowners to me affords no subject of exultation. Their misfortune is sufficiently trying without the burthen of reproach. Their situation has nothing in it to excite envy, but it has strong claims to our commiseration and assistance. They sought, by assuming the attitude of intimidation, to extort from their employers what they knew they could not expect from the justice of their cause. They required, in fact, though not in plain terms, an increase of wages, contrary to the contract they had entered into, and at variance with the interests of their masters. The result of their dissentions has not been alone the failure of their designs: it seems to have altered the nature of their employment. The effect appears to be a change from a permanent to an uncertain and precarious dependence. Their occupations before this struggle were known and settled from year to year, but now their engagements are for short periods only. The coalowner may gain by this alteration, because he can always command a choice of workmen, and is not subject to any serious injury by the …caprice of his servants; but the keelman, I apprehend, must be a loser, for there are so many of his fraternity beyond the demand for their labour that he can expect little encouragement but what must depend on his own good conduct.

It is this excess of labour beyond the demand which calls for serious consideration. These men attribute their privations to the existence of machinery. They call for the abolition of the spouts, but they are regardless of the rights of others while they urge what is most conducive to their own interests. They forget that by the same rule that they are justified, when under no prohibitory engagements, to obtain the best price they can for their services, the coalowners are at liberty to employ their capital (which is to them what labour is to their servants) in the way they think most advantageous. The question of evils and benefits of machinery is much too complicated and extensive for a short letter; but the discussion at all is plainly merely gratuitous, for the result can in no way establish the right of the keelmen to demand the destruction of machinery. It requires but a superficial glance to perceive that, though machinery may be injurious to particular individuals, it is of the first national importance. But machinery has not much increased of late years in this neighbourhood, and it is only advanced as the great cause of the existing inconvenience because the inconvenience would cease in a great measure on the abolition of the spouts. The superabundance of keelmen is to be attributed to other causes. Many of them who are now idle were more profitably employed during the late wars than they could have been in their present occupations; but perhaps the greatest cause of the superabundance is to be assigned to the practice which has prevailed almost universally of every keelman educating his family to follow his own avocation. Thus we are not to conclude that the demand for the services of keelmen is now less than it has been for many years, but that the candidates for employment are much more numerous. I am fully aware of the difficulty of prescribing for the employment of a superabundant population. It is not easy to point out in what other mode men might maintain themselves than the one to which they have always been accustomed. Though they have necessarily acquired a particular aptitude for one employment only, their labour might doubtless in many instances be transferred into new channels. With regard to their children, it seems obvious that they ought to a certain extent be educated for some other calling. It would be very desirable that a fund could be established for this purpose. The keelmen would naturally contribute their mite, however trifling it should be, and their employers might do a most essential service to the community, and acquire the highest honour to themselves, by liberally subscribing towards such a project.

I am, Sir, your's truly,

H.

420. Cutting from *The Northern Reformer's Magazine*, c. 1823[1]
[NCL, J. Bell, *Collections relative to the River Tyne: its Trade and the Conservancy thereof*, vol. II, ff. 266–8]

In the late disputes between the Keelmen and the Coal Owners on the Tyne very important questions are involved, interesting not only to the parties immediately concerned, but also to the community at large. In the first place is observable the aristocratic nature of our institutions, and the laws emanating from them, by which the more opulent classes are enabled to oppress the labouring and productive classes, and by the aid of combination, vagrancy, and emigration laws, to set what price they please on their labours. Hence the great increase of pauperism and poor rates, of prisons and penitentiaries.

The price of labour is regulated by demand – an article of sale and purchase. How impolitic and unjust, therefore, to call in the aid of the military and the magistracy to settle differences of this kind of daily occurence. Unfortunately in this case the keelmen had no court of justice and equity to appeal to, for the redress of grievances under which they laboured, nor any other apparently practical mode of bettering their condition, than that which they pursued, namely, quietly withdrawing themselves from their labour till a period arrived when it might be deemed more valuable. They may be charged with folly and imprudence, and even with misconduct by some who have paid little attention to the peculiar circumstances in which they are placed, or by those who are interested and leagued against them; and some acts of riotous and violent behaviour on the part of the keelmen during their stop may be referred to in justification of the severities exercised against them; but the question is, did the keelmen possess any means of obtaining what is called a legal remedy? In the courts of their neighbourhood, where many of the magistrates are Coal Owners, and most of them some way or other connected with the trade, where even the Counsel employed against them are Coal Owners, could the keelmen hope for or expect an impartial hearing, or any redress of the grievances which were the subject of complaint?

The keelmen were charged of course with a combination, and though many of them were not bound, yet, by means of the vagrant laws, the magistrates were enabled to punish them, without being guilty of any other misdemeanour than that of leaving their employment. Though it was notorious that a combination existed among the Coal Owners to restrict the vend, thereby enhancing the price of coals, none of the mercenary editors of the newspapers had the courage or the honesty to notice the circumstance, though not only the keelmen, but the shippers of coals and others in the trade, as well as the public, were evidently suffering more extensively from this conspiracy than from the combination of the keelmen. Here the journalists betrayed their trust, as guardians of the public interest, joined the opulent party most connected with their own interests, and filled their papers constantly with communications from 'the special committee for managing the affairs of the coal trade during the stop', and with declamations against the 'refractory keelmen', recommending to their employers and to the magistrates additional severities against them.

[The increase in the number of spouts and the larger quantities of coal loaded by them has 'considerably diminished the number of keels and keelmen', but the editor of the *Tyne Mercury* attributed the keelmen's distresses to the great increase of their number from their imprudent habit of bringing up all their boys to the same occupation. This is untrue, only one boy being allowed to a keel when three men are employed], but, on this subject, the Editor has, in more instances, evinced a most deplorable ignorance, and his employers must, for a remuneration, be content with the pretended zeal he has displayed in their service.

[The increase in spouts, 'however objectionable as nuisances' must augment the revenues of the Conservators of the Tyne], but no advantage or emolument which they may derive from these erections can be a suffcent apology for any dereliction of the public interest.

The parts of the above in square brackets are summaries of longer parts of the article which, to a large extent, repeat what is stated in the keelmen's four Addresses.

¹ The cutting is numbered pages 57–60.

THE DECAY OF THE KEELMEN'S HOSPITAL

421. Petition of the Stewards of the Keelmen's Hospital, 1 September 1852 [TWA 394/49]

To the Worshipful the Mayor and Aldermen and Councillors of the Borough of Newcastle upon Tyne in Council assembled, the humble petition of Robert Harrison, Benjamin Minnikin, David Christie and Robert Caverhill, Stewards of the Keelmen's Hospital, Newcastle upon Tyne, Sheweth

That the said Keelmen's Hospital was built at the sole charge of the Keelmen of Newcastle upon Tyne for the benefit of themselves and their widows in the year 1701. That in the year 1730 the Society was embodied by 200 of the keelmen of the Town who voluntarily agreed to make contributions of one penny per tide for the purpose of keeping up the Hospital, and that the clock was put up in 1772, each member contributing six shillings towards the expence.

That on Monday the 5ᵗʰ July last past the Cupola or Clock Tower of the said Hospital was struck by lightning and considerably damaged. That the building of the said Hospital is insured in the West of England Fire Office, but as the policy does not cover the damage by any other accident than fire, the Office could have legally disclaimed any liability to make good the damage; the Office, however, made a gift to the Hospital of the sum of £10. 0s. 0d. towards making good such damage. That £9. 5s. 0d. of the above sum has been paid to the bricklayers and carpenters, and in all about £11. 0s. 0d. has been already expended, and that it will take £9 or £10 more to restore the clock alone to its former state, independent of the building.

That since the decay of the keelmen's trade, the funds of the Hospital have also fallen to decay; the sick allowance is discontinued, the limited resources of the Society being applied towards the funerals of deceased members and widows, and there is consequently no fund applicable to the necessary repairs of the said Hospital. That the Keelmen's Hospital has no connection with the Keelmen's fund established by Act of Parliament and does not receive any support or benefit therefrom. That, in consequence of the extreme poverty of the Institution of the Keelmen's Hospital, it has been considered a proper case to appeal to the public for their support on the occasion.

That in case such appeal should be responded to, it has been considered that it would be extremely desirable and for the benefit of the public and of the Institution that there should be a minute hand and an illuminated glass dial added to the clock, which it is understood might be effected, as well as the other necessary repairs required, for about £45, and when it is considered that the nearest public clocks to that of the Hospital are those of the Exchange, Sandhill, All Saints and St Ann's, the two latter of which have no minute hands and are therefore useless at night, it is hoped that the object contemplated will meet the generous support of the public. That your petitioners as such Stewards of the said Hospital have already used considerable exertion for the purpose of effecting the reparations and improvements contemplated by private subscriptions, but hitherto without effect, except as to the sum of £4 10s. 0d. – the amount received from a few benevolent individuals on the occasion, and your petitioners are apprehensive that they will not be able to effect the objects desired without the generous aid and assistance of your honorable Council. Your petitioners therefore humbly pray that your honorable Council will be graciously pleased to take the subject of their petition into consideration, and afford your petitioners, as such Stewards and for and on behalf of the said Hospital, in order to their effecting the repairs and improvements aforesaid such aid and assistance in the premises as to your honours shall seem meet. And your petitioners shall ever pray &c.[1]

[1] For the subsequent history of the hospital, see Introduction, p. xxvii.

BIBLIOGRAPHY

PRIMARY SOURCES

Durham Cathedral Library

Additional Manuscript 97

Durham County Record Office

Clayton and Gibson Papers

National Coal Board Records

Strathmore Papers

Durham University Special Collections

The Earl Grey Papers

Miscellaneous Books, GRE/v/Misc.6

Shafto Papers

House of Lords Record Office

The Magistrates' Bill to control the Keelmen's Charity (manuscript, 1712), petitions against it, and associated papers

Newcastle City Library

Bell, J., *Collections Relative to the Tyne its Trade and Conservancy* (6 volumes of manuscript and printed material)

Brockie, William, *The Keelmen of the Tyne*, booklet with press cuttings attached

North of England Institute of Mining and Mechanical Engineers

The Bell Collection for a History of Coal Mining (22 volumes of manuscripts, press cuttings and other printed material)

William Brown's Letter Book

Easton Papers

Watson Collection

Northumberland Archives

Ridley Papers

The National Archives

Admiralty Records

Home Office Papers

State Papers

Tyne and Wear Archives

A large body of manuscripts concerning the keelmen (Accession 394)

Cotesworth Papers

Ellison Papers

Keelmen's Hospital Society Minute Book, 1740–1842; Cash Books 1734–5, 1735–7, 1737–40, 1771–97 (includes names of members, deaths, reasons for exclusions), 1735–1823; Keelmen's Hospital Memoranda of daily and weekly occurrences, 1770–96; Sick and poor book, 1740–69; Register of Members, 1769–1888

Records of the Hostmen's Company

Records of Newcastle Corporation: Common Council Minute Books, 1699–1718, 817–24; Estate and Property Sub-committee Minute Book, 1890–98; Letter Book, 1771; Petitions to the Common Council, 1799–1850; Typescript Calendars of the Common Council Books and Petitions

Newspapers

Durham Chronicle

Durham County Advertiser

Gateshead Observer

Mercurius Politicus

Newcastle Advertiser

Newcastle Chronicle

Newcastle Courant

Newcastle Guardian

Newcastle Journal

Newcastle Weekly Chronicle Supplement

Northern Reformer's Magazine

Review of the State of the English Nation

Star

Times

Tyne Mercury

SECONDARY SOURCES

Aspinall, A., *The Early English Trade Unions* (London, 1949)

Brand, J., *History and Antiquities of the Town and County of Newcastle upon Tyne*, 2 volumes (London, 1789)

Brockie, William, *The Keelmen of the Tyne*, n.d.

Cruickshanks, E., Handley, S., and Hayton, D.W., eds, *History of Parliament, The Commons, 1690-1715*, 5 volumes (Cambridge, 2002)

Curnock, Nehemiah, *Journal of the Reverend John Wesley*, 8 volumes (London, 1909–16)

Defoe, Daniel, *A Review of the State of the British Nation*, vol. VIII, Number 139

Dendy, F.W., ed., *Extracts from the Records of the Hostmen's Company of Newcastle upon Tyne*, Surtees Society, CV, 1901

Dunn, Matthias, *A Treatise on the Winning and Working of Collieries* (London and Newcastle, 1852)

Ellis, Joyce, 'Urban Conflict and Popular Violence: The Guildhall Riots of 1740 in Newcastle upon Tyne', *International Review of Social History*, XXV (1980), pp. 332–49

Ellis, Joyce M., ed., *Letters of Henry Liddell to William Cotesworth*, 21 November and 4 December 1710, Surtees Society, CXCVII, 1987

Fewster, Joseph M., 'The Keelmen of Tyneside in the Eighteenth Century', *Durham University Journal*, new series, XIX (1957–8), pp. 24–33, 66–75, 111–23

Fewster, Joseph M., 'The Last Struggles of the Tyneside Keelmen', *Durham University Journal*, new series, XXIV (1962–3), pp. 5–15

Fewster, Joseph M., *The Keelmen of Tyneside, Labour Organisation and Conflict in the North-East Coal Industry, 1600-1830* (Woodbridge, 2011)

Fewster, Joseph M., ed., *Morpeth Electoral Correspondence 1766-1776*, Surtees Society, 221, 2017

Furbank, P.N., and Owens, W.R., *A Critical Bibliography of Daniel Defoe* (London, 1998)

Guthrie, J., *The River Tyne, its History and Resources* (Newcastle, 1880)

Healey, George Harris, ed., *The Letters of Daniel Defoe* (Oxford, 1955)

Heslop, R. Oliver, 'Keels and Keelmen', NEIMME, NRO 3410/ZD/71

Historical Manuscripts Commission, *The Manuscripts of the Earl of Carlisle, preserved at Castle Howard* (London, 1897)

Hostmen, *The Case of Charles Atkinson, John Johnson, John Simpson, and great numbers of the Trading Hoastmen, commonly called Fitters, of the Town and County of Newcastle upon Tyne* [1712] (Lincolns Inn Tracts, M.P., 102)

Hughes, Edward, *North Country Life in the Eighteenth Century, the North East, 1700-1750*

Hughes, Edward, ed., *The Diaries and Correspondence of James Losh, 1811-23*, Surtees Society, CLXXII, 1962

Johnson, R.W., *The Making of the Tyne, A Record of Fifty Years' Progress* (Newcastle, 1895)

Keelmen, *The Case of the Poor Skippers and Keel-men of Newcastle, Truly Stated: With Some Remarks on a printed Paper, called and pretended to be their Case* [1712] (British Library 8223 E 9 (32))

Keelmen, *A Farther Case relating to the poor Keelmen* (c. 1712)

Keelmen, *Four Addresses of the Keelmen of the River Tyne* (Newcastle, 1823)

Keelmen, *Articles of the Keelmen's Hospital and Society with Rules and Regulations for the Hospital, to which is added an Account of the Hospital and Society from their beginning to the present time* (Newcastle, 1829)

Law Reports, *The English Reports, King's Bench Division*, volumes 102, 108, 111 (Edinburgh, 1910)

Levine, David, and Wrightson, Keith, *The Making of an Industrial Society – Whickham 1560-1765* (Oxford, 1991)

McKay, John, 'Keels and Keelmen', *Newcastle Weekly Chronicle Supplement*, 9 November 1889

Mander, Francis, 'The Tyneside Keelmen's Strike of 1710: Some Unpublished Documents', *Gateshead and District Local History Society, Bulletin*, No. 1, 1969

Marshall, John, ed., *Proceedings at Law in the Case of the King versus Russell and others relative to the Coal Staiths erected at Wallsend on the River Tyne* (Newcastle, 1830)

Milne, Maurice, 'Strikes and Strike-Breaking in North East England, 1815-44: the Attitude of the Local Press', *International Review of Social History*, 22 (1977), pp. 226–40

Mitchell, Andrew, *An Address to the Society of Keelmen on the River Tyne, with a correct Table of the Dues of the River* (Newcastle, 1792)

Moore, John Robert, *A Checklist of the Writings of Daniel Defoe* (Bloomington, 1960)

Murray, Alexander, *An Account of the Keelmen's Hospital and Society… and an Address to Young Keelmen* (Newcastle, 1781)

Namier, Sir Lewis B., and Brooke, John, eds, *The History of Parliament, The Commons, 1754-1790*, 3 volumes (London, 1964)

Nicholson, J.I., 'Keels and Keelmen', *Newcastle Weekly Chronicle Supplement*, 9 November 1889

Oxford Dictionary of National Biography (Oxford, 2004)

Parliament, House of Commons, *Journals of the House of Commons*, XV (1705–8), XVII (1711–14), XXXII (1768–70), XLIII (1788), LXXV (1819–20)

Parliament, House of Lords, *Manuscripts of the House of Lords*, n.s. IX; *Journals of the House of Lords*, XIX (1709–14)

Patent Rolls, *Calendar of Patent Rolls, Richard II, 1381-85* (London, 1897)

Richardson, M.A., *The Local Historian's Table Book of Remarkable Occurrences chiefly illustrative of the History of the Northern Counties*, Historical Division, 4 volumes (Newcastle, 1841–4)

Robinson, John, *The Delaval Papers, How they were Discovered, with numerous Family Letters and others of National and General Interest* (Newcastle, n.d.)

Rogers, Nicholas, *The Press Gang, Naval Impressment and its Opponents in Georgian Britain* (London, 2007)

Rowe, D.J., 'The Strikes of the Tyneside Keelmen in 1809 and 1819', *International Review of Social History*, XIII (1968), pp. 58–75.

Rowe, D.J., 'The Decline of the Tyneside Keelmen in the Nineteenth Century', *Northern History*, IV (1969), pp. 111–31.

State Papers, *Calendar of State Papers of the Reign of Charles I, Domestic Series, V, 1631-33* (reprint Liechtenstein, 1967); *Addenda, 1625-49* (London, 1897)

Sutherland, C.H.V., *English Coinage 600-1900* (London, 1982)

The Northern Reformer's Magazine (Newcastle, 1823)

Turnbull, Les, *The World of William Brown, Railways – Steam Engines – Coalmines* (NEIMME, 2016)

Watson, Harry D., 'Newcastle Keelmen in the 18th Century: the Scottish Connection', *Journal of Northumberland and Durham Family History Society*, vol. 13, No. 3 (1988)

Welford, Richard, 'Early Newcastle Typography 1639-1800', *Archaeologia Aeliana*, 3rd series, III (1907), pp. 16–17.

INDEX OF PERSONS

Note: Many of the names below (particularly those of the keelmen) were rendered phonetically by contemporaries. It is highly likely, for example, that Thomas Croudess was related to his skipper, Robert Croudes. Robert Croudes himself may well be the same man as Robert Croudas (also a skipper). George Millar and George Miller are probably one and the same, since both were skippers of keelboats at the same time; likewise Alexander Caldcleugh and Alexander Carclough. Names have, however, been preserved as they appeared in the documents, unless there is strong evidence to the contrary.

INDEX OF PLACES